THE GREAT WAR

TROWBRIDGE SOLDIERS

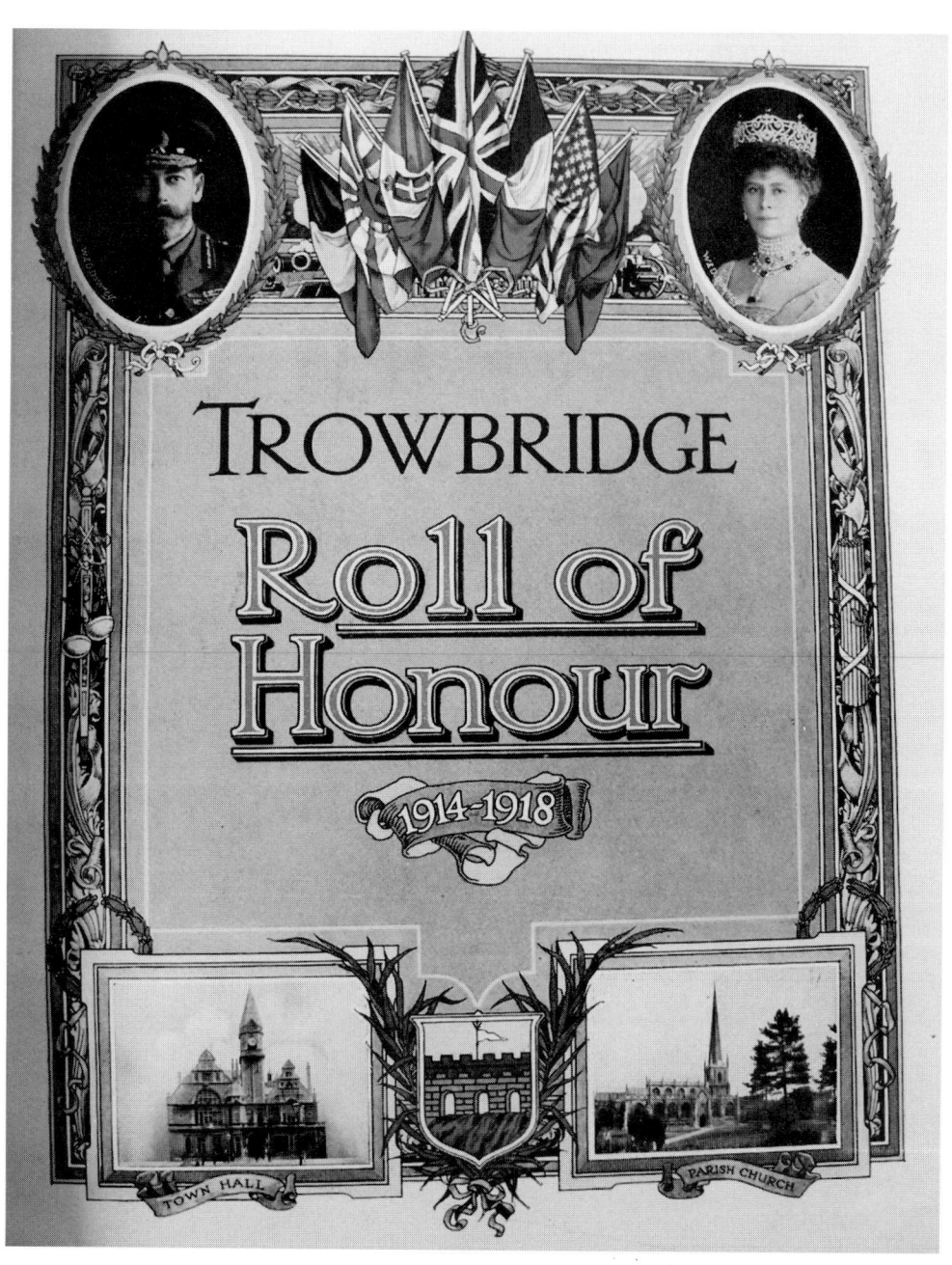

Title page from Towbridge Roll of Honour By the Rev. Harry Sanders

THE GREAT WAR

TROWBRIDGE SOLDIERS

RICHARD BROADHEAD

To Matt
Best wishes
Richard Broadhead
01249 760555.

Trowbridge Territorials at the Secretariat Delhi, India, who have volunteered for service in Mesopotamia (modern day Iraq) to fight Turkish forces. Left to right: William Arthur Ruddle, died of disease in Mesopotamia October 1916 - John Henry Mackett, killed in action near Gaza, Palestine, November 1917 - Leslie Gayton, captured at Kut by Turkish forces died of illness or disease while a prisoner of war - Edward Ernest Preen, captured at Kut by Turkish forces died of enteric fever while a prisoner of war - Harold Francis Cosser, wounded at the Battle of Cestiphon and evacuated to Kut where he was captured by Turkish forces died of illness or disease in Adana, Turkey.

First published 2010

O&B Services
The Annexe
Poynder Place
Hilmarton, SN11 8SQ

© Richard Broadhead 2010

The right of Richard Broadhead to be identified as the Author
Of this work has been asserted in accordance with the
Copyrights, Designs, and Patents Act 1988.

All rights reserved, no part of this book may be reprinted
or reproduced or utilised in any form or by any electronic,
mechanical, or other means, now known or hereafter invented
including photocopying and recording, or in any information
storage or retrieval system, without the permission in writing
from the Publishers.

British Library Cataloguing in Publication Data.
A catalogue record for this book is available from the British Library.

ISBN 978 0 9563825 11

CONTENTS

	Foreword	
	Introduction	
Chapter 1	The War of Hate - 1914	9
Chapter 2	1915 - The War that should have been over by Christmas	25
Chapter 3	Belgium & France	37
Chapter 4	Gallipoi	42
Chapter 5	Loos	61
Chapter 6	Jutland	81
Chapter 7	The Somme	90
Chapter 8	1917	124
Chapter 9	Arras	138
Chapter 10	Passchendaele	164
Chapter 11	Cambrai	187
Chapter 12	1918	199
Chapter 13	Kaiserschlact	206
Chapter 14	A Black Day for the German Army	232
Chapter 15	Armistice Day - Monday 11 November 1918	259
Chapter 16	Remembrance	279
	Trowbridge Men Not Remembered by the CWGC	285
	Maps	286
	A-Z of Memorials	290

Foreword

This is the third of Richard Broadhead's books about those from Wiltshire who fought and died in The Great War; this one is a tribute to those from Trowbridge. The magnitude of the research he has undertaken is daunting; painstakingly he has recorded the names of all those listed on the War memorials in, and around, Trowbridge; then examined records held in The National Archives, a number of Regimental and Corps Museums and The Commonwealth War Grave Commission. Then hardest of all I judge, he has read through the newspapers of those days both national and local, searching for details of the men of Trowbridge who gave their lives.

The 16 Chapters listed near the front of the book reflect the great, and awful confrontations of The Great War. I say awful for it was a war of attrition, where both sides poured their manpower onto the battlefield hoping to exhaust their opponents before they themselves were exhausted. I found the most moving Chapter to be that covering Gallipoli, where so many fell and "have no known grave" from the 5th Wiltshires. Their faces and many others, look out from the pages, their lives cut short; their faces are the faces of Wiltshire's Sons today, their address in many cases still exist in and around Trowbridge and if one was to knock on the front door of one of those addresses it is very possible that a member of the same family might answer the door.

Trowbridge's first casualty is Lieutenant LFH Mundy of the Royal Horse Artillery (RHA), stationed at Trowbridge, who died serving a gun of L Battery RHA at Nery France. Three members of L Battery won the VC that day including Captain EK Bradbury who died beside Lieutenant Mundy. The Battery is now titled L (Nery) Battery RHA in honour of the gallantry shown by those, like Mundy, who died rather than yield. Where is that Battery today? As I write it is in Afghanistan but akin to the front doors I have mentioned above it is stationed in Tidworth in Wiltshire.

In the Bible one reads, "...some there be that have no memorial and it is as though they have never been.." - this excellent book is a magnificent memorial to Wiltshire, to Trowbridge and above all to those who fell and are listed in the 16 Chapters. "We will remember them".

Brigadier Robert Hall
Chairman Wiltshire Council

May 2010

Introduction

I have been visiting War Memorials and attending Remembrance Services for a number of years. Since writing about the men and women who died during the Great War I have realised how little we know about these people who we are asked to remember. After nearly 100 years in many places all we have is a list of names of men who we are told gave there lives for our freedom and we simply imagine muddy Flanders Trenches and lines of white head stones. The parents and nearly all the brother and sisters of the dead have now passed from this life and with the passing of the last Tommy, Harry Patch, there is no one left who can tell future generation of the first hand experiences, fears and hopes.

Trowbridge Soldiers is about the men affiliated with the town in some way who died in the Great War. I have tried to give the reader information that helps to build a picture of the lives of the fallen. Not everybody wanted to be a soldier, sailor or airman, and not all the men wanted to go to war. The older men had families and before you condemn a man for not volunteering look at our comfortable life today with our houses and children and ask would you give up all you have for an uncertain future? Many men did volunteer but precious few knew what was in store for them nor how, if they returned the conflict wound change their lives. I recently spoke to the relatives of a veteran of the Great War and they informed me that when he returned he was not the same man who had left Trowbridge.

This book is not a list of names of the fallen but tells their stories and I have tried to bring the fallen back to life. Who was J. Smith listed on Trowbridge War Memorial? You will find his story as you read the book, he was not a native of Trowbridge but his sweetheart, Edith lived in Waterworks Road Trowbridge.

We must also thank the foresight of the Rev. Harry Sanders who compiled a book The Trowbridge Roll of Honour which he compiled at the end of the war and from which I have taken some of the photos of the fallen. Not all of those associated with Trowbridge appeared in the Roll of Honour Book or on the War Memorial, but I have tried to bring all these men together. Some of the men from Trowbridge are not remembered by the Commonwealth War Graves Commission, many are buried in Trowbridge Cemetery and I will endeavour to have these forgotten men recognised.

I have included in this book the stories of the men of the 2/4th Battalion Wiltshire Regiment whose names appear on the Memorial in St.James Church, Trowbridge even though many of them did not come from Trowbridge their Memorial is here and will forever be a part of the Towns History. I would like to thank all those parishioners of local churches who have guided me to various memorials within their place of worship and have allowed me to take photographs. Most of all I would like to thank my long-suffering wife, Anita, who has supported me beyond the call of duty during the writing of this book and of course to my two lovely boys, Jack-Harry and Tom who were kind enough to give me leave from playing games with them, and whom I sincerely hope never have to serve their country in such a way as those listed herein.

This book is not about the battles of the First World War or the men who directed the battles, it is a book about the great men who left their towns, whether as a volunteer or a conscript, to fight for our future. If we forget their sacrifice we open the door for future conflicts, which will mean that their deaths were to have been in vain.

CROMWELL
PRESS GROUP

Cromwell Press, Trowbridge based Book Printers, are delighted to support Richard's book which is of significant local historical interest and congratulate him on the success of his project

If you are interested in having your book printed we can offer various solutions from Digital through to Litho Printing, Design and scanning

Tel: 01225 711400   www.cromwellpressgroup.co.uk

H.J Knee Ltd and the Knee family would like to dedicate this space to the memory of our workers, both friends and family, who fought in the Great War.
Let those who come after see to it that their names be not forgotten

1
THE WAR OF HATE, 1914

In August 1914 the fuse was lit that would ignite a conflict that would change the world; it was to be given many names: the Great European War; The Great War for Civilisation and the First World War being but a few. There were many reasons for the commencement of hostilities, but once mobilisation of men had started, it triggered a domino effect throughout Europe and then on across the world.

Patriotism spread through countries like a plague, and, like a plague, it almost immediately claimed its victims. Men volunteered to fight for good and God against evil, in a war where keen, willing participants would be home for Christmas. The British Army was small but well trained, and had been developed to protect and control the British Empire, while relying on the powerful British Navy to protect the world trade routes.

In the August of 1914, Soldiers of the British Expeditionary Force marched across Belgium, a country that Great Britain had the treaty to protect, across fields where one hundred years earlier, the Duke of Wellington had defeated Napoleon Bonaparte. They marched to the town of Mons. The Great War had begun.

23 AUGUST 1914 – THE BATTLE OF MONS, BELGIUM
26 AUGUST 1914 – THE BATTLE OF LE CATEAU, FRANCE

Trowbridge's First Casualty

Lieutenant Lionel Francis Hastings Mundy
Service No.   N/A
Place of Birth: Hastings, Sussex
Date of Death: 03/09/1914
Memorial: Trowbridge
War cemetery: Baron Communal Cemetery
Theatre of war: France
Next of Kin: Lionel & Ella Tisdale Mundy
Address: 92 Brook Green, Hamersmith, London

Royal Horse Artillery
Age: 28
Home Country: England
Cause of death: Died of wounds

Lionel, whose home was at Barnet, was stationed at Trowbridge with H Battery Royal Horse Artillery and was a very popular officer. He took a keen interest in all kinds of sports and was a prime mover in a series of military competitions which took place at the Barracks in the summer of 1913, in which members of the battery showed great proficiency. He was an enthusiastic follower of the Avon Vale Hounds and in July 1914 took part in the Wilts Lawn Tennis Tournament at the County Ground, Trowbridge. He was 28 years of age and had joined the army in 1906. A local report stated that by his heroic death the army has been robbed of another of its gallant band of officers.

Lionel had arrived in France on Sunday 16 August 1914. On 1 September 1914 at Nery in France, L battery were preparing to march when Germans took the British by surprise. The area was raked by shrapnel and machine gun fire and both men and horses were lying dead and wounded. Captain Edward Kinder Bradbury shouted:

"Who'll volunteer to get the guns into action" all who could stand shouted "me!"

An account by an artillery officer reveals what took place:

"Bradbury was the real hero. He got the gun into action and gave orders. Mundy knelt on one side and did ranging officer, and Bradbury, Campbell and Giffard with the battery Sergeant-Major, gunner and driver served the gun. Bradbury had one leg taken off above the knee but still went on; Campbell was killed, Mundy was hit in both legs; the major, coming back hastily, was hit in the throat as he arrived. Bradbury had his other leg taken off, Giffard was badly wounded, and still they kept the last gun firing: and when I Battery and the other Brigade came up they found that the Germans had left their guns and bolted. Wasn't it magnificent!

Poor Mundy got home but died there, and only the Major who saw nothing of it and Giffard who stopped five bullets survived."

Lionel is buried at Baron Communal Cemetery, France, with sixteen other men who died during the fighting in September 1914.

Lionel Mundy did not get home, Gunner Clout who had witnessed much of the fighting wrote to his wife from his hospital bed in Portsmouth:

"I saw poor Mundy die by my side, he said " Goodbye Clout. Don't forget to have a look at the garden if you live to get home. Tell them what we have done."

Gunner Clout finished the letter to his wife writing,

"It's been murder not war."

Lionel Francis Hastings Mundy

6 SEPTEMBER 1914 - THE BATTLE OF THE MARNE, FRANCE
9 SEPTEMBER 1914 - THE BATTLE OF FERE CHAMPENOISE, FRANCE
14 SEPTEMBER 1914 - FIRST BATTLE OF THE AISNE, FRANCE

Stoker 1st Class Rowland Herbert Stafford   *HMS Aboukir Royal Navy*
Service No.   K/3801   Age: 23
Place of Birth: Minterne Magna, Dorset   Home Country: England
Date of Death: 22/09/1914   Cause of death: Killed in action
Memorial: Southwick
War cemetery: Portsmouth Naval Memorial
Theatre of war: At sea
Next of Kin: Hedley George & Emily Jane Stafford

Address: Goose Street, Southwick, Wiltshire

Rowland, known as Herbert, was the second son of Hedley & Emily Stafford and on Tuesday 22 September 1914 he was serving on the Aboukir which was on patrol in the North Sea with her sister ships H.M.S. Hogue and H.M.S. Cressy. At 6am the Aboukir was torpedoed by the German Submarine U9, the explosion broke the ships back and she sank in 20 minutes with the loss of over 500 men. The Cressy and the Hogue thought the Aboukir had hit a mine and attempted to pick up survivors. Hogue was then hit by two torpedoes and sank. The Captain of the Cressy realised he was under attack but unfortunately it was two late and the Cressy was hit by another two torpedoes causing the ship to sink. The action lasted less than two hours and cost the lives of over 1400 men. One of these was Herbert who is remembered on the Portsmouth Naval Memorial.

25 SEPTEMBER 1914 - THE BATTLE OF ALBERT, FRANCE

Private Robert Henry Blake   *1st Bn Wiltshire Regiment*
Service No.   7719   Age: 27
Place of Birth: Southwick, Wiltshire   Home Country: England
Date of Death: 26/09/1914   Cause of death: Died of wounds
Memorial: Trowbridge
War cemetery: City of Paris Cemetery
Theatre of war: France
Next of Kin: George & Martha Blake
Address: Salters Yard, Trowbridge, Wiltshire

Robert Henry Blake, who was aged 27, was well known in Trowbridge having been employed at Messrs Mcall's cloth mills before being recalled to the colours on the outbreak of war. Robert had served seven years with the Wiltshire Regiment, fought through the Boer War, and had seen service in India. He formed one of the company selected for a tour of the County when the Wiltshire Regiment made there memorable march through Wiltshire in 1914.
Robert had arrived in France on Friday 14 August 1914 and after their arrival the Wiltshire Regiment took part in all the major actions of 1914 including the battle of Aisne.
At 5am on 14 September 1914 the 1st Wilts had marched as advance guard to the brigade through Brenelle to high ground east of Chassemy and moved on to cross the river Aisne at Vailly. A bridge had been built by the Royal Engineers under fire from German Artillery. The British 8th & 9th Brigades who had crossed the river under cover of darkness were fighting on the north bank of the river Aisne. The 8th Brigade asked for assistance and the 1st Wilts set off and were told to go via the woods and cross the railway bridge between Vailly and Presles. The bridge was demolished however a plank had been placed across the breach. As the 1st Wilts approached the bridge they saw men of the 9th Brigade falling back in retreat toward the bridge and the 1st Wilts took up positions to cover the 9th Brigades retirement. Lieutenant Colonel Bird of the Royal Irish Rifles arrived and ordered an advance to seize a hill north of the Aisne held by part of the 9th Brigade.

The 1st Wilts crossed the broken bridge and took up an outpost line at dusk and entrenched. The Germans made a half hearted attack at about 11pm which was not successful. On Tuesday 15th September the position was shelled and there were several casualties and it would appear that Robert Henry Blake sustained wounds in his right arm and left foot. A letter was received by his parents on 28 September, the letter was dated 22 September explaining that Robert had been wounded but had every hope of recovery and was eagerly looking forward to being transferred home. Shortly after Robert's mother received a letter, dated 24 September, from the Lady Superior of the Hospital Pasteur, Rue de Varigirard, Paris. In the letter the Lady Superior explained:

"I am sorry to let you know your son is seriously ill with tetanus, subsequent to his wounds. His case is bad and we fear all we can possibly do will prove useless. We attend and care for your dear brave child with all our heart, and pray Almighty God to comfort you and Mr Blake."

A Parcel of comforts was immediately dispatched and urgent enquiries made to the young fellows progress, but no further news was obtained until October 10 when another letter was received from the Mother Superior in which the following appeared:

"Our Divine Lord called your dear, brave son on Saturday 26 September. We did our best to soothe and revive him, but you know tetanus is such a bad affliction and your son had been badly wounded in arm and foot. A Clergyman attended to him and was at the Cemetery. Robert spoke very little since he came; in fact he was in a bad way on his arrival. He however, felt very pleased when he heard the English spoken; we have some Irish Sisters in the Hospital. I am sorry that my other letter did not reach you, as I quite understand your anxiety. God help you through this hard trial. May He rest in peace the soul of your dear son."

Robert died at the Hospital Pasteur, Paris on Sunday 26 September 1914 and is buried at the City of Paris Cemetery, Bagneux, France, with thirty other members of the British Expeditionary Force who died during this period of fighting. The letters arrived prior to any official notification from the War Office.

Robert Henry Blake

Albert Ernest Little

1 OCTOBER 1914 - THE BATTLE OF ARRAS, FRANCE

Private Albert Ernest Little
Service No.: 7078
Place of Birth: Semington, Wiltshire
Date of Death: 13/10/1914
Memorial: Trowbridge
War cemetery: Le Touret Memorial
Theatre of war: France
Next of Kin: Alfred & Annie Little
Address: Carpenters Arms Yard, Trowbridge, Wiltshire

1st Bn Wiltshire Regiment
Age: 26
Home Country: England
Cause of death: Killed in action

Albert had arrived in France on Friday 14 August On Tuesday 13 October 1914 the 1st Battalion Wiltshire Regiment advanced over the river Loisne, north east of Bethune, France, in pursuit of the German forces. At 8.45pm C Company returned from the firing line near La Couture and reported 9 killed and eight wounded. One of those killed was Albert. He is remembered on the Le Touret Memorial, France, along with over 13,000 men who fell in this area during the fighting in 1914 and 1915 and who have no known grave.

Private George Blackman
Service No.: 9086
Place of Birth: Yatton Keynell, Wiltshire
Date of Death: 18/10/1914
Memorial: Southwick
War cemetery: Le Touret Memorial
Theatre of war: France
Next of Kin: Henry & Annie Blackman
Address: Frome Road, Southwick, Wiltshire

1st Bn Wiltshire Regiment
Age: 18
Home Country: England
Cause of death: Killed in action

Prior to his enlistment in the army eighteen year old George was a gardener; he arrived in France with the Wiltshires on 14 August 1914. On Sunday 18 November 1914 the Wiltshires were attempting to advance at Ligny-le-Grand, south of Aubers, France. The German positions were too strong and they only managed to gain about 300 yards of ground. The Germans then shelled the British trenches and George was one of three men killed. He is remembered on the Le Touret Memorial and has no known grave.

19 OCTOBER 1914 - THE FIRST BATTLE OF YPRES

Lance Sergeant Walter Sidnell
Service No.: 10539
Place of Birth: Trowbridge, Wiltshire
Date of Death: 22/10/1914
Memorial: Trowbridge
War cemetery: Le Touret Memorial
Theatre of war: France
Next of Kin: Frederick & Annie Sidnell
Address: 48 Park Street, Trowbridge, Wiltshire

1st Bn Royal Scots Fusiliers
Age: 22
Home Country: England
Cause of death: Killed in action

Walter Sidnell and the plaque in Holy Trinity Church

Walter enlisted in the Royal Scots Fusiliers at Ayr, Scotland in February 1912. After remaining at Ayr for a short time he was transferred to 2nd Battalion then stationed in Londonderry, Ireland. In January 1913, he was sent with a draft to join the 1st Battalion at Pretoria, South Africa, he returned to England with the Regiment in April 1914, and was stationed at Gosport until the outbreak of the war when the Regiment were among the first to go with the Expeditionary Force to France. Sailing from Southampton on 10 August 1914 he arrived in France on Monday 14 August 1914.

He took part in the Battle of Mons and several other engagements, and was killed in action at Ypres on Thursday 22 October 1914, after very fierce fighting and after remaining in the trenches for several days. He was a young man of fine physique and was 22 years old.

Walter was a popular soldier and was spoken highly of as a promising non-commissioned officer. He had many friends in Bath and was formerly in service as a footman with Mrs Morgan, of the Royal Crescent, where he was held in high esteem. While living in Bath he pluckily went to the assistance of a Detective-Sergeant, for which he was the recipient of a present from the Chief Constable of Bath.

Walters mother and father received many letters of sympathy; in particular the Bishop of Salisbury wrote:

"I sympathise with you with all my heart in your great sorrow that has come to you suddenly. May God help and comfort you. Your son has died for his country and is now with him who died for us all, and who will help you bear all and look forward to the great meeting when no parting or death can come."

Walter was serving in the 3rd Division of the British Expeditionary Force and the several other engagements he took part in would have almost certainly included The Rearguard action at Solesmes, the Battle of Le Cateau, the Battle of the Marne, The Battle of Aisne and the Battles around Ypres, where he fell. Walter was the brother of William Sidnell who died in 1916 and Stafford Herbert Sidnell who died in 1920. Walter has no known grave.

Private George Hawkins   *2nd Bn Wiltshire Regiment*

Service No.	8547		Age:	27
Place of Birth:	Hilperton, Wiltshire		Home Country:	England
Date of Death:	22/10/1914		Cause of death:	Killed in action
Memorial:	Melksham			
War cemetery:	Ypres Menin Gate			
Theatre of war:	Belgium			

Next of Kin: James & Louisa Hawkins
Address: Bowerhill, Melksham, Wiltshire

Regular soldier George arrived in France on 7 October 1917 and was posted as missing at Beseare, Belgium on Thursday 22 October 1914. No news was heard of George until a letter from a sergeant Hale explaining that George had been killed fighting for his country and had nine wounds on his body. His brothers Alfred and Herbert were to die in 1917, George is remembered on the Ypres Menin Gate and has no known grave.

Private Herbert James Hurn   *2nd Bn Wiltshire Regiment*
Service No.   3/9418   Age: 21
Place of Birth: Trowbridge, Wiltshire   Home Country: England
Date of Death: 23/10/1914   Cause of death: Killed in action
Memorial: Trowbridge
War cemetery: Tyne Cot Memorial
Theatre of war: Belgium
Next of Kin: Alfred Hooper & Georgina Hurn
Address: 23 Broad Street, Trowbridge, Wiltshire

Herbert had arrived in France with the 2nd Battalion Wiltshire Regiment on Wednesday 7 October 1914. Just over two weeks later on Friday 23 October 1914 the 2nd Battalion Wiltshire Regiment were in the front line trenches at Beslare, south east of Zonnebeke, Belgium,. The Germans bombarded the British causing many casualties and doing much damage to the trenches. One of six fatalities the Wiltshires suffered on this day was Herbert.
He is buried in Tyne Cot Cemetery, Belgium, 'Tyne Cottage' was the name given by the Northumberland Fusiliers to a barn which stood near the level crossing on the Passchendaele-Broodseinde road which had been part of the German defences. Herbert is one of over 11,000 men who were casualties of the First World War buried or commemorated at Tyne Cot Cemetery.

Right: Herbert Hurn

Far right: William Hall

Private William Hall   *2nd Bn Wiltshire Regiment*

Service No.	3/9327	Age:	24
Place of Birth:	Hilperton, Wiltshire	Home Country:	England
Date of Death:	24/10/1914	Cause of death:	Killed in action
Memorial:	Trowbridge		
War cemetery:	Ypres Menim Gate		
Theatre of war:	Belgium		
Next of Kin:	Frank & Fanny Hall		
Address:	Dymott Square, Hilperton, Trowbridge, Wiltshire		

William had arrived in France with the 2nd Battalion Wiltshire Regiment on Wednesday 7 October 1914. Just over two weeks later on Saturday 24 October 1914 the 2nd Battalion Wiltshire Regiment were holding the front line trenches at Beslare, south east of Zonnebeke, Belgium.

At 5.30am as the day was breaking the Germans attacked with a superior force but the enemy were driven back with heavy casualties.

The Germans then renewed the attack and after 2 hours of continuous fighting, in which the Germans had hundreds of casualties, the enemy broke through the British lines. The Wiltshires suffered very heavy casualties, a total of sixty six of their members were killed and a large number captured.

A special note was inserted in the Wiltshires War Diary concerning the gallant work of Captain Comyn, the medical officer and stretcher bearers who for the previous three days and nights were continuously handling wounded or burying dead.

William is remembered on the Ypres Menin Gate Memorial, Belgium with over 54,000 men who have no known grave and died in Belgium during the Great War.

Lance Corporal William Lewington   *1st Bn Wiltshire Regiment*

Service No.	7776	Age:	27
Place of Birth:	Axford, Wiltshire	Home Country:	England
Date of Death:	24/10/1914	Cause of death:	Killed in action
Memorial:	Marlborough & Ramsbury		
War cemetery:	Le Touret Memorial		
Theatre of war:	France		
Next of Kin:	Annie Lewington (wife) - Stephen & Eleanor Lewington (parents)		
Address:	Trowbridge – Axford, Wiltshire		

William was a reservist; he had left the army and married Annie Hawey in 1913. He was a postman in Marlborough but at the outbreak of war he was called up and his wife Annie returned to her home at Trowbridge with their infant child. William had arrived with the 1st Wiltshires in France on Friday 14 August and on Saturday 14 October they were in trenches at Neuve Chapelle facing a German night attack which was beaten off during the early hours of the morning. At 9.45am the Germans began to shell Neuve Chapelle village and the British trenches. This ceased after a couple of hours but then continued from 2pm to 7pm causing a great deal of damage to the village and the British trenches. The War Diary for the day lists the following casualties;

"2nd Lieut Riddell slightly wounded. 8 men killed, 36 wounded and 23 men missing. It is feared that most of these 23 men were buried in the dug outs."

It is likely William was one of those who was initially listed as missing. He is remembered on the Le Touret Memorial and has no known grave.

Private William Avons *1st Bn Wiltshire Regiment*
Service No. 6152   Age: 32
Place of Birth: Hilperton, Wiltshire   Home Country: England
Date of Death: 26/10/1914   Cause of death: Killed in action
Memorial: Hilperton
War cemetery: Le Touret Memorial
Theatre of war: France
Next of Kin: Frederick Charles & Annie Avons
Address: Dymott Square, Hilperton, Wiltshire

In August 1915 Mr and Mrs Avons received news of their eldest son William, who had been posted as "missing" since October 1914, and of who no information had been obtainable. William was a single man in the reserve, and at the outbreak of war had been working for Mr Mathews of Hilperton as a wheelwright. He was recalled to the colours and went out with D Company the 1st Wiltshire Regiment, to France. His name was included on the list of the "missing," and although through the efforts of Miss Fredericks of Beechcroft, Burnham, Bucks, inquiry was made through the German prisoner camps and else where, mystery shrouded his fate until the Enquiry Department for wounded and missing established by the British Red Cross and Order of St. John, obtained some reliable information.

Miss Fredericks writing from Burnham, on 24 August 1915 said:

"Dear Mrs Avons, I deeply regret being the bearer of sad news to you, but perhaps the previous letter from the Red Cross may have prepared you a little for the information now received about your son William, and which I have enclosed. Your brave lad has given his life for his King and country, and what more glorious death could come to our dear ones?
In the midst of your deep sorrow you must feel proud of him. And surely there could not have been a more beautiful time after desperately fighting all day long against a terrible foe, for him to have gone to his everlasting rest in the evening. How terrible this war is. Our splendid young men sacrificing their lives, while for women the sacrifice is double. May you have comfort and strength given you to bear your great sorrow. May your other brave lads come back to you in safety. With the sincerest sympathy from Hilda Fredericks."

The letter forwarded by Miss Fredericks from the Red Cross was as follows:

British Red Cross and Order of St. John, August 19 1915.
Private Avons, 6152, 1st Wilts, D Company.

"Dear Madam, You have asked us for information of Private W. Avons who was reported wounded and missing on the 26 October 1914. You will understand that it is difficult at this time to get any information about events in the early part of the war, but we are informed by a Private Kinch, who is now in the 26th General Hospital at Etaples, that he saw Private Avons carried by stretcher bearers to the dressing station, which was a chateau off the Aisne, in the evening. The day of this event was not given, but it is presumably in the early weeks of September 1914, when the fighting on the Aisne took place. Private Kinch says that Private Avons was dead, and that he has no doubt of his identity. Yours truly, for Sir Louis Mallett C.R.P".

Frederick & Annie Avons had three other sons serving (one with the Royal Field Artillery in the Dardenelles, one in France and one in the North Sea), and a son in law, Driver Telfer, in the Royal Horse Artillery.

Far left: William Avons

Left: Clifford Nelson Bailey

It is now known that William was one of those listed missing after desperate fighting around Neuve Chapelle, France on Monday 26 October 1914. The Germans moved up within two hundred yards of the British lines, the Wiltshires deployed 3 platoons from C Company and attacked their foe driving the Germans back at bayonet point into the burning village of Neuve Chapelle. Soon after the British lost control of the village of Neuve Chapelle. William is remembered on the Le Touret Memorial, France and has no known grave.

Corporal William Henry Forsyth   *1st Bn Wiltshire Regiment*

Service No.	7389
Place of Birth:	Trowbridge, Wiltshire
Date of Death:	26/10/1914
Memorial:	Not known
War cemetery:	Le Touret Memorial
Theatre of war:	France
Next of Kin:	Job & Mary J Forsyth
Address:	Semington, Wiltshire

Age:	33
Home Country:	England
Cause of death:	Killed in action

William had arrived in France on Friday 14 August 1914 with the 1st Battalion Wiltshire and on Monday 26 October the Wiltshires were at the village of Neuve Chapelle. The Germans shelled the British position and the Regiment on the left of the Wiltshires mostly cleared out leaving their trenches. At 4.30pm the Wiltshires were informed that the Germans had broken into the trenches on the left and 2 platoons were sent and reserves moved up just in time to meet the Germans debouching from the west side of the village of Neuve Chapelle. Two platoons from C Company held the Germans near the farm that was being used as the Wiltshires HQ. As darkness was falling the Germans moved up within two hundred yards of the British lines, the Wiltshires deployed 3 platoons from C Company and attacked their foe driving the Germans back at bayonet point into the burning village of Neuve Chapelle. It is likely at this point William was reported missing.

Some months later Job & Mary Forsyth received an official communication from the War Office presuming William had been killed in action on the day he had been declared missing. William is remembered on the Le Touret Memorial, France and has no known grave

Private Clifford Nelson Bailey *1st Bn Wiltshire Regiment*
Service No.   7718   Age: 25
Place of Birth: Trowbridge, Wiltshire   Home Country: England
Date of Death: 30/10/1914   Cause of death: Killed in action
Memorial: Trowbridge
War cemetery: Ypres Town Cemetery
Theatre of war: Belgium
Next of Kin: John & Anna Maria Bailey
Address: 98 Mortimer Street, Trowbridge, Wiltshire

Clifford arrived in France on Saturday 12 September 1914 having been a soldier prior to the commencement of hostilities. Little is known of the fate that became of Clifford. He was reported missing in November 1914. After the war his remains were found and he was buried in Ypres Town Cemetery Extension.

Private Frederick Dike *2nd Bn Royal Welsh Fusiliers*
Service No.   10606   Age: 25
Place of Birth: Trowbridge, Wiltshire   Home Country: England
Date of Death: 30/10/1914   Cause of death: Killed in action
Memorial: Not known
War cemetery: Pont Du Hem Military Cemetery La Gorgue
Theatre of war: France
Next of Kin: Anne Dike
Address: 245 Sumner Road, Peckham, London

Frederick, who had been employed as a florist, enlisted in the South Wales Borders on 1 October 1908 and after 2 years service he purchased his discharge on the 3rd of June 1910, the cost of which was £18. On 12 May 1911 Frederick rejoined the Army enlisting in the Royal Welsh Fusiliers and on 19 December 1912 he was posted to India. His Battalion returned from India to England on 11 March 1914. The 2nd Royal Welsh Fusiliers had been at Portland in Dorset at the point of mobilisation and landed at Rouen France on Tuesday 11 August 1914. On Friday 30 October 1914 Frederick was with the Royal Welsh Fusiliers in trenches near Fromelles, France. There had been fierce fighting for many days and there were over 150 dead Germans lying in front of the British trenches. It is likely Frederick was killed when the Royal Welsh Fusiliers counter attacked after the Germans had broken through the British lines on the left of the Royal Welsh Fusiliers trenches. The Royal Welsh Fusiliers had 4 fatalities on this day, Frederick was one of them and he is buried in Pont Du Hem Military Cemetery at La Gorgue, France.

Pioneer Edwin Stephen Ford *1st Bn   Wiltshire Regiment*
Service No.   6713   Age: 28
Place of Birth: Tondu, Glamorgan   Home Country: Wales
Date of Death: 31/10/1914   Cause of death: Killed in action
Memorial: Trowbridge
War cemetery: Le Touret Memorial
Theatre of war: France
Next of Kin: Sarah Anne Ford (wife) - Alfred & Elizabeth Ford (parents)
Address: 15 Brewery Street, Pembroke Dock – 26 Westbourne Road, Trowbridge

Edwin had joined the Wiltshires on 4 February 1903 at the age of 17 and 1 month into 1907 he married his wife Sarah Anne. Prior to the outbreak of war he worked as a labourer for

Far left: Edwin Ford

Left : Ernest Meaden

the Great Western Railway. It is probable that Edwin was a reservist and was called up at the outbreak of war. He arrived in France on Friday 14 August 1914 and fought with the Wiltshires in many of the engagements they were involved in. Edwin was listed as missing in action on Saturday 31 October 1914 but it is likely he was killed near Neuve Chapelle during German attacks in the days leading up to this, when much confusion reigned and at one point 150 members of the 1st Battalion Wiltshire Regiment were marked as missing. Edwin is remembered on the Le Touret Memorial and has no known grave.

Private Ernest Meaden   *1st Bn Wiltshire Regiment*
Service No.   5713
Place of Birth: Trowbridge, Wiltshire
Date of Death: 31/10/1914
Memorial: Trowbridge
War cemetery: Le Touret Memorial
Theatre of war: France
Next of Kin: Edith Mary Meaden (wife) - John & Louisa Meaden (parents)
Address: Bristol - 9 Thomas Street, Trowbridge, Wiltshire

Age: 30
Home Country: England
Cause of death: Killed in action

It is likely Ernest was a reservist, after being called back to the colours he was sent to Weymouth for training and while there he married his sweetheart Edith Mary Maine on 29 August 1914. He arrived in France on Monday 21 September 1914 and a little over a month later he was listed at missing in action at Neuve Chapelle, France. Ernest left a widow who was pregnant with his son. He is remembered on the Le Touret Memorial and has no known grave.

Private Frederick Francis Frame   *1st Bn Northumberland Fusiliers*
Service No.   936
Place of Birth: Trinity, Jersey
Date of Death: 01/11/1914
Memorial: Trowbridge
War cemetery: Ypres Menin Gate
Theatre of war: Belgium
Next of Kin: Frederick William & Anna Selina Frame
Address:,   Trowbridge, Wiltshire

Age: 31
Home Country: England
Cause of death: Died

Frederick had served in India prior to the Great War and had arrived in France on Thursday 27 August 1914. He was reported missing on Sunday 1 November 1914 and later was reported as having died on that date. His cousin Arthur Edward Frame was killed in action on 16 February 1915, both are remembered on the Ypres Menin Gate.

Private Walter Moore   *1st Bn Wiltshire Regiment*

Service No.	7124
Place of Birth:	Wingfield, Wiltshire
Date of Death:	04/11/1914
Memorial:	Trowbridge
War cemetery:	Bethune Town Cemetery
Theatre of war:	France
Next of Kin:	Berkley & Matilda Anne Moore
Address:	Laurel Cottage, Wingfield, Trowbridge, Wiltshire

Age: 33
Home Country: England
Cause of death: Died of wounds

Walter had originally joined the Wiltshires on 4 October 1904 at the age of 18 years and ten months. He arrived in France on Friday 14 August 1914 and took part in all the engagements that the 1st Battalion Wiltshire Regiment were involved in during 1914. He died of wounds at the 33rd Casualty Clearing Station based at Bethune, France.

7 NOVEMBER 1914 - BRITISH & INDIAN FORCES LAND AT MESOPOTAMIA TO PROTECT BRITISH OIL INTERESTS

Trooper Walter Leo Letora   *3rd Dragoon Guards*

Service No.	375
Place of Birth:	Trowbridge, Wiltshire
Date of Death:	13/11/1914
Memorial:	Trowbridge
War cemetery:	Ypres Menin Gate
Theatre of war:	Belgium
Next of Kin:	Francis & Eliza Letora
Address:	14 Newtown, Trowbridge, Wiltshire

Age: 23
Home Country: England
Cause of death: Killed in action

Right: Frederick Fancis Frame

Far right : Leo Letora

Walter known as Leo was serving with the 3rd Dragoon Guards in Egypt prior to the Great War and arrived in France on Saturday 31 October 1914. He had only been at the front a few days when he was killed by a shell on Friday 13 November 1914. The day before his death he was praised by his officer for his courage and pluck. He is remembered on the Ypres Menin Gate and has no known grave. In 1917 the following memoriam appeared in a local paper:

"In loving memory of our dearest son and brother who fell in action at Ypres
Now a mother's heart is aching
For a son she loved so well
He gave his life for his country
In honours cause he fell"

Private Sidney Percy Hartley   *1st Bn Dorsetshire Regiment*
Service No.   9494   Age: 19
Place of Birth: Trowbridge, Wiltshire   Home Country: England
Date of Death: 19/12/1914   Cause of death: Died
Memorial: Trowbridge
War cemetery: Netley Military Cemetery
Theatre of war: Home
Next of Kin: John & Mary Hartley
Address: 18 Middle Rank, Trowbridge, Wiltshire

Sidney was employed as a fish hawker. He enlisted in the 1st Battalion Dorsetshire Regiment on 8 January 1913 arriving in France on Sunday 16 August 1914. He was evacuated from France on 17 December 1914 and died on Saturday 19 December 1914, of sickness or disease at Netley Military Hospital. His family inserted the following memoriam in a local paper:

"Had he asked us well we know
We should say Lord spare this blow
Yes with streaming tears should pray
Lord we love him let him stay
From his sorrowing Mother, Brothers and Sister's"

Far left: Sidney Percy Hartley

Left: Felix Charles Hurbert Hanbury-Tracey

Lieutenant Felix Charles Hurbert Hanbury-Tracey *2nd Bn Scots Guards*
Service No.	N/A
Place of Birth:	Buckingham Gate, London
Date of Death:	10/12/1914
Memorial:	All Saints Church, Eastbourne
War cemetery:	Ploegsteert Memorial
Theatre of war:	Belgium
Next of Kin:	Madeline Hanbury-Tracy (wife) – Charles 4th Baron Sudeley (parent)
Address:	46, Montague Square, London

Age: 30
Home Country: England
Cause of death: Killed in action

Felix was Educated at Harrow and the Royal Military College Sandhurst and received a commission with the Scots Guards on 8 May 1901. He retired form the army in 1907 and on 11 June 1908 he married Madeline Llewellyn at Lacock, Wiltshire. He arrived in France on 7 November and on the night of the 18-19 December he took part in an attack on German positions at Fromelles with the 2nd Battalion Scots Guards. He was slightly wounded during the start of the attack but carried on and led his men. He was then seriously wounded on the parapet of the German Trench. Some of his men attempted to carry him to safety but he ordered them to leave him where he was and not risk their lives.The Germans counterattacked recapturing the trench and Felix died in German hands a few hours later. He was subsequently buried by his captors. A few days later during the 1914 Christmas truce information was received from the Germans that Felix had been buried in Fromelles German cemetery, he is today remembered on the Ploegsteert Memorial. A memorial service was held at Trowbridge and Madeline, his wife laid a wreath of myrtle, which had been grown at Lackham from a spray taken from her bridal bouquet.

18 DECEMBER 1914 - BATTLE OF GIVENCHY, BELGIUM

Sergeant Stanley Alfred Elkins *2nd Welsh Regiment*
Service No. 9673
Place of Birth: Trowbridge, Wiltshire
Date of Death: 22/12/1914
Memorial: Not Known
War cemetery: Le Touret Memorial
Theatre of war: France
Next of Kin: Arthur & Annie Elkins

Age: 27
Home Country: Wales
Cause of death: Killed in action

Regular soldier Stanley arrived in France on Saturday 22 August 1914. He was killed in action on Tuesday 22 December 1914 and is remembered on the Le Touret Memorial. He has no known grave.

25 DECEMBER 1914 - UNOFFICIAL CHRISTMAS TRUCE

Private Frederick Philip Cole *1st Wiltshire Regiment*
Service No. 6449
Place of Birth: Lacock, Wiltshire
Date of Death: 26/12/1914
Memorial: Not known
War cemetery: Ypres Menin Gate
Theatre of war: Belgium
Next of Kin: Frederick William & Lydia Cole
Address: 41 Hillside View, Peasedown, Somerset

Age: 29
Home Country: England
Cause of death: Killed in action

Frederick was an apprentice painter with Gowen and Stevens of Trowbridge, and enlisted in the Wiltshires on the 12 October 1903 at the age of 18 yeas and 7 months. At the outbreak of war he was working in Weston-Super-Mare and was engaged to be married. However, being on reserve he was called up and returned to the Wiltshires, arriving in France on Friday 14 October 1914, and he took part in all the actions the Wiltshire Regiment were involved in. Frederick was killed in action on Boxing day 1914. At Kemmel in Belgium there was no Christmas truce and the 1st Battalion Wiltshire Regiments war diary states;

"In trenches. Germans did a good deal of shelling, but most of their shells did not burst. A good deal of sniping in trenches. Cold and frost. 2 killed, 1 wounded."

In December 1915 the following memoriam was inserted in a local paper:

"In loving memory of Frederick Philip Cole killed in action while serving with the 1st Wiltshire Regiment on Boxing Day 1914
For him the Warfare's over
The sounds of battle cease
Angels have bourne his soul away
To realms of endless peace"

Members of the Wiltshire Regiment in the trenches winter 1914-15

2
1915 - THE WAR THAT SHOULD HAVE BEEN OVER BY CHRISTMAS

Private Richard Thomas Knight *2nd Bn Wiltshire Regiment*
Service No.   3/9969   Age: 21
Place of Birth: Marlborourgh, Wiltshire   Home Country: England
Date of Death: 02/01/1915   Cause of death: Died
Memorial: Trowbridge & Marlborough
War cemetery: Merville Communal Cemetery
Theatre of war: France
Next of Kin: Annie Knight (parent)
Address: 13 Stand Lane, Marlborourgh, Wiltshire

Richard was a baker at the outbreak of hostilities. It is likely he was one of the first to volunteer for service and arrived in France with a draft of Kitchener's Army men on 11 December 1914. He was one of twenty men who were admitted to hospital with sickness between 18 December 1914 and the New Year due to the cold weather. He died of sickness on Saturday 2 January 1915 at one of the casualty clearing stations based at Merville, France. In December 1917 the following memoriam was inserted in a local paper:

"In loving memory of Richard Knight who died of wounds
Angels call the roll up yonder
Muster day in heaven proclaim
Call the role and at the summons
He will answer to his name
From his sorrowing Mother and Dad and Sisters"

Private George Hooper   *2nd Bn Welsh Regiment*
Service No.   1786   Age: 26
Place of Birth: Trowbridge, Wiltshire   Home Country: England
Date of Death: 23/01/1915   Cause of death: Killed in action
Memorial: Trowbridge
War cemetery: Browns Road Military Cemetery Festubert
Theatre of war: France
Next of Kin: George & Laura Young
Address: 12 Upper Bond Street, Trowbridge, Wiltshire

George was the eldest son of Laura Young, and had arrived in France on 29 November 1914. He was killed in action at Givenchy, France on Saturday 23 January 1915. His brother, William Young, was to be killed at Gallipoli in November 1915.

Far Left: Richard Thomas Knight

Left: George Hooper

Driver Thomas Rogers   *192nd HT Coy Army Service Corps*
Service No.   S2/015426
Place of Birth: Oldham, Lancashire
Date of Death: 28/01/1915
Memorial: Not known
War cemetery: Trowbridge Cemetery
Theatre of war: Home
Next of Kin: Walter & Sophia Rogers
Address: St Anne's On Sea, Lancashire

Age: 22
Home Country: England
Cause of death: Died

Thomas, a shop assistant, volunteered for service with the Army Service Corps and was posted to Trowbridge. He died at Trowbridge Isolation Hospital after a short illness and was the first soldier to die from the barracks. He was buried in Trowbridge Cemetery with full military honors which was attended by family members and 250 officers and men of the Army Service Corps.

Far left: The gave of Thomas Rogers in Trowbridge Cemetery.

Left: Arthur Edward Frame

Sergeant Arthur Edward Frame   *2nd Bn Northumberland Fusiliers*
Service No. 920
Place of Birth: Trowbridge, Wiltshire
Date of Death: 16/02/1915
Memorial: Trowbridge
War cemetery: Ypres Menim Gate
Theatre of war: Belgium
Next of Kin: Fanettu Ford (sister
Address: 13 Marlborough Buildings, Trowbridge, Wiltshire.

Age: 30
Home Country: England
Cause of death: Killed in action

Arthur had served in the army for ten years at the commencement of hostilities and arrived on the continent on 16 January 1915. He was shot through the head while serving on the Ypres front in Belgium on Tuesday 16 February 1915. His cousin Frederick Francis Frame was reported missing on Sunday 1st November 1914, both are remembered on the Ypres Menim Gate.

Private Joseph Samuel Fincher   *3rd Bn South Wales Borderers*
Service No. 14148
Place of Birth: Trowbridge, Wiltshire
Date of Death: 24/02/1915
Memorial: Not Known
War cemetery: Bristol Arnos Vale Cemetery
Theatre of war: Home
Next of Kin: Mary J. Fincher (wife) - Naomi Fincher (parent)

Age: 50
Home Country: Wales
Cause of death: Died

Joseph married Mary J. Morgan in South Wales in 1890, he died of illness or disease at Bristol on Wednesday 24 February 1915.

10 March 1915 - Battle of Neuve Chapelle

Lance Coporal William Albert Hurn   *2nd Bn Wiltshire Regiment*
Service No. 3/9417
Place of Birth: Trowbridge, Wiltshire
Date of Death: 10/03/1915
Memorial: Trowbridge
War cemetery: Le Touret Memorial
Theatre of war: France
Next of Kin: John & Selina Hurn
Address: 21 Shails Lane, Trowbridge, Wiltshire.

Age: 21
Home Country: England
Cause of death: Killed in action

William had arrived in France on 20 October 1914, he was killed in action on Wednesday 10 March 1915 at Neuve Chapelle. He was a corporal in the regiment but gave up his stripes to become an officers servant. Captain Strawson wrote to Mrs Hurn informing her of her husband's death stating his officer was also believed to have been killed. William was only 21 and left a widow and one daughter.
At 7.30am on Wednesday 10 March 1915 an artillery bombardment commenced and at 8.05am ceased. The Wiltshires in the trenches described the bombardment as being the most tremendous they had ever seen or heard, both in point of noise and in actual effect. The shrieking of the shells in the air, their explosions, and the continuous thunder of the batteries all merged into one great volume of sound. The discharges of the guns were so rapid that they sounded like

the fire of a gigantic machine gun. During the thirty five minutes it continued the British could show themselves and even walk about in perfect safety. The 2nd Wiltshire's had waited in the support trenches in the area of Cameron Lane since their arrival at 5.30am and during the morning British wounded streamed past and at 1pm they received orders to advance. They advanced along Cameron Lane, in company lines at 25 yard intervals. At about 2.30pm the 2nd Wiltshire's arrive at the second support trenches in the rear of Neuve Chapelle. D and C Companies pushed forward to the old British Trench, during this time the Battalion was under German shell fire.

The 2nd Wiltshire's were now given orders of clearing the German trenches on the left of Min Du Pietre and then connecting the trench with the old British trench. D and C Companies now moved forward to capture the German trench at the road junction 250 yards south of the Moated Grange. At this point there was some delay as Captain Gilson was shot in the leg, Captain Makin took Command and another delay followed. Both C and D Companies advanced between the British and German trenches; a bombing party worked along the German trench and 108 prisoners were taken. There was hardly any resistance for the trenches, which in places were literally blotted out and were filled with dead and dying Germans, partially buried in earth and debris, and the majority of survivors were in no mood for further fighting. When the leading company got within 50 yards of the Moated Grange, hot rifle fire opened up from the direction of the trench. A body of Germans ensconced in some enclosure. The 2nd Wilts advanced and another 100 yards of German trench were captured. The chief difficulty the 2nd Wiltshire's experienced was the fire from machine guns in the houses. At this point no further progress could be made that day.

It was an imposing sight at dusk, to see the village around on fire as a result of shells poured into them, largely from our guns. A sergeant in the 2nd Wiltshire's sent a post card home after Neuve Chapelle saying,

"Have been doing great things, am well up to now, but had a few escapes - bullets through trousers and coat."

On Wednesday 10 March the 2nd Wiltshire's had 8 fatalities, 6 men and 2 officers. William was one of the men and the officer he served was one of the officers. William is remembered on the Le Touret Memorial, France, along with over 13,000 names of men who fell in this area before 25 September 1915 and who have no known grave.

Far left: William Albert Hurn

Left: Thomas Pritchard Adlam

Private Thomas Pritchard Adlam — *2nd Bn Wiltshire Regiment*
Service No. 11026
Place of Birth: Caversham, Berkshire
Date of Death: 12/03/1915
Memorial: Trowbridge
War cemetery: Le Touret Memorial
Theatre of war: France
Next of Kin: Wilfred & Jane Adlam
Address: 105 Dursley Road, Trowbridge, Wiltshire
Age: 21
Home Country: England
Cause of death: Killed in action

Volunteer Thomas arrived in France on 11 December 1914 and was killed in action at Neuve Chappelle, France on Friday 12 March 1915. He was the son of Wilfred and Jane Adlam, another of whose sons were killed in 1911 by a fall of cheese at the Wilts Farmers branch on the Down. The death of Thomas had not been officially notified when another Trowbridge man, who was in the trenches near to Thomas, wrote to his own parents on 19 March 1915:

"I am quite well. I have been in four days hard fighting, and I never want to see such sight again as I saw in these four days. We lost several in our regiment, and poor Adlam was killed. You will remember him; he belonged to the Conigre chapel. The bullet that killed him killed two other men as well. We are now back from the firing line"

At Neuve Chappelle on 12 March there was confusion in the trenches after the Germans carried out a bombing attack, 44 men died on the day and between 10 and 13 March 1915 the 2nd Battalion Wiltshire Regiment had 295 casualties, of this number 172 were missing and it was later found that seventy three had died. Because of the confusion of the battle and the failure of the Neuve Chappelle attacks many bodies were lost. Thomas is remembered on the Le Touret Memorial, France, along with over 13,000 names of men who fell in this area before 25 September 1915 and who have no known grave.

Lance Coporal Walter Powell — *2nd Bn Duke of Cornwall's Light Infantry*
Service No. 8032
Place of Birth: Trowbridge, Wiltshire
Date of Death: 14/03/1915
Memorial: Trowbridge
War cemetery: Ypres Menin Gate
Age: 31
Home Country: England
Cause of death: Killed in action

Below: Ypres Menin Gate - Right: Walter Powell

Theatre of war: Belgium
Next of Kin: Frederick & Eliza Powell
Address: 2 Harmony Place, Lower Studley, Trowbridge, Wiltshire

Walter joined the army in 1907, before that he was employed at the brush works in Trowbridge. He arrived in France with the 1st Battalion Duke of Cornwall's Light Infantry. He was wounded in the head and arm early in the war and returned to England for convalescence returning to the firing line again in December with the 2nd Battalion Duke of Cornwall's Light Infantry. On Sunday 14 March 1915 Walter was in trenches in front of St.Eloi, the trenches connected to a defensive position called the Mound, which was described as an artificial heap about 30 feet high by about half acre.

At 5pm the Germans exploded mines under the Mound and the British trenches; this was followed by a terrific German bombardment and the whole area was plastered by shells. A German infantry attack followed capturing the British trenches and forcing what was left of the defenders to flee. Walter was initially reported missing but later the news reached Frederick & Eliza that Walter had been killed in action. He is remembered on the Ypres Menin Gate.

Private Charles Edward Bailey *1st Bn Royal West Kent Regiment*
Service No.   L/5679
Age: 35
Place of Birth: Trowbridge, Wiltshire
Home Country: England
Date of Death: 22/03/1915
Cause of death: Killed in action
Memorial: Not known
War cemetery: Aeroplane Cemetery
Theatre of war: Belgium
Next of Kin: Edith Maud Bailey (wife)
Address:,   Maidstone, Kent.

Charles joined the army on 16 October 1900 at Maidstone. He married Edith Maud Webb in 1908 and left the army in 1909 but as a reservist he was called up at the outbreak of hostilities and arrived in France on 6 February 1915. He was killed in action on Monday 22 March 1915 near Zonnebecke Belgium. He left a widow and two young sons.

Private Herbert Pictor *3rd Bn Monmouthshire Regiment*
Service No.   2171
Age: 26
Place of Birth: Trowbridge, Wiltshire
Home Country: England

Far left: Herbert Pictor

Left: Henry Alfred George Fryer

Date of Death:	24/03/1915	Cause of death:	Killed in action
Memorial:	Trowbridge		
War cemetery:	Wulvergem Churchyard		
Theatre of war:	Belgium		
Next of Kin:	Henry & Emma Pictor		
Address:	9 St. Thomas's Passage, Trowbridge, Wiltshire		

Herbert was employed by Butt & Sons, Trowbridge but working in Wales at the outbreak of the Great War. He was one of the first to volunteer for service in early August enlisting in the Monmouthshire Regiment. He was one of four brothers to have joined the New Army. Herbert had a cheerful and optimistic nature and arrived in France on 13 February 1915. Captain Gardner, Herbert's company officer wrote:

"I wish to express on behalf of myself, brother officers and men of this Regiment our deepest sympathy with you in the loss of your son, Private Pictor. As you have no doubt already been informed, he was killed on the 24 March, and I am sure it will be of consolation to you to know his death was painless. He will be much missed by all who knew him. He was a gallant fellow and died a glorious death serving his King and country."

Private Henry Alfred George Fryer   *1st Bn Wiltshire Regiment*

Service No.	3/19	Age:	32
Place of Birth:	Trowbridge, Wiltshire	Home Country:	England
Date of Death:	11/04/1915	Cause of death:	Died of wounds
Memorial:	Trowbridge		
War cemetery:	Dickebusch New Military Cemetery		
Theatre of war:	Belgium		
Next of Kin:	Lena Fryer (wife) - Harry W G & Rose Fryer (parents)		
Address:	10 Upper Bond Street - Islington Green, Trowbridge, Wiltshire		

Henry, a labourer, married Lena Smith in 1902, he arrived in France on 22 October 1914. It is likely he was one of 4 men wounded Sunday 11 April 1915 at Elzenwalle, Belgium. He is buried near by at Dickebusch New Military Cemetery.

Sergeant Robert Michael Moffatt   *97th Bty Royal Field Artillery*

Service No.	33674	Age:	29
Place of Birth:	Trowbridge, Wiltshire	Home Country:	England
Date of Death:	16/04/1915	Cause of death:	Died
Memorial:	Not known		
War cemetery:	Helles Memorial		
Theatre of war:	Gallipoli		
Next of Kin:	Robert & Catherine Moffatt		
Address:	10 Hill Street, London		

Robert was employed at Woolwich Arsenal and at the outbreak of war he volunteered for service with the Royal Field Artillery. He arrived on the Gallipoli Peninsular on 2 April 1915. He died of illness or disease two weeks later on Friday 16 April 1915. It is likely his grave was lost after the Allies evacuated Gallipoli and he is remembered on the Helles Memorial.

17 APRIL 1915 - THE CAPTURE OF HILL 60, BELGIUM

Private William James Underwood   *3rd Bn Royal Fusiliers*
Service No.   7420   Age: 36
Place of Birth: Trowbridge, Wiltshire   Home Country: England
Date of Death: 26/04/1915   Cause of death: Killed in action
Memorial: Trowbridge
War cemetery: Ypres Menin Gate
Theatre of war: Belgium
Next of Kin: John & Hannah
Address: 4 Cross Street, Trowbidge, Wiltshire

William was killed in action on Monday 26 April 1915 during the Second Battle of Ypres. He is remembered on the Ypres Menin Gate and has no known Grave.

28 APRIL 1915 - FIRST BATTLE OF KRITHIA, GALLIPOLI, TURKEY

Private Roland John Burton   *1st Bn Dorsetshire Regiment*
Service No.   3/8649   Age: 29
Place of Birth: Trowbridge, Wiltshire   Home Country: England
Date of Death: 02/05/1915   Cause of death: Killed in action
Memorial: Trowbridge
War cemetery: Divisional Cemetery
Theatre of war: Belgium
Next of Kin: John & Elizabeth Burton
Address: 31 Dursley Street, Trowbridge, Wiltshire

Roland, a collier, volunteered for service enlisting on 3 September 1914. He had initially joined the Somerset Light Infantry but was transferred to the Dorset Regiment. After his training he arrived in France on 8 April 1918. On 1 May 1915 Roland was with the Dorset's at Hill 60, an artificial mound some 60 feet tall made up of earth which had been spoil from a nearby railway cutting. During the evening and without warning the Germans opened a severe bombardment of Hill 60. This was followed by thick white and yellow clouds of gas being released from nozzles in front of the German trenches. The gas was so dense that it took almost immediate effect.
A Lieutenant serving in the Dorset Regiment wrote an account of his first experience of asphyxiating gas.

"I expect you have heard how the Germans on this 'Hill 60' played us the dirtiest trick that any British Regiment has had to put up with. The Canadians did not have it like we did, they had it from 400 to 500 yards away, whereas our trenches are at most 40 yards from the Germans. I saw more of the affair than anyone else, so I can tell you exactly what happened. At about seven o'clock I came out of my dug out and saw a hose sticking over the German parapet, which was starting to spout out a thick yellow cloud with a tinge of green in it. The gas came out with a hiss that you could hear quite plainly. I at once shouted to my men to put on respirators (bits of flannel), then I got mine and went and warned the Captain, who did not yet have his respirator on. The Huns began a terrible bombardment, not so much at us but at our supports and our dressing station.

Now, either they had miscalculated the direction of the wind or else it had changed, for the gas did not come directly toward us, but went slantwise, then our trench being so close the gas went into part of the German trenches as well as into ours. They bolted from theirs when they got a wiff of the filthy stuff, a few of our men staggered away down the hill, some got into a wood behind it and died there, as the ground was low and the gas followed them, others only got as far as the mine head and communication trenches. The company in support on my left moved up into the firing line, as did also half of my platoon, consequently, I was left with a few men to do all the rescue work.. My men were splendid; they all came with me into the gas, except the ones I ordered to stay behind, and we must have saved scores of lives. The men in most cases were lying insensible in the bottom of the trenches, and quite a number were in the mine head, which was the worst possible place. The best place after the first rush of gas was the firing line, being the highest point.

I was the only officer not in the firing line, and I should think quite 200 men passed through my hands, some died with me and some died on the way down. The Battalion had, I believe, 337 casualties. I can't understand how it was I was not knocked out; it must have been the work I had to do. I was simply mad with rage, seeing strong men drop to the ground and die in this way. They were in agonies. I had to argue with many of them as to whether they were dead or not. Why we got it so bad was because of our closeness of our trenches to the Germans, and this affair does away with the idea that it is not deadly. I saw two men staggering in over a field in our rear last night, and when I went to look for them this morning they were both dead. Altogether, I suppose 100 or 120 men and two or three officers are dead or will die of the stuff. I am absolutely sickened. Clean killing is at least comprehensible, but this murder by slow agony, it absolutely knocks me. The whole civilised world ought to rise up and exterminate those swine across the hill."

Roland died from the effects of poison gas on Sunday 2 May 1915 and is buried at Divisional Cemetery, Belgium.

Sapper Laurence Hubert Jones *9th Field Coy Royal Engineers*
Service No.: 23350
Place of Birth: Trowbridge, Wiltshire
Date of Death: 03/05/1915
Memorial: Trowbridge
War cemetery: Potijze Chateau Grounds Cemetery
Theatre of war: Belgium

Age: 21
Home Country: England
Cause of death: Killed in action

Right: Roland John Burton

Far Right: Laurence Hubert Jones

Next of Kin: Ernest Augustus & Elizabeth Jones
Address: 6 Victoria Road, Trowbridge, Wiltshire

Laurence, known as Hubert, was a carpenters apprentice, he was for several years a member of the Parish Church Choir, a teetotaller and a non-smoker. He was described as always ready to help someone else. Hubert, who was aged 21, had served nearly three years in the Army and went to France with the Expeditionary Force in August 1914. Since then many cheery letters have been received from him in which, whilst predicting that the war would be of long duration, he mentioned that he had not applied for any furlough (leave), as there were many men in his division whose circumstances rendered it more urgent.

"It is my sad duty to write and tell you that your brother Sapper H. Jones, was killed on the afternoon of the May 2nd. He was buried by his comrades the following day, and a small wooded cross was erected to his memory. I know that you will all be very much upset by this news but it may come as some comfort for you to know that your brother was killed instantaneously by a shell, and he has given his life for his country. His section sergeant told me yesterday that he was one of the best men in his section. I know that god will comfort you in your affliction. Your brother's grave has been carefully recorded, and it's position will be permanently marked at the first opportunity."

It is interesting to note that official records state Laurence was killed on 3 May while Captain Townsend clearly states he was killed on 2 May. Laurence's Brother William George would be killed in 1918. The following memoriam was inserted in a local paper in 1918:

"Can we forget him? No, we loved him too dearly
For his memory to fade from our life like a dream;
Our lips need not speak, for our hearts mourn sincerely,
For grief often dwells where it is seldom seen.
Never forgotten. by his sorrowing Mother, Father, Sisters and Brothers

Private William Joseph Bennett   *1st Bn Somerset Light Infantry*
Service No.   7932   Age: 25
Place of Birth: Trowbridge, Wiltshire   Home Country: England
Date of Death: 04/05/1915   Cause of death: Died of wounds
Memorial: Trowbridge
War cemetery: Perth Cemetery China Wall
Theatre of war: Belgium
Next of Kin: Lily Bennett (wife)
Address: 6 Castle Street, Trowbridge, Wiltshire.

William Joseph Bennett, known as Joseph, of the 1st Battalion, Somerset Light Infantry was killed in action on Tuesday 4 May 1915 at the age of 25. Joseph, who had lost his parents, was early in life adopted by his aunt Mrs W. Rosborough, Castle Street. He Joined the Somerset's and served for a number of years in Malta and China, where he was selected to form one of the guard at the British Legation, Peking. He was an enthusiastic sportsman and played centre forward for his regiment and possessed many trophies as a crack rifle shot. On obtaining his discharge he was employed by Spencer's Foundry, Melksham, and in August 1913 he married at Studley, Miss Lily Eade of that village, who with her little son, was left to mourn the loss of a good husband.

Whilst serving in France Joseph sent home much interesting news, also particulars of the regimental sports which were held back from the firing line. Here Joseph succeeded in winning the quarter-mile race, got into the semi final of the 100 yards, and with his team, won the inter

Right: William Joseph Bennett

Far Right: Herbert Harold Hector L. Stillman

platoon race. He was very popular in the regiment and his early death was much deplored. Joseph Bennett was wounded during the fighting and evacuated from St. Julien north east of Ypres to a casualty clearing station. An account stated at the time that that it was a most unpleasant and trying time and the Somersets were under continuous heavy shell fire from both flanks.

Private Herbert Harold Hector L Stillman   *1st Bn York & Lancaster Regiment*

Service No.	10219	Age:	21
Place of Birth:	Trowbridge, Wiltshire	Home Country:	England
Date of Death:	04/05/1915	Cause of death:	Killed in action
Memorial:	Trowbridge		
War cemetery:	Ypres Menin Gate		
Theatre of war:	Belgium		
Next of Kin:	Samuel J & Emily Stillman		
Address:	Dursley Road, Trowbridge, Wiltshire.		

Herbert, known as Harold, had been employed as a blacksmiths striker and enlisted in the army at Bath in August 1912 at the age of 18 years and 11 months. In December 1913 he left for India with the York & Lancaster Regiment where he was serving at Jubbulpore at the outbreak of the Great War. The York & Lancaster Regiment returned to Europe and arrived in France on 15 January 1915. He was killed in action during the Second Battle of Ypres where his Battalion had been under constant attack from German forces. To give an example of the ferocity of the fighting, on the morning of 8 May the 1st Battalion York & Lancaster Regiment received a draft of 487 newly trained replacement troops - equivalent to about half of the battalion's normal strength. Harold is remembered on the Ypres Menin Gate and has no known grave.

6 MAY 1915 - SECOND BATTLE OF KRITHIA, GALLIPOLI, TURKEY

9 MAY 1915 - THE BATTLE OF AUBERS RIDGE, FRANCE

Private William Ewart Earney *1st Bn South Wales Borderers*
Service No. 15148 Age: 27
Place of Birth: Trowbridge, Wiltshire Home Country: England
Date of Death: 09/05/1915 Cause of death: Killed in action
Memorial: Trowbridge
War cemetery: Le Touret Memorial
Theatre of war: France
Next of Kin: Rosina Earney (wife) – Henry & Sarah Earney (parents)
Address: Blaina, Wales - 8 Harford Street, Trowbridge

On Saturday 29 May 1915 Mrs Rosina Earney received the news of the death of her husband who was serving in the South Wales Borderers. William was the fourth son of Henry & Sarah Earney but had been living for seven years in Blaina, South Wales. He was well known in Trowbridge, where he had been employed at the engine sheds, and was a scholar at the Tabernacle Sunday School, having passed through each of the classes and received his Bible on attaining the Bible Class. He was also for some years a member of the Boys' Brigade where he was very popular. William, who left a wife and young baby, enlisted in November 1914 in the 1st South Wales Borderers, and after two months training at Brecon and Pembroke Dock, left for the trenches in January 1915. He was described as a splendid fellow, absolutely fearless, and was quickly given the dangerous work of advancing before the regiment and clearing the way by bomb throwing, in which he was quite an expert. He went through the Neuve Chappelle fight and the attack on Hill 60, He was mortally wounded on Sunday 9 May 1915 at Richebourg l'Avoue, this being the first day of the battle of Aubers Ridge which is always remembered by the shell scandal that followed it. Shells were in short supply and many of the shells in use were of poor manufacturing quality and either fell short or were duds and failed to explode. This led to an inadequate bombardment. The 1st South Wales Borderers were to take part in the southern attack on Sunday 9 May, just before 4pm they started to advance and were cut down without reaching the German Trenches. The 3rd Brigade which the 1st South Wales Borderers were a part, suffered 1000 casualties within minutes. There were more than 11,000 British casualties on 9 May 1915 and the 1st South Wales Border suffered 233, of which 9 were officers. Many of the soldiers bodies who fell in the Battle of Aubers Ridge remained on the battlefield until 1919 mixed with the remains of soldiers who fell in subsequent battles. William Earney has no known grave and is remembered on Le Touret Memorial.

Far Left: William Ewart Earney

Left: Albert Harrison

3
BELGIUM & FRANCE

Private Albert Harrison   *2nd Bn Gloucestershire Regiment*

Service No.	5665	Age:	35
Place of Birth:	Chipping Norton, Oxfordshire	Home Country:	England
Date of Death:	09/05/1915	Cause of death:	Killed in action
Memorial:	Trowbridge		
War cemetery:	Ypres Menin Gate		
Theatre of war:	Belgium		
Next of Kin:	Hannah Harrison (wife) - James & Eliza Harrison (parents)		
Address:	East Brent, Somerset - 35 Gloucester Road Trowbridge		

Albert Harrison, eldest son of James & Eliza Harrison was serving with the 2nd Battalion Gloucestershire Regiment, when he was killed in action on Sunday 9 May 1915 at the age of 35. Albert, who with his wife resided at East Brent, Somerset, had served with the Gloucesters for 12 years in South Africa, St. Helena, and India and was a time expired man. In 1912 he took a second term in the reserve and was called up in August 1914 and completed his training at Woolwich, leaving for France in November 1914. In January 1915 he was invalided home with severe frost bite, and after treatment at a Gravesend Hospital and a short furlough he returned to France, where he had been through several engagements.

On 9 May 1915 the 2nd Battalion Gloucestershire Regiment were in trenches along the eastern edge of Sanctuary Wood at 6.30am when the Germans opened up with a terrific bombardment from the front and from the right. After 10 minutes the bombardment ended and the German infantry opened up with very heavy rifle fire which ceased after 15 minutes. This patern continued and much damage was done to the front line. At 7.15am the enemy attacked and the Germans were pouring into the left hand side of the trenches, however the Gloucesters killed 350 of the German attackers. The Gloucesters attempted to bomb the Germans out of the trenches but they only had the primitive Jam tin bombs which proved very unreliable and were forced to retreat because the Germans had more and superior hand grenades. After the failure of the bombing raid a counter attack was attempted, but due to the poor state of the ground the Gloucester could only manage to get within about 15 yards of the German positions and established a firing line; reserves were urgently sent forward but by this time the Gloucesters in the original attack were wiped out.

No news was heard from the men in the advance trenches and scouts were sent forward but returned with the news that the trenches had been blotted out. At the end of a very hard days fighting the Gloucesters had nearly 150 casualties at Sanctuary Wood near Zillebeke, east of Ypres, Belgium, including the Commanding Officer Lieutenant Colonel Tulloh. Albert is remembered on the Menin Gate at Ypres with over 54,000 other Soldiers who fell in the Ypres Salient during the First World War and have no known grave.

Far left: William Dallimore

Left: Wilfred Ernest Treasure

Private William Dallimore   *3rd Bn Monmouthshire Regiment*
Service No.   2403   Age: 27
Place of Birth: Bradford on Avon, Wiltshire   Home Country: England
Date of Death: 11/05/1915   Cause of death: Killed in action
Memorial: Trowbridge
War cemetery: Ypres Menin Gate
Theatre of war: Belgium
Next of Kin: Mildred Dallimore (wife) - Richard & Mary Dallimore (parents)
Address: Newtown, Ebbw Vale, Monmouth -16 Timbrell Street, Hilperton

William was a coal miner when he married Mildred Blanchard at the end of the year in 1909 at Bedwellty Monmouthshire. He volunteered for service and arrived on the continent on 13 February 1915. In May 1915 the 3rd Battalion Monmouthshire Regiment were engaged in heavy fighting during the Second Battle of Ypres. In fact the 83 Brigade, of which they were a part, had lost so many men that it was formed into a composite battalion (formed of all the different member regiments) under the command of Lieutenant Colonel Gough. They then proceeded to positions in the line at Potijze, Belgium. It is likely that this is where William was killed on Tuesday 11 May 1915. He is remembered on the Ypres Menin Gate.

Lance Corporal Wilfred Ernest Treasure   *10th Hussars*
Service No.   7127   Age: 23
Place of Birth: Yeovil, Somerset   Home Country: England
Date of Death: 13/05/1915   Cause of death: Killed in action
Memorial: Trowbridge
War cemetery: Ypres Menin Gate
Theatre of war: Belgium
Next of Kin: William James & Mary Violetta Treasure
Address: Mansourah, Bythesea Road, Trowbridge, Wiltshire

Regular Soldier Wilfred was with the 10th Hussars in August 1914 at Potchefstroom in South Africa, at the outbreak of hostilities. He arrived on the continent on October 1914. He was reported missing on Thursday 13 May 1915 during the Battle of Fresenberg which took place near Potijze, Belgium. Later his death was accepted and the lising changed to killed in action. He is remembered on the Ypres Menin Gate.

Right: John Thomas Long

Far right: A British Lancer displaying lance and sword.

15 MAY 1915 - THE BATTLE OF FESTUBERT, BELGIUM

Private John Thomas Long   *4th Dragoon Guards*

Service No.	7888
Place of Birth:	Trowbridge, Wiltshire
Date of Death:	15/05/1915
Memorial:	Trowbridge
War cemetery:	Ypres Menin Gate
Theatre of war:	Belgium
Next of Kin:	Thomas & Rosina Long (parents)
Address:	3 Hardings Yard, Newtown, Trowbridge, Wiltshire.

Age: 30
Home Country: England
Cause of death: Died of wounds

Violet Long of Bradford Road, Trowbridge received the following from S.S.M. Fraser, of C Squadron, 4th Dragoon Guards, with the British Expeditionary Force in France, apprising her of the death of her brother:

"It is with deep regret that I have to inform you that No.7888 Private J. Long, was killed in action at Ypres on Monday 10 May. He was shot through the brain whilst doing his duty, he died nobly as he lived. His death is deeply regretted by his comrades, by whom he was beloved. He was buried by his comrades, who paid their last respects to one they well loved. A small cross bearing his name and that of his regiment was erected at the head of the grave. The officers and N.C.O.'s and men wish me to convey to you their deepest sympathy in your loss."

John Long was the eldest son of the late Thomas & Rosina Long, of Newtown, and was 30 years of age. He had served 12 years, his time expiring in April 1914. He rejoined in August 1914 at the outbreak of war, and went straight to the front. His younger brother Nelson Long was also at the front serving with the South Wales Borderers. After the German gas attack that opened the 2nd Battle of Ypres the British were forced to retreat with heavy losses and it is likely that John Long lost his life at the battle of Frezenberg, east of Ypres toward Zonnebeke in Belgium. It is interesting to note that in the letter from S.S.M. Fraser, the date of death given as Monday 10 May 1915 and Commonwealth War Graves Commission records the death as Saturday 15 May 1915, this could be a cause of the confusion of battle. Also in S.S.M. Fraser's letter it state John was buried, many graves were lost due to the amount of shelling at Yrpes in Belgium and it would appear that John's was one of the lost graves. John is remembered on the Menin Gate at Ypres and has no known grave.

Private Stephen Bathard	*6th Bn Austrailian Infantry AIF*
Service No.: 2056	Age: 29
Place of Birth: Potterne, Wiltshire	Home Country: Australia
Date of Death: 17/05/1915	Cause of death: Died of wounds
Memorial: Not Known	
War cemetery: Alexandria Chatby Military and War Memorial Cemetery	
Theatre of war: Gallipoli	
Next of Kin: Stephen D & Mary J Bathard	
Address: Dunge Farm, West Ashton, Wiltshire	

Stephen, known as Steve, was a farm hand and emigrated from England arriving in Australia on 2nd October 1907 where he was in business with his brother Tom. He volunteered for service with the Australian army on 26 September 1914, his parents received the following letter from one of his comrades:

"I write in order to extend my deepest sympathy with you in the loss you have suffered by the heroic end of your brave boy, Steve. I am an old fried of your sons, having known Tom for over ten years, and I was the first to meet Steve when he landed in Melbourne. We were sworn comrades, and I have grown to look upon them as brothers. Steve and I spent a great deal of time together; in fact we both volunteered on the same day, but I had the hard luck to be rejected on account of defective eyesight; otherwise I should have been beside my poor mate when he fell. It is a great pitty you did not see him before he reached the front. He looked every inch a soldier. The brave fellow had his wish, as he often used to say that he would like to fall in Australian uniform with the bonnie blue flag of Australia floating over him. I am sure we are proud of the fact that he fell on the glorious field under circumstances which will go down in history to the end of time. During his residence in Australia he made many friends, and he was popular wherever he went. In all the places where he had lived memorial services were held and flags were at half mast"

On 13 May 1915 Steve was shot in the head, most likely from a stray bullet as his company were at rest. He was evacuated to a hospital ship and taken to a base hospital in Alexandria, Egypt where he died of wounds on Monday 17 May 1915. The following is an extract from an Australian newspaper:

"At the branch church, Galaquil East, a solemn service was held in the presence of the whole of our members and adherents in memory of a brave young man Private Stephen Bathard, who recently gave his life in the service of King and country at the Dardenelles. He made many warm friends during his stay of about three years at Galaquil East. He was a member of the choir, and was ready to assist in any way. The pastor spoke very feelingly regarding the young man's life and his great sacrifice. In the loving memory of their departed brother, members joined in this impressive service, feeling the frailty of life and the comfort of Christ's words for the life to come. A solo, 'Shadows,' was sung, and the whole congregation stood while the dead march in 'Saul' was played"

Two parcels of Steve Bathard's personnel property were returned to his parents and consisted of letters, book, name stamp, razor, strop, sweater, disc, wallet, pocket-book, photos and testament.

He is buried in Alexandria Chatby Military War Memorial Cemetery, Egypt.

Bugler Fred Gardiner   *15th Bn Central Ontario Regiment*

Service No.	77520	Age:	30
Place of Birth:	Trowbridge, Wiltshire	Home Country:	Canada
Date of Death:	21/05/1915	Cause of death:	Killed in action
Memorial:	Trowbridge		
War cemetery:	Vimy Memorial		
Theatre of war:	France		
Next of Kin:	James & Martha Gardiner		
Address:	9 Yerbury Street, Trowbridge, Wiltshire		

Fred, of the 48th Canadian Highlanders, met his death on Thursday 20 May whilst fighting in the trenches with the Canadians. He was the sixth son of the late James & Martha Gardiner of Yerbury Street and was aged 30. He was an old employee at the G.W.R.engine sheds at Trowbridge and in 1901, in company with his brother Herbert, he left for Canada, where the brothers bought some land, built a house, and were successfully embarking as fruit farmers. On the outbreak of war both brothers offered their services to the Motherland and were accepted, Fred, joining the 30th Battalion, whilst his younger brother was sent to the 3rd Contingent, their farm being placed in the hands of a caretaker and legal advisor. On arrival in England in the early part of 1915, the 30th Battalion went into training at Shorncliffe, and left for France on 2 May, where 3 weeks later, Fred, who had transferred to the Highlanders, met his death.

On Sunday 16 May his mother, Martha, received a letter from Fred in which he said his regiment was going into action. Although not fearing the result it was quite possible he might be killed and if this happened his relatives must not mourn for him, but receive the consolation that he had given all for his King and country. Within a few days of the receipt of that letter the sad news was received from his company officer that the end which he had foretold had come true and Fred, had been shot in the trenches. Included in the letter was the sum of £7, which the deceased soldier had handed to a comrade to forward to his mother if he met his death. Fred's two other brothers Frank and George offered their services on the outbreak of war, but were rejected as medically unfit. Between 20 and 22 May 1915 the 3rd Canadian Brigade of which the 48th Canadian Highlands were part, were south of Neuve Chapelle where the battle of Festubert was taking place. Fred's Regiment were in the area of the orchard known after as the Canadian Orchard and it is likely that this is where he met his death. The Canadian troops reported many problems with their standard Ross rifle, which as many as 50% may have been faulty with a tendency to jam. Fred is remembered on Vimy Memorial and has no known grave.

Fred Gardiner

4
GALLIPOLI

On Sunday 25 April 1915, British forces were landed on the Gallipoli Peninsula, the British and French Navies had been attempting to force a passage through the Dardanelles Narrows with a view to put pressure on Germany's allies, the Ottoman Empire, to aid Russia.
The ships were stopped by mines and the Turkish Forts that dominated the Dardanelles. A plan was conceived to land British, Commonwealth and French troops on the Gallipoli Peninsula, to capture the forts and march north to Constantinople, thus knocking the German allies out of the war and relieve pressure on Russia.

2nd Lieutenant William James De Vere Scott　*8th Bn Manchester Regiment*
Service No . N/A　Age: 25
Place of Birth: Trowbridge, Wiltshire　Home Country: England
Date of Death: 29/05/1915　Cause of death: Killed in action
Memorial: Trowbridge
War cemetery: Helles Memorial
Theatre of war: Mesopotamia
Next of Kin: James & Julia Scott
Address: 19 The Down, Trowbridge, Wiltshire

William was a school master and the eldest son of James and Julia Scott of Trowbridge. He volunteered for service and was commissioned into the 1/8th Battalion Manchester Regiment which was raised in Ardwick in August 1914. They landed at Alexandria, Egypt on 25 September 1914 and arrived on the Gallipoli Peninsular on 6 May 1915. William was killed in action on Saturday 29 May 1915, he has no known grave and is remembered on the Helles Memorial.

Far left: William James De Vere Scott

Left: Charles Bray

4 June 1915 - Third Battle of Krithia, Gallipoli, Turkey

Private Charles Bray *1st Bn Cheshire Regiment*
Service No.   10322
Age: 35
Place of Birth: Trowbridge, Wiltshire
Home Country: England
Date of Death: 10/06/1915
Cause of death: Killed in action
Memorial: Trowbridge
War cemetery: Ypres Menin Gate
Theatre of war: Belgium
Next of Kin: Ethel Wilkins (sister)
Address: 23 Timbrell Street, Trowbridge, Wiltshire

Charles, the son of Mary Anne Bray and a labourer, had been a player with Trowbridge Football Club. He had served with the Wiltshire Regiment in the South African war and rejoined the colours at the outbreak of war. He re-enlisted at Chester on 12 August 1914. He arrived in France on 26 January 1915 and was wounded on 5 May 1915. Charles was killed in action in Belgium on Thursday 10 June 1915 and he is remembered on the Ypres Menin Gate.

Private George Henry Shrapnell *1st Bn Wiltshire Regiment*
Service No.   6288
Age: 31
Place of Birth: Trowbridge, Wiltshire
Home Country: England
Date of Death: 13/06/1915
Cause of death: Died of wounds
Memorial: Trowbridge
War cemetery: Bedford House Cemetery
Theatre of war: Belgium
Next of Kin: Mabel Shrapnel (wife) – Samuel & Jane Shrapnell (parents)
Address: 5 Mortimer Street, Trowbridge, Wiltshire.

George, a reservist, had originally enlisted with the Wiltshires on 6 May 1903 at the age of 18 years and 3 months. He was the son of Samuel and Jane Shrapnell and married Mabel Jane Woodman in 1907 and resided with his wife and 3 Children at 5 Mortimer street, Trowbridge, Wiltshire. George was called up in August 1914, but for some time was an inmate of a military hospital, where he underwent an operation for varicose veins. Ultimately he went into training at Weymouth and in October 1914 left with a draft arriving in France on 23 October 1914, where he was attached to his old regiment. George's official confirmation of his death was on Sunday 13 June 1915 from wounds received the previous day. On Saturday the 12 June 1915 the 1st Battalion the Wiltshire Regiment were at rest near Ypres, Belgium, during the afternoon an accident occurred with a grenade which William Pope from Walthamstow and an officer were killed and 23 other men, including George, were injured.
George is buried in Bedford House Cemetery which is 2.5 Kilometres south of Ypres town centre. Bedford House, also known as Woodcote House, was the name given by the Army to the Chateau Rosendal, a country house in a small wooded park with moats. Although it never fell into German hands, the house and the trees were gradually destroyed by shell fire.

Private Herbert Claude Horton *1st Bn Wiltshire Regiment*
Service No.   3/316
Age: 40
Place of Birth: Trowbridge, Wiltshire
Home Country: England
Date of Death: 15/06/1915
Cause of death: Killed in action
Memorial: Trowbridge

Far left: George Henry Shrapnell

Left: Herbert Claude Horton

War cemetery: Ypres Menin Gate
Theatre of war: Belgium
Next of Kin: Henry & Elizabeth A Horton
Address: 3 Brickplatt, Trowbridge, Wiltshire

Herbert, a bricklayer, had originally enlisted with the Rifle Brigade on 28 March 1898 in London. He served during the South African war and was discharged from the army on 27 March 1910 described as medically unfit for further service and his character was described as very good. At the outbreak of hostilities Herbert volunteered for service joining the 1st Battalion Wiltshire Regiment and arrived on the continent on 11 November 1914. He was killed in action on Tuesday 15 June 1915 as the Wiltshires fought near Hooge, Belgium. He is remembered on the Ypres Menin Gate and has no known grave.

Private Robert Henry White   *1st Bn Wiltshire Regiment*
Service No.   7382   Age: 32
Place of Birth: Hilperton, Wiltshire   Home Country: England
Date of Death: 16/06/1915   Cause of death: Killed in action
Memorial: Trowbridge
War cemetery: Ypres Menin Gate
Theatre of war: Belgium
Next of Kin: Levi & Clara White
Address: 10 Islington Road, Trowbridge, Wiltshire.

Robert enlisted with the Wiltshires on 24 August 1905 at the age of 22 years and 4 months. He arrived on the continent on 14 August 1914. On Wednesday 16 June 1915 the 1st Battalion Wiltshire Regiment were in Belgium on the Menin Road. At 2.50am the British artillery commenced a bombardment between Roulers railway and the southern edge of Ypres wood. At 4.20 am the Wiltshires went forward and entered the German trenches. During the next 5 hours they gradually advanced with grenade throwers driving the Germans back. When the Wiltshires were about 50yards from the village of Hooge, the Germans began advancing down communication trenches under the cover of heavy fire and their own bomb (grenade) throwers. After about 90 minutes the Wiltshires supply of grenades was exhausted and the Germans succeeded in driving the Wiltshires from the recently captured trenches. The Wiltshires counter attacked without success and many men were shot down. The Germans then bombarded the British in the remainder of the captured trenches finally shelling with gas shells.

Robert was initially reported missing in action, later he was reported killed. He is remembered on the Ypres Menin Gate and has no known grave.

Gunner Thomas Victor Cross   *Howitzer Brigade RMA*
Service No.   RMA/11310
Place of Birth: Calne, Wiltshire
Date of Death: 20/06/1915
Memorial: Trowbridge
War cemetery: Bully-Grenay Communal Cemetery French Extension
Theatre of war: France
Next of Kin: Lily Cross (wife); Thomas & Rosa Cross (parents)
Address: 37 Lower Bond Street, Trowbridge, Wiltshire

Age: 27
Home Country: England
Cause of death: Died of wounds

Thomas was employed by the Great Western Railway at Bristol, having left the Royal Marines in 1911 after 7 years service. He married Lily Elkins early in 1914 and as a reservist he rejoined his depot at Portsmouth at the commencement of hostilities. Thomas was sent to Coventry, where he watched the casting and making of some dozen big guns and in February 1915 he took the last of these guns to the continent. He was initially moved to Ostend, Belgium, then Dunkirk, France and then onto serve with the Marine Howitzer Brigade near Bethune, France. Lily received a letter from Thomas in which he assured his wife that there was little chance of him being killed because he was so far behind the trenches. Shortly afterwards however, came the sad news from Eastney Barracks, that he had died of wounds at the Hospital at Le Brebis the previous day.

Bombardier Harry J Burbidge   *HMS St.Vincent RMA*
Service No.   RMA/9707
Place of Birth: Staverton, Wiltshire
Date of Death: 21/06/1915
Memorial: Trowbridge
War cemetery: Osmondwall Cemetery
Theatre of war: Home

Age: 32
Home Country: England
Cause of death: Died

Right: Robert Henry White

Far right: Thomas Victor Cross

Far left: Harry J Burbidge

Left: Frederick John Perrett

Next of Kin: Elizabeth Burbidge (wife) - Andrew & Eliza Burbidge (parents)
Address: 39 The Halve, Trowbidge, Wiltshire

Harry enlisted in the Royal Marine Artillery on 4 September 1901 at Trowbridge and in the summer of 1906 he married Elizabeth Rose Drewett at Portsmouth. He had a long career in the RMA and served on many ships. He died most likely of illness or disease on Monday 21 June 1915 and was buried in Osmondwall Cemetery in Scotland. In June 1915 the following memoriam was inserted in a local paper:

"Forget Him? Never will
We loved him here, we love him still;
Nor love him less, although he's gone
From us to his eternal Home
One of the best"

Lance Coporal Frederick John Perrett   *1/4th TF Bn Wiltshire Regiment*
Service No.   1202   Age: 29
Place of Birth: Steeple Ashton, Wiltshire   Home Country: England
Date of Death: 24/06/1915   Cause of death: Died
Memorial: Trowbridge
War cemetery: Delhi War Cemetery
Theatre of war: India
Next of Kin: Helen Perrett (wife) - John & Sarah Perrett (parents)
Address: 18 Prospect Place, Trowbridge - Bleet, Hinton, Wiltshire.

Fred was a maltster's labourer and in the spring of 1905 he married Helen Louisa C Charmbury. He had served about 10 years with the Territorials, acting as company cook. He had undergone a course of instruction in camp cooking at Aldershot, and in 1914 won a first class certificate. On the outbreak of war Fred Perrett was one of the first to volunteer for foreign service, and on arrival in India with the 1/4th Battalion he again took a course of instruction in cooking, the different diet issued in India necessitating a complete change in manor and method In his letters home he gave many interesting accounts of his experiences, and with one exception always stated that he was in good health. On Sunday 27 June 1915 Helen of 18 Prospect Place received the distressing news that her husband, Frederick John Perrett, of the 1st Battalion 4th Wiltshire Regiment, had died in Delhi Hospital from Malaria. Fred left a widow and four children and had been for many years an employee at Messers Ushers Malthouse.

The Following letter was received by Helen Perrett from 2nd Lieutenant Henry F. Angus OC "B" Double Company, 1st-4th Wilts Redg

"It is with very great regret that I have to inform you of the death of Lance Corporal Perrett. He went into hospital with malaria fever, which is not usually a very serious illness. It is something that we expect to get sooner or later. Your husband had a very high fever and the end seems to have come quite suddenly. The funeral took place the following day, Friday 25 June 1915, in Delhi Cemetery. The Company followed the gun carriage to the Station Hospital, and the funeral was carried out with military honours
We all of us feel the deepest sympathy with you in the loss you have sustained. Your husband has given his life for his country at a very critical time. It would have been impossible for a brave man not to act as he has acted and the terrible loss which you and your children have to bear is part of the price that has to be paid in this war. We feel very deeply what it must mean to you. From all sides i have heard the highest regard of Lce.-Corpl. Perrett. He has occupied a warm place in the hearts of many of his comrades."

30 JUNE 1915 - ALLIED CASUALTIES AT GALLIPOLI REACH 42,434

Acting CSM Edward Charles Thornton *1st Bn Somerset Light Infantry*
Service No.: 6676 Age: 30
Place of Birth: East Farnham, Wiltshire Home Country: England
Date of Death: 06/07/1915 Cause of death: Killed in action
Memorial: Trowbridge
War cemetery: Talana Farm Cemetery
Theatre of war: Belgium
Next of Kin: Mary Ann E Thornton (wife) - Edward & Anne Thorton (parents)
Address: 15 Frome Road, Trowbridge - Kingsbridge, Devon

Edward Thornton was aged 30 and had served 12 years in the Somersets, of which he had been a reservist for nine years. He had been employed for the past eight years as chief parcel porter at Trowbridge Railway Station. He was very popular with his colleagues and was held in high esteem by the officials of the Great Western Railway who regarded him as a thoroughly reliable, trustworthy and painstaking employee. He had married Mary Ann E Cottle in the spring of 1908 and was called to the colours in August 1914 and rejoined his regiment as a corporal at Taunton. His keenness and enthusiasm during training bought further promotion, and before leaving for the front in January 1914 he was made a sergeant, the further distinction of company sergeant major being conferred on the field of battle for gallant conduct.
On Monday 12 July 1915 Mary received the sad news that her husband Edward had been killed in action. The letter was from the commanding officer of A Company the 1st Battalion Prince Albert's Somerset Light Infantry in which he stated:

"I regret to inform you that your husband, C.S.M. Thornton was killed in action on Tuesday 6 July 1915. He was shot through the head and killed instantaneously. I am very sorry to have to write to you this sad news, as your husband was one of the best men in the Somersets, and had done very well out here; he was very popular with the men and feared nothing. All A Company join me in saying how sorry we are to have lost him."

A further communication was received from Corporal Fred Taylor, of the Somersets, who after expressing his and his comrades sympathy adds:

"He asked me many weeks ago to write if ever anything occurred, and it is with saddened heart that I take the first opportunity of doing so, as he was the best and truest friend I have met in this country. He was always doing some kindness, and it was only last Saturday that he saved my life from this awful gas. The officers, non-commissioned officers, and men all deeply deplore his loss."

Edward was of an optimistic nature and in his letters home, after speaking of the heavy fighting the regiment had gone through, he stated that he had been gassed, but had got through successfully and was eagerly looking forward to a return home.

The Germans first use of gas on the western front was near Langemarck on 22 April 1915 when they attacked using a cloud of Chlorine gas, a bluish-white mist rolling forward on the wind, gas was used frequently during the second Battle of Ypres and continued to be used by both sides throughout the First world war.

Edward did not return home his body lies in Talana Farm Cemetery named by Boer war veterans after the battle of Talana Hill on 20 October 1899 in South African war. The 1st Somerset took part in the Second Battle of Ypres, taking part in the actions in April and May at St Julien, Frezenburg and Bellewaarde. Edward was shot through the head and at this time the British Infantryman had no head protection as steel helmets were only first introduced in late 1915.

25 JULY 1915 - NASRIYA IN MESOPOTAMIA IS CAPTURED BY BRITISH FORCES

30 JULY 1915 - GERMANS ATTACK WITH FLAME THROWERS AT HOOGE, BELGIUM

6 AUGUST - BATTLE OF SARI BAIR AND LANDINGS AT SUVLA BAY AND ACHI BABA, GALLIPOLI, TURKEY

Left: Edward Charles Thornton

Below: Allied troops at Gallipoli

GALLIPOLI

In January 1916 a report in the local paper lead with the headline '5th WILTS ALMOST ANNIHILATED'. It referred to Sir Ian Hamilton, who had been the commander of the Gallipoli Peninsula Operations, with the dispatches describing the events of the 6 to 10 August 1915 when a great attack had taken place from the Anzac area.

The aims were to break out of Anzac and cut off the bulk of the Turkish forces on the peninsula from Constantinople and to gain a commanding position for the artillery to cut off the Turkish army with sea traffic.

The 5th Wiltshire Regiment were part of the left covering column and were to march northwards along the beach and seize a hill called Damakjelik Bair some 1400 yards north of Table Top. This would enable 9th corps to be aided as it landed south of Nibrunei Point, while protecting the flank of the other assaulting columns.

During the main attack a hill, Chunuk Bair, had been taken and on the night of Monday 9 and Tuesday 10 August 1915 the 5th Battalion Wiltshire Regiment and the 6th Loyal North Lancashire Regiment were chosen to hold this position. The Loyal north Lancashire's arrived first and their commanding officer, even though it was dark, recognised how dangerously the trenches were sited. He at once ordered that observation posts were dug on the actual crest of the hill.

The Wiltshire's were delayed by the rough terrain of the intricate country. They did not reach the position until 4a.m. The war diary disagrees with this time stating that the Wiltshire's arrived at 3a.m. and lies the blame on a New Zealand officer who was their guide. When the Wiltshire's did arrive they were told to lie down in what was believed erroneously, to be a covered and safe position.

At daybreak on Tuesday 10 August, the Turks delivered a grand attack from the line Chunuk Bair Hill Q against the Wiltshire's and the Loyal North Lancashire's, which were already weakened in numbers by previous fighting. First the British were shelled and then at 5.30a.m., were assaulted by a huge column, consisting of a division plus a regiment and three battalions. The Loyal North Lancashire Regiment were overwhelmed in their shallow trenches by the sheer weight of the Turkish attack while the Wilts Regiment were caught out in the open and were literally almost annihilated. The War diary for the Wiltshires states the Turks attacked 15 minutes after machine guns opened fire at 4.30a.m . It also gives an indication of how desperate the British were to escape from the fighting. During the desperate fighting Lieutenant Colonel J. Carden commanding the 5th Wiltshire's was killed.

Another account is given from Captain (then Lieutenant) Bush who was honoured for his conspicuous service during the Gallipoli campaign. According to the dispatches, the Wiltshire's and another regiment had a whole division of Turks and two other Battalions against them on August 10, 1915. Fire was opened on them at dawn with terrible results. Those who could, retired down a narrow gully, only to come under fire from more machine guns, and here, the two remaining senior officers being killed, Lieutenant Bush found himself left in command. He immediately, with the help of two sergeants, rallied the men and lined them against the side of the gully just out of reach of the machine guns. He, himself, went up and across the gully, finding a fairly practicable though terribly steep way up, got the men across by twos and threes, and led them to a place of safety under the top of the cliffs. Leaving them with the two remaining subalterns with orders not to move till after dark, if he did not return, and then to make their way to the beach, he went across the open, under machine gun and rifle fire about 300 yards, finally reaching a New Zealand trench. From there he was passed down to Headquarters, and was able to pass word along the line to look out for the men as they came in after dark. A party was sent out to clear the bottom of the gully - about 150 to 200 men came in that night. Lieutenant Bush was invalided home about 10 days afterwards, with dysentery. Some of the men of the 5th Wiltshire's lay hidden and survived the attack returning to their unit as late as 26 August 1915. Almost 150 members of the 5th Wiltshire's were killed on Tuesday 10 August 1918 the majority have no known grave and are remembered on Helles Memorial.

Far left: Leonard Arthur Cox

Left: Charles Leonard Smart

Corporal Leonard Arthur Cox   *5th Bn Wiltshire Regiment*
Service No.   9449
Place of Birth: Southwick, Wiltshire
Date of Death: 10/08/1915
Memorial: Trowbridge
War cemetery: Helles Memorial
Theatre of war: Gallipoli
Next of Kin: Samuel & Annie Cox
Address: 17 Gladstone Road, Trowbridge, Wiltshire

Age: 22
Home Country: England
Cause of death: Died of wounds

Leonard was a railway engine stoker. He volunteered for service in 1914 and arrived on the Gallipoli Peninsular on 30 June 1915. He was officially reported wounded on August 10 1915, after the Wiltshires were almost annihilated at Gallipoli. He was then reported wounded and missing and his parents inserted his picture in a local paper asking for news of their son. On the Christmas Eve 1916 Samuel & Annie Cox were notified that their son was presumed killed on Tuesday 10 August 1915. It is likely he died in the gully of Sazli Beit from his wounds. He is remembered on the Helles Memorial and has no known grave.

Private Charles Leonard Smart   *5th Bn Wiltshire Regiment*
Service No.   10778
Place of Birth: Stroud, Gloucestershire
Date of Death: 10/08/1915
Memorial: Trowbridge
War cemetery: Helles Memorial
Theatre of war: Gallipoli
Next of Kin: Amelia Smart
Address: 24 Shails Lane, Trowbridge, Wiltshire.

Age: 19
Home Country: England
Cause of death: Killed in action

Charles, a shop assistant, volunteered for service with the 5th Battalion Wiltshire Regiment and arrived on the Gallipoli Peninsular on 12 July 1915. He was reported missing after the Wiltshires were described as annihilated; later he was reported killed in action on Tuesday 10 August 1915. He is remembered on the Helles Memorial and has no known grave.

GALLIPOLI

Private Hubert John Clark   5th Bn Wiltshire Regiment
Service No.: 9677
Age: 23
Place of Birth: Hilperton, Wiltshire
Home Country: England
Date of Death: 10/08/1915
Cause of death: Killed in action
Memorial: Hilperton
War cemetery: Helles Memorial
Theatre of war: Gallipoli
Next of Kin: John & Mary Clark
Address: Dymont Square, Hilperton, Wiltshire.

Hubert, a baker, volunteered for service with the 5th Battalion Wiltshire Regiment and arrived on the Gallipoli Peninsular in July 1915. The Military records record his name as Herbert, but after extensive research no Herbert or Herbert John could be found. He was one of the casualties when the Wiltshires were described as almost annihilated on Tuesday 10 August 1915. He is remembered on the Helles Memorial and has no known grave.

Lance Corporal George Randall   5th Bn Wiltshire Regiment
Service No.: 3/228
Age: 42
Place of Birth: Conigre, Wiltshire
Home Country: England
Date of Death: 10/08/1915
Cause of death: Killed in action
Memorial: Hilperton - Hilperton Church Memorial - Trowbridge
War cemetery: Helles Memorial
Theatre of war: Gallipoli
Next of Kin: Rosina K Randall (wife) – Jane Randall (parent)
Address: 40 Islington, Trowbridge, Wiltshire.

George was a canal labourer working for the Great Western Railway and he had married Rosina Kate Parker in 1896. At the age of 42 he would have been at the upper end of the age limit for serving with the army. He volunteered for service in 1914 and arrived on the Gallipoli Peninsular in July 1915. He was one of the casualties when the Wiltshires were described as almost annihilated on Tuesday 10 August 1915. He was officially reported missing in September 1915 and some time later it was assumed he had been killed in action. He is remembered on the Helles Memorial and has no known grave.

Private William Charles Elkins   5th Bn Wiltshire Regiment
Service No.: 9327
Age: 18
Place of Birth: Whiteparish, Wiltshire
Home Country: England
Date of Death: 10/08/1915
Cause of death: Killed in action
Memorial: Not known
War cemetery: Helles Memorial
Theatre of war: Gallipoli
Next of Kin: John and Selina Bethiah Elkins
Address: Hop Gardens, Whiteparish, Wiltshire.

Eighteen year old William, a woodman, was an under age soldier as at this period of the war the age required to serve overseas was nineteen. When he enlisted he stated his residence was Hilperton, and it is likely he was employed in the area when he volunteered for service in 1914, arriving on the Gallipoli Peninsular in July 1915. He was one of the casualties when the Wiltshires were described as almost annihilated on Tuesday 10 August 1915. He was officially reported missing in September 1915 and at some time later it was assumed he had been killed in action. He is remembered on the Helles Memorial and has no known grave.

Private James Henry Hillman   *5th Bn Wiltshire Regiment*

Service No.	9362
Place of Birth:	Rhymey, Wales
Date of Death:	10/08/1915
Memorial:	Not known
War cemetery:	Helles Memorial
Theatre of war:	Gallipoli
Next of Kin:	Henry and Mary Hillman
Address:	Bath, Somerset.
Age:	37
Home Country:	England
Cause of death:	Killed in action

Military records state that James was born in Trowbridge, Wiltshire, however he was actually born in Rymey, Gwent but was brought up in Trowbridge. He was employed as an ostler which was a person who looked after horses used in the brewing industry. He volunteer for service and arrived on the Gallipoli Peninsular in July 1915. He was one of the casualties when the Wiltshires were described as almost annihilated on Tuesday 10 August 1915. He was officially reported missing in September 1915 and at some time later it was assumed he had been killed in action. He is remembered on the Helles Memorial and has no known grave.

Private Herbert Marshman   *1/5th Bn Welsh Regiment*

Service No.	2079
Place of Birth:	Trowbridge, Wiltshire
Date of Death:	10/08/1915
Memorial:	Trowbridge
War cemetery:	Helles Memorial
Theatre of war:	Gallipoli
Next of Kin:	William & Louisa Marshman
Address:	Horse Road, Hilperton, Trowbridge, Wiltshire
Age:	21
Home Country:	England
Cause of death:	Killed in action

Twenty one year old Herbert was a baker, he volunteered for service in 1914 joining the 1/5th Battalion Welsh Regiment at Pontypridd, Glamorgan. He arrived on the Gallipoli Peninsular on 9 August 1915, when the British landed troops at Suvla Bay. He was killed in action the following day, Tuesday 10 August 1915, and it is likely his grave was lost during subsequent fighting. He is remembered on the Helles Memorial, his step brother Harry Loxley was to die in November 1917.

Private Herbert Reynolds   *4th Bn South Wales Borderers*

Service No.	12664
Place of Birth:	Trowbridge, Wiltshire
Date of Death:	11/08/1915
Memorial:	Not Known
War cemetery:	East Murdos Military Cemetery
Theatre of war:	Gallipoli
Next of Kin:	William Reynolds (brother)
Address:	52 Newall Street, Albertillery, Monmouthshire
Age:	19
Home Country:	Wales
Cause of death:	Died

William was a miner and lodged with his brother at his Uncle and Aunt's house in Albertillery, Monmouthshire. He volunteered for service in 1914 with the 4th Service Battalion South Wales Borderers. This was a Battalion that was recruited to serve for the duration of the war and part of Kitchener's appeal for more men. William was sent for training first at Tidworth, then Chiseldon, then Cirencester. He arrived on the Gallipoli Peninsular on 15 July 1915. At some time after this date he was evacuated to a hospital on the Greek Island of Murdos where he died on Wednesday 11 August 1915 of illness or disease.

Right: Albert George Ricketts

Far right: William Job White

Private Albert George Ricketts   *5th Bn Wiltshire Regiment*
Service No.   18061   Age: 36
Place of Birth: Trowbridge, Wiltshire   Home Country: England
Date of Death: 12/08/1915   Cause of death: Died of wounds
Memorial: Trowbridge
War cemetery: Helles Memorial
Theatre of war: Gallipoli
Next of Kin: Eliza Ricketts (wife) – James & Emma Ricketts (parents)
Address: 27 Charles Street, Silverton, Kent - 2 Islington, Trowbridge.

Albert, known as George, was employed as a furnace man and had married Eliza Shotter at West Ham, London, in 1899. He volunteered for service with the 5th Battalion Wiltshire Regiment and arrived on the Gallipoli Peninsular on 12 July 1915. He was wounded during the fighting on 10 August 1915 and died on Thursday 12 August 1915. It is likely he died in the gully of Sazli Beit, and is almost certain that news of his death did not reach England until November 1915. He is remembered on the Helles Memorial and has no known grave. In August 1916 Eliza Ricketts inserted the following memoriam in a local paper.

"In proud and affectionate memory of my Husband and the officers and men who fell with him at Gallipoli August 10 1915 - Hero's all."

Private William Job White   *6th Bn Leinster Regiment*
Service No.   1167   Age: 23
Place of Birth: Trowbridge, Wiltshire   Home Country: England
Date of Death: 12/08/1915   Cause of death: Died of wounds
Memorial: Trowbridge
War cemetery: Embarkation Pier Cemetery
Theatre of war: Gallipoli
Next of Kin: Job & Ellen White
Address: 40 Islington, Trowbridge, Wiltshire.

William, aged 23, was well known in Trowbridge. He was educated at the Parochial Schools, and was a splendid athlete, he took part in the school sports, captaining the football eleven which won the elementary school cup in 1906-7, and was a member of the school cricket eleven and won a silver medal. After leaving school his interest in sport continued, and for several years he was the captain and leading member of the Trowbridge United Football Club, runners up of the Knock Out cup, and he was often seen in the ranks and did good service for both the Town and Reserve teams. His liking for the military was but natural, his father having been an Army pensioner, with nine years 55 days' service in India.

William was the only son in a family of 10 and was the mainstay of his widowed mother, who, it is needless to state was almost broken-hearted at the loss of her son. Ellen White had a brother Job Holloway, serving with the 2nd Wilts in France, a brother in law, Private J.Gingell with the 4th Wilts in India. Private William Holloway, a nephew, was with the 3rd Wilts at Weymouth, and three other relatives were serving with various regiments, one nephew having been wounded. By the end of the war both Job and William Holloway were to die and are also on Trowbridge War Memorial. William had originally enlisted in the Wiltshire Regiment but it was over subscribed and he was transferred to the Irish 6th Leinster Regiment which like many Irish regiments at this time was in need of recruits. This transfer happened to many Wiltshire volunteers.

The 6th Leinster Regiment landed on Gallipoli at Suvla Bay, in August and it is likely William was wounded in the fighting around Sari Bair. He is buried at Embarkation Pier Cemetery which was an area occupied by the headquarters of two divisions, and later by a casualty clearing station. The pier was made for the purpose of evacuating wounded from the battle of Sari Bair, but it came under heavy rifle and shell fire and was abandoned after just two days.

Private Roland Cook Keates   *Grenadier Guards*
Service No.   Not known   Age: 24
Place of Birth: Westbury, Wiltshire   Home Country: England
Date of Death: 14/08/1915   Cause of death: Died
Memorial: Not known
War cemetery: West Ashton Church
Theatre of war: Home
Next of Kin: Ebenezer & Rosina Keates
Address: Brookbank Cottage, Yarnbrook

Roland had served with the Grenadier Guards prior to the war and held the distinction of being the tallest man in the British Army, standing six feet seven and a half inches. At the end of his term of service he left the army and was placed on the army reserve, he was then recalled to the colours at the outbreak of hostilities presenting himself at Devizes Barracks. He was

Roland Cook Keates was the tallest soldier in the British Army - his grave at West Ashton Church

returned as medically unfit and discharged from the army in November 1914 and was sent for treatment at Winsley Sanatorium under London specialists. After a long painful illness he died on Saturday 14 August 1915. Roland was buried in West Ashton Churchyard with full military honours, he is not remembered by the Commonwealth War Grave Commission. His brother Donald Keates would be killed in November 1918.

Private Joseph Earle   *8th Bn Royal Welsh Fusiliers*
Service No.   24025
Age: 32
Place of Birth: Trowbridge, Wiltshire
Home Country: England
Date of Death: 18/08/1915
Cause of death: Died of wounds
Memorial: Trowbridge
War cemetery: Helles Memorial
Theatre of war: Gallipoli
Next of Kin: Mabel Emily Earle (wife) - Joseph & Jane Earle (parents)
Address: 52 Shails Lane, Trowbridge, Wiltshire

Joseph, aged 32, had been employed as a labourer when he married Mabel Emily Clift at Trowbridge on 19 July 1907. She was the daughter of Philip Clift, an old army man and a well known member of the Trowbridge National Guard. Joseph had enlisted with the Wiltshire Militia on 2 January 1905, and after serving for 3 years he transferred to the National Reserve. He volunteered for service with the 5th Wiltshires on 27 August 1914 but after eight months service, transferred to the Royal Welsh Fusiliers. This may have been due to his disciplinary record with the Wiltshires, when he was absent without leave on two occasions and was given detention for causing a disturbance in his billet. In June 1915 8th Royal Welsh Fusiliers sailed for Alexandria in Egypt and on 4 July 1915 had been transported to the Greek Island of Mudros in preparation for landing on Gallipoli. By 16 July 1915 the 8th Royal Welsh Fusiliers landed at Cape Helles on the southern tip of the Gallipoli Peninsula. At the end of July 1915 the 8th Royal Welsh Fusiliers left and returned to Mudros and between 3-5 August 1915 landed at Anzac Cove. Joseph was admitted to the 16th Casualty Clearing Station on Wednesday 18 August 1915 with a gunshot wound to the back and died there the same day. His grave was later lost and he is remembered on the Helles Memorial with over 21,000 Commonwealth soldiers who have no known grave.

Right: Joseph Earle

Below: British gun at Gallipoli

Lance Corporal William James Pepler   *5th Bn Royal Irish Regiment*
Service No. 910
Age: 21
Place of Birth: Southwick, Wiltshire
Home Country: England
Date of Death: 18/08/1915
Cause of death: Died
Memorial: Not known
War cemetery: Portianos Military Cemetery
Theatre of war: Gallipoli
Next of Kin: James & Fanny Pelper
Address: Frome Road, Southwick, Wiltshire.

Twenty one year old William was employed as an analyst with Wilts United Dairies and was a keen sportsman playing in defence for Southwick Football Club and a member of the local Cricket Club. He was also the secretary of the Southwick Men's Institute and had a large circle of friends in the area. In September 1914 he volunteered for service with the Somerset Light Infantry but was transferred to the Royal Irish Regiment. He was first sent to Longford, Ireland and then to Basingstoke where he was selected because of his clerical abilities to serve with Headquarters staff. At the end of June 1915 he left England for the Dardenelles. He contracted enteric fever and was evacuated to one of the military hospitals based on the island of Lemnos where he succumbed to the illness on Wednesday 18 August 1915. He is buried in Portianos Military Cemetery

Corporal Sydney John Chandler   *8th Bn Northumberland Fusiliers*
Service No. 6469
Age: 22
Place of Birth: Trowbridge, Wiltshire
Home Country: England
Date of Death: 19/08/1915
Cause of death: Killed in action
Memorial: Not known
War cemetery: Helles Memorial
Theatre of war: Gallipoli
Next of Kin: George & Jane Chandler
Address: Kington St. Michael, Wiltshire

Twenty two year old Sydney a Domestic Gardener volunteered for service with the 8th Service Battalion Northumberland Fusiliers at Sheffield. The Northumberland Fusiliers arrived on Gallipoli Peninsular in early August. He was killed in action on Thursday 19th August 1915 and is remembered on the Helles Memorial.

21 AUGUST 1915 - ANZAC ATTACK AT ANAFARTA, SUVLA BAY AND THE START OF THE BATTLE OF SCIMITAR HILL, GALLIPOLI

Private Charles Elms   *1st Bn Somerset Light Infantry*
Service No. 17439
Age: 27
Place of Birth: Corsham, Wiltshire
Home Country: England
Date of Death: 28/08/1915
Cause of death: Killed in action
Memorial: Trowbridge
War cemetery: Mesnil Ridge Cemetery Mesnil-Martinsart
Theatre of war: France
Next of Kin: James & Annie Elms
Address: 4 Bennett's Yard, The Halve, Trowbridge, Wiltshire.

Charles was employed as a coal carter and volunteered for service arriving in France on 22

GALLIPOLI

Above: Allied troops bathing at Gallipoli

Right: Arthur Charles Potter

June 1915. He was killed in action on Saturday 28 August 1915. His brothers John and James were also killed during the Great War

Private Arthur Charles Potter   *6th Bn Royal Munster Fusiliers*

Service No.	3208	Age:	18
Place of Birth:	Eddington, Wiltshire	Home Country:	England
Date of Death:	30/08/1915	Cause of death:	Killed in action
Memorial:	Trowbridge		
War cemetery:	Helles Memorial		
Theatre of war:	Gallipoli		
Next of Kin:	George & Pheobe Potter		
Address:	28 Bradford Road, Trowbridge, Wiltshire		

Arthur was the sixth son of George & Pheobe Potter and previous to the commencement of hostilities was employed at Sawtells bedding factory, Holt. With the first call for volunteers he offered his services, was accepted at Devizes and with 1,100 other Wiltshire lads was drafted to Irish regiments. After a short training at the Curraugh Camp and later in England he was sent to the Dardanelles, landing on the Peninsula on 14 August 1915. He met his death 16 days later whilst taking part in a bayonet charge. The sad news reached Trowbridge and many expressions of sympathy and condolence had been extended to both George & Pheobe Potter, who are comforted in the knowledge that their son died a heroes death. Arthur was landed at Suvla Bay on the Gallipoli Peninsula and it is interesting to read in his letter below that he thought he was landing on Lemnos which was the HQ for British forces. Writing to his brother the day before he was killed, Arthur said:

"We landed on the island named Lemnos on Saturday 14th August, about six in the morning. We were the second regiment to land here about four hours after the Manchester's. We had our work cut out, and the Turks were waiting for us but we drove them back a lot, but not without suffering. Then we were fighting like the devil for 14 days without a minutes rest and then came four days off, which we spent digging roads (worse than being in trenches). On Monday the 16 we made a big attack at 7.15 in the morning without a drop of water and the sun was fearfully hot, but by the time the sun had set we had driven the Turks back about a

mile. We had many casualties. Dick Wells is entered as missing, Cecil Ferris badly wounded and Leonard Groves, Tom Keen and Fred Knight slightly wounded. Nothing further happened until Sunday, when the enemy hoisted a white flag, but they did not get it all their own way and we would not cease fire. We followed this with a bayonet charge and captured the trenches, but it left us with about six officers to the battalion. On Saturday 21 August we were shifted off the hills into the valley, where we advanced about a mile under heavy shrapnel fire into the Turks' trenches, which had been taken the day before. On the next day we advanced and dug ourselves in 200 yards away from the enemy, and we have been holding it since. That is a week now. Our troops got cut up badly here as they were led into a trap and the dead they left behind were terrible. They are still lying about now as the enemy snipers are very busy, and the stench is enough to knock one down at 30 yards."

It is likely that Arthur died on the fighting at Hill 60 on the Gallipoli peninsula south of Suvla Bay. He is remembered on Helles Memorial and has no known grave. Arthur's brothers John and Robert were also destined to be killed in the following years. Arthur was also an under age soldier as in 1915 soldiers could only fight overseas if they were 19 years of age.

Brig. Gen. Paul Aloysius Kenna VC DSO   *Cdg 3rd Mounted Brigade*
Service No.: N/A
Age: 53
Place of Birth: Liverpool
Home Country: England
Date of Death: 30/08/1915
Cause of death: Died of wounds
Memorial: Not Known
War cemetery: Lala Baba Cemetery
Theatre of war: Gallipoli
Next of Kin: Angela Mary Kenna (wife) – James & Julia Kenna (Parents)
Address: Trowle House, Trowbridge, Wiltshire

Paul was born in Liverpool in 1862, he was the son of James & Julia Kenna and educated at St. Augustine's College, Stoneyhurst, and Sandhurst. In 1886 he was commissioned into the 2nd West Indian Regiment and after two years service in the West Indies and East Africa he transferred to the 21st Lancers. In 1893 and 1894 he was one of the best polo players in the British Army in India and he rode more than 300 National Hunt and Flat winners before concentrating on show-jumping later in his sporting career. In 1895 he received the Royal Humane Society's Medal for saving a drowning man from the River Liffey. He served in the Second Sudanese War (1896-1899).and in 1898 he received the Victoria Cross and an extract from "London Gazette." dated 15 November 1898, records the following:-

"At the Battle of Khartoum, on 2nd September 1898, Captain P.A. Kenna assisted Major Crole Wyndham, of the same regiment, by taking him on his horse, behind the saddle (Major Wyndham's horse having been killed in the charge), thus enabling him to reach a place of safety; and after the charge of the 21st Lancers, Captain Kenna returned to assist Lieutenant de Montmorency, who was endeavouring to recover the body of second Lieutenant R.G. Grenfell."

Paul served as Assistant Provost Marshal in South Africa 1899-1902, he then served in Somaliland Campaign 1904 and in 1905 he married Angela Mary Hibbert and was promoted to Colonel and made Aide-de-Camp to King Edward VII. In 1910 and 1911 he led the Great Britain show jumping team in America and then The Great British in 1912 Stockholm Olympics. However the team arrived late and the horses performed badly. After the poor performance Paul was responsible for influencing the preparation and training of horses for future Olympics. He was promoted to Brigadier General in 1914 and commanded the Nottinghamshire and Derbyshire Regiment, he was then transferred to the Yeomanry of the 2nd Mounted Division at Gallipoli. He was wounded by a shell on 29 August 1915, in the attack on Turkish positions at Chocolate Hill, east of Suvla Bay, and he died of his wounds on Monday 30 August 1915. He is buried at Lala Baba Cemetery Galipoli.

> *31 AUGUST 1915 - THE ALLIES LOSSES AT GALLIPOLI DURING AUGUST NUMBER 40,000 SOLDIERS, FROM DEATH DUE TO FIGHTING OR THROUGH DYSENTERY AND OTHER DISEASES*

Captain William Campbell Adamson   *6th Sqdn Royal Flying Corps*
Service No.   N/A   Age: 28
Place of Birth: Careston Castle, Forfarshire   Home Country: Scotland
Date of Death: 05/09/1915   Cause of death: Killed in action
Memorial: Hilperton Church & Careston Church
War cemetery: Harelbeke New British Cemetery
Theatre of war: Belgium
Next of Kin: Margaret Stancomb Adamson (wife) - William & Nora Adamson (parents)
Address: Whyte House Weeke, Winchester, Hampshire - Careston Forfarshire

William was the only son of William & Nora Adamson of Careston Castle, Forfarshire. In the spring of 1913 he married Margaret Stancomb Mann at Hilperton Church and gained his flying certificate on 17 July 1914. At the out break of the war he was one of the first airmen to serve on the continent arriving in France on 9 October 1914. On Sunday 5 September 1915 he was on patrol over the German lines near Zandvoorde, Belgium when he was confronted by three hostile aircraft. William succeeded in chasing off all three but his biplane was hit by an enemy anti aircraft shell and his machine came down in a flat spiral and it went down behind enemy lines. It was hoped William was alive when the machine landed and he had been taken prisoner and he was listed as missing. Fellow officers in his squadron dropped a message to the German air corps asking for details of him. At this time in the war it was usual for air forces to communicate in this way. A few days later news was received that William had met his death in action. It was conveyed in the following letter from a Major in command of the squadron:

Above: Paul Aloysius Kenna

Right: William Campbell Adamson

"I am much grieved to have to inform you that he was lost yesterday afternoon, Sept, 5th. He was putting up a magnificent fight against some German aeroplanes, and his machine was unfortunately hit by a German anti aircraft gun, and fell in the German lines. I have known him in the squadron since March. He has always done some excellent work. I do not know of any officer who will be more missed." William left a widow and a baby son.

Private Frank Woodward *2/4th TF Bn Wiltshire Regiment*
Service No.   3138   Age: 29
Place of Birth: Malmesbury, Wiltshire   Home Country: England
Date of Death: 20/09/1915   Cause of death: Died
Memorial: Malmesbury & Trowbridge St. James Church
War cemetery: Kirkee 1914-1918 Memorial
Theatre of war: India
Next of Kin: George & Elizabeth Woodward
Address: 11 Elm Grove Terrace, Tiverton, Bath

Frank was a footman and having enlisted with the 2/4th Battalion Wiltshire Regiment was sent to India for garrison duties. He died on Monday 20 September 1915 of illness or disease at Poona Hospital, India. He was buried in a cemetery in Poona but the Commonwealth War Graves Commission do not tend the graves of some service men in India but he is remembered on the Kirkee 1914-1918 Memorial.

Private Stanley John Swayne *2/4th TF Bn Wiltshire Regiment*
Service No.   2607   Age: 21
Place of Birth: Salisbury, Wiltshire   Home Country: England
Date of Death: 20/09/1915   Cause of death: Died
Memorial: Salisbury & Trowbridge St. James Church
War cemetery: Kirkee 1914-1918 Memorial
Theatre of war: India
Next of Kin: Thomas & Fanny Swayne
Address: 1 Waverley Place, Gigant Street, Salisbury

Stanley was the younger son of Thomas and Fanny Swayne of Salisbury. After volunteering in 1914 he left for India in December 1914 to replace regular troops who had been stationed in India at the start of the war. He died of illness, at Poona, India on Monday 20 September 1915.

Lance Corporal George Percy Coward *2nd Bn South Wales Borderers*
Service No.   11224   Age: 19
Place of Birth: North Bradley, Wiltshire   Home Country: Wales
Date of Death: 20/09/1915   Cause of death: Killed in action
Memorial: Not Known
War cemetery: Helles Memorial
Theatre of war: Gallipoli
Next of Kin: William and Mary Coward
Address: 4 King's Parade British, Talywain, Monmouthshire

It is likely nineteen year old George, a coal miner, volunteered for service with the South Wales Borderers. He arrived on the Gallipoli Peninsular on 22 August 1915 and was killed in action just under a month later on Monday 20 September 1915. He has no known grave and is remembered on the Helles Memorial.

5
LOOS

Private William Tom Jefferies   *6th Bn Wiltshire Regiment*
Service No.: 12182
Place of Birth: Westbury, Wiltshire
Date of Death: 25/09/1915
Memorial: Not known
War cemetery: Loos Memorial
Theatre of war: France
Next of Kin: Lily Jefferies (wife) - Noah & Fanny Jefferies (Parents)
Address: 4 New Court, Trowbridge - 18, New Buildings, Westbury

Age: 26
Home Country: England
Cause of death: Killed in action

William was a printer. He married Lillian Saunders in Westbury in the summer of 1912 and volunteered for service in 1914. After undergoing training William was sent to France on 19 July which was his birthday. He was killed on the first day of the battle of Loos, France when the British used gas for the first time. The 6th Battalion Wiltshire Regiment were in trenches at Rue de Callioux, at 5.50am asphyxiating gas was released and the attack commenced at 6.30am the objective was Rue d'Auvert and the initial assault was carried out by advancing through saps (trenches dug into no mans land). However the attacks were repulsed and the saps became full. On the left D company got out of the trench and attacked but were held up and suffered heavy casualties. The war diary for the day states:

"Owing to the wet weather considerable difficulty was experienced in bringing back the wounded."

One of William's colleague's wrote to Noah & Fanny Jefferies stating that William had been killed in action. This probably reached them before the official confirmation because he was listed as missing on a casualty list that was issued on 4 October 1915. He has no known grave and is remembered on the Loos Memorial.

Sergeant William George Sainsbury   *1st Bn Wiltshire Regiment*
Service No.: 5021
Place of Birth: Trowbridge, Wiltshire
Date of Death: 26/09/1915
Memorial: Not known
War cemetery: Brandhoek Military Cemetery
Theatre of war: Belgium
Next of Kin: Not known
Address: West Lavington, Wiltshire

Age: 35
Home Country: England
Cause of death: Killed in action

William was an old soldier and probably on reserve at the outbreak of hostilities; he arrived in

France on 14 April 1915. While the Battle of Loos was taking place to the south, the 1st Battalion Wiltshire Regiment were in very wet trenches at Hooge, Belgium. While the Wiltshires were being relieved fighting broke out and artillery support was called for. With so many men in the trenches they became congested and then the Germans retaliated, shelling the British fire trenches. The Wiltshires casualties were 2 killed and 20 wounded. One of those killed was William; he is buried in Brandhoek Military Cemetery, Belgium.

27 SEPTEMBER 1915 - BRITISH GUARDS DIVISION CAPTURE HILL 70 AT LOOS, FRANCE

Sergeant Frank Thompson — *3rd Bn Grenadier Guards*
Service No.: 11083
Place of Birth: Trowbridge, Wiltshire
Date of Death: 27/09/1915
Memorial: Not Known
War cemetery: Loos Memorial
Theatre of war: France
Next of Kin: Rose Thompson (wife) - Arthur and Martha Thompson (parents)
Address: 47 Roberts Road, High Wycombe, Buckinghamshire.
Age: 30
Home Country: England
Cause of death: Killed in action

Police officer Frank was the third son of Arthur and Martha Thompson and in the spring of 1911 he married Rose M. Colliass at Maidenhead. He was 6 foot 3 inches tall and volunteered for service joining the Grenadier Guards and arriving in France on 27 July 1915. The first news of Frank's death was received from a Sergeant Sulivan of the Royal Motor Transport who sent some of Frank's letters he had picked up on the battlefield and stated that Frank had been killed in a charge on German positions. It is likely his remains were lost during subsequent fighting and he is remembered on the Loos Memorial.

Private William Edward Hodges — *6th Bn East Kent Regiment*
Service No.: G/3498
Place of Birth: Hilperton, Wiltshire
Date of Death: 29/09/1915
Memorial: Holt
War cemetery: Lapugnoy Military Cemetery
Theatre of war: France
Next of Kin: Susan Watts (parent)
Address: Holt, Wiltshire.
Age: 28
Home Country: England
Cause of death: Died of wounds

William was a wireman working on the tramway in Edmonton, Middlesex. He volunteered for service and arrived in France on 31 August 1915, less than a month later he was dead. He had been wounded in the Battle of Loos and evacuated to one of the casualty clearing stations, Lapugnoy, France and died of his wounds on Wednesday 29 September 1915.

Captain William Edwin Jenkins — *2nd Bn Northumberland Fusiliers*
Service No.: N/A
Place of Birth: Trowbridge, Wiltshire
Date of Death: 01/10/1915
Memorial: Trowbridge
War cemetery: Loos Memorial
Theatre of war: France
Age: 33
Home Country: England
Cause of death: Killed in action

Far right: William Edwin Jenkins

Right: William Percy Alfred Young

Next of Kin: William Harry & Emily Jenkins
Address: 43 Castle Street, Trowbridge, Wiltshire

William was a career soldier after joining the army in his teens as a private he attained the rank of Captain. He arrived in France on 18 January 1915 and in September 1915 he was with the 2nd Battalion Northumberland Fusiliers at the Battle of Loos. William was reported killed between 1-3 October 1915 and later it was assumed he had died on Friday 1 October 1915. He is remembered on the Loos Memorial and has no known grave.

> 5 OCTOBER 1915 - A BRITISH AND FRENCH FORCE LANDS AT SALONIKA, GREECE TO SUPPORT SERBIA
>
> TUESDAY 12 OCTOBER 1915 - ENGLISH NURSE EDITH CAVELL WAS SHOT BY THE GERMANS FOR HELPING BRITISH PRISONERS OF WAR ESCAPE FROM BELGIUM TO NEUTRAL HOLLAND

Corporal Ernest Pullen   *10th Bn Lancashire Fusiliers*

Service No.: 7193
Place of Birth: Monkton Farliegh, Wiltshire
Date of Death: 02/11/1915
Memorial: Hilperton
War cemetery: Ypres Menin Gate
Theatre of war: Belgium
Next of Kin: George & Allice Pullen
Address: Staverton, Trowbridge, Wiltshire.

Age: 24
Home Country: England
Cause of death: Killed in action

Prior to the Great War 24 year old Ernest was a motor tyre builder in Manchester, he volunteered and signed up for the duration of the war, joining the 10 Service Battalion Lancashire Fusiliers. He arrived in France on 15 July 1915 and his unit was sent to the trenches south of Ypres, Belgium and shadowed an experienced infantry battalion as part of their training. Ernest was one of two members of the Lancashires to be killed on Tuesday 2 November 1915. He is remembered on the Ypres Menin Gate and has no known grave.

Private William Percy Alfred Young *8th Bn Royal Welsh Fusiliers*
Service No. 24048 Age: 20
Place of Birth: Trowbridge, Wiltshire Home Country: England
Date of Death: 03/11/1915 Cause of death: Killed in action
Memorial: Trowbridge
War cemetery: Green Hill Cemetery
Theatre of war: Gallipoli Next of Kin: Laura Young (parent)
Address: 12 Upper Bond Street, Trowbridge, Wiltshire.

William Young was 20 years of age and had originally joined the Wiltshire Regiment, but was transferred to the Welsh Fusiliers. He arrived on the Gallipoli Peninsular in July 1915; his father was serving in France with a Navvies Battalion. Laura Young received the following letter from the Rev. E.Teale Church of England Chaplain, 41st Field Ambulance, 40th Brigade, 13th Division, Mediterranean expeditionary force:

"Thursday 4 November 1915, I very much regret to inform you that your son was killed yesterday. He was on his way to the regimental washing tanks when a bullet hit him in the back and passed into his heart. Your boy's death was instantaneous, he had no time to leave any last messages. It is sometimes a comfort to know that one who has been killed in war passed out of this life into the wider life beyond painlessly. Your boy would not have any suffering of any kind, he would hardly know he was hit.
I buried him in a site set apart as a cemetery not many yards from the spot he was killed. This site will always be a permanent memorial to those who have given their lives on this part of the peninsula. The official description for the site is 105 H.I. Suvla. The men of his regiment have put a wooden cross on the grave with his name and regiment, written thereon.
I am very sorry indeed that you were called upon to bear this loss, it is a sorrow which you and your family share in common with thousands of other families in England today. You must have some joy in knowing that your boy willingly answered the Nation's call and made his sacrifice at this critical time. He was very much liked by his regiment and the men who attended his funeral spoke very kindly of him."

This was Laura's second son to die in the war, George Hooper fell on 23 January 1915 in France. William is buried in Green Hill Cemetery along with nearly 3,000 servicemen of the Great War, of which 2,472 of the burials are unidentified.

Lt. Commander Robert Pennington Williams *HMS Pembroke Royal Navy*
Service No. N/A Age: 41
Place of Birth: Keynsham, Somerset Home Country: England
Date of Death: 08/11/1915 Cause of death: Died
Memorial: Not Known
War cemetery: Great Yarmouth Gorleston Cemetery
Theatre of war: Home
Next of Kin: Alice Williams (wife) - Gabriel & Catherine Williams (parents)
Address: Not Known - George Hotel, Trowbridge, Wiltshire

Prior to the South African War Robert lived in India, he left India and volunteered for service with Lunsden's Horse, in which he served for a year, he was awarded the Queens Medal with 3 bars. At the outbreak of the Great War Robert was a ships captain with the British Indian Steam Navigation Company and was given a commission in the Royal Naval Reserve. He was given command of the Caronia, an armed merchant ship, and spent many months in the North Sea. On the day he sailed he married Alice Webbley at Bristol. Due to illness caused by the

Far Right: Robert Pennington Williams

Right: Edgar Jesse Gregory

extreme cold he was given sick leave and transferred to the Naval Barracks at Chatham which he commanded. His health again broke down and he died on Monday 8 November 1915 and he was buried at Great Yarmouth Gorleston Cemetery.

22 NOVEMBER 1915 - THE BATTLE OF CTESIPHON, MESOPOTAMIA

Private Edgar Jesse Gregory *2/4th TF Bn Wiltshire Regiment*
Service No.   T3127   Age: 25
Place of Birth: Melksham, Wiltshire   Home Country: England
Date of Death: 22/11/1915   Cause of death: Killed in action
Memorial: Melksham & Trowbridge St. James Church
War cemetery: Basra Memorial
Theatre of war: Mesopotamia
Next of Kin: Noah and Jane Gregory
Address: Sandridge Lane, Bromham

Edgar, known as Jesse and a carpenter, volunteered for service enlisting with the 2/4th Battalion Wiltshire Regiment and was sent to India for garrison duties. When men were required for Mesopotamia he came forward and was sent to what is modern day Iraq on 25 August 1915. He was killed in action on Monday 22 November 1915 at the Battle of Ctesiphon, Iraq, in action against Turkish forces. He is remembered on the Basra Memorial and has no known grave. The following memoriam was inserted in a local paper by Jessie's parents in 1917:

In loving memory of our dear son and brother
Two years have passed and we still miss him
Friends may think the wound is healed
But they little know the sorrow
Deep within the heart concealed
Never forgotten by his Father, Mother, Brother and Sisters

Private Arthur Tanner	*2/4th TF Bn Wiltshire Regiment*

Service No.	3175	Age:	29
Place of Birth:	Kington St Michael, Wiltshire	Home Country:	England
Date of Death:	22/11/1915	Cause of death:	Killed in action
Memorial:	Kington St Michael & Trowbridge St. James Church		
War cemetery:	Basra Memorial		
Theatre of war:	Mesopotamia		
Next of Kin:	Alfred James & Jane Tanner		
Address:	Kington St Micheal, Wiltshire		

Arthur, a farm labourer, volunteered for service with the 2/4th Battalion Wiltshire Regiment and was initially sent to India for garrison duty. When a call came for men to fight in Mesopotamia Arthur again volunteered and arrived in modern day Iraq on 25 August 1915. He was killed on Monday 22 November 1915 at the Battle of Ctesiphon, Iraq, in action against Turkish forces. He is remembered on the Basra Memorial and has no known grave.

Private Levi Erasmus Garrett	*2/4th TF Bn Wiltshire Regiment*

Service No.	1706	Age:	21
Place of Birth:	Warminster, Wiltshire	Home Country:	England
Date of Death:	22/11/1915	Cause of death:	Killed in action
Memorial:	Trowbridge St. James Church - Warminster		
War cemetery:	Basra Memorial		
Theatre of war:	Mesopotamia		
Next of Kin:	Lillian Garrett (wife) - Joseph and Sarah Ann Garrett (parents)		
Address:	13 Victoria Road, Bugley, Warminster - Longbridge Deverill		

When 21 year old Levi, a farm Labourer, married Lillian Prince in the spring of 1914 they had no knowledge of the war that was to come. Levi volunteered to serve with the 2/4th Battalion Wiltshire Regiment for garrison duties in India. After a call for more men to fight in Mesopotamia Levi again volunteered and arrived in Mesopotamia modern day Iraq where on, 25 August 1915, where he was attached to the 1st Battalion Oxford & Bucks Light Infantry. He was killed in action on Monday 22 November 1915 at the Battle of Ctesiphon, Iraq, in action against Turkish forces. He is remembered on the Basra Memorial and has no known grave.

Private George Henry Swaine	*2/4th TF Bn Wiltshire Regiment*

Service No.	2937	Age:	26
Place of Birth:	Semington, Wiltshire	Home Country:	England
Date of Death:	22/11/1915	Cause of death:	Killed in action
Memorial:	Trowbridge St James Church Memorial		
War cemetery:	Basra Memorial		
Theatre of war:	Mesopotamia		
Next of Kin:	Alfred & Celia Swaine		
Address:	Canal Bridge, Semington, Wiltshire		

George, a farm labourer, was the eldest son of Alfred & Celia Swaine, he volunteered for service enlisting with the 2/4th Battalion Wiltshire Regiment and was sent to India for garrison duties. When men were required for Mesopotamia he came forward and was sent to what is modern day Iraq on 25 August 1915. He was killed in action on Monday 22 November 1915 at the Battle of Ctesiphon, Iraq, in conflict with Turkish forces. He is remembered on the Basra Memorial and has no known grave. News of his death reached his parents in January 1916 and a memorial service was held at the Wesleyan Chapel in Semington.

Sergeant Robert Berrett		*2/4th TF Bn Wiltshire Regiment*	
Service No.	1587	Age:	22
Place of Birth:	Steeple Ashton, Wiltshire	Home Country:	England
Date of Death:	22/11/1915	Cause of death:	Killed in action
Memorial:	Steeple Ashton & Trowbridge St James Church Memorial		
War cemetery:	Basra Memorial		
Theatre of war:	Mesopotamia		
Next of Kin:	Francis Walter & Caroline Berrett		
Address:	Church Street, Steeple Ashton, Wiltshire		

Robert, known as Bob, worked with his father and brother as wheelwrights in Steeple Ashton and he was well known in the village, was a member of the choir and played a prominent role in the football and cricket teams. Bob was with the Territorials before the war broke out and went to India with the Regiment in 1914. While at Poona he volunteered for service in Mesopotamia arriving on 25 August 1915. He was killed in action on Monday 22 November 1915 at the Battle of Ctesiphon, Iraq, while fighting Turkish forces. He is remembered on the Basra Memorial and has no known grave. His brother Arthur was killed in June 1915 while serving in France with the 1st Battalion Wiltshire Regiment. His parents inserted the following memoriam in a local paper:

"Into the field of battle he bravely took his place,
And fought and died for England and the honour of his race.
He sleeps not in a native land, but beneath a foreign sky,
Far from those who loved him, but in a hero's grave he lies.
From his sorrowing Father, Mother, Brothers and Sisters."

Lance Corporal Alfred Edward V Beck		*2/4th TF Bn Wiltshire Regiment*	
Service No.	3160	Age:	22
Place of Birth:	Fisherton, Wiltshire	Home Country:	England
Date of Death:	22/11/1915	Cause of death:	Killed in action
Memorial:	Salisbury & Trowbridge St James Church Memorial		
War cemetery:	Basra Memorial		
Theatre of war:	Mesopotamia		
Next of Kin:	Henry & Ellen Beck		
Address:	Fisherton Anger, Salisbury, Wiltshire		

Alfred, known as Edward, was a gas fitter and a Wiltshire Territorial. At the outbreak of war he was sent to India to serve at Poona; while there he volunteered for service in Mesopotamia arriving on 25 August 1915 and was attached to the Oxford and Buckinghamshire Light Infantry. He was killed in action on Monday 22 November 1915 at the Battle of Ctesiphon, Mesopotamia, which is about 20 miles south of Baghdad in modern day Iraq. He is remembered on the Basra Memorial and has no known grave.

Lance Coporal Frederick John Sawyer		*2/4th TF Bn Wiltshire Regiment*	
Service No.	2301	Age:	20
Place of Birth:	Melksham, Wiltshire	Home Country:	England
Date of Death:	22/11/1915	Cause of death:	Killed in action
Memorial:	Melksham & Trowbridge St James Church Memorial		
War cemetery:	Basra Memorial		
Theatre of war:	Mesopotamia		
Next of Kin:	Frederick & Florence Sawyer		

Address: Chapel Court, Melksham, Wiltshire

Twenty year old Frederick, known as Fred, was a grocers assistant with Norris and Archard in Melksham. At the commencement of hostilities he joined the Wiltshire Territorials and was sent to India to serve at Poona. He volunteered to serve in Mesopotamia arriving on 25 August 1915 and was attached to the Dorset Regiment.

Fred was killed in action on Monday 22nd November 1915 at the Battle of Ctesiphon, Mesopotamia Frederick and Florence Sawyer, his parents, received the following letter from Quarter Master Sergeant Wyatt who was based at Poona in India:

"I expect you are surprised to hear from me, but as Quarter Master Sergeant of his company and a friend of your son I thought I would write a few lines to say how deeply I deplore his loss. Personally I feel it as much as if I had lost a brother. I knew him well at Marlborough and since we have served together our friendship had grown. I have had no greater shock throughout the war than when I heard of his death, and so it was throughout the Company; to a man we all liked him and respected him. He has lived a perfectly clean life since he joined, and no man ever heard a foul word from his lips. As a soldier he was one of the best, if not the best lance corporal in our regiment. Undoubtedly he would have been promoted long before this had he not gallantly volunteered to serve his country at the Gulf. A colour sergeant was badly wounded and Fred went to bandage his wounds with a field bandage. He was struck in the left forearm, almost severing the arm, but still kept on with his act of mercy. Another bullet struck him in the thigh but disregarding this he tried to complete his task; another bullet struck him in the stomach and he dropped."

Fred is remembered on the Basra Memorial and has no known grave.

Private Arthur William Webb   *1st Bn Wiltshire Regiment*

Service No.	6789	Age:	30
Place of Birth:	Trowbridge, Wiltshire	Home Country:	England
Date of Death:	22/11/1915	Cause of death:	Died of wounds
Memorial:	Not Known		
War cemetery:	Bailleul Communal Cemetery Extension Nord		
Theatre of war:	France		
Next of Kin:	Rebecca Webb (wife) - William & Rose Webb (parents)		
Address:	16 Carter Street - Trowbridge, Wiltshire		

Arthur, a paint grinder originally enlisted with the Wiltshires on 15 January 1904 at the age of 18 years and 1 month. At the end of the year in 1906 he married Rebecca Ibell in Chester, Cheshire; he was also on the National Reserve and was one of the first to be mobilised and called back to his unit. He arrived in France on 31 August 1914 and it is likely he would have taken part in all the engagements the Wiltshires were involved with. He was wounded toward the end of 1915 and evacuated to one of the casualty clearing stations based at Bailleul, France, where he succumbed to his wounds on Monday 22 November 1915.

Captain Charles Gordon Bond   *2nd Bn Wiltshire Regiment*

Service No.	N/A	Age:	34
Place of Birth:	Savernake, Wiltshire	Home Country:	England
Date of Death:	25/11/1915	Cause of death:	Killed in action
Memorial:	Trowbridge		
War cemetery:	Guards Cemetery Windy Corner Cuinchy		
Theatre of war:	France		

Charles Gordon Bond

Next of Kin: Dorothy M B Pembroke (wife) - Rev. Gordon J E & Helen M Bond (parents)
Address: Ormonde, Victoria Road, Trowbridge - Savernake, Wiltshire

Charles was commissioned to the Wilshire Regiment in 1900, he married Dorothy M B Pembroke on 18 December 1907. At the commencement of hostilities he was the Adjutant of the 1/4th Battalion and went to India with them. He was transferred to the 2nd Battalion Wiltshire Regiment in 1915 and arrived in France on 23 November 1915. On Thursday 25 November the Wiltshires were in trenches at Givenchy, France, during the evening the Royal Engineers exploded two mines, a small one and a large one causing a huge crater. The Wiltshires rushed forward and took the fortified crater with little opposition. At this point of the war the Wiltshires did not have steel helmets and during the rush forward Charles was killed by a piece of falling earth.
Charles was well respected and a special memorial service was held in Delhi, India by his former battalion. He is buried in Guards Cemetery Windy Corner Cuinchy, France.

Private Albert Walter Cullimore   *2/4th TF Bn Wiltshire Regiment*
Service No.   2658   Age: 25
Place of Birth: Biddestone, Wiltshire   Home Country: England
Date of Death: 28/11/1915   Cause of death: Died of wounds
Memorial: Biddestone & Trowbridge St. James Church
War cemetery: Kut War Cemetery
Theatre of war: Mesopotamia
Next of Kin: Albert & Ellen Cullimore
Address: Pickwick, Corsham, Wiltshire

Albert, known as Walter and a labourer, volunteered for service with the 2/4th Battalion Wiltshire Regiment and was sent to India for Garrison duties. After a call for more men for the Mesopotamia campaign he again volunteered arriving on 25 May 1915. He was wounded in fighting most likely at Ctesiphon in November 1915. He died of his wounds on Sunday 28 November 1915.

> *5 DECEMBER 1915 - BRITISH FORCE AT KUT ARE SURROUNDED BY TURKISH TROOPS*
>
> *8 DECEMBER 1915 - EVACUATION OF GALLIPOLI BEGINS*

Rifleman Walter Foyle		*8th Bn Rifle Brigade*	
Service No.	S/10461	Age:	23
Place of Birth:	North Bradley, Wiltshire	Home Country:	England
Date of Death:	09/12/1915	Cause of death:	Killed in action
Memorial:	North Bradley		
War cemetery:	La Brique Military Cemetery No2		
Theatre of war:	France		
Next of Kin:	Miss Jane Newman (friend) - Elizabeth Gibbons (parent)		
Address:	56 Pearscroft Road, Fulham - Church Lane, North Bradley, Wiltshire		

Walter was a steam roller driver and volunteered for service for the duration of the war with the 8th Service Battalion Rifle Brigade on 7 May 1915. He arrived in France on 3 August 1915 and was killed in action near La Brique, France, on Thursday 9 December 1915 and is buried in La Brique Military Cemetery No2. His personal possessions were sent to his friend Miss Jane Newman and consisted of; 1disc, 4 photo's, 12 letters and 1 Gospel of St. Mathew.

Bombardier Sidney Edwards		*81st Bde Royal Field Artillery*	
Service No.	61914	Age:	27
Place of Birth:	Orpington, Kent	Home Country:	England
Date of Death:	28/12/1915	Cause of death:	Died of wounds
Memorial:	Not Known		
War cemetery:	Le Touquet Paris Plage Communal Cemetery		
Theatre of war:	France		
Next of Kin:	William & Amelia Edwards		
Address:	Post Office Cottage, Wingfield, Wiltshire		

Sidney was the second son of William & Amelia Edwards. He volunteered for service with the Royal Field Artillery and arrived in France on 6 November 1915. He was wounded in subsequent fighting and died of his wounds at The Duchess of Westminister's Hospital based at Le Touquet.

Private William Henry Burden		*2/4th TF Bn Wiltshire Regiment*	
Service No.	1795	Age:	21
Place of Birth:	Marlborough, Wiltshire	Home Country:	England
Date of Death:	28/12/1915	Cause of death:	Died of wounds
Memorial:	Marlborough & Trowbridge St. James Church		
War cemetery:	Amara War Cemetery		
Theatre of war:	Mesopotamia		
Next of Kin:	John & Emily Burden		
Address:,	Marlborough, Wiltshire		

Twenty one year old William volunteered and enlisted with the 2/4th Battalion Wiltshire Regiment and was sent to India for Garrison duties. He then came forward in a response for more men for the Mesopotamia campaign arriving on 25 August 1915 and was attached to the 1st Battalion Oxford and Bucks Light Infantry. He was wounded in fighting, most likely at Ctesiphon in November 1915, and succumbed to his wounds on Tuesday 28 December 1915 at one of the hospitals based at Amara in modern day Iraq.

Lance Sergeant Ernest Arthur Gomm   *6th Bn Wiltshire Regiment*
Service No. 19038   Age: 22
Place of Birth: Willingdon, Sussex   Home Country: England
Date of Death: 02/01/1916   Cause of death: Died of wounds
Memorial: Trowbridge
War cemetery: Merville Communal Cemetery
Theatre of war: France
Next of Kin: Daisy H E Gomm (wife) - William F. & Sarah A. Gomm (parents)
Address: 28 Gloucester Road, Trowbridge, Wiltshire

Ernest, known as Arthur, was a shop assistant and he married Daisy H E Walker in the spring of 1915. He volunteered for service for the duration of the war and arrived in France on 8 September 1915. On Boxing Day 1915 the Wiltshires were in trenches East of Bethune, France, between Copse Street and the La Bassee Road. Arthur received a severe bullet wound from a German sniper and was evacuated to a military hospital at Merville, France, where he died on Sunday 2nd January 1915. His brother Stanley Gomm was to die in 1918.

Private Alexander James Hayter   *16th Bn Kings Royal Rifle Corps*
Service No. C/1083   Age: 20
Place of Birth: Milbourne Port, Somerset   Home Country: England
Date of Death: 02/01/1916   Cause of death: Killed in action
Memorial: Trowbridge & United Free Church Memorial
War cemetery: Woburn Abbey Cemetery Cuinchy
Theatre of war: France
Next of Kin: Annie Hayter (parent)
Address: 15 Drynham Road, Trowbridge

Right: Ernest Arthur Gomm

Far right: Alexander James Hayter

Twenty year old Alexander, known as Alec, was a former member of Trowbridge Church Lads Brigade and at the outbreak of hostilities he was serving as an apprentice to printer Frank Slugg. He volunteered for service on 23 November 1914 and arrived in France on 16 November 1915. On 1 January 1915 Alec posted a letter to Mr Slugg, and in it he wrote he was looking forward to the end of the war, and stated that the Germans seemed to have had enough of it at the front. Alec was killed on Sunday 2 January 1915 at La Bassee France when the Germans exploded a mine beneath the British trenches. He was buried in Woburn Abbey Cemetery Cuinchy on the same day, the news reached Trowbridge on Alec's 21st birthday.

4 JANUARY 1916 - THE BATTLE OF SHEIK SA'AD, MESOPOTAMIA - AN ATTEMPT TO RELIEVE THE BRITISH GARRISON IN KUT

Private Edward Patrick Rodgers　*Royal Defence Corps*
Service No.　Not known　Age:　50
Place of Birth:　Liverpool, Lancashire　Home Country:　England
Date of Death:　08/01/1916　Cause of death:　Died
Memorial:　Trowbridge
War cemetery:　Trowbridge Cemetery
Theatre of war:　Home
Next of Kin:　Elizabeth Rodgers　(wife) - Patrick and Mary Rodgers (parents)
Address:　85 Mortimer Street, Trowbridge, Wiltshire

Edward was an old soldier and had spent 18 years in the Royal Horse Artillery and the Royal Field Artillery. He had been awarded the Burmah medal and clasp for service in 1885 to 1887. In civilian life he was a stone masons labourer and had married Elizabeth Ann Hobbs in 1896. At the outbreak of hostilities, Edward had enlisted with the Royal Defence guarding vulnerable installations and was initially stationed near Bristol but in late 1915 he was sent to Wallingford near Reading. He went on guard on the evening of Friday 8 January and after finishing his duty he went to his lodgings and while talking to his landlady's son he fell down and died. Edward died of heart failure. His body was conveyed to Trowbridge where he was buried with full military honours. Edward's son Albert and daughter Amy were to die in November 1918 and are buried in Trowbridge Cemetery. On the Trowbridge War Memorial his name is spelt Rogers, he is not remembered by the Commonwealth War Graves Commission.

Far left: Edward Patrick Rodgers

Left: Charles William Potter

> *9 JANUARY 1916 - GALLIPOLI EVACUATION COMPLETED*
>
> *24 JANUARY 1916 - THE MILITARY SERVICE ACT IS PASSED IN PARLIAMENT CONSCRIPTION WILL COMMENCE IN MAY 1916*

Sergeant Charles William Potter — *2nd Dragoon Guards*
Service No. 5577
Place of Birth: Ipswich, Suffolk
Date of Death: 26/01/1916
Memorial: Trowbridge
War cemetery: Vermelles British Cemetery
Theatre of war: France
Next of Kin: William Henry & Lydia Annie Potter
Address: 40 Frome Road, Trowbridge, Wiltshire

Age: 23
Home Country: England
Cause of death: Killed in action

William had been employed as an apprentice at Haden's foundry and when the establishment closed he worked for Petter's of Yeovil. He left the workshop and joined the army at his earliest opportunity, joining the Queen's Bays. At the outbreak of war Williams regiment was one of the first to be sent to France and he arrived there on 14 August 1914. He fought at Mons, the Marne and Ypres and was wounded in October 1914. William was promoted and given charge of the machine gun section, he was killed in action during a heavy bombardment on Wednesday 26 January 1916 near Vermelles, France. His brother Robert Stanley Potter was to bekilled in 1918.

Private Henry James Bethell — *4th Bn Wiltshire Regiment*
Service No. 3626
Place of Birth: Trowbridge, Wiltshire
Date of Death: 07/03/1916
Memorial: Trowbridge
War cemetery: Trowbridge Cemetery

Age: 54
Home Country: England
Cause of death: Died

Henry James Bethell and his grave in Trowbridge Cemetery

Theatre of war: Home
Next of Kin: Ruth Blanche Bethell (wife) - Henry & Harriet Bethell (parents)
Address: 10 Adcroft Street, Trowbridge, Wiltshire

Henry, a boot maker, was over 50 years of age when he volunteered for service, though he was too old to serve on the continent older men were used to guard installations in Great Britain. Henry was stationed at Newcastle and he was taken ill in February 1916 and died on Tuesday 7 March at Seaton Delaval, Whitley Bay.

Private Arthur Henry Bailey   *1st Bn Gloucestershire Regiment*
Service No.: 15348
Age: 36
Place of Birth: Trowbridge, Wiltshire
Home Country: England
Date of Death: 10/03/1916
Cause of death: Killed in action
Memorial: Trowbridge
War cemetery: Maroc British Cemetery
Theatre of war: France
Next of Kin: Robert & Matilda Bailey
Address: 10 New Road, Trowbridge, Wiltshire

Arthur was the third son of Robert and Matilda Bailey and prior to the Great war he was a coal miner working in South Wales. He volunteered for service with the Gloucester Regiment and spent his last leave in Trowbridge leaving for the front two days before Christmas 1915. On Friday 10 March 1916 Arthur was with the Gloucesters in trenches at the Double Crasssier sector near Maroc, France. He was killed by a heavy German bombardment which lasted for the next 3 days causing the Gloucester's over twenty fatalities.

Private John Crabbe   *7th Bn York & Lancaster Regiment*
Service No.: 16617
Age: 25
Place of Birth: Trowbridge, Wiltshire
Home Country: England
Date of Death: 11/03/1916
Cause of death: Died of wounds
Memorial: Not known
War cemetery: Voormezeele Enclosure No1 and No2
Theatre of war: Belgium
Next of Kin: Mrs Crabbe (wife) - John & Jennet Crabbe (parents)
Address: 2 Avon Crescent Trowbridge - Cumberland Road, Bristol, Gloucestershire

John volunteered for service, arriving in France on 13 July 1915. He died of wounds on Saturday 11 March 1916 and was buried in Voormezeele Enclosure No1 and No2, Belgium.

Driver Benjamin Daly   *1st Div Amm Col Royal Field Artillery*
Service No.: 63613
Age: 23
Place of Birth: Cork, Ireland
Home Country: England
Date of Death: 15/03/1916
Cause of death: Died of wounds
Memorial: Trowbridge
War cemetery: Nouex Les Mines Communal Cemetery
Theatre of war: France
Next of Kin: Hilda Daly (wife) - James Daly (parent)
Address: 5 Mortimer Lane, Basingstoke, Hampshire - Innishannon, Co. Cork

Benjamin joined the Royal Artillery at 18 years of age and arrived in France on 16 August

Right: Arthur Henry Bailey

Far right: William Jacobs

1914. He married Hilda Self at the end of 1915 in Hampshire and they lived at 3 Marlborough Buildings, Hilperton Road, Trowbridge. He was shot by a sniper near Loos, France on Wednesday 15 March 1915 and died of his wounds. His wife, Hilda, inserted the following memoriam in a local paper;

In loving memory of my dear husband
Not gone from memory not gone from love
But gone to our Father's Home
His loving wife Hilda

Private William Jacobs		*1st Bn Wiltshire Regiment*	
Service No.	10728	Age:	32
Place of Birth:	Woolwich, Kent	Home Country:	England
Date of Death:	19/03/1916	Cause of death:	Died
Memorial:	Trowbridge & Hilperton		
War cemetery:	Trowbridge Cemetery		
Theatre of war:	Home		
Next of Kin:	Laura Annie Jacobs (wife) - John & Mary Jacobs (parents)		
Address:	12 Wyke Road, Trowbridge, Wiltshire		

William had been employed as a painter and decorator with Ushers Brewery before the Great War. He volunteered for service and arrived in France on 13 July 1915. He was evacuated from France and died of illness or disease at the 5th Southern General Hospital, Portsmouth on Sunday 19 March 1916. He was buried in Trowbridge with a full Military Funeral.

5 APRIL 1916 - FIRST BATTLE OF KUT

Private Alfred Charles Bishop		*2/4th TF Bn Wiltshire Regiment*	
Service No.	2393	Age:	25
Place of Birth:	Brentford, Essex	Home Country:	England

Date of Death: 06/04/1916 Cause of death: Died
Memorial: Trowbridge
War cemetery: Basra Memorial
Theatre of war: Mesopotamia
Next of Kin: Thomas & Susan Bishop
Address: 5 Drynham Lane, Trowbridge, Wiltshire

Alfred worked for Ushers Brewery and he was a Territorial soldier with the 2/4th Territorial Battalion of the Wiltshire Regiment. At the outbreak of hostilities the Wiltshire Regiments territorial battalions were sent to India, arriving in January 1915, to replace the regular battalions. During 1915 volunteers were asked to support the British in Mesopotamia fighting the Turkish forces. Alfred was one of the volunteers and he arrived in Mesopotamia on 28 August 1915. On 29 April 1916 the British and Indian Force at Kut in modern day Iraq surrendered after being under siege from Turkish forces. Over 10,000 troops were surrendered and of those nearly 1500 were sick. Alfred was initially reported as missing at Kut and later officially reported to have died from illness during the siege on Thursday 6 April 1916. He is remembered on the Basra Memorial and has no known grave.

Lance Corporal Geoffrey Hayward Manning   *2/4th TF Bn Wiltshire Regiment*
Service No. 200816   Age: 24
Place of Birth: Melksham, Wiltshire   Home Country: England
Date of Death: 06/04/1916   Cause of death: Killed in action
Memorial: Melksham & Trowbridge St. James Church Memorial
War cemetery: Basra Memorial
Theatre of war: Mesopotamia
Next of Kin: Arthur & Mary Manning
Address: High Street, Melksham, Wiltshire

Geoffrey was employed by a wine merchant and was also a Wiltshire Territorial. At the outbreak of war he was sent to India to serve in Poona allowing Regular troops to be released to fight. He volunteered for service in Mesopotamia arriving on 25 August 1915. He was killed in action at the siege of Kut in modern day Iraq on Thursday 6 April 1916 while fighting Turkish forces. He is remembered on the Basra Memorial and has no known grave.

Private Henry Hutchins   *2/4th Bn Wiltshire Regiment*
Service No. 1809   Age: 22
Place of Birth: Preshute, Wiltshire   Home Country: England
Date of Death: 06/04/1916   Cause of death: Killed in action
Memorial: Marlborough - Devizes Odd Fellows & Trowbridge St James Church
War cemetery: Basra Memorial
Theatre of war: Mesopotamia
Next of Kin: Edward & Sarah Ann Hutchins
Address: Tan Yard, London Road, Marlborough

Henry worked for a tailor shop, was a keen member of the Odd fellow's lodge and also a Wiltshire Territorial. He was sent to India to serve in Poona allowing regular troops to be released to fight. He volunteered for service in Mesopotamia arriving on 25 August 1915. He was killed in action at the siege of Kut in modern day Iraq on Thursday 6th April 1916 while fighting Turkish forces. He is remembered on the Basra Memorial and has no known grave. His brother William Edwad Hutchins was to be killed in April 1918.

Sergeant Thomas Huan Archdale Hurley   *5th Bn Wiltshire Regiment*
Service No.   3/180   Age: 45
Place of Birth: Bath, Somerset   Home Country: England
Date of Death: 09/04/1916   Cause of death: Killed in action
Memorial: Trowbridge
War cemetery: Basra Memorial
Theatre of war: Mesopotamia
Next of Kin: Annie Hurley (wife) - Edward & Unity Hurley (parents)
Address: 27 Castle Street, Trowbridge – Bath Somerset

Thomas was a hairdresser and ran a shop in Church Street, Trowbridge. He married Annie Simons in the spring of 1903 and lived with his family in Castle Street. He volunteered for service, joining the 5th Service Battalion Wiltshire Regiment and served at Gallipoli arriving on 30 June 1915 and then on to Mesopotamia. At 4.20am on Sunday 9 April 1916 the Wiltshires were advancing towards the Turkish positions at Sannaiyat in modern day Iraq, to relieve the besieged city of Kut. During the advance the Wiltshires lost direction due to hostile enemy fire and the British were scattered and forced to dig in 650yards from Turkish positions. During the day many wounded crawled into the Wiltshires positions or were collected. The Wiltshires casualties were 23 killed, 165 wounded and 39 missing. Thomas was initially reported wounded and later wounded and missing and eventually killed in action. He is remembered on the Basra Memorial and has no known grave.

Private Herbert Reginald Clift   *5th Bn Wiltshire Regiment*
Service No.   10556   Age: 25
Place of Birth: Staverton, Wiltshire   Home Country: England
Date of Death: 19/04/1916   Cause of death: Killed in action
Memorial: Trowbridge & Hilperton
War cemetery: Basra Memorial
Theatre of war: Mesopotamia
Next of Kin: Henry & Annie Clift
Address: 19 Wyke Road, Hilperton Marsh, Trowbidge, Wiltshire

Herbert was employed at Melksham Rubber Works and played centre forward for Town

Right: Alfred Charles Bishop

Far Right: Thomas Huan Archdale Hurley

Far left: Herbert Reginald Clift

Left: James Andrews

Football Club. He volunteered for service arriving in France on 11 November 1914, joining the 2nd Battalion Wiltshire Regiment. During the winter of 1914 Herbert suffered from frost bite and was evacuated to England and after his recovery he was sent to Egypt and then on to Mesopotamia, where he joined the 5th Battalion Wiltshire Regiment.

He was killed in action on Wednesday 19 April at Bait Isa in modern day Iraq, while fighting Turkish forces. He is remembered on the Basra Memorial and has no known grave. In April 1917 his family inserted the following memoriam in a local paper:

"To the memory of a Dear One
His voice his touch his smile
These love springs flowing o'er
Earth for it's little while
Shall never know them more
From his loving parents, Sister and Brothers"

Private James Andrews   *5th Bn Wiltshire Regiment*
Service No.: 12488   Age: 35
Place of Birth: Steeple Ashton, Wiltshire   Home Country: England
Date of Death: 23/04/1916   Cause of death: Died of wounds
Memorial: Trowbridge & Keevil
War cemetery: Amara War Cemetery
Theatre of war: Mesopotamia
Next of Kin: Rose Anne Andrews (wife) - George and Lucy Andrews (parents)
Address: 21 St Thomas Road, Trowbridge, Wiltshire

James, a farm labourer, originally joined the Wiltshires on 10 January 1898 at the age of 17 years and 3 months. At the outbreak of the Great War he volunteered for service and arrived in France on 11 December 1914. He was wounded on 27 January 1915 and evacuated to England. After his recovery he was transferred to the 5th Battalion Wiltshire Regiment and sent to Mesopotamia, modern day Iraq. He was wounded during the relief of Kut and evacuated to a base hospital at Amara where he succumbed to his wounds on Sunday 23 April 1916. In April 1917 his wife inserted the following memoriam in a local paper;

"In loving Memory
Died of wounds at Amara Persian Gulf
Sleep on dear one in a far off land
In a grave we may never see
But as long as life and memory last
We will remember thee
Fondly remembered by his wife and children"

Private William Henry Archer   *2/4th TF Bn Wiltshire Regiment*
Service No.   201223   Age: 25
Place of Birth: Cricklade, Wiltshire   Home Country: England
Date of Death: 03/05/1916   Cause of death: Died
Memorial: Cricklade & Trowbridge St James Church Memorial
War cemetery: Basra Memorial
Theatre of war: Mesopotamia
Next of Kin: William H & Annie Archer
Address: The Laurels, 10 Abingdon Court Road, Cricklade, Wiltshire.

William, a clerk for the Great Western Railway, joined the Wiltshire Territorials and was sent to India arriving in 1915 at Poona. He volunteered to serve in Mesopotamia and was captured by the Turkish forces at the fall of Kut in modern day Iraq on 29 April 1916. He died most likely of disease on Wednesday 3 May 1916 while a prisoner of war. He is remembered on the Basra Memorial and has no known grave.

Private Willie Froom   *2/4th TF Bn Wiltshire Regiment*
Service No.   201103   Age: 21
Place of Birth: Newbury, Berkshire   Home Country: England
Date of Death: 03/05/1916   Cause of death: Died
Memorial: Devizes & Trowbridge St. James Church
War cemetery: Basra Memorial
Theatre of war: Mesopotamia
Next of Kin: George & Mary Froom
Address: 48 Escourt Street, Devizes, Wiltshire

Twenty one year old Willie, a baker, enlisted with the 2/4th Wiltshire Regiment and was sent to India for Garrison duties. He volunteered for service in Mesopotamia, modern day Iraq. While serving it is likely he became ill and died of sickness or disease. He is remembered on the Basra Memorial and has no known grave.

Pioneer Albert Ford   *6th Labour Bn Royal Engineers*
Service No.   120340   Age: 41
Place of Birth: Trowbridge, Wiltshire   Home Country: England
Date of Death: 03/05/1916   Cause of death: Died
Memorial: Trowbridge
War cemetery: St Sever Cemetery Rouen
Theatre of war: France
Next of Kin: Ada Louisa Ford (wife) – Eli Ford (parent)
Address: 35 Mount Pleasant, Trowbridge, Wiltshire

Albert was employed by Ushers Brewery and in 1903 he married Ada Louis Doel. He volunteered for service joining the Royal Engineers on 18 September 1915 and arrived in France on 2 October 1915. On 1 May 1916 Albert was admitted to Number 1 Stationary Hospital with pneumonia and was described as very ill. Ada was informed by a sister at the hospital that Albert was comfortable and everything was being done for him and she hoped to write in a day or so when he was much better. The following letter was written by the sister on 5 May 1916;

"I am writing to let you know about your husband's death. He was very ill when brought into the hospital, and although everything possible was done for him he never recovered, but passed very quietly away at 7.30pm on the evening of Wednesday 3rd May. He was very patient and it may comfort you to know that he did not suffer any pain. I am sorry to be the bearer of bad news."

Albert is buried in St. Sever Cemetery, Rouen, France. He left a widow and 5 children.

Private John Hopgood   *2/4th TF Bn Wiltshire Regiment*
Service No. 201338   Age: 20
Place of Birth: Fisherton, Wiltshire   Home Country: England
Date of Death: 09/05/1916   Cause of death: Died
Memorial: Salisbury & Trowbridge St. James Church
War cemetery: Basra Memorial
Theatre of war: Mesopotamia
Next of Kin: Frederick & Mary Selina Hopgood
Address: 20 East Street, Salisbury

A year after the end of the war in November 1919, Frederick and Mary Hopgood discovered the fate of their eldest son John known as Jack, who had been a member of the approximately 10,000 strong garrison at Kut that was surrendered to the Turks on 29 April 1915. They believed he was a prisoner of the Turks and hoped that he would be returned at the end of the war. John died on Tuesday 9 May 1916 at Shamran, Meopatamia, as the garrison of Kut were marched north through the desert. John was only twenty years old and is remembered on the Basra Memorial, Iraq. He has no known grave.

Albert Ford

6
JUTLAND

On Wednesday 31 May 1916 the only major naval battle of the First World War began and was to be come known as the Battle of Jutland. It took place off the Northwest coast of Denmark and when the battle ended on Thursday 1st June 1916, both the British and the German Navy's claimed victory; although the British lost more ships, the German fleet returned to port and remained there for the rest of the War. A number of Trowbridge men lost their lives in the battle, and the shock that was felt in the town was also felt in towns and cities throughout Great Britain.

Able Seaman Frederick Butcher   *HMS Black Prince Royal Navy*

Service No.	J/23292	Age:	18
Place of Birth:	Trowbridge, Wiltshire	Home Country:	England
Date of Death:	31/05/1916	Cause of death:	Died
Memorial:	Trowbridge		
War cemetery:	Portsmouth Naval Memorial		
Theatre of war:	At Sea		
Next of Kin:	Benjamin W & Annie Butcher		
Address:	58 Mortimer Street, Trowbridge, Wiltshire		

Eighteen year old Frederick had attended Trinity School in Trowbridge and upon leaving worked for Yates. He Joined the Navy as a Boy and had only been transferred to mans service a few weeks before the war broke out. He was killed in the sinking of H.M.S. Black Prince on Wednesday 31 May 1916. He is remembered on the Portsmouth Naval Memorial. Frederick had three brothers in the army and one, Harold, was to die of wounds in 1917.

Leading Seaman Edward Clifford Jones   *HMS Black Prince Royal Navy*

Service No.	238805	Age:	24
Place of Birth:	Hilperton Marsh, Wiltshire	Home Country:	England
Date of Death:	31/05/1916	Cause of death:	Killed in action
Memorial:	Not Known		
War cemetery:	Portsmouth Naval Memorial		
Theatre of war:	At Sea		
Next of Kin:	Harry & Eliza Jones		
Address:	Southwick Trowbridge		

Edward was a baker's boy and joined the Navy at the age of fifteen and signed on for 12 years mans service. He joined the Black Prince in April 1914 and was killed in action on Wednesday 31 May 1916. He is remembered on the Portsmouth Naval Memorial.

Far left: Frederick Butcher

Left: Robert Potter

Private Robert Potter   *HMS Lion Royal Marine Light Infantry*
Service No.   PLY/13118
Place of Birth: Eddington, Wiltshire
Date of Death: 31/05/1916
Memorial: Trowbridge
War cemetery: Plymouth Naval Memorial
Theatre of war: At Sea
Next of Kin: George & Phoebe Potter
Address: 28 Bradford Road, Trowbridge, Wiltshire

Age: 30
Home Country: England
Cause of death: Killed in action

Before joining the Royal Marines Robert worked at the railway engine sheds in Trowbridge, he was the eldest son of George & Phoebe Potter. He enlisted on 24 August 1904 and at the outbreak of the Great War he was serving on H.M.S. Lion. At the battle of Jutland the Lion was Admiral Beatty's flagship and Robert was killed in action. He may have been killed when one of the Lion's gun turrets received a direct hit as he was one of 99 fatalities suffered by the Lion at Jutland. George & Phoebe Potter had 5 sons serving in the forces and three were to be killed during the war, Arthur in 1915 and John in 1917. Robert is remembered on the Plymouth Naval Memorial.

Stoker 1st Class Esley John Rawlings   *HMS Queen Mary Royal Navy*
Service No.   306928
Place of Birth: Trowbridge, Wiltshire
Date of Death: 31/05/1916
Memorial: Trowbridge
War cemetery: Portsmouth Naval Memorial
Theatre of war: At Sea
Next of Kin: Florence M Rawlings
Address: 42 Union Street, Trowbridge, Wiltshire

Age: 31
Home Country: England
Cause of death: Killed in Action

Esley enlisted in the Navy in 1904 and in the spring of 1909 he married Florence Maria Davis in Trowbridge. In 1914 he had almost completed his terms of service with the Navy but with the commencement of hostilities his service was extended. He died most likely due to drowning on Wednesday 31 May 1916 in the sinking of the Queen Mary. As a Stoker he would have

Right:: Esley John Rawlings

Far rightt: Henry Woodman

worked in the ships engine room and there would have been little chance of escape on that fateful day. The Queen Mary suffered 1266 fatalities and had only 8 survivors. Esley is remembered on the Portsmouth Naval Memorial.

Elec. Art. 3rd Class Henry Woodman   *H.M.S. Queen Mary*

Service No.	M/1011	Age:	29
Place of Birth:,	Trowbridge	Home Country:	England
Date of Death:	31/05/1916	Cause of death:	Killed in action
Memorial:	Trowbridge		
War cemetery:	Portsmouth Naval Memorial		
Theatre of war:	At Sea		
Next of Kin:	Samuel & Sarah Woodman		
Address:	26 Timbrell Street, Trowbridge, Wiltshire		

Henry, known as Harry, was a scholar of the British School and he won the George Nelson Haden scholarship at the Technical School and served an apprenticeship with Haden's. He was also a scholar at the Emanuel Sunday School and was the youngest son of Samuel & Sarah Woodman. Harry had joined the Navy in 1908 and was appointed to the Queen Mary when the ship was commissioned at Portsmouth in 1913.

In early June 1916 rumours reached Trowbridge of a Great sea Battle and that some local men had been killed. One of these was Harry who died in the sinking of HMS Queen Mary along with over 1200 members of her crew.

Arrangement had been made for Harry's marriage to Miss Roberts of Hilperton during his next leave . He is remembered on the Portsmouth Naval Memorial. The following memoriam was inserted in a local paper:

"In loving memory
Keep back those tears they must not swell
'Twas God who took him all is well
From Father, Mother, Brothers and Sisters"

Stoker 1st Class John James Foreman   *HMS Queen Mary Royal Navy*

Service No.	K/15000
Place of Birth:	Crockerton, Wiltshire
Date of Death:	31/05/1916
Memorial:	North Bradley
War cemetery:	Portsmouth Naval Memorial
Theatre of war:	At Sea
Next of Kin:	John James & Ellen Foreman
Address:	Wood Marsh, North Bradley, Wiltshire

Age: 24
Home Country: England
Cause of death: Killed in action

John, a farm labourer and known as James, was the eldest son of John James & Ellen Foreman. He was killed in the sinking of the Queen Mary on Wednesday 31 May 1916. As a stoker he would have worked in the engine room and would have had little chance of escape. He is remembered on the Portsmouth Naval Memorial.

Electrical Art. 4th Class Arthur John Richards   *HMS Indefatigable Royal Navy*

Service No.	M/7749
Place of Birth:	Horningsham, Somerset
Date of Death:	31/05/1916
Memorial:	Trowbridge - Frome - Christ Church & St. Johns Church Frome
War cemetery:	Plymouth Naval Memorial
Theatre of war:	At Sea
Next of Kin:	Mrs Richards (wife) - John & Caroline Richards (parents)
Address:	65 Frome Road, Trowbridge - 46 Keyford, Frome

Age: 28
Home Country: England
Cause of death: Killed in action

Arthur, known as John and a cabinet maker, enlisted in the Navy in June 1914 joining H.M.S. Defiance. He was then transferred to H.M.S. Indefatigable which he joined on 31 December 1914 at Malta. John was killed in action on Wednesday 31 May 1916 during the battle of Jutland. He was one of 1,017 of the crew who were killed when the ship was sunk by German shell fire. He left a widow and two children and is remembered on the Plymouth Naval Memorial.

Arthur John Richards

Private William Harry George Andrews   2/4th TF Bn Wiltshire Regiment
Service No   2217   Age: 19
Place of Birth: Telisford, Wiltshire   Home Country: England
Date of Death: 31/05/1916   Cause of death: Died
Memorial: Bradford on Avon & Trowbridge St. James Memorial
War cemetery: Baghdad North Gate War Cemetery
Theatre of war: Mesopotamia
Next of Kin: L/cpl George & Elizabeth Andrews
Address: 15 Frome Road, Bradford on Avon, Wiltshire

Nineteen year old William was employed as a clerk at Spencer Moulten Company in Bradford on Avon and was also a Wiltshire Territorial. At the outbreak of war he was sent to India to serve at Poona where he volunteered for service in Mesopotamia being attached to the Oxford and Buckinghamshire Light Infantry. He was captured by Turkish Forces at the fall of Kut in modern day Iraq on 29 April 1916. At the end of September 1916 Elizabeth Andrews received an official notice from the war office that her son had died of disease while a prisoner of war on Wednesday 31 May 1916. In May 1917 while her husband was serving in India Elizabeth inserted the following memoriam in a local paper:

"Far from home and kindred there is a silent grave
Of one we loved so dearly and yet we could not save
His king and country called him he bravely did his best
But god saw fit to take him to his eternal rest"

Elec.Art.3rd Class Herbert Howard Rogers   H M S Royal Navy
Service No.   M/1737   Age: 28
Place of Birth: Trowbridge, Wiltshire   Home Country: England
Date of Death: 01/06/1916   Cause of death: Killed in action
Memorial: Trowbridge
War cemetery: Portsmouth Naval Memorial
Theatre of war: At Sea
Next of Kin: Alice Alma Rogers (wife) - Edward & Ellen Rogers (parents)
Address: 81 Gunner Street Kingston, Portsmouth - 32 Timbrell Street, Trowbridge

Herbert, known as Bert, had served an apprenticeship at Hadens of Trowbridge prior to joining the Navy. He married Alice Alma Robinson in Portsmouth in November 1915. Bert had previously had a narrow escape from drowning when the cruiser he had been serving on was mined and sunk. He was killed in action on Thursday 1 June 1916 along with 185 crew of the Destroyer Tipperary and is remembered on the Portsmouth Naval Memorial. In May 1917 his parents inserted the following memoriam in a local paper;

"Softly at night the stars are gleaming
O'er a far distant ocean grave
Where there sleepeth without dreaming
One we loved so dearly but could not save"

2 JUNE 1916 - THIRD BATTLE OF YPRES. BELGIUM

Private Walter Slade   7th Bn Bedfordshire Regiment
Service No.   17400   Age: 20
Place of Birth: Trowbridge, Wiltshire   Home Country: England

Far left:: Herbert Howard Rogers

Left: William Alfred Wheeler

Date of Death: 03/06/1916 Cause of death: Killed in action
Memorial: Not Known
War cemetery: Bronfay Farm Military Cemetery Bray Sur Somme
Theatre of war: France
Next of Kin: Not Known
Address: Not Known.

Walter was a waiter in London, he volunteered for service joining the 7th Service Battalion Bedfordshire Regiment. He arrived in France on 12 August 1915 and was killed in action on Saturday 3 June 1916.

5 JUNE 1916 - LORD KITCHENER IS DROWNED AFTER HMS HAMPSHIRE SINKS AFTER HITTING A MINE

Bugler William Alfred Wheeler   *HMS Hampshire RMLI*
Service No.   PO/18390   Age: 16
Place of Birth: Southwick, Wiltshire Home Country: England
Date of Death: 05/06/1916   Cause of death: Died
Memorial: Not Known
War cemetery: Portsmouth Naval Memorial
Theatre of war: At Sea
Next of Kin: William & Mary Anne Wheeler
Address: 2 Wyndsom Place, Southwick, Wiltshire.

Sixteen year old William joined the Royal Marine Light Infantry on 26 January 1915, the minimum recruitment age for the Royal Marines was 15 years of age and boys went to sea at 16 years. The Hampshire was his first ship and he died after the Hampshire hit a mine in the North Sea. Lord Kitchener was also lost on the Hampshire as he had been en route to Russia. William is remembered on the Portsmouth Naval Memorial.

Private Ebeneezer Walter T Mattock   *14th Bn Quebec Regiment*
Service No.   464396   Age: 33
Place of Birth: Trowbridge, Wiltshire Home Country: Canada

Date of Death:	12/06/1916	Cause of death:	Killed in action
Memorial:	Trowbridge		
War cemetery:	Ypres Menim Gate		
Theatre of war:	Belgium		
Next of Kin:	Tom & Julia Mattock		
Address:	54 Granville Terrace Dursley Road, Trowbridge, Wiltshire		

When Ebeneezer, known as George, left school he worked in the cloth mills in Trowbridge in 1906 he emigrated to Canada and was employed as an iron worker. He volunteered for service on the pacific coast and on 28 September 1915 he joined the Canadian army and came back to Europe. On Monday 12 June 1916 George was reported wounded and missing during fighting at Zillbeke, Belgium. At the end of August 1916, Tom and Julia Mattock received the news that George had been killed in action on the day he was reported missing. He is remembered on the Ypres Menin Gate and has no known grave.

Private Henry Howard Stevens   *16th Manitoba Regiment*

Service No.	78013	Age:	28
Place of Birth:	Hilperton, Wiltshire	Home Country:	England
Date of Death:	13/06/1916	Cause of death:	Killed in Action
Memorial:	Hilperton		
War cemetery:	Ypres Menin Gate		
Theatre of war:	Belgium		
Next of Kin:	Thomas & Priscilla Stevens		
Address:	Timbrell Street, Trowbridge, Wiltshire		

Henry was the youngest son of Thomas and Priscilla Stevens. He had emigrated to Canada to join his brother where they both worked in farming. In July 1914, he returned to England for a holiday but was prevented from returning to Canada because of the outbreak of hostilities. He then worked for the Wiltshire Conservative Benefit Society's office at Trowbridge. With the arrival of the first Canadian forces in England, Henry had the opportunity to serve with some old friends and after gaining permission he joined the Canadian Infantry and left for France in March 1916. At 1am on 13 June 1915 a terrific bombardment started on German positions at Mount Sorrel near Zillebeke, Belgium. After the barrage lifted the Canadians

Far right: Ebeneezer WalterT Mattock

Right: Henry Howard Stevens

advanced toward Halifax trench which they had been given 10 minutes to secure before the Canadians continued on to Montreal and Brown Pig trench. The first news of what became of Henry arrived in a letter from a private E.P.Adie who stated that Henry had been reported missing on Tuesday 13 June 1916, he went on to write;

"Your brother and I were close friends and we were both together when we started the charge. Unfortunately I got caught in some barbed wire and by the time I had cleared myself from it your brother was away ahead. I never saw him again. Henry was a man well loved for his good natured and cheery disposition and he is greatly missed by all of us who are left in the platoon."

Private Arthur Henry Waterhouse   *26th Bn Royal Fusiliers*
Service No.   23921   Age: 20
Place of Birth: Totland Bay, Isle of Wight   Home Country: England
Date of Death: 19/06/1916   Cause of death: Died of wounds
Memorial: Trowbridge
War cemetery: Bailleul Communal Cemetery Extension Nord
Theatre of war: France
Next of Kin: William John & Louisa Mary Waterhouse
Address: Raveloe, Totland Bay, Isle of Wight.

Twenty year old Arthur was an employee of Capital and Counties Bank in Fore Street, Trowbridge. He volunteered for service with the 26 Service Battalion Royal Fusiliers, known as the Banker's Battalion formed in London on 17 July 1915 which was composed of bank clerks and accountants. Arthur arrived in France on 4 May 1916 and his unit began familiarisation with trench warfare in the areas of Ploegsteert and the Douve valley. During this familiarisation which it is likely took them into front line trenches, Arthur was wounded and evacuated to a casualty clearing station at Bailleul, France, where he succumbed to his wounds.

Private Frank Roland Holloway   *8th Bn Wiltshire Regiment*
Service No.   18923   Age: 20
Place of Birth: Bristol, Gloucestershire   Home Country: England

Far Left: Arthur Henry Waterhouse

Left: Frank Roland Holloway

Date of Death: 21/06/1916 Cause of death: Died
Memorial: Trowbridge
War cemetery: Staverton St.Paul Churchyard
Theatre of war: Home
Next of Kin: Frederick James & Emily Holloway
Address: 13 Marsh Road, Hilperton, Wiltshire

Frank was the only son of Fred & Emily Holloway. He was employed at the Avon Rubber Company and regularly played for the Marsh United Football Club. Being a member of the territorials, whom he joined on 28 August 1912, Frank was sent to Salisbury Plain for training and on 22 February 1915 was transferred to the 8th Bn Wiltshire Regiment. While on service he contracted rheumatism and consumption (tuberculosis), which may have been due to a lack of accommodation for so many new troops. slept on the floor on straw in disused factories. On 26 June 1915 he was discharged from the army and he lived in a consumptive hut in his parent's garden. He died on Wednesday 21 June 1916 and his funeral was described as being semi-military. In 1918 his parents inserted the following memoriam;

"He suffered much he murmured not
We watched him day by day
With aching hearts until he passed away
Twas hard to part with one we loved
But Jesus called him home
From this dark world of sin and pain
To rest upon His throne
Never forgotten by his loving Mother, Father and Sisters"

Wiltshires on the way to the front at the Somme

7
THE SOMME

> *24 June 1916 - A Week Long British Artillery Bombardment Commenced*

Lance Corporal William Sidnell *155th Field Coy Royal Engineers*
Service No.   99884
Age: 29
Place of Birth: Trowbridge, Wiltshire
Home Country: England
Date of Death: 28/06/1916
Cause of death: Died of wounds
Memorial: Trowbridge
War cemetery: Bethune Town Cemetery
Theatre of war: France
Next of Kin: Frederick & Annie Sidnell
Address: 48 Park Street, Trowbridge, Wiltshire

William was an employee of the Great Western Railway; he joined them in 1904 as a cleaner and was registered as a fireman in December 1905. Owing to ill health, he was unable to continue working on the footplate and in July 1914, he took an indoor job at the Westbury locomotive department. In May 1915 he joined the Royal Engineers at Chatham and arrived in France on 19 December 1915 and saw some action at Loos. It is likely he was near Mazingarbe, France making preparations for the Battle of the Somme when he was wounded on Wednesday 28 June 1916 and evacuated to Bethune where he died at one of the casualty clearing stations.

Frederick and Annie Sidnell received the following letter from the Bishop of Salisbury.

"I am indeed grieved to hear that a second son has been taken from you and you have my deep sympathy and prayer in your sore affliction. You have given of your best to the services of your country, and they have given themselves. Surely we may feel that those who have died for others must be very near and dear to Him who died for us all. May God help and comfort you."

Sapper R.W. Young the only other Trowbridge man from William's company wrote the following to Frederick and Annie Sidnell;

"Willie was always quiet and reserved and he was liked by all the N.C.O's and men of his section and anyone who ever came in contact with him. Never a shouting sort of chap, whatever he said was confidential. He had put in an application to be transferred to a railway company and was expecting to be moved at any time."

William's brother's Walter had been killed in December 1914 and Stafford Herbert was to die in 1920.

THE SOMME

Right:: William Sidnell

Far Right: James Elms

Private James Elms	*5th Bn Wiltshire Regiment*
Service No.: 3/9933	Age: 18
Place of Birth: Semington, Wiltshire	Home Country: England
Date of Death: 29/06/1916	Cause of death: Died
Memorial: Trowbridge	
War cemetery: Amara War Cemetery	
Theatre of war: Mesopotamia	
Next of Kin: James & Annie Elms	
Address: Semington Lane, Melksham, Wiltshire	

Eighteen year old James was an under age soldier, it is likely he was 17 years of age when he volunteered for service. He first served in Egypt and then Mesopotamia. He died of heatstroke on Thursday 29 June 1915 at one of the hospitals based in Amar in modern day Iraq. His brothers Charles and John Elms were also to be killed in the war.

> *1 JULY 1916 - START OF THE SOMME OFFENSIVE WITH ALMOST 750,000 ALLIED SOLDIERS ATTACKING ON A 25 MILE FRONT*
>
> *58,000 BRITISH TROOPS ARE CASUALTIES ON THE FIRST DAY*

Private George Knight	*25th Bn Northumberland Fusiliers*
Service No.: 25/337	Age: 34
Place of Birth: Trowbridge, Wiltshire	Home Country: England
Date of Death: 01/07/1916	Cause of death: Killed in action
Memorial: Not known	
War cemetery: Thiepval Memorial	
Theatre of war: France	
Next of Kin: Janet Johnstone Knight (wife) - George & Catherine Knight (parents)	
Address: Front Street, Witton Gilbert, Durham - Consett, Durham	

George was a coal miner and at the start of 1908 he married Janet Johnstone Hannah at Chester Le Street, Durham. He volunteered for service with the 25th Service Battalion Northumberland

Fusiliers known as the 2nd Tyneside Irish. He arrived in France in January 1916 and on the first day of the Battle of the Somme, 1 July 1916, George was in trenches North of La Boisselle. Two minutes before zero hour the British exploded a mine of 40,600 pounds of explosives, at Ysap opposite the Northumberlands positions; the 25th Battalion were in the third wave and were attacking down Mash Valley and had to cross 800 yards of no man's land. The Northumberland's were cut down by machine gun fire from Ovilliers, La Boisselle and trenches on the right of the attack. George was one of those killed in action at Mash Valley on Saturday 1 July 1916 and he is remembered on the Thiepval Memorial with over 72,000 fatalities who have no known grave.

Private Walter James Sheppard *1st Bn Somerset Light Infantry*
Service No.   7054   Age: 28
Place of Birth: Trowbridge, Wiltshire   Home Country: Wales
Date of Death: 01/07/1916   Cause of death: Killed in action
Memorial: Not Known
War cemetery: Serre Road Cemetery No 1
Theatre of war: France
Next of Kin: Mary Sheppard (wife) - John and Elizabeth Sheppard
Address: 30 Russell Street, Llanelly, Carmarthenshire - Trowbridge

Regular soldier Walter had arrived in France on 21 August 1914. On 1 July 1916 the Somersets were in Trenches opposite the German position of the Quadrilateral. At 7.20am the British exploded a huge mine containing over 20 tons of explosives under the German position of Hawthorn Redoubt south of Beaumont Hamel. Ten minutes later the Somersets advanced which was initially successful and they reached the 1st line of the German trenches. However, the British were short of grenades and there was a terrific grenade fight and only when fresh supplies of grenades had been brought up could the Somersets proceed. As they advanced to the German second like trenches, enemy soldiers who had hidden in deep dugouts appeared in the front line and firing rifles and machine guns shot down many of the Somersets. After dark the Somersets were relieved and made their way back to the old British front line. Walter was one of those killed during this attack.

Private William Harris   *6th Bn Wiltshire Regiment*
Service No.   19352   Age: 28
Place of Birth: Trowbridge, Wiltshire   Home Country: England

Far left: William Harris

Left: Sidney Herbert Reynolds

Date of Death: | 02/07/1916 | Cause of death: | Killed in action
Memorial: | Trowbridge
War cemetery: | Thiepval Memorial
Theatre of war: | France
Next of Kin: | Amy Harris (wife) - Charles & Edith Harris (parents)
Address: | 42 Fore Street, Trowbridge - 56 Bradford Road, Trowbridge

William, a wool salesman, had married Amy Edith Lyles at the start of the year in 1910. He volunteered for service with the 6th Service Battalion Wiltshire Regiment and on 2 July 1914, the 2nd day of the Battle of the Somme, he was with the Wiltshires attacking German trenches south of La Boisselle, France. The Wiltshires succeeded in capturing the enemies first and second trench lines and their casualties were 39 killed, 242 wounded and 35 missing. William was one of those reported missing. He is remembered on the Thiepval Memorial and has no known grave.

Private Sidney Herbert Reynolds　　　　　　*6th Wiltshire Regiment*

Service No. | 12101 | Age: | 22
Place of Birth: | Trowbridge, Wiltshire | Home Country: | England
Date of Death: | 04/07/1916 | Cause of death: | Died of wounds
Memorial: | Trowbridge
War cemetery: | Heilly Station Cemetery Mericourt Labbe
Theatre of war: | France
Next of Kin: | George & Laura Reynolds
Address: | 76 Mortimer Street, Trowbridge, Wiltshire

Sidney was a wire mattress maker and had volunteered for service in September 1914 with the 6th Service Battalion Wiltshire Regiment arriving in France on 19 July 1915. He was wounded and evacuated to the 36th Casualty Clearing Station at Heilly, France where he succumbed to his wounds on Tuesday 4 July 1916. In June 1917 George and Laura Reynolds inserted the following memoriam in a local paper;

"In loving memory of our dear son
We mourn the loss of the son we loved
And did our best to save
Beloved in life regretted gone
Remembered in his grave
One year has passed and we still miss him
From his sorrowing Mother Father and Brothers"

Private Walter Trollope　　　　　　*1st Bn Wiltshire Regiment*

Service No. | 5925 | Age: | 32
Place of Birth: | Horningsham, Wiltshire | Home Country: | England
Date of Death: | 05/07/1916 | Cause of death: | Died of wounds
Memorial: | Trowbridge
War cemetery: | Thiepval Memorial
Theatre of war: | France
Next of Kin: | Elizabeth Mary Trollope (wife) - Thomas & Mary Trollope (parents)
Address: | 19 Thomas Street, Trowbridge, Wiltshire

Walter was an army reservist and was employed by the Great Western Railway as a fitter in the engine shed. He married Elizabeth Mary Jones in Trowbridge in 1905 and was called to

Far left: Walter Trollope

Left: Arthur Jesse Rawlings

the colours at the outbreak of war. He arrived in France on 12 September 1914 and on 5 July the Wiltshires were attacking Leipzig Salient on the Somme. At 7pm the Wiltshires attacked the German line and were met by heavy rifle and machine gun fire and the left of the attacking company was very badly cut up. When they reached their objective the Wiltshires were so few in numbers that they were forced to temporarily withdraw but still managed to take the objective. It is likely Walter was wounded during this attack and died of his wounds either in no man's land or in the captured German trenches. Walter left a widow and five young children and is remembered on the Thiepval Memorial.

Private Arthur Jessie Rawlings   *1st Bn Wiltshire Regiment*
Service No. 11027
Place of Birth: Trowbridge, Wiltshire
Date of Death: 06/07/1916
Memorial: Trowbridge
War cemetery: Thiepval Memorial
Theatre of war: France
Next of Kin: James & Dorcas Rawlings
Address: 11 Duke Street, Trowbridge, Wiltshire
Age: 29
Home Country: England
Cause of death: Killed in action

Arthur, known as Jesse, was a carter at a flour mill and he married Mary Rodd in the spring of 1908. He volunteered for service at the outbreak of war and arrived in France on 27 October 1914. He was killed in action on Thursday 6 July at Leipzig Salient on the Somme which the Germans had bombarded all day with bombing, trench mortars and rifle grenades. He left a widow and three small children.

Private Andrew Lochhead   *2/4th TF Bn Wiltshire Regiment*
Service No. 2857
Place of Birth: Glasgow, Scotland
Date of Death 06/07/1916
Memorial: Melksham & Trowbridge St. James Church
War cemetery: Amara War Cemetery
Theatre of war: Mesopotamia
Next of Kin: Andrew & Helen Lochhead
Age: 25
Home Country: England
Cause of death: Died

Address: Boxwood Cottage, The Forest, Melksham

Andrew was the youngest son of Andrew and Helen Lochhead. He was employed as a printer and had been a keen member of Melksham Shooting Club where he became a crack shot winning a number of prizes and competitions. He followed the temperance principles and while working in Cheltenham he joined the Lodge of the Good Templars. At the outbreak of war he returned to Melksham and enlisted with the 2/4th Battalion Wiltshire Regiment and was sent on garrison duties in India. He subsequently volunteered for active service in Mesopotamia arriving on 25 August 1915 and was attached to the 1st Battalion Oxford & Bucks Light Infantry. In June 1916 Andrew's parents received news that their son was in hospital with enteric fever where he was to die from the disease on Thursday 6 July 1916. Andrew and Helen Lochhead's eldest son John had died from enteric fever while serving in the Boer War.

Captain George Guy Hermon-Hodge   *Royal Horse Artillery*
Service No.   N/A   Age: 32
Place of Birth: Checkendon, Berkshire   Home Country: England
Date of Death: 07/07/1916   Cause of death: Died of wounds
Memorial: Trowbridge
War cemetery: Gezain Communal Cemetery Extension
Theatre of war: France
Next of Kin: 1st Baron Wyfold of Accrington & Baroness Wyfold
Address: Wyfold, Oxfordshire.

George was the son of Robert Trotter Hermon-Hodge, 1st Baron Wyfold and Frances Caroline Hermon. Prior to the Great War he commanded the Royal Horse Artillery Battery based at Trowbridge, where he lived at Wigfield Road. He was a fine horseman and a good shot and served mainly in Ireland, where he was very popular. He arrived in France on 14 September 1914 and died of wounds on Friday 7 July 1916 at the Battle of the Somme.

CSM Walter George Lester DCM MID   *1st Bn Wiltshire Regiment*
Service No.   4591   Age: 38
Place of Birth: Trowbridge, Wiltshire   Home Country: Canada

Right: Andrew Lochhead

Far right: George Guy Hermon-Hodge

Date of Death:	07/07/1916
Memorial:	Trowbridge
War cemetery:	Thiepval Memorial
Theatre of war:	France
Next of Kin:	Annie Alice Jane Lester (wife) – John & Annie Lester (parents)
Address:	Arcola, Saskatchewan – 19 New Road, Trowbridge

Cause of death: Killed in action

Walter stood 6 foot 3 inches tall and had been in the Army for 20 years having served 10 years in India and 3 years in South Africa. Just one year before the war in 1913 he married Annie Alice Jane Bridges at Andover, Hampshire. Being a regular soldier he was one of the first to be mobilized arriving on the continent on 14 August 1914 and he was the first man from Trowbridge to be mentioned in Sir John French's first list of Dispatches. During the retreat from Mons, Belgium, for days while under heavy shell fire, he cheered and continually rallied his men and kept them supplied with ammunition. He was awarded the Distinguished Conduct Medal. He was wounded on 19 May 1916 but continued with his duties and on 6th July 1916 he took part in an assault on the Leipzig Salient at the Battle of the Somme. At 1.15am in the early hours of Friday 7 July 1916 the Germans mounted a counter attack against the trenches the Wiltshires had captured. The enemy rushed forward and managed to reach the edge of the trench and dropped bombs and opened fire. Walter was killed instantly and his commanding officer wrote to Annie Lester expressing his sympathy and stating:

"Her consolation must be the knowledge that her husband died a heroes death on the battlefield."

Prior to his death Walter had been recommended for a commission and it is likely he would have been promoted to a lieutenant. This would be Annie Lester's second bereavement, having lost her only child with pneumonia in the same year. Walter is remembered on the Thiepval Memorial and has no known grave, his brother Jessie Lester was to be killed in 1918.

Private George Henry Purnell   *9th Bn Welsh Regiment*

Service No.	16884		Age:	27
Place of Birth:	Studley, Wiltshire		Home Country:	England
Date of Death:	07/07/1916		Cause of death:	Killed in action
Memorial:	Trowbridge			
War cemetery:	Thiepval Memorial			

Far left: Walter George Lester

Left: George Henry Purnell

Theatre of war: France
Next of Kin: William George & Louisa Purnell
Address: 87 Dursley Road, Trowbridge, Wiltshire.

George volunteered for service with the 9th Service Battalion Welsh Regiment and arrived in France on 18 July 1915. At 8.15am on Friday 7 July 1916 the 9th Welsh were preparing to attack German trenches between Baliff Wood and the northeast end of La Boiselle at the Somme. The 9th Welsh advanced behind a creeping barrage which would enable them to cross the 300 yards of no man's land and get as close as possible to the German trenches. The bombardment and attack were successful. However because of an error in timing the 9th Welsh initially ran into barrage causing a large number of casualties. It is likely George was killed by the British artillery barrage. He is remembered on the Thiepval Memorial and has no known grave. His brother Frederick Mathew Purnell was to be killed in 1918.

Private William Arthur Reynolds   *2nd Bn Wiltshire Regiment*
Service No. 3/9267
Age: 26
Place of Birth: Trowbridge, Wiltshire
Home Country: England
Date of Death: 08/07/1916
Cause of death: Killed in action
Memorial: Not known
War cemetery: Thiepval Memorial
Theatre of war: France
Next of Kin: Lucy Reynolds (wife) - Arthur William & Edith Reynolds (parents)
Address: 4 Morris Street, Robdurne Road, Swindon - 6, Cardiff Road., Abercynon

William had been a coal miner when he married Lucy Barke in the summer of 1913 in Swindon. He volunteered for service and arrived in France on 7 October 1914. He was killed in action on Saturday 8 July 1916 during the attacks on the at Maltz Horn Valley and and Trones Wood. He is remembered on the Thiepval Memorial and has no known grave.

Sergeant Alfred William Frederick Shuttleworth   *27th Bde Royal Field Artillery*
Service No. 62540
Age: 21
Place of Birth: Trowbridge, Wiltshire
Home Country: England
Date of Death: 24/07/1916
Cause of death: Killed in action
Memorial: Not Known
War cemetery: Thiepval Memorial
Theatre of war: France
Next of Kin: Not Known
Address: Not Known

Alfred was born in Trowbridge. He was killed on Monday 24 July 1914 during preparations for an attack on Delville Wood at the Somme, most likely by German counter battery fire. He is remembered on the Thiepval memorial and has no known grave.

Lance Corporal Francis Mortimer Propert   *2nd Bn Royal Welsh Fusiliers*
Service No. 31198
Age: 26
Place of Birth: Wingfield, Wiltshire
Home Country: England
Date of Death: 24/07/1916
Cause of death: Died of wounds
Memorial: Not known
War cemetery: Heilly Station Cemetery Mericourt Labbe
Theatre of war: France

Next of Kin: David & Elizabeth Propert
Address: Southwick, Wiltshire

Francis, known as Frank, was a gamekeeper prior to the Great War. He initially joined the Royal Artillery but was transferred to the Royal Welsh Fusiliers. He was wounded in fighting in July 1916 at High Wood and Delville Wood at the Somme and died of his wounds at one of the casualty clearing stations based at Heilly, France.

Pioneer Brian Wilfred Francis Maguire   *1st Bn Kings Royal Rifle Corps*

Service No.	R/16798
Place of Birth:	Maidstone, Kent
Date of Death:	27/07/1916
Memorial:	Trowbridge
War cemetery:	Serre Road Cemetery No 2
Theatre of war:	France
Next of Kin:	Patrick & Winifred Maguire
Address:	55 Bradley Road, Trowbridge, Wiltshire
Age:	19
Home Country:	England
Cause of death:	Killed in action

Nineteen year old Brian was educated at Trowbridge High School and was successful in passing the Oxford Local Examination at the age of 15 and a year later qualified for the County University Scholarship for entry into the Civil Service. Brian made the decision to join a commercial business in London and it was where he was working at the outbreak of war. Being under age he wrote to his parents for permission to enlist, which they gave him, but he failed the medical test and was rejected because of his poor eye sight. He made many other attempts to volunteer and in November 1915 his 13th application was accepted and he joined the Kings Royal Rifles. After initial training he was volunteered for the machine gun section and passed a special training course. In June 1916 he was selected from the section he belonged to go to the front with a draft of machine gunners. He was killed in action on Thursday 27 July 1916 at Delville Wood at the Somme.

Private Arthur Frederick Nicholls   *1st Bn Wiltshire Regiment*

Service No.	12330
Place of Birth:	Bradford on Avon, Wiltshire
Age:	22
Home Country:	Wales

Left: Wilfred Francis Maguire

Below: Member of the Wiltshire regiment after an attack at Thiepval displaying captured German Equipment.

Date of Death:	28/07/1916	Cause of death:	Died of wounds
Memorial:	Not known		
War cemetery:	Couin British Cemetery		
Theatre of war:	France		
Next of Kin:	Ethel Nicholls (wife) - Alfred and Mary Nicholls (parents)		
Address:	5 Tyntyla Ave, Llwynypia, Glamorganshire – Trowbridge		

Arthur, a railway porter, married Ethel Ham in 1915 at Pontypridd, Glamorgan. He volunteered for service with the Wiltshire Regiment arriving on the continent on 21 September 1915. He died of wounds received in fighting at the Somme and was buried in Couin British Cemetery.

Private Samuel Starr   *17th Bn Welsh Regiment*

Service No.	25129	Age:	42
Place of Birth:	Frome, Somerset	Home Country:	Wales
Date of Death:	29/07/1916	Cause of death:	Died of wounds
Memorial:	Not known		
War cemetery:	Bethune Town Cemetery		
Theatre of war:	France		
Next of Kin:	Susan Starr (wife) – William & Agnes Starr (parents)		
Address:	22 Glanant St. Hirwaun, Glamorganshire – Gloucester Road, Trowbridge		

Samuel was a colliery repairman, he married Susannah Hedges in Trowbridge in 1893 and he joined the 17th Service Battalion Welsh Regiment which was a Bantam Battalion. A Bantam Battalion was made up of men who were considered too short for the army, but as the need for men grew these battalions were formed. Samuel would have arrived in France with the 17th Welsh in early June 1916 and then onto intensive trench training in the Lens area. It is almost certain Samuel was wounded during this period of training and trench familiarisation and was evacuated to a casualty clearing station where he later died.

2nd Lieutenant Geoffrey Raymond Palmer   *10th Bn West Riding Regiment*

Service No.	N/A	Age:	28
Place of Birth:	Kettering, Northamptonshire	Home Country:	England
Date of Death:	30/07/1916	Cause of death:	Killed in action
Memorial:	Trowbridge		
War cemetery:	Thiepval Memorial		
Theatre of war:	France		
Next of Kin:	James & Katherine Palmer		
Address:	The Drive, Kettering, Northamptonshire.		

Geoffrey was a science master at the High School in Wingfield Road, he was a skilled musician and was always available to share his talents with any good cause and had a wide range of friends in Trowbridge. He volunteered for service as a private with the Gloucester Regiment and was given a commission on 2 May 1915 with the West Riding Regiment. He arrived in France on 1 July 1916 and was killed in action on Sunday 30 July 1916 during an attack on Gloster Alley at the Somme. He is remembered on the Thiepval memorial and has no known grave.

Private Arthur George Hiscox   *2/4th TF Bn Wiltshire Regiment*

Service No.	1636	Age:	23
Place of Birth:	Trowbridge, Wiltshire	Home Country:	England
Date of Death:	30/07/1916	Cause of death:	Died

Memorial:	Chippenham – Melksham & Trowbridge St. James Church
War cemetery:	Basra Memorial
Theatre of war:	Mesopotamia
Next of Kin:	James & Alice Hiscox
Address:	Avondale Road, Melksham, Wiltshire

Twenty three year old Arthur, a labourer, had volunteered to go to India with the Wiltshires to relieve regular regiments. He arrived in Bombay in January 1915 and when a call was made for volunteers to go to Mesopotamia he volunteered and arrived in what is modern day Iraq on 28th August 1915. He was attached to the Oxford and Buckinghamshire Light Infantry and was captured by the Turkish forces at the surrender of Kut on 29April 1916. He was one of over 10,000 British troops marched through the desert, into captivity at Mosul in modern day Iraq. In December 1916 news reached Trowbridge that Arthur had died of dysentery at Mosel while a prisoner of the Turks and a letter was received via the Red Cross Society in Geneva stating:

"We fear that any word of ours must inevitably prove very inadequate at this time, but we trust that it may be of some slight consolation to you in your sorrow to know from the signature at the end of this document, it is evident that Private Arthur Hiscox received as much medical care and attention as possible under the circumstances from one of his own countrymen, and also that his last moments were passed in the presence of familiar comrades who had shared, we may suppose, at least some weeks of his captivity with him at Mosul. Will you allow us to express our sincere sympathy with you in your sad loss, and our deep regret that your suspense and anxiety should be ended in so sad a manner."

Arthur is remembered on the Basra memorial and has no known grave. In August 1918 his parents inserted the following memoriam in a local paper:

"Out in that foreign land
Lies one we all love well
We could not hold his dying hand
We could not say farewell
"Until the Day Breaks"
From his loving Mother, Dad, Sisters and Brothers"

Private Leonard Percy Watson   *1st Wiltshire Regiment*

Service No.	22733	Age:	23
Place of Birth:	Trowbridge, Wiltshire	Home Country:	England
Date of Death:	07/08/1916	Cause of death:	Died of wounds
Memorial:	Winsley		
War cemetery:	Etaples Military Cemetery		
Theatre of war:	France		
Next of Kin:	Alfred & Alice Watson		
Address:	Hartley Winsley, Bradford on Avon, Wiltshire		

Leonard was employed by the Bradford Co-operative Society. He was wounded in the first week of the Battle of the Somme, most likely during fighting at the Leipzig salient. He was evacuated to one of the military hospitals based at Etaples, France, where he died from illness as a result of his wounds on Monday 7 August 1916. In 1918 his parents inserted the following memoriam in a local paper:

"We miss him when the morning comes

Right: Leonard Percy Watson

Far right: Frederick Gore

We miss him as the night draws on;
We miss him here, we miss him there,
We miss our sonny everywhere,
Fondly remembered by his Mother, Father, Brothers and Sisters."

Rifleman Arthur Henry Hulbert		*17th Bn Kings Royal Rifle Corps*	
Service No.	10207	Age:	23
Place of Birth:	Southwark, Surrey	Home Country:	England
Date of Death:	08/08/1916	Cause of death:	Killed in action
Memorial:	Not known		
War cemetery:	Essex Farm Cemetery		
Theatre of war:	Belgium		
Next of Kin:	Margaret Hulbert (wife) – George & Elizabeth Hulbert (parents)		
Address:	Not known - 56 St Pauls Road, Walworth		

Arthur was employed by a printer and lived in Trowbridge prior to the Great War which was his mothers home town. He volunteered for service with the Kings Royal Rifle Corps and arrived in France on 20 December 1914. It is likely he was wounded and evacuated to England and toward the end of 1915 he married Margaret Connor at Lewes, Sussex. He was transferred to the 17th Battalion Kings Royal Rifle Corps and was killed in action on Tuesday 8 August 1916 near Ypres, Belgium.

Private Frederick Sidney Elliott		*2/4th Bn Ox & Bucks Light Infantry*	
Service No.	5392	Age:	18
Place of Birth:	Trowbridge, Wiltshire	Home Country:	England
Date of Death:	16/08/1916	Cause of death:	Killed in action
Memorial:	Not known		
War cemetery:	Thiepval Memorial		
Theatre of war:	France		
Next of Kin:	Herbert & Elizabeth Elliott		
Address:	58 Abbey Road, Osney, Oxford		

Under age Frederick was the eldest son of Herbert and Elizabeth Elliott who had lived at Bradford Road in Trowbridge. He volunteered for service with the Oxford and Buckinghamshire Light Infantry and arrived in France in May 1915. He was killed in action on Wednesday 16 August 1916 at the Somme and is remembered on the Thiepval Memorial. He has no known grave.

Corporal Frederick Gore   *8th Bn Rifle Brigade*
Service No.   2669
Place of Birth: Trowbridge, Wiltshire
Date of Death: 17/08/1916
Memorial: Trowbridge
War cemetery: Thiepval Memorial
Theatre of war: France
Next of Kin: Jessis & J Gore
Address   24 The Halve, Trowbridge, Wiltshire
Age: 24
Home Country: England
Cause of death: Killed in action

Frederick enlisted in the Rifle Brigade in February 1908 and had previously worked at the Wiltshire Times printing works. He had served in Egypt and at the outbreak of hostilities he was in India. He returned to Europe with the Rifle Brigade arriving in France on 20 December 1914. In February 1915 whilst in the trenches he was shot by a sniper, the bullet penetrating his body a fraction of an inch below his heart, smashing two ribs and exiting under the shoulder blade. He was evacuated to England and after treatment he returned to the firing line. Then in November 1915 he was again wounded by shrapnel bullets in his left leg and foot, which necessitated many painful probings for splinters at a base hospital. He made a rapid recovery and was returned to duty and in June 1916, he was granted a few dys leave and he returned to Trowbridge. He was killed in action during the afternoon of Friday 18 August 1916 north of Delville Wood. In his last letter home, written just two days before his death, he stated:

"Poor old Fritz was having all he wanted and a little more, and I hope it won't be long before we get him on the run."

Frederick is remembered on the Thiepval Memorial and has no known grave. He had two brothers and two brother-in-laws serving in the army, his brother Ernest was to win the Military Medal.

Rifleman Alfred William Firman   *20th Bn Kings Royal Rifle Corps*
Service No.   C/9579
Place of Birth: Trowbridge, Wiltshire
Date of Death: 18/08/1916
Memorial: Not known
War cemetery: Carnoy Military Cemetery
Theatre of war: France
Next of Kin: William & Flora Firman (foster parents)
Address: Yate Rocks, Yate, Gloucestershire.
Age: 19
Home Country: England
Cause of death: Killed in action

Born Alfred William Smith in Trowbridge in 1896 he was the son of Flora Smith who married William Firman in Rochester Kent in 1903. Alfred was an Ostler who looked after horses on a farm and some time before the war he changed his name to Firman. After joining the Rifle Corps he arrived at Le Harvre, France, with them at the end of March 1916. He was killed in action near Guillemont at the Somme on Friday 18 August 1916.

Private Albert Edward Baker   *1st Bn Wiltshire Regiment*
Service No.   18225   Age: 33
Place of Birth: Trowbridge, Wiltshire   Home Country: England
Date of Death: 24/08/1916   Cause of death: Killed in action
Memorial: Trowbridge
War cemetery: Thiepval Memorial
Theatre of war: France
Next of Kin: Kate Elizabeth Baker (wife) - Edmund & Matilda Baker (parents)
Address: 1 Hawkins Buildings, Hilperton Road, Trowbidge – Keynsham

Albert was employed in the press shop at Kemp and Hewitt's Mill and during the evenings he was an auxiliary postman delivering letters to North Bradley and Hilperton. He had married Kate Elizabeth Elkins in 1902 and they had five children. Albert was a member of Kemps and Hewitt's team in the Trowbridge Air Rifle League and had served a term with the Wiltshire Volunteers. He was also a member of the National Reserve. In December 1914 he volunteered for service and less than 2 months later he was at the front, arriving in France on 23 February 1915. He was killed in action at the Leipzig Salient near Thiepval on Thursday 24 August 1916 during a heavy German bombardment. The news reached Kate Baker in early September 1914 and a letter from a comrade stated that Albert's body was found near an observation post, which had been entirely destroyed by the enemy's fire. The letter also described Albert's burial but his grave location was lost and he is today remembered on the Thiepval Memorial.

Private Albert Brunker   *1/8th Bn Royal Warwickshire Regiment*
Service No.   4970   Age: 21
Place of Birth: Trowbridge, Wiltshire   Home Country: England
Date of Death: 27/08/1916   Cause of death: Killed in action
Memorial: Trowbridge
War cemetery: Thiepval Memorial
Theatre of war: France
Next of Kin: Edward Albert & Matilda Brunker
Address: 4 Bradford Road, Trowbridge, Wiltshire

Twenty one year old Albert was the only son of Edward and Matilda Brunker and he was

Right: Albert Edward Baker

Far right: Albert Brunker

employed at Aplin's mineral water manufactory. He joined the army in March 1916 and on Sunday 27 August 1916 he was involved with the Warwicks in an attack on Constance trench and Pole trench at the Somme. The Warwicks ran into the British barrage and in mid September news was received in Trowbridge that Albert had been killed in action on that day. He is remembered on the Thiepval Memorial and has no known grave.

Private Samuel Marshman   *26th Bn Australian Infantry AIF*
Service No.   521   Age: 31
Place of Birth: Southwick, Wiltshire   Home Country: England
Date of Death: 28/08/1916   Cause of death: Killed in action
Memorial: Southwick
War cemetery: Villers Bretonneux Memorial
Theatre of war: France
Next of Kin: George & Esther Marshman
Address: Southwick, Wiltshire

Samuel had emigrated to Australia arriving on 27 July 1907 and was employed as a baker. He volunteered for service with the Australian army on 8 April 1915 and after completing his training was sent to Gallipoli via Egypt in September 1915. After the evacuation of Gallipoli he was sent back to Alexandria in Egypt and then on to France arriving at Marseilles in March 1916. He was killed in action during fierce fighting near Mouquet Farm at the Somme on Monday 28 August 1916. His personal possessions were returned to his sister Annie and consisted of a matchbox, a gift box, photos, cards, cigarette holder in case, cigarette case, mirror, card wallet, bible, letters, charm, 2 hankerchiefs, disc and a notebook. He is remembered on the Villers Bretonneux Memorial with over 10,000 Australians who died at the Somme and have no known grave.

Gunner Albert Ash   *6th Amm. Col Royal Field Artillery*
Service No.   15393   Age: 33
Place of Birth: Trowbridge, Wiltshire   Home Country: England
Date of Death: 30/08/1916   Cause of death: Died
Memorial: Not known
War cemetery: Baghdad North Gate War Cemetery
Theatre of war: Mesopotamia
Next of Kin: Levi & Emily Mortimer
Address: Norrington Gate Farm, Broughton Gifford, Wiltshire

Regular soldier Albert arrived in Mesopotamia in November 1914. It is likely he was captured at the fall of Kut when the British surrendered to the Turkish forces and died of disease on Wednesday 30 August 1916.

Private Samuel Henry Billett   *6th Bn Wiltshire Regiment*
Service No.   22137   Age: 19
Place of Birth: Hilperton, Wiltshire   Home Country: England
Date of Death: 01/09/1916   Cause of death: Killed in action
Memorial: Trowbridge & Hilperton
War cemetery: Kemmel Chateau Military Cemetery
Theatre of war: Belgium
Next of Kin: Samuel & Alice Billett
Address: 3 Wilts Hilperton, Trowbridge, Wiltshire

Nineteen year old Samuel, known as Harry, had worked in the gardens of Mr E.C. Beaven at Arboyne Holt and joined the 6th Service Battalion Wiltshire Regiment in November 1915 arriving in France in early 1916. He was wounded in the arm in July 1916 but was soon able to rejoin his unit. In the early hours of Friday 1st September the Wiltshires relieved the 9th Welsh Battalion at trenches near Kemmel Belgium. The British trenches had a light bombardment by the Germans and during this bombardment they suffered 2 fatalities, one of whom was Samuel. The first intimation of his death was in a letter from Private C. Stillman which was dated 4 September. In this letter he wrote on behalf of the platoon to express their sympathy with Samuel and Alice Billett in the death of one of the best lads in the platoon and also explained that Harry had been killed instantaneously. Harry's parents inserted the following memoriam in a local paper in August 1917:

"Our darling son and brother
His heart was always in our home
He always tried to do his best
Until there came that sudden call
And God called him to rest
He was loved by all who ever knew him
Fondly loved by Father, Mother Sister and Brother"

Private Albert Victor Lane *1st Bn Wiltshire Regiment*
Service No.   22732   Age: 22
Place of Birth: Tormartin, Glos   Home Country: England
Date of Death: 03/09/1916   Cause of death: Died of wounds
Memorial: Trowbridge
War cemetery: Thiepval Memorial
Theatre of war: France
Next of Kin: Mr & Mrs Lane
Address: 18 Innox Road, Trowbridge, Wiltshire

Albert was employed at the Avon Rubber Works in Melksham. He joined the Wiltshires in January 1916 and after a period of training at Weymouth he was sent to France. The last letter received from him in autumn 1916 stated that he had just had a term of rest at a rear base and was about to go back to the trenches. On Sunday 3 September 1916 at 5.10 am, the Wiltshires

Right: Samuel Henry Billett

Far right: Albert Victor Lane

were at Leipzig Salient, at the Somme, preparing to assault German positions. As soon as they left the safety of their trenches the Wiltshires were subjected to "Whizbang", German artillery bombardment and machine gun fire. Some of the attackers were wiped out by the British barrage and because of the number of casualties the attack failed. Nothing was heard of Albert for over ten months even though his parents wrote to the War Office, the Red Cross and the Salvation Army. In July 1917 his parents received official news that Albert had been killed in action on 3 September 1916. He is remembered on the Thiepval Memorial and has no known grave. His parents inserted the following memoriam in a local paper:

"In loving memory of a dear son and brother
Could we have raised his dying head
Or heard his last farewell
The grief would not have seemed so hard
To those who loved him well
No one knows the silent heartache
Only those can tell
Who have lost those loved the dearest
Without saying Farewell
From his sorrowing Father, Mother, Brothers and Sister"

Lance Corporal James Dicks — *8th Bn Royal Dublin Fusiliers*
Service No.: 15923
Place of Birth: Trowbridge, Wiltshire
Date of Death: 09/09/1916
Memorial: Trowbridge
War cemetery: Thiepval Memorial
Theatre of war: France
Next of Kin: Not known
Address: Not known
Age: Not known
Home Country: England
Cause of death: Killed in action

James originally joined the Wiltshire Regiment but like many local men was transferred to the Royal Dublin Fusiliers. He was killed on Saturday 9 September during a German counter attack near Mouquet Farm at the Somme, France. He is remembered on the Thiepval Memorial and has no known grave.

Rifleman Charles Edward Griffiths — *16th Bn London Regiment*
Service No.: 5946
Place of Birth: Trowbridge, Wiltshire
Date of Death: 10/09/1916
Memorial: Not known
War cemetery: Thiepval Memorial
Theatre of war: France
Next of Kin: Thomas & Sarah J Griffiths
Address: 80 Douglas Street, London
Age: 38
Home Country: England
Cause of death: Killed in action

Charles was a commercial clerk. He joined the 16th Battalion London regiment known as the Queens Westminster Rifles arriving in France in 1916. At 7am on Sunday 10 September 1916 he was with the 16th Londons preparing to assault German positions south east of Leuze Wood near Combles at the Somme. As they went forward they were halted by German machine gun fire from Loop trench and the sunken Combles Road. It is probable that Charles was killed during this attack. He is remembered on the Thiepval Memorial and has no known grave.

Right: The Military Medal

Far right: Leonard Doel

Sergeant Leonard Doel MM		1st Bn Wiltshire Regiment	
Service No.	9927	Age:	21
Place of Birth:	Hilperton, Wiltshire	Home Country:	England
Date of Death:	10/09/1916	Cause of death:	Died of wounds
Memorial:	Not known		
War cemetery:	Abbeville Communal Cemetery Extension		
Theatre of war:	France		
Next of Kin:	Alice Mortimer (parent)		
Address:	9 New Road, Trowbridge		

Leonard was a gardener and volunteered for service at a recruiting meeting held at the school room West Ashton on 29 August 1914. He joined the 1st Battalion Wiltshire Regiment and after completing his training arrived in France on 15 January 1915. Leonard was promoted to Sergeant in 1916 because of his good work and ability and was recommended for a Military Medal. He was wounded by a German sniper on 3 September 1916 at the Leipzig Salient, during the battle of the Somme. He was evacuated to the 1st South African Hospital, Abbeville, France and succumbed to his wounds on Sunday 10 September 1916. Leonard's aunt received the following letter from Captain Brown, Leonard's commanding officer:

"I have just heard that your nephew has died of wounds, and I am writing to tell you how extremely sorry I am. He was sitting in the trench with me at the time, when a sniper's bullet passed through the earth of the parapet and penetrated his right shoulder and probably, I expect, perforated his lung. He was acting Sergeant Major at the time, and not only was he invaluable as machine gun instructor, but he was quite the most promising boy in the company. He was such a good fellow too, and this makes it doubly sad. I can only offer my deepest sympathy and tell you what a very great loss he is to myself and the company."
P.S. "It was on the morning of September 3rd after our attack, that he was hit and I had recommended him for a Military Medal."

Chaplain Archibald Cullen of the 1st South African Hospital, Abbeville, France, wrote the following to Leonard's family:

"There was one little incident connected with the gallant fellow's last hours which deserves to be remembered. On the day that Sergeant Doel died there was in the next bed to himself, a

man, who was not nearly so badly wounded as himself, but whose groans and complainings were disturbing the whole war. "For Gods sake," said Doel, "shut you teeth, man and make a fight of it. You have got a chance I haven't". He died like a brave Christian man and a gallant soldier."

In November 1916 Leonard was posthumously awarded the Military Medal.

Private William George Leonard Marshman   *1/4th TF Bn Wiltshire Regiment*
Service No.		2885
Place of Birth:	Calne, Wiltshire
Date of Death:	11/09/1916
Memorial:		Trowbridge St. James Church
War cemetery:	Kirkee 1914-1918 Memorial
Theatre of war	India
Next of Kin:		Annie Maria Marshman (wife) - Thomas & Harriet Marshman (parents)
Address:		London Road, Calne - West Street, Lacock

Age:			42
Home Country:	England
Cause of death:	Died

During the Great War the 1/4th Wiltshire Regiment was on Garrison duty in India. Many older soldiers or soldiers who were wounded and not fit to fight were sent for Service. Forty two year old William died of malaria, a Wiltshire officer said at the time that all the soldiers suffered from malaria but some were worse than others.

> *15 SEPTEMBER 1916 - FIRST USE OF THE BRITISH SECRET WEAPON THE "TANK" - GREAT ADVANCES WERE MADE AND A TANK DROVE DOWN THE MAIN STREET OF FLERS*

Bugler Henry Arthur Walton   *27th Manitoba Regiment*
Service No.		71128
Place of Birth:	Bradford on Avon, Wiltshire
Date of Death:	15/09/1916
Memorial:		Bradford on Avon
War cemetery:	Vimy Memorial
Theatre of war:	France
Next of Kin:		Arthur and Fanny Walton
Address:		8 Market Street, Bradford on Avon, Wiltshire

Age:			25
Home Country:	Canada
Cause of death:	Killed in action

Before he emigrated to Canada in 1913 Henry was employed at Avon Rubber works and lived at 14A British Row, Trowbridge. He was also a member of Bradford Church Lads Brigade. He enlisted in the Canadian infantry on 22 December 1914 and then travelled to England in 1915. He arrived in France in September 1915. He suffered from shell shock at St. Eloi and after his recovery he returned to the front. Friday 15 September 1916 was the first time tanks were used at the Battle of Flers – Courcelette at the Somme. The 27th regiment were attacking north east toward Courcelette. Henry was a runner with A company and would have been exposed to much danger as he carried messages across the battlefield. He was posted as missing on this day and is remembered on Vimy Memorial and has no known grave. His cousin David Parfit was to be killed fighting with the Canadians on 26 September 1916. On leaving for the front Henry wrote to his old Church Lads Brigade Captain:

"I trust the Brigade is still going strong. It is at a time like this when a fellow sees the benefit he gets through joining it. I can always look back and think of the happy times I spent in the

THE SOMME

Above: Vimy Memorial - Right: Henry Arthur Walton

Brigade, and I feel even today proud to think that I once belonged to it. If it had existed at Keewatin, I should have joined it there. As for the 27th, naturally I am also proud of it. We have had a good name so far, and I hope to keep it up."

Private Frederick William Hooper	*1/8th Bn Royal Warwickshire Regiment*
Service No. 5297	Age: 20
Place of Birth: Southwick, Wiltshire	Home Country: England
Date of Death: 18/09/1916	Cause of death: Died of wounds
Memorial: Not known	
War cemetery: Boulogne Eastern Cemetery	
Theatre of war: France	
Next of Kin: Harry and Eliza Hooper	
Address: Frome Road, Southwick, Wiltshire	

Twenty year old Frederick known as Fred was a Brush maker and joined the Warwickshire Regiment arriving in France in 1916. He was wounded at the Battle of the Somme and evacuated to a base hospital at Boulogne where he died of his wounds on Monday 18th September 1916. His parents inserted the following Memoriam in a local paper in 1918:

"In loving memory of our dear son and brother
Who died of wounds in Boulogne France
Days of Sadness still come o'er us
Secret tears do often flow
Memory keeps our loved one near us
Though it's now two years ago
We think and talk of him
And think how he died
To think he could not say good-bye
Before he closed his eyes
Could we but kneel beside his grave
and shed a silent tear
But now he sleeps somewhere in France
The one we loved so dear
Ever Remembered by his loving Mother, Father, Sisters and Brothers"

Private Frank Woodward   *2/4th TF Bn Wiltshire Regiment*

Service No.	3138	Age:	29
Place of Birth:	Malmesbury, Wiltshire	Home Country:	England
Date of Death:	20/09/1915	Cause of death:	Died
Memorial:	Malmesbury & Trowbridge St. James Church		
War cemetery:	Kirkee 1914-1918 Memorial		
Theatre of war:	India		
Next of Kin:	George & Elizabeth Woodward		
Address:	11 Elm Grove Terrace, Tiverton, Bath		

Frank was a footman and having enlisted with the 2/4th Battalion Wiltshire Regiment was sent to India for garrison duties. He died on Monday 20 September 1915 of illness or disease at Poona Hospital, India. He was buried in a cemetery in Poona but the Commonwealth War Graves Commission do not tend the graves of some service men in India but he is remembered on the Kirkee 1914-1918 Memorial.

Private Frederick Henry Sparey   *2/4th TF Bn Wiltshire Regiment*

Service No.	4177	Age:	28
Place of Birth:	Codford St Peter, Wiltshire	Home Country:	England
Date of Death:	25/09/1916	Cause of death:	Died
Memorial:	Trowbridge St James		
War cemetery:	Kirkee 1914-1918 Memorial		
Theatre of war:	India		
Next of Kin:	Beatrice Bessie Sparey (wife) - Henry & Emma Sparey (parents)		
Address:	42 Gorringe Road, Bemerton		

Postman Frederick married Beatrice Miles in 1913 just one year prior to the commencement of hostilities. He enlisted with the 2/4th Battalion Wiltshire Regiment and was sent to India for garrison duties. He died of illness or disease on Monday 25 September 1916.

CSM David George Parfitt   *8th Manitoba Regiment*

Service No.	602	Age:	25
Place of Birth:	Whetstone, Middlesex	Home Country:	Canada
Date of Death:	26/09/1916	Cause of death:	Killed in action
Memorial:	Not Known		
War cemetery:	Vimy Memorial		
Theatre of war:	France		
Next of Kin:	Fred & Elizabeth Parfitt		
Address:	Keewatin, Ontario		

David was a miller and a member of Bradford on Avon Church lads Brigade; his parents worked as steward and stewardess of the Bradford conservative club. He emigrated to Canada in 1911 where he was employed with the Lake of the Woods Milling Company and two years later his parents followed. He volunteered for service on 21 September 1914 and was with the first Canadian contingent to arrive in England and then landed in France in February 1915. He was badly gassed at Ypres in 1915 and later suffered from dysentery. On Tuesday 26 September 1916 the 8th Battalion were attacking German positions at Heeian trench at the Somme. As he assaulted they were met by German machine gun fire from Zollern trench. David was last seen at the head of D company while leading an attack and was reported missing, believed killed. He is remembered on Vimy Memorial and has no known grave. His cousin Henry Walton had been killed on 15 September 1916.

Right: David George Parfitt

Far right: Reginald Etwell

Gunner Walter Frank Webb		*18th Heavy Battery RGA*	

Service No.: 66175
Place of Birth: Yarnbrook, Wiltshire
Date of Death: 26/09/1916
Memorial: North Bradley
War cemetery: Sarigol Military Cemetery Kriston
Theatre of war: Salonika
Next of Kin: Charles & Mary Anne Webb
Address: North Bradley, Wiltshire
Age: 27
Home Country: England
Cause of death: Died

Walter was a bricklayer. He joined the Royal Garrison Atillery and was sent to Salonika, Greece where the British were fighting the Bulgarians. He was taken ill and admitted to the 21st Stationary Hospital where he died of illness or disease. During the Salonika campaign, for every fatality in battle three soldiers died from disease.

Sergeant Reginald Etwell   *11th Bn Royal Fusiliers*

Service No.: 6381
Place of Birth: Twerton, Somerset
Date of Death: 30/09/1916
Memorial: Trowbridge
War cemetery: Puchevillers British Cemetery
Theatre of war: France
Next of Kin: Arthur & Sarah Etwell
Address: 15 Harford Street, Trowbridge
Age: 19
Home Country: England
Cause of death: Died of wounds

Under age soldier Reginald volunteered for service at 17 years of age and at 19 he was a sergeant with the Royal Fusiliers. He arrived in France on 26 July 1915 and was wounded during fighting at the Somme. He was evacuated to a casualty clearing station at Puchevillers, France where he died on Saturday 30 September 1916. It is interesting to note his medal card states he died on 12 October 1918.

Private Reginald John Yerbury   *1/8th TF Bn Middlesex Regiment*

Service No.: 3345
Place of Birth: Trowbridge, Wiltshire
Age: 19
Home Country: England

Date of Death: 30/09/1916 Cause of death: Died of wounds
Memorial: Private Memorial Window, Bradford on Avon
War cemetery: Etaples Military Cemetery
Theatre of war: France
Next of Kin: Walter C & Emma Alethea Yerbury
Address: Brooklyn, Stroud Road, Gloucester

Reginald, a bank clerk, volunteered for service on 7 September 1914 at Ealing at the age of eighteen years and two months. He travelled on the troopship Nessian, via Gibraltar, and arrived at Marseilles, France on 25 July 1915. He was wounded with gunshot wounds to his head and legs at around midnight on Monday 11 September when two companies of the 1/8th Middlesex assaulted German positions on the Ginchy - Morval Road, near Leuze Wood at the Somme. He was evacuated to the St. John Ambulance Brigade Hospital at Etaples, France, but succumbed to his wounds at 6.15am on Saturday 30 September 1916 and was buried in the military cemetery. In April 1917, his personal positions were returned to his mother, Emma Yerbury and consisted of a wallett, letters, cards, photos, disc, silver wrist watch (broken), metal cigarette case, match box, address book and cheque book. He is remembered on a private memorial window in Holy Trinity Church, Bradford on Avon.

Lance Corporal Frank Henry Angell   *1st Bn Wiltshire Regiment*
Service No. 12118   Age: 30
Place of Birth: Trowbridge, Wiltshire   Home Country: England
Date of Death: 05/10/1916   Cause of death: Killed in action
Memorial: Trowbridge
War cemetery: Thiepval Memorial
Theatre of war: France
Next of Kin: Ellen Angell (wife) - William and Louisa Angell (parents)
Address: 64 Trowbridge Road, Bradford on Avon - High St., Hilperton

Frank was a shop assistant and in the summer of 1909 he married Frances Ellen L Gorton at Bradford on Avon. He volunteered for service with the Wiltshires arriving in France on 20 July 1915 and on Thursday 5 October 1916 he was in muddy trenches at Stuff Redoubt at the Somme. It is likely he was killed during shelling the Wiltshires encountered in the morning. He is remembered on the Thiepval Memorial and has no known grave. Ellen Angell and Franks parents inserted the following memoriam in a local paper in September 1917:

Far left: Frank Henry Angell

Left: Reginald George Box

*"In Sweet Remembrance of a good and faithful husband and Daddie who gave his life on the Somme
He hath fought the good fight
The silent grief in the soul
No human eyes may trace
For many a broken heat lies hid
Behind the Smiling Face
From those he loved his wife and children Ida and Jeffcot*

*Under a Grassy mound he sleeps,
And a simple cross of wood
Has been planted there that all may know
He died as a soldier should.
From his Loving Father, Mother, Will, Ruth, Herbert."*

Private Frederic Merritt   *7th Wiltshire Regiment*
Service No.: 12413   Age: 25
Place of Birth: Coldwaltham, Sussex   Home Country: England
Date of Death: 06/10/1916   Cause of death: Died
Memorial: Not known
War cemetery: Salonika Lembet Road Military Cemetery
Theatre of war: Salonika
Next of Kin: Dora May Merritt (wife) - James and Eliza Merritt (parents)
Address: Frome Road, Southwick -.Southwick

Factory worker Frederic married Dora M Brown at the beginning of 1915. He volunteered and enlisted with the 7th Service Battalion Wiltshire Regiment, arriving in France on 21 September 1915 and then in November 1915 the Wiltshires were transferred to Salonika, Greece. He died of illness or disease on Friday 6 October 1916 in one of the British Hospitals based at Salonika. During the Salonika campaign, for every fatality in battle three soldiers died from disease.

Rifleman Reginald George Box   *1/12th Bn London Regiment*
Service No.: 6360   Age: 21
Place of Birth: North Bradley, Wiltshire   Home Country: England
Date of Death: 07/10/1916   Cause of death: Killed in action
Memorial: Trowbridge
War cemetery: Thiepval Memorial
Theatre of war: France
Next of Kin: Frederick & Rosina Box
Address: 89 Lower Studley, Trowbridge, Wiltshire

Reginald was employed as a butcher at Case and Sons and enlisted under the Derby Scheme in 1915. The Derby Scheme was introduced by Lord Derby and allowed men to enlist and not be called up until the army had need for them. Reginald was called up in April 1915 and passed fit only for home duties, with the 9th Battalion Middlesex Regiment. He was sent for training in London and his fitness improved so much that in late September 1916 he was sent to France for duty joining the 1/12th London Regiment, known as the Rangers. Two weeks later Frederick and Rosina Box received a letter from one of Reginald's comrades explaining he had been killed on 7 October. No official news was heard from the war office and Reginald's parents wrote to his commanding officer who replied that Reginald was alive on 14 October 1916. Official information was received in mid November 1916 with the information that Reginald had in fact been killed in action on Saturday 7th October 1916. On that day the Rangers had assaulted a German position called Dewdrop trench, during the Battle of Ancre Heights at the Somme. The attack failed and Reginald, who was just 21 years of age, met his death on practically his first visit to the trenches. He is remembered on the Thiepval Memorial and has no known grave.

Private William Arthur Ruddle   *1/4th TF Bn Wiltshire Regiment*

Service No.	2471	Age:	25
Place of Birth:	Westbury, Wiltshire	Home Country:	England
Date of Death:	07/10/1916	Cause of death:	Died
Memorial:	Trowbridge		
War cemetery:	Amara War Cemetery		
Theatre of war:	Mesopotamia		
Next of Kin:	William A Rhoda Ruddle		
Address:	20 Mortimer Street, Trowbridge, Wiltshire		

William was employed as a warehouseman with the grocers, J. Sainsbury and was also a territorial soldier with the 1/4th Territorial Battalion Wiltshire Regiment. He volunteered for garrison duties in India leaving in October 1914. While in India he volunteered to serve in Mesopotamia with the 2nd Battalion Dorset Regiment and arrived in modern day Iraq on 20 May 1915. He died of illness or disease on Saturday 7 October 1916 at one of the base hospitals at Amara in modern day Iraq.

Driver George Henry Shrapnell   *5C Res. Brig. Royal Field Artillery*

Service No.	43199	Age:	26
Place of Birth:	Trowbridge, Wiltshire	Home Country:	Wales
Date of Death:	09/10/1916	Cause of death:	Died
Memorial:	Trowbridge		
War cemetery:	Mountain Ash Maesyrarian Cemetery		
Theatre of war:	Home		
Next of Kin:	Cecillia Shrapnell (Wife) – Mary A Shrapnell (Grandparent)		
Address:	Mountain Ash, Glamorganshire – Trowbridge		

George was a regular soldier and had married Cecilia Williams in 1913 in Mountain Ash, Glamorgan. He was wounded in June 1916, most likely the result of an accident, and died on Monday 9 October 1916.

Private Frank Oliver Stokes   *1st Bn Wiltshire Regiment*

Service No.	19566	Age:	30
Place of Birth:	Holt, Wiltshire	Home Country:	England
Date of Death:	09/10/1916	Cause of death:	Killed in action
Memorial:	Trowbridge & Holt		
War cemetery:	Grandcourt Road Cemetery Grandcourt		
Theatre of war:	France		
Next of Kin:	Nellie Stokes (wife) – Samuel & Mary H. Stokes (Parents)		
Address:	Midlands, Holt - 17 Thomas Street, Trowbridge, Wiltshire		

Frank was employed at Beaven's Leather Works and in 1911 he married Ellen K. Coles known as Nellie; he was a keen footballer and played in goal for Holt football team. He joined the army on 22 April 1915, enlisting with the 5th Battalion Wiltshire Regiment and was sent with a draft to Gallipoli arriving on 15 October 1915. He was evacuated from Gallipoli on 26

November 1915 with frostbitten feet and spent the next eight months in hospital, first on Malta and then at Netley, Hampshire. He was discharged from hospital at the end of June 1916 and was then sent to Weymouth for the next 3 months. On 22 September 1916 he was sent to France to join the 1st Battalion Wiltshire Regiment. Frank was killed in action on Monday 9th October 1916, when the Wiltshires were at Stuff Redoubt, South of Thiepval at the Somme. On the day of his death he wrote to his wife Nellie and remarked that his chum, poor Fred Angell had gone, (he was killed on 5 October 1916). In 1917 Nellie inserted the following memoriam:

"In ever loving memory of my dear husband and daddie
One year has passed and still we miss him
Friends may think the wound is healed
But they little know the sorrow
Deep within the heart concealed
We often sit and think of him
When we are all alone
For memory is the only thing
That grief can call it's own
Like ivy on the withered oak
All other things decay
But our love for him will e'er keep green
and never fade away
Never to be forgotten by his sorrowing Wife and children, Kathleen and Charles"

Private Frank Edward Eliza Elliott		*1st Bn Royal Warwickshire Regiment*	
Service No.	18735	Age:	21
Place of Birth:	Trowbridge, Wiltshire	Home Country:	England
Date of Death:	12/10/1916	Cause of death:	Killed in action
Memorial:	Trowbridge		
War cemetery:	Thiepval Memorial		
Theatre of war:	France		
Next of Kin:	Watson Elliot		
Address:	The Chestnuts, Timbrell Street, Trowbridge, Wiltshire		

Frank was a carpenter and it is likely he joined the army under the Derby Scheme, joining firstly

Right: William Arthur Ruddle

Far Right: Frank Oliver Stokes

the Somerset Light Infantry and then the 1st Battalion Royal Warwickshire Regiment. He was killed in action on Thursday 12 October 1916 when the Warwicks advanced 500 yards across no man's land and dug in south of Hazy Trench east of Lesboeufs at the Somme. He is remembered on the Thiepval Memorial and has no known grave.

Private George Cornish *2nd Bn Wiltshire Regiment*
Service No. 10277 Age: 38
Place of Birth: Warminster, Wiltshire Home Country: England
Date of Death: 17/10/1916 Cause of death: Killed in action
Memorial: Not known
War cemetery: Thiepval Memorial
Theatre of war: France
Next of Kin: Emily Florence Cornish (wife) - George and Annie Cornish (parents)
Address: The Market Place, Westbury – Trowbridge

George was a County Court Bailiff and married Florence Emily King in 1897. He volunteered for service with the Wiltshire Regiment arriving in France on 19 January 1915. On Tuesday 17 October 1916 the Wiltshires were in Flers Trench at the Somme. The weather was described as awful with rain and frost and the British trenches were shelled intermittently throughout the day. It is likely George was killed during the German shelling. He is remembered on the Thiepval Memorial and has no known grave

18 NOVEMBER 1916 - THE END OF THE BATTLE OF THE SOMME

Private Charles William Baden *2nd Bn Wiltshire Regiment*
Service No. 22605 Age: 24
Place of Birth: Trowbridge, Wiltshire Home Country: England
Date of Death: 18/10/1916 Cause of death: Killed in action
Memorial: Trowbridge
War cemetery: Warlencourt British Cemetery
Theatre of war: France
Next of Kin: Rose A. Baden
Address: 57 The Down, Trowbridge, Wiltshire

Far left: Frank Edward Elliott

Left: Charles William Badden

Charles was a coal miner, he had married Rose A. Stevens in the summer of 1910 in Glamorgan and it is likely he joined the Wiltshires under the Derby Scheme. On Wednesday 18 October the Wiltshires were in trenches north of Flers at the Somme and were preparing to assault German positions. As they reached the enemy wire the Germans machine gunned the Wiltshires, some of who managed to enter the German trench but were then machine gunned out due to a lack of bombs (hand grenades). The Wiltshires estimated casualties at the time was 364, it is probable Charles was reported missing during this attack and later reported killed.

Sergeant William George Bendall   *2nd Bn Wiltshire Regiment*
Service No.   7378   Age: 28
Place of Birth: Trowbridge, Wiltshire   Home Country: England
Date of Death: 18/10/1916   Cause of death: Killed in action
Memorial: Trowbridge
War cemetery: Warlencourt British Cemetery
Theatre of war: France
Next of Kin: Edward & Martha Bendall
Address: 49 Islington, Trowbridge, Wiltshire

William had been a member of the Church Lads Brigade in which he rose to the rank of sergeant and at the age of 17 he joined the local volunteer company and a few weeks later joined the regular army. He had served with the Wiltshires in Africa, India and Gibraltar and had arrived with his Battalion in Belgium on 7 October 1915. He was wounded in the head by shrapnel at Festubert in 1915, steel helmets were not issued until the start of 1916; he had been promoted in the field for what was described as consistent and conspicuous gallantry. He was posted missing on Wednesday 18 October when the Wiltshires were in trenches north of Flers at the Somme as described for Charles Baden. William was the only son of Edward and Martha Bendall and after numerous fruitless enquiries official news was received in July 1917 that their son had been killed in action on the day he was reported missing.

Private Herbert Nelson Reynolds   *2nd Bn Wiltshire Regiment*
Service No.   23661   Age: 25
Place of Birth: Trowbridge, Wiltshire   Home Country: England
Date of Death: 18/10/1916   Cause of death: Killed in action

Right: William George Bendall

Far Right: Herbert Nelson Reynolds

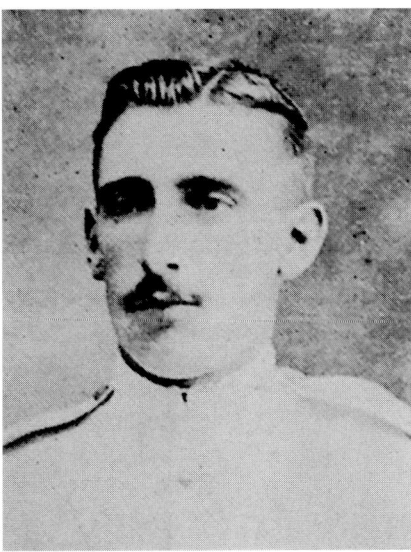

Memorial:	Melksham
War cemetery:	Warlencourt British Cemetery
Theatre of war:	France
Next of Kin:	Herbert & Alice Reynolds
Address:	2 Scotland Road, Melksham, Wiltshire

Herbert, known as Bert, was the only son of Herbert and Alice Reynolds and was employed at Avon India Rubber works in Melksham. He was called up in the early part of 1916 and sent to France in June 1916 with the 2nd Battalion Wiltshire Regiment. He was posted missing on Wednesday 18 October when the Wiltshires were in trenches north of Flers at the Somme as described for Charles Baden. Official information was received in May 1917 that Bert had been killed in action on the day he was reported missing. His parents inserted the following memoriam in October 1918:

"In ever loving memory of our dear son Bert
We think of him in silence no eye can see us weep
But ever in our aching hearts his memory we shall keep
Not here, but in a better land
Some day we'll understand
We never thought his time so short in this world to remain
When from our home he went away he thought to come again.
Ever remembered by Mother, Father and Sisters"

Private William Alfred G. Wilkins		*1st Bn Wiltshire Regiment*	
Service No.	24136	Age:	24
Place of Birth:	North Bradley, Wiltshire	Home Country:	England
Date of Death:	21/10/1916	Cause of death:	Killed in action
Memorial:	Trowbridge		
War cemetery:	Thiepval Memorial		
Theatre of war:	France		
Next of Kin:	Lucy Wilkins (wife) - William & Elizabeth Wilkins (parents)		
Address:	91 Mortimer Street, Trowbridge – North Bradley		

William, known as Willie, was employed in the Butchers shop of Bowyer, Philpott and Payne and had married Lucy F. Billett in 1915. He was the first member of North Bradley Baptist Chapel to be killed. Willie joined the army under the Derby Scheme in November 1915 at Trowbridge Town Hall. He was called up in April 1916 with the first married groups and sent to Bovington Camp, and after 3 month training he was sent with a draft to France joining the Wiltshires. On Saturday 21 October 1916 the Wiltshires were North of Mouguft Farm near Thiepval and were support for the successful attack made by the 75th Brigade Stump Road during the Battle of Ancre Heights at the Somme. It is likely Willie was killed by shell fire and he is remembered on the Thiepval Memorial but has no known grave. A memorial service was held for Willie at the North Bradley Baptist Church and one of his sisters who could not attend wrote the following:

"We did not realise what a dreadful thing war was until it had ruthlessly robbed us of a loved one."

Private William Albert Baker		*2/4th TF Bn Wiltshire Regiment*	
Service No.	200973	Age:	25
Place of Birth:	Langley Burrell, Wiltshire	Home Country:	England
Date of Death:	30/10/1916	Cause of death:	Died

Far left: William Alfred G. Wilkins

Left: Jack Oswald Couldridge

Memorial:	Chippenham & Trowbridge St James Church Memorial
War cemetery:	Baghdad North Gate War Cemetery
Theatre of war:	Mesopotamia
Next of Kin:	Mr F A & Mrs L A Baker
Address:	20 River Street, Chippenham, Wiltshire

William, a farm labourer, was the eldest son of Albert and Louisa Baker and a Wiltshire Territorial. He was sent to India at the outbreak of hostilities and served at Poona. He volunteered for service in Mesopotamia arriving in 1916 and was captured at the fall of Kut to Turkish forces on 29 April in the same year. He died most likely of disease on Monday 30 October 1916 while a prisoner of war. His parents were informed he had died at Adana in Turkey, official records state he is buried at Baghdad North Gate War Cemetery in Iraq.

2nd Lieutenant Jack Oswald Couldridge *12th Bn Worcestershire Regiment*

Service No	N/A	Age:	22
Place of Birth:	Bideford, Devon	Home Country:	England
Date of Death:	06/11/1916	Cause of death:	Killed in action
Memorial:	Trowbridge		
War cemetery:	Thiepval Memorial		
Theatre of war:	France		
Next of Kin:	James & Charlotte Couldridge		
Address:	16 Uffingham Road, St. Annes Park, Bristol		

Jack was a clerk at the Capital and Counties Bank in Fore Street, Trowbridge. He initially joined the Wiltshire Regiment and attained the rank of Lance Sergeant. On 22 January 1916 he received a commission with the 12th Battalion Worcestershire Regiment. He was attached to the 2nd Battalion Worcestershire Regiment, who on 5 November 1916, were taking part in the Battle of Transloy Ridges at the Somme. They were in trenches near Lesboeufs and were taken to a sunken road by French guides. After a short barrage the Worcesters scrambled to their feet and began to advance and were met by a heavy German barrage with machine guns crashing and stuttering down the sunken lane. The bank of the sunken lane was steep and proved difficult to climb. It is at this point Lieutenant E.P.Bennett went forward with a spade and cut a step in the bank and signalled to the Worcestors to advance. The attack was successful and Lieutenant Bennett was awarded the Victoria Cross. During the narrative of this event is mentioned "a dead little Lieutenant" who Lieutenant Bennett passes and this is believed to be Jack Couldridge. Jack was initially posted as missing on 8 November 1916 and later he was listed as being killed in action on 6 November 1916. He is remembered on the Thiepval Memorial and has no known grave.

Major Allen Llewellyn Palmer   *1st Royal Wiltshire Yeomanry*

Service No.	N/A	Age:	34
Place of Birth:	Trowbridge, Wiltshire	Home Country:	England
Date of Death:	15/11/1916	Cause of death:	Died
Memorial:	Trowbridge & Lacock Church & Village		
War cemetery:	St Pierre Cemetery Amiens		
Theatre of war:	France		
Next of Kin:	Brig. Gen. George & Madeleine Palmer		
Address:	Berryfield, Bradford on Avon, Wiltshire		

Allen was educated at Harrow and Sandhurst and he obtained a commission in the 14th Hussars in May 1901. He served in the South African war receiving the Queens Medal and two clasps. He resigned his captaincy in 1907 and was commissioned into the Royal Wiltshire Yeomanry in 1908. From 1910 to 1911 he was the A.D.C. to the Governor of Bombay and was master of the Hounds at Ootacamund, India. After his return to England he became Joint Master of the Cattistock Hunt and had strong interests in agriculture and was an active member of many agricultural societies in Wiltshire. In December 1915 he left for France with his Regiment. On 29 October 1916 Allen underwent an operation after being taken seriously ill with appendicitis at No. 1 New Zealand Stationary Hospital at Amiens, France. News reached Allen's parents that he was seriously ill and his father left Trowbridge early on the morning of Wednesday 15 November but before he could reach his son he had died of peritonitis. On the day of Allen's funeral a memorial service was held simultaneously in Trowbridge. In April 1917 Allen's parents donated a pair of Flags and their sons' sword to the Parish Church in Trowbridge. In 1923 his parents donated eight bells to Christchurch, Bradford on Avon in memory of Felix Hanbury-Tracy, their son in law who was killed in action in December 1914 and their two sons, Michael George who died in 1911 and Allen who died in November 1916. Allen Llewellen Palmer was described as a real English Gentleman.

Private George Hamilton Cameron Jackman   *2nd Bn D.C.L.I.*

Service No.	3/576	Age:	20
Place of Birth:	Trowbridge, Wiltshire	Home Country:	England
Date of Death:	17/11/1916	Cause of death:	Killed in action
Memorial:	Not known		
War cemetery:	Doiran Memorial		
Theatre of war:	Salonika		
Next of Kin:	John Charles & Sarah Elizabeth Jackman		
Address:	20 Stoneycroft Road, Woodford Bridge, Woodford Green, Essex		

Twenty year old George was called up for service and after training was sent to Salonika, Greece to join the Duke of Cornwall's Light Infantry, the DCLI. On 15 November 1916 the DCLI were at Kakarska to view Tumbitza and Pheasant Wood. At Karkarska there was an observation post and Bulgarian mounted patrols came into sight of the post, all that could be seen was a grassy plain and wooded valley beyond. Orders were received to attack Tumbitza at 6.30am on Friday 17 November 1916. The village was occupied by 30 to 40 Bulgars and it was said that they always ran away when a British patrol arrived. The Commanding Officer of the DCLI received no information about the ground to be covered and the only view he had received was from the observation post 4 miles from the objective. At 5.15am on the 17 November 1916

Right: Allen Llewellyn Palmer

Far right: Sydney Ernest J. Green

Below: Allen Llewellyn Palmer's Sword in St. James Church, Trowbridge.

the DCLI reached the Pheasant Wood. At 6.15am B Company of the DCLI advanced toward the bridge at Tumbitza they were met by heavy rifle and machine gun fire and forced to retire. During the evening patrols were sent out to collect the wounded but the dead had to be left. The DCLI suffered 20 men killed and one of these was George. He is remembered on the Doiran Memorial and has no known grave.

Private Sydney Ernest J Green   *7th Bn Wiltshire Regiment*

Service No.	16071	Age:	24
Place of Birth:	Southwick, Wiltshire	Home Country:	England
Date of Death:	23/11/1916	Cause of death:	Died
Memorial:	Trowbridge		
War cemetery:	Liverpool Anfield Cemetery		
Theatre of war:	Home		
Next of Kin:	Ernest & Alice L Green		
Address:	15 Gladstone Road, Trowbridge, Wiltshire		

At the outbreak of war Sydney returned to Trowbridge from Cardiff and volunteered for service. He was sent to the Oxfordshire and Buckinghamshire Light Infantry but then transferred to the 7th Service Battalion Wiltshire Regiment. Having completed his training he arrived in France on 21 September 1915 and in November 1915 the Wiltshires were transferred to Salonika, Greece. Sydney was wounded on 4 September after forward positions were shelled and initially evacuated to hospital in Malta. From there he was sent to Mill Road Auxiliary Hospital at Liverpool where he developed dysentery. While weak from his wounds he succumbed to the illness and died on Thursday 23 November 1916.

Private Percy William James Brown *2/4th TF Bn Wiltshire Regiment*
Service No.   2787   Age: 19
Place of Birth: Warminster, Wiltshire   Home Country: England
Date of Death: 06/12/1916   Cause of death: Died
Memorial: Trowbridge St. James Church Memorial - Warminster
War cemetery: Baghdad North Gate War Cemetery
Theatre of war: Mesopotamia
Next of Kin: William & Amy Agnes Brown
Address: 41 Pound Street, Warminster, Wiltshire

Nineteen year old Percy was a Wiltshire Territorial and was sent to India arriving in January 1915 serving at Poona. He volunteered for service in Mesopotamia and landed on 25 August 1915. He was captured at the fall of Kut to Turkish Forces on 29 April 1916 and died most likely of disease on Wednesday 6 December 1916.

Gunner John Francis Keevil   *47th Siege Bat. RGA*
Service No.   73517   Age: 28
Place of Birth: Avebury, Wiltshire   Home Country: England
Date of Death: 19/12/1916   Cause of death: Killed in action
Memorial: Trowbridge
War cemetery: Bernafay Wood British Cemetery Montauban
Theatre of war: France
Next of Kin: Gladys Keevil (wife) - Frederick W. F. & Kate Keevil (parents)
Address: Bratton. Wiltshire - 8 Bloomfield Avenue, Bath

John, known as Jack, was the youngest son of William and Kate Keevil, he was educated at Kingsholme School, Weston-Super-Mare and was employed by Lloyds Bank at Fore Street, Trowbridge. He married Glayds Bird at Edington on 28 April 1915 and was called up in April 1916 joining the Royal Garrison Artillery. He became a signaller which would have left him in an exposed position during bombardments. He was killed in action Tuesday 19 December 1916.

Lance Corporal Joseph Harry Barnes   *2/4th TF Bn Wiltshire Regiment*
Service No.   3186   Age: 23
Place of Birth: Christchurch, Hampshire   Home Country: England
Date of Death: 21/12/1916   Cause of death: Died
Memorial: Trowbridge St James Church Memorial
War cemetery: Baghdad North Gate War Cemetery
Theatre of war: Mesopotamia
Next of Kin: George & Frances Barnes
Address: 6 Church Lane, Christchurch, Hampshire

Joseph was a plumber and a territorial serving with the Wiltshires. At the out break of war he went to India arriving in January 1915 and served in Poona. He volunteered for service in Mesopotamia and was captured at the fall of Kut by Turkish forces. He died of illness or disease as a prisoner of war on Thursday 21 December 1916.

Private Charles Alfred Grant   *1/8th Bn Royal Warwickshire Reg.*
Service No.   5010   Age: 32
Place of Birth: Trowbridge, Wiltshire   Home Country: England
Date of Death: 22/12/1916   Cause of death: Died

Memorial: North Bradley
War cemetery: St Sever Cemetery Extension Rouen
Theatre of war: France
Next of Kin: Alfred & Emily Grant
Address: Yarnbrook, Wiltshire

Charles was the only son of Alfred & Emily Grant and was a mason employed by Linzey and Son of Trowbridge. He was called up and joined the Royal Warwickshire Regiment on 21 March 1916. He became ill and was admitted to No. 9 General Hospital based at Rouen, France and died of dysentery on Friday 22 December 1916.

Private Ernest Bennett *1st Bn Wiltshire Regiment*
Service No. 10078
Age: 30
Place of Birth: Calne, Wiltshire
Home Country: England
Date of Death: 25/12/1916
Cause of death: Died
Memorial: Trowbridge
War cemetery: Trowbridge Cemetery
Theatre of war: Home
Next of Kin: Emily Bennett (wife) - Henry & Elizabeth Bennett (parents)
Address: 9 Mortimer Street, Trowbridge - Calne

Ernest was a carter and had married Emily Hitchens on 6 December 1913. He volunteered for service at the outbreak of hostilities and arrived in France on 28 November 1914. In February 1915 he was evacuated from France and sent to Liverpool Hospital suffering from frost-bite and rheumatism and after several months' treatment he was discharged from the army. He died at his home on Christmas morning 1916 leaving a widow and two small children. He was buried in Trowbridge Cemetery with full military honours. He is not listed on the Commonwealth War Graves Commission web site or in the soldiers died in the Great War listing

Right: John Francis Keevil

Far right: Ernest Bennett

8
1917

Private George Victor Jim Elmes *F Bn Tank Corps*
Service No.   6921   Age: 19
Place of Birth: Derry Hill, Wiltshire   Home Country: England
Date of Death: 03/01/1917   Cause of death: Died
Memorial: Chippenham
War cemetery: Trowbridge Cemetery
Theatre of war: Home
Next of Kin: Nelson Jim & Hannah Elmes
Address: 6 Park Lane, Chippenham, Wiltshire

George was a member of the newly formed Tank Corps originally named the Machine Gun Corps Heavy. He was a new recruit and in training at Bovington, Dorset (which later became home of the Tank Corps). He was taken ill on New Years Day 1917 while travelling to his home from Bovington to visit his mother. At Trowbridge he was found to be so seriously ill that he was admitted to the Red Cross hospital where he died two days later of illness. He was buried with full military honors at Trowbridge Cemetery.

Private Hubert George Helps *44th Bn New Brunswick Regiment*
Service No.   460741   Age: 35
Place of Birth: Bradford on Avon, Wiltshire   Home Country: England
Date of Death: 07/01/1917   Cause of death: Killed in action
Memorial: Hilperton Church Memorial
War cemetery: Villers Station Cemetery Viller Au Bois
Theatre of war: France
Next of Kin: Sidney G & Kate Helps
Address: 4 Ivy Terrace, Bradford on Avon

Hubert was a tinsmith and enlisted with the Canadian army on 11 August 1915. On Sunday 7 January he was with the 44th Battalion near the front line at Vimy Ridge. The war diary for the day states:

"1pm. No unusual occurrence to report. Enemy Trench Mortars very active between 3pm & 8pm. Our Artillery very active in retaliation about 5pm onwards 1 O.R. Killed, 2 O.R. wounded reported."

The one other rank killed was Hubert and he is buried in Villers Station Cemetery.

Private Howard Stanley Hillman *5th Bn Wiltshire Regiment*
Service No.   25838   Age: 22
Place of Birth: Southwick, Wiltshire   Home Country: England
Date of Death: 16/01/1917   Cause of death: Killed in action
Memorial: Not known

War cemetery:	Amara War Cemetery
Theatre of war:	Mesopotamia
Next of Kin:	Albert J & Hannah Hillman
Address:	Southwick, Wiltshire

Howard was employed by Barnes Brothers Steam Rollers with whom he travelled around the country, his employers had asked for an exemption from military service and whilst this had been given several times he was called up in August 1916. After training at Weymouth he was sent to India, spending Christmas day at sea, and on arrival he was sent to join the 5th Battalion Wiltshire Regiment in Mesopotamia, modern day Iraq. On Tuesday 16 January 1917 the Wiltshires were in action against Turkish forces near Kut at the Abdul Hassan bend on the Tigris River at Hai Street and Swindon Street trenches. Howard was killed in his first action most likely by a sniper. He is buried in Amara War Cemetery in modern day Iraq.

Private Leslie Gayton *1/4th TF Bn Wiltshire Regiment*

Service No.	200723	Age:	32
Place of Birth:	Trowbridge, Wiltshire	Home Country:	England
Date of Death:	17/01/1917	Cause of death:	Died
Memorial:	Trowbridge		
War cemetery:	Basra Memorial		
Theatre of war:	Mesopotamia		
Next of Kin:	Frank & Sarah Gayton		
Address:	21 Eastbourne Villas, Trowbridge, Wiltshire		

Leslie was a warehouseman working for a woollen cloth company, he was also a territorial soldier and at the outbreak of war he volunteered to serve in India replacing regular army battalions. While serving in India a call was made for men to serve in Mesopotamia and Leslie was one of those who came forward. He arrived in Mesopotamia on 25 May 1915 and was captured at the fall of Kut on 29 April 1916. He was then marched north through the dessert into captivity. He died of illness or disease as a prisoner of the Turks on Wednesday 17 January 1917. He is remembered on the Basra memorial and has no known grave

Private Henry Arthur White *2nd Bn Leinster Regiment*

Service No.	5393	Age:	36
Place of Birth:	Bedminster, Somerset	Home Country:	England

Far left: Leslie Gayton

Left: Henry Arthur White

Date of Death:	21/01/1917	Cause of death:	Killed in action
Memorial:	Trowbridge		
War cemetery:	Maroc British Cemetery		
Theatre of war:	France		
Next of Kin:	Elizabeth Mabel White (wife) - George & Emily White (parents)		
Address:	5 Surrey Place, Trowbridge - Farleigh Castle, Freshford		

Henry was a coach painter and married Elizabeth Mabel Francis in 1911. He was called up originally joining the Wiltshire Regiment but was transferred to the 2nd Battalion Leinster Regiment. He was killed in action on Sunday 21 January 1917.

CSM Rupert Charles Rowe   *5th Bn Wiltshire Regiment*

Service No.	6238	Age:	32
Place of Birth:	Steeple Langford, Wiltshire	Home Country:	England
Date of Death:	21/01/1917	Cause of death:	Killed in action
Memorial:	Wootton Bassctt		
War cemetery:	Amara War Cemetery		
Theatre of war:	Mesopotamia		
Next of Kin:	Beatrice Elizabeth Rowe (wife) - James & Sarah Rowe (parents)		
Address:	1 Home Mill Buildings, Trowbridge – Steeple Langford		

Rupert, known as Bert, had originally enlisted with the Wiltshires in 1903 and after leaving the army was employed as a railway porter for the Great Western Railway. In the summer of 1908 he married Beatrice Elizabeth Musto at Chipping Sodbury. As a reservist he was called to the colours in 1914 joining the 5th Battalion Wiltshire Regiment and was sent to Gallipoli arriving on 30 June 1915. After the evacuation of Gallipoli they were sent to Egypt and then on to Mesopotamia in February 1916. On Sunday 21 January 1917 the Wiltshires were in action against Turkish forces near Kut at the Abdul Hassan bend on the Tigris River at Hai Street and Swindon Street trenches. Bert was killed in action while the Wiltshire were making preparations for an attack on Turkish positions. Beatrice Rowe inserted the following memoriam in a local paper in January 1919:

"In proud and devoted memory of my beloved husband
Call him not dead my brave noble hero
Death is too cold a word for such as he
Nay rather say he sleeps in happy dreaming
Awaking to heavens everlasting day
and we who mourn must weep not
Because he loved us we are blessed indeed
Never forgotten by his devoted wife and five little ones"

Brigadier General Walter Long DSO CMG   *Cdg 56th Inf Bde General Staff*

Service No.	N/a	Age:	37
Place of Birth:	Charles Street, Middlesex	Home Country:	England
Date of Death:	28/01/1917	Cause of death:	Killed in action
Memorial:	West Ashton		
War cemetery:	Couin New British Cemetery		
Theatre of war:	France		
Next of Kin:	Hon Sibell Long OBE (wife) – Walter H. & Doreen Long (parents)		
Address:	West Ashton, Wiltshire		

Walter, known as Toby, was the eldest son of Right Hon. Walter H. and Lady Doreen Long

Walter Long and his memorial window in West Ashton Church

and was educated at Harrow leaving there in July 1898. He obtained a commission with the Royal Scots Greys in 1899. In November 1899 he went with the Scots Greys to South Africa and took part in the ride under Sir John French at the relief of Kimberly. He was badly wounded at Dronfield, South Africa when a Boer shot at him at short range injuring his arm. He was mentioned in dispatches several times and gained a D.S.O. and the Queen's and King's Medals, each with two clasps. Toby was a keen sportsman playing both cricket and polo for his regiment, he was also a fine horseman and won a great many steeple chases. He was a champion light weight boxer and was for two years middle weight champion in the British Army. On 17 December 1910 he married Sibell Vanden Bempde-Johnstone OBE, granddaughter of Baron Derwent and they had a son, also named Walter, who became 2nd Viscount Long. At the outbreak of the Great War Toby went to France with the British Expeditionary Force and during the retreat from Mons it was said that he risked his own life to save a wounded man but told the man he saved to tell no one of his bravery. He was killed in action while taking his brigade into action at Hebuterne, France on Sunday 28 January 1917. Toby's father received the following letter from the King:

"The Queen and I are deeply grieved to hear that your son has been killed in action after such a distinguished career, and in the prime of youth. I regret that my Army has lost one of its young and promising Generals. We offer you and Lady Doreen our heartfelt sympathy in your great sorrow."

The Times military correspondent wrote:

"The death of General Long will be lamented by a wide circle of friends. He was the best type of officer of the old Army, adored by his soldiers and a man to whom duty always came first. He was never off duty for a day while in France. His good leading brought him command of a Brigade in November 1916 and he plainly marked out for further advancement. Always cheery, he was popular with everyone and was a fine example to others."

Memorial services were held for Toby at St. Margarets, Westminster, St. Mary's Steeple Ashton and in December 1919 Memorial Tablets and a Memorial Window were unveiled at West Ashton Church by Viscout French who had been the Commanding Officer of the British Expeditionary Force at the start of the War.

Sergeant Horace William Sherman   *5th Wiltshire Regiment*
Service No.: 3/593
Place of Birth: Debenham, Suffolk
Date of Death: 01/02/1917
Memorial: Trowbridge
War cemetery: Basra Memorial
Theatre of war: Mesopotamia
Next of Kin: Kate Sherman (wife) – George & Eliza Sherman (parents)
Address: 16 Lower Broad Street, Trowbridge - Suffolk
Age: 38
Home Country: England
Cause of death: Killed in action

On 23 December 1896 Horace enlisted in Ipswich with the Royal Horse Artillery at 18 years of age. He had served 18 years in locations such as India and China and left the army in April 1914 while posted to Trowbridge. On leaving he married Kate Wilcox and found employment with Blake's Brewery. On the outbreak of war he volunteered for service with the Wiltshire Regiment arriving in France on 11 November 1914. He was severely wounded in May 1915 and after his recovery and home leave he was sent to Mesopotamia, modern day Iraq. He was wounded again on 23 April 1916 during a Turkish counter attack at Bait Isa, Iraq. Horace was sent to India to recover and then returned to his unit in Mesopotamia. He was killed in action on Thursday 1 February 1917. The War Diary states that 1 man was killed while the Wiltshires were supporting an attack by the 8th Battalion Cheshire Regiment between Moscow trench and Rome trench in Mesopotamia. He is remembered on the Basra Memorial and has no known grave. Kate Sherman inserted the following memoriam in a local paper:

"In ever loving memory of my dear husband
Sleep on dear one in an unknown grave
Your dear life you nobly gave
No loved ones were with you to say goodbye
Burt safe in Gods keeping now you lie"

Horace left a widow and a little boy, Horace Henry, aged 9 months, whom he never saw.

Lieutenant Herbert Charles Collins   *24th Bn Manchester Regiment*
Service No.: N/A
Place of Birth: Comilla Tippera, India
Age: 27
Home Country: England

Horace William Sherman

Date of Death:	11/02/1917	Cause of death:	Died
Memorial:	Trowbridge		
War cemetery:	Etaples Military Cemetery		
Theatre of war:	France		
Next of Kin:	Ela B Collins (wife) - Arthur Herbert & Esther Ida Collins (parents)		
Address:	34 Broad Street, Warwick, Warwickshire		

Charles was educated at Clifton College and married Ela B Dodd at Warwick late in 1914. He died of disease on 11 February 1917 at a base hospital at Etaples, France. Charles had two brothers who served in the war, Arthur who survived was an English cricketer and most famous as a 13-year-old schoolboy, for achieving the highest-ever recorded score in cricket, he scored 628 not out over four afternoons in June 1899. Norman Cecil Collins, was killed at the Somme in August 1916

Private Edward Ernest Preen   *1/4th TF Bn Wiltshire Regiment*

Service No.	200088	Age:	24
Place of Birth:	Exeter, Devon	Home Country:	England
Date of Death:	12/02/1917	Cause of death:	Died
Memorial:	Trowbridge		
War cemetery:	Baghdad North Gate War Cemetery		
Theatre of war:	Mesopotamia		
Next of Kin:	Mrs Mattock (sister) – Charles & Mary Preen (parents)		
Address:	9 Clark's Place Ashton Street, Trowbridge – South Wales		

Edward was a weaver employed by Salter & Co. Mills and McCalls. He was a territorial soldier and at the outbreak of war volunteered to serve in India replacing regular army battalions. While serving in India a call was made for men to serve in Mesopotamia and Leslie was one of those who came forward. He arrived in Mesopotamia on 25 May 1915 and was captured at the fall of Kut on 29 April 1916. He was then marched north through the dessert into captivity. He died on Monday 12 February from enteric fever while a prisoner of the Turks. Edward's father and 4 brothers were also serving in the army, Arthur was awarded the Military Medal and Howard Joseph Preen was killed in July 1917.

Private Walter H Pinchin   *7th Coy Machine Gun Corps*

Service No.	72525	Age:	31
Place of Birth:	Trowbridge, Wiltshire	Home Country:	England
Date of Death:	14/02/1917	Cause of death:	Killed in action
Memorial:	Trowbridge		
War cemetery:	Berks Cemetery Extension		
Theatre of war:	Belgium		
Next of Kin:	George & Selina Pinchin		
Address:	18 Eastbourne Road, Trowbridge		

Walter was a printer employed at the Wiltshire Times and then by Mr Dotesio at Bradford on Avon. He volunteered for service in August 1914 joining the Wiltshire Regiment and arrived in France on 11 December 1914. He was seriously wounded in the back in September 1915 and after his recovery he returned to the front in November 1916, transferring to the Machine Gun Corps. On Saturday 17 February Walter's mother received a letter in which he said how he was in the best of health and that he was glad that warmer weather was approaching. Soon after the following letter was received from Walter's Commanding Officer, Major A. Douglas Sparkes:

Left: Edward Ernest Preen

Far left: Walter H. Pinchin

"Trenches, 14 February 1917
It is with the deepest sorrow that I have to tell you that your son, No. 72525 Private W. Pinchin, was killed in action this afternoon. He was one of a party carrying up rations to the front when a shell killed him instantly. Officers and men feel for you in your sad loss, which is very, very much. We will have a cross erected over his grave and tend it with care, for that little we can do for our fallen comrade. Accept my heartfelt sympathy and do not hesitate to ask if I can do anything for you."

Gunner Robert Angell		*73rd Coy Royal Garrison Artillery*	
Service No.	137364	Age:	28
Place of Birth:	Ogbourne St George, Wiltshire	Home Country:	England
Date of Death:	19/02/1917	Cause of death:	Died
Memorial:	Not known		
War cemetery:	Kirkee 1914-1918 Memorial		
Theatre of war:	India		
Next of Kin:	George & Rhoda Angell		
Address:	Staverton, Wiltshire.		

Robert, a farm labourer, was used to dealing with horses and joined the Royal Garrison Artillery where his skills would have been in demand, horses being used to pull the heavy guns. He was sent to India where he died of illness or disease on Monday 19 February 1917. He is buried, but many graves in India are not tended by the Commonwealth War Grave Commission and he is remembered on the Kirkee 1914-1918 Memorial.

Private George Nelson Smith		*1/4th TF Bn Hampshire Regiment*	
Service No.	202000	Age:	19
Place of Birth:	Trowbridge, Wiltshire	Home Country:	England
Date of Death:	24/02/1917	Cause of death:	Killed in action
Memorial:	Trowbridge		
War cemetery:	Basra Memorial		
Theatre of war:	Mesopotamia		
Next of Kin:	Frederick & Ellen Smith		
Address:	3 Stainers Building, Castle Street, Trowbridge		

Right: George Nelson Smith

Far right: Edward Victor Mattock

Before enlisting George was employed by Cleeveland's Butchers in Silver Street, Trowbridge and was described as a bright lad with a brimful of good spirits. He volunteered for service with the Hampshire Regiment in 1915 and was sent to Mesopotamia in 1916. At the end of April 1916 two companies of the 1/4th Battalion Hampshire Regiment had surrendered to Turkish forces at the fall of Kut in modern day Iraq. George was with the remainder of the Hampshires that formed a composite battalion with the 1/5th Battalion the East Kent Regiment. The Commonwealth War Graves Commission give the date of George's death as 24 February 1917. However other sources indicate he was killed in action on Friday 23 February 1917 as British forces attempted to cross the river Tigris north of Kut at the Shurman Loop. When the British boats were over half way across the river they were met by heavy but erratic fire from Turkish forces who retreated allowing the British to establish a bridgehead. It is likely George was killed during this attack and he is remembered on the Basra Memorial and has no known grave.

Gunner Charles Brinkworth   *101st Bde Royal Field Artillery*

Service No.	16917	Age:	40
Place of Birth:	Trowbridge, Wiltshire	Home Country:	England
Date of Death:	24/02/1917	Cause of death:	Died
Memorial:	Not known		
War cemetery:	Pieta Military Cemetery		
Theatre of war:	Malta		
Next of Kin:	Alice Brinkworth (wife)		
Address:	17 Worrell Street Kingsholm, Gloucester, Gloucestershire		

Charles worked for a railway contractor and had volunteered for service, initially being sent to France arriving on 5 September 1915, but was soon transferred to Salonika, Greece. He became ill and was evacuated to a military hospital based at Malta where he died on Saturday 24 February 1917.

25 FEBRUARY 1917 - KUT EL AMARA IS RE-OCCUPIED BY THE BRITISH

Rifleman Edward Victor Mattock	*12th Bn Kings Royal Rifle Corps*

Service No.	R/16534	Age:	25
Place of Birth:	Trowbridge, Wiltshire	Home Country:	England
Date of Death:	27/02/1917	Cause of death:	Killed in action
Memorial:	Trowbridge		
War cemetery:	Thiepval Memorial		
Theatre of war:	France		
Next of Kin:	Edward J & Fannie Mattock		
Address:	36 The Furlong, Trowbridge, Wiltshire		

Edward was the eldest son of Edward and Fannie Mattock. He was employed by E. Taylor & Co. Bedding manufacturers and was a member of the "Mount Ararat" Lodge of Oddfellows. He enlisted on 3 December 1915 and was sent to the front on 8 March 1916. He was killed in action at Combles, France, on Tuesday 27 February 1917 during the German retreat to the Hindenburg Line and the subsequent British advance in the early part of 1917. His death was instantaneous and he was buried side by side with eight comrades from his battalion at a position called "Lone Tree", which was lost in later fighting. He is now remembered on the Thiepval Memorial. Edward had two brothers serving with the forces and in March 1918 they inserted the following memoriam in a local paper:

"He sleeps beside his comrades,
In an unknown grave over the foam,
But his name is written in letters of love
On the hearts he left at home.
From his sorrowing Brothers, Fred B.E.F. France and Tom, London.

Private Edward Leonard Sutton	*2/4th TF Bn Wiltshire Regiment*

Service No.	200330	Age:	20
Place of Birth:	Holt, Dorset	Home Country:	England
Date of Death:	28/02/1917	Cause of death:	Died
Memorial:	Trowbridge St James Church		
War cemetery:	Kirkee 1914-1918 Memorial		
Theatre of war:	India		
Next of Kin:	George Pemberton & Laura Sutton		
Address:	14 The Avenue, Wilton, Wiltshire.		

Edward, a felt maker, enlisted with the 2/4th Battalion Wiltshire Regiment and was sent to India to replace regular army units on garrison duties. He died of illness or disease on Wednesday 28 February 1917. Even though Edward was buried the Commonwealth War Graves Commission do not tend the graves of servicemen in India but remember them on memorials.

Sergeant William Harold Singer	*2/4th TF Bn Wiltshire Regiment*

Service No.	201034	Age:	21
Place of Birth:	Marlbourgh, Wiltshire	Home Country:	England
Date of Death:	05/03/1917	Cause of death:	Died
Memorial:	Trowbridge St James - R Shop Memorial Swindon		
War cemetery:	Kirkee 1914-1918 Memorial		
Theatre of war:	India		
Next of Kin:	Willie J & Harriet Singer		
Address:	78 Cheltenham Street, Swindon, Wiltshire		

William known as Willie, was a fitter at the Great Western Railway Works at Swindon. He enlisted with the 2/4th Battalion Wiltshire Regiment and was sent to India on garrison duties. He died of enteric fever on Monday 5 March 1917. He was buried but the Common wealth War Graves Commission do not maintain graves in India and he is today remembered on the Kirkee 1914-1918 Memorial.

Private Alfred Smith *9th Bn Gloucestershire Regiment*
Service No.   16005
Place of Birth: Bulkington, Wiltshire
Date of Death: 06/03/1917
Memorial: Trowbridge
War cemetery: Karasouli Military Cemetery
Theatre of war: Salonika
Next of Kin: Abigail Smith (wife) - Ambrose & Anne Smith (parents)
Address: 10 Gas Works Road, Trowbridge

Age: 27
Home Country: England
Cause of death: Killed in action

Alfred, known as Alfie, was a well known footballer and a member of Trowbridge reserve team who in 1910-11 made a record for the club by winning four cups. He was employed as a hawker and in 1911 he married Abigail Farr at Trowbridge. He was one of the first to volunteer from Trowbridge joining the 9th Battalion Gloucestershire Regiment arriving in France on 21 September 1915, moving to Salonika in November 1915. He was killed in action on Tuesday 6 March 1917 south west of Doiran, Greece and was initially buried at Horseshoe Hill Military cemetery but relocated to the Karasouli Military Cemetery at the end of the war. He left a widow and two small children.

> *11 MARCH 1917 - BAGHDAD IS CAPTURED BY THE BRITISH - 15 MARCH 1917 - RUSSIAN TSAR NICHOLAS II ABDICATES FOLLOWING THE START OF THE RUSSIAN REVOLUTION - 18 MARCH 1917 - GERMANS RETIRE TO THE HINDENBURG LINE*

Gunner Richard Carey Parsons *3rd Div Canadian Field Artillery*
Service No.   311917
Place of Birth: Seend, Wiltshire
Date of Death: 19/03/1917
Memorial: Not known
War cemetery: Brookwood Military Cemetery
Theatre of war: Home
Next of Kin: Caroline Parsons (wife)
Address: 231 Ferry Road, St James, Winnipeg, Canada

Age: 43
Home Country: Canada
Cause of death: Died

Richard married Caroline Ford in 1894 and in 1907 left England for Canada where he was employed as a machinist for the Canadian Northern Railway. He enlisted in the Canadian Artillery on 12 January 1916 and after training he travelled to England. He died of illness or disease at Brook War Hospital Woolwich on Monday 19 March 1917. His son William served with the same unit and his uncle lived at Westbourne Road, Trowbridge.

> *25 MARCH 1917 - BATTLE OF JEBEL HAMRIN, MESOPOTAMIA*
>
> *26 MARCH 1917 - THE FIRST BATTLE OF GAZA, PALESTINE*

Far left: Alfred Smith

left: Frank Tadd

Lance Coporal Frank Tadd *Royal Marine Light Infantry*
Service No.   PO/8831   Age: 40
Place of Birth: Trowbridge, Wiltshire   Home Country: England
Date of Death: 27/03/1917   Cause of death: Died
Memorial: Trowbridge
War cemetery: Portsmouth Naval Memorial
Theatre of war: At Sea
Next of Kin: Beatrice Alice Tadd (wife) - Thomas & Harriet Tadd (parents)
Address: 15 Abercrombie Street Landport, Portsmouth – Trowbridge

Frank was a regular marine and had served at the first naval battle of Heligoland and was present at the landing and evacuation of Gallipoli. He was on his way home to England on the SS Thracia when she was hit by a Torpedo from the German submarine U69 and sank twelve miles north of Belle Ile, an island off the coast of Brittany. Frank had almost completed 21 years service with the marines.

Private Albert Edward Willis *5th Bn Wiltshire Regiment*
Service No.   19000   Age: 33
Place of Birth: Swindon, Wiltshire   Home Country: England
Date of Death: 29/03/1917   Cause of death: Killed in action
Memorial: Trowbridge
War cemetery: Basra Memorial
Theatre of war: Mesopotamia
Next of Kin: Constance Mary H Willis (Wife) - Rebecca Willis (parent)
Address: 3 Edinburgh Buildings, The Halve, Trowbridge, Wiltshire

Albert, a farm labourer, had married Constance Mary H Fryer in the summer of 1906. He enlisted with the 5th Battalion Wiltshire Regiment and was first sent to Gallipoli arriving in December 1915. After the evacuation of Gallipoli the Wiltshires were sent to Mesopotamia in February 1916. At 9am on Thursday 29 March 1917 Albert was with the Wilshires near the Nahrwan Canal at Baghdad in Iraq. As they advanced they were met by heavy shell and machine gun fire. Albert was one of 27 men killed, he is remembered on the Basra Memorial and has no known grave.

Lieutenant Raymond George Vincent   *73rd Bn Canadian Infantry*

Service No.	N/A	Age:	30
Place of Birth:	London, London	Home Country:	England
Date of Death:	29/03/1917	Cause of death:	Killed in action
Memorial:	Melksham		
War cemetery:	Barlin Communal Cemetery Extension		
Theatre of war:	France		
Next of Kin:	Violet Vincent (wife) - Thomas G. & Alice E. Vincent (parents)		
Address:	Prospect House, Trowbridge, Wiltshire		

Raymond, a clerk, arrived in Canada in 1910 and volunteered for service with the Canadian Army on 5 August 1916 and after training was sent to Europe. He was killed in action on Thursday 29 March 1917 during fighting at Vimy Ridge in France.

Lance Coporal Alfred Hawkins   *2nd Bn Wiltshire Regiment*

Service No.	8651	Age:	23
Place of Birth:	Whaddon, Wiltshire	Home Country:	England
Date of Death:	02/04/1917	Cause of death:	Died of wounds
Memorial:	Melksham		
War cemetery:	Warlincourt Halte British Cemetery Saulty		
Theatre of war:	France		
Next of Kin:	James & Louisa Hawkins		
Address:	Bowerhill, Melksham, Wiltshire		

Regular soldier Alfred was the youngest son of James and Louisa Hawkins and had arrived in France on 7 October 1914. He died of wounds at a casualty clearing station based near the villages of Warlincourt and Saulty, France, on Monday 2 April 1917. His brothers Herbert and George were also to die in the war and in April 1918 James Hawkins inserted the following memoriam in a local paper:

"One year has gone and still we miss him
Some may think the wound is healed
But they little know the Sorrow

Right: Albert Edward Willis

Far Rightt: Reginald George Vincent

That lies within our hearts concealed
He's gone one of the best and now we mourn him
The only hope that is left us now is his brothers safe return"

6 APRIL 1917 - THE UNITED STATES DECLARES WAR ON GERMANY

Private George B Banks *2nd Bn Welsh Regiment*
Service No.   5891
Place of Birth: Bradford on Avon, Wiltshire
Date of Death: 07/04/1917
Memorial: Trowbridge
War cemetery: Cologne Southern Cemetery
Theatre of war: Germany
Next of Kin: George & Emily Banks
Address: 2 John Street, Barry, Glamorgan

Age: 28
Home Country: Wales
Cause of death: Died

George was a surface worker at a colliery, it is likely he had served in the army and was on reserve as he was called up and sent to France arriving on 21 September 1914. He was captured by the Germans during fighting some time in the first two years of the war. He died on Saturday 7 April 1917 while a prisoner of war.

Lance Coporal William Purnell *6th Bn Wiltshire Regiment*
Service No.   22604
Place of Birth: Beckington, Somerset
Date of Death: 07/04/1917
Memorial: Trowbridge
War cemetery: Elzenwalle Brasserie Cemetery
Theatre of war: Belgium
Next of Kin: Edward & Mary Ann Purnell
Address: 10 Harford Street, Trowbridge, Wiltshire

Age: 25
Home Country: England
Cause of death: Killed in action

William was employed as a clerk at the offices of Wiltshire Workings Men's Conservative Society. He had been rejected by the army several times because of defective eyesight, but was

George B. Banks

Right: William Purnell

Far right: George Herbert Harman

finally accepted at the end of 1915. On his first journey to France he was invalided home and spent three months in hospital and returned to the front in March 1917. He was killed by German shelling while on sentry duty in trenches at Elzenwalle Brasserie near Voormezeele, Belgium on Saturday 7 April 1917. His birthday was on the 22 April and if he had lived he would have been 26 years of age.

Rifleman George Herbert Harman *1/16th Bn London Regiment*
Service No.   7125   Age: 21
Place of Birth: Trowbridge, Wiltshire   Home Country: England
Date of Death: 08/04/1917   Cause of death: Killed in action
Memorial: Trowbridge
War cemetery: Agny Military Cemetery
Theatre of war: France
Next of Kin: Joseph & Mary Jane Harman
Address: 32 Duke Street, Trowbridge, Wiltshire

George was employed by Norris and Sons as a railway parcel van man and was a member of the Pioneer Society. He joined the army in February 1916 initially joining the Somerset Light Infantry, and then was transferred to the London regiment. He was killed in action near Agny, 5 Km southwest of Arras on Easter Sunday during preparations for the the First Battle of the Scarpe.

9
ARRAS

The Nivell Offensive started on Monday 9 April 1917, it was a joint action between the French and British The British attack took place at Arras.

Lance Corporal Arthur John Ayres　　　　　　*2nd Bn Wiltshire Regiment*
Service No.　　　25547　　　　　　　　　　Age:　　　　　　39
Place of Birth:　　Frome, Somerset　　　　　　Home Country:　England
Date of Death:　　09/04/1917　　　　　　　　Cause of death:　Killed in action
Memorial:　　　　Trowbridge
War cemetery:　　Neuville-Vitasse Road Cemetery
Theatre of war:　　France
Next of Kin:　　　Arthur John & Harriet Ayres
Address:　　　　 88 Bradford Road, Trowbridge, Wiltshire

Arthur, a wood mattress maker, had been employed by Chapman and Company bedding manufactures for over 20 years. He joined the army in March 1916 and after training at Bovington Camp in Dorset with the Somerset Light Infantry he was transferred to the Wiltshire Regiment and proceeded to France in July 1916. He was killed in action on the morning of Easter Monday 1917 when the Wiltshires attacked the Hindenburg line near Neuville-Vitasse, 3Km south west of Arras.

Left: Arthur John Ayres - Below: Ruins of Arras Hotel de Ville

Rightt: John Elms

Far Right: Charles Edward Miller

Private John Elms		*2nd Bn Wiltshire Regiment*	
Service No.	8481	Age:	26
Place of Birth:	Corsham, Wiltshire	Home Country:	England
Date of Death:	09/04/1917	Cause of death:	Killed in action
Memorial:	Trowbridge		
War cemetery:	Neuville-Vitasse Road Cemetery		
Theatre of war:	France		
Next of Kin:	James & Annie Elms		
Address:	Semington Lane, Melksham, Wiltshire		

Regular solider John had served for four years with the Wiltshires at the outbreak of hostilities. He arrived in France on 7 October 1914. He was wounded at Loos in September 1915 and after a short stay in hospital he returned to the front only to be wounded again in December 1916. He was killed in action on the morning of Easter Monday 1917 when the Wiltshires attacked the Hindenburg line near Neuville-Vitasse, 3Km south west of Arras. Arthur's Company Officer, Lieutenant Rudman, wrote the following letter to Annie Elms:

"My deepest sympathy lies with you in your great bereavement and I hope you will find consolation in the fact that your son proved to be one of the bravest men in the company, and died a true soldier's death fighting for his country. His loss was and is keenly felt by his comrades and all who knew him. In the death of your son we have lost one of the smartest and one of the finest soldiers in the company and all the officers remaining join in assuring you of our deepest sympathy."

When Annie Elms received this letter she had lost three sons, Johns brother's Charles killed in 1915 and James died in 1916.

Private Charles Edward Miller		*2nd Bn Wiltshire Regiment*	
Service No.	20601	Age:	23
Place of Birth:	Bristol, Gloucestershire	Home Country:	England
Date of Death:	09/04/1917	Cause of death:	Killed in action
Memorial:	Trowbridge		

War cemetery: Wancourt British Cemetery
Theatre of war: France
Next of Kin: Charles & Emily Miller
Address: 19 Court Street, Trowbridge, Wiltshire

Charles was a labourer on a farm. He joined the Wiltshire Regiment in 1915 and after completing his training he arrived in France on 1 October 1915. He was killed in action on the morning of Easter Monday 1917 when the Wiltshires attacked the Hindenburg line near Neuville-Vitasse, 3Km south west of Arras.

Private Douglas Robert Pinchin *2nd Bn Wiltshire Regiment*
Service No. 33251
Age: 22
Place of Birth: Hilperton, Wiltshire
Home Country: England
Date of Death: 09/04/1917
Cause of death: Killed in action
Memorial: Hilperton
War cemetery: Bucquoy Road Cemetery Ficheux
Theatre of war: France
Next of Kin: Frederick & Lucy Pinchin
Address: Hilperton Manor, Hilperton, Wiltshire

Douglas volunteered for service with the Wiltshire Yeomanry at the outbreak of hostilities. He was sent to France at the end of 1916 being transferred to the 2nd Battalion Wiltshire Regiment. He was killed in action on the morning of Easter Monday 1917 when the Wiltshires attacked the Hindenburg line near Neuville-Vitasse, 3Km south west of Arras. Douglas's elder brother George Pinchin, a vet in Rhodesia, died after an attack of malarial fever on 13 May 1917.

Private Arthur Howard Lane *2nd Bn Wiltshire Regiment*
Service No. 3/9763
Age: 25
Place of Birth: Lower Studley, Wiltshire
Home Country: England
Date of Death: 09/04/1917
Cause of death: Killed in action
Memorial: Not Known
War cemetery: Arras Memorial
Theatre of war: France
Next of Kin: Alice Lane (wife) - William A & Ellen Lane (parents)
Address:, Edington, Wiltshire – North Bradley

It is likely Arthur, a farm labourer, was either a territorial or was on the national reserve and he was called up or volunteered for service with a regular battalion arriving in France on 20 October 1914. While on leave from the army he married Alice Carr on 5 October 1916 and returned to the front shortly after. He was killed in action on the morning of Easter Monday 1917 when the Wiltshires attacked the Hindenburg line near Neuville-Vitasse, 3Km south west of Arras. In April 1914 his young widow inserted the following memoriam in a local paper:

"In ever loving memory of my dear husband killed in action in France
We shall never forget his loving face
As he bade his last goodbye
And left his home forever
On the battlefield to die
Far away from his home and his loved ones
Laid to rest in that far away land
Never more shall our eyes behold him

Never more shall we clasp his hand
His loving ways and smiling face
A pleasure to recall
Though there is nothing left to answer
But his photo on the wall
Ever remembered by his loving wife and children"

Private William Bray		*2nd Bn Wiltshire Regiment*	
Service No.	21318	Age:	33
Place of Birth:	Trowbridge, Wiltshire	Home Country:	England
Date of Death:	09/04/1917	Cause of death:	Killed in action
Memorial:	Not known		
War cemetery:	Arras Memorial		
Theatre of war:	France		
Next of Kin:	James & Emily Bray		
Address:	Horse Road, Hilperton, Wiltshire		

William had left Trowbridge in 1901 and was employed in the collieries at Mountain Ash in South Wales. His work had been considered as being of national importance at the commencement of hostilities. In June 1915 William enlisted in the army joining the Wiltshires and after the completion of his training he arrived in France on 9 December 1915. In January 1917 he was fortunate to receive leave from the army and returned to Trowbridge and when he spoke to his relatives he was very optimistic about the future. However he returned to France and did not see the end of the war. He was killed in action on the morning of Easter Monday 1917 when the Wiltshires attacked the Hindenburg line near Neuville-Vitasse, 3Km south west of Arras. William's brother Albert was to die form wounds in March 1918.

Private George Hillier		*2/4th TF Bn Wiltshire Regiment*	
Service No.	202086	Age:	41
Place of Birth:	Horton, Wiltshire	Home Country:	England
Date of Death:	11/04/1917	Cause of death:	Died
Memorial:	Melksham & Trowbridge St. James Church Memorial		
War cemetery:	Kirkee 1914-1918 Memorial		

Right: William Bray

Far Right: George Hillier

Theatre of war: India
Next of Kin: Thomas & Anne W Hillier
Address: 9 Union Street, Melksham, Wiltshire

At 41 years of age George had almost reached the upper age limit for the army when he left Melksham, where he had for many years been an employee of the Avon India Rubber Works and a tobacco factory. He joined the army on 11 April 1915 and after training was sent to India arriving on 5 March 1916. He died of blood poisoning at Ahmednagar, India on Wednesday 11 April 1917. The Commonwealth War Grave Commission do not maintain servicemen's graves in India and he is remembered on the Kirkee 1914-1918 Memorial.

Private Walter Robert Adams   *1st Bn Hampshire Regiment*
Service No.: 32980
Age: 26
Place of Birth: Trowbridge, Wiltshire
Home Country: England
Date of Death: 15/04/1917
Cause of death: Killed in action
Memorial: Not Known
War cemetery: Arras Memorial
Theatre of war: France
Next of Kin: Robert & Lizzie Adams
Address: Not known

William had originally been a member of the 9th Resevere Cavalry Regiment but was transferred to Hampshire Regiment. He was killed in action near Warncourt Ridge on Sunday 15 April 1917 during the Battle of Arras. He is remembered on the Arras Memorial and has no known grave.

Private Charles George York   *1st Bn Dorsetshire Regiment*
Service No.: 3/6418
Age: 24
Place of Birth: Bradford on Avon, Wiltshire
Home Country: England
Date of Death: 16/04/1917
Cause of death: Died of wounds
Memorial: Trowbridge
War cemetery: Nesle Communal Cemetery
Theatre of war: France
Next of Kin: Ethel York (wife) - Charlie & Emily York (parents)
Address: 11 Edinburgh Buildings, The Halve, Trowbridge - Bradford on Avon

Charles, known as Charlie, was employed as a labourer prior to the war and had been a member of the Dorset Militia for three years. He married Ethel Golding during the summer of 1914 and was called up at the commencement of hostilities arriving in France on 23 October 1914. He had served in the battles of the Aisne, Loos and the Somme, and it is likely he was wounded in action during actions between the 13-14 April near Cepy Farm, north of St. Quentin, France. He succumbed to his wounds on Monday 16 April 1917 at No.21 Casualty Clearing Station Nesle, a village 20km south of Peronne, France. Ethel York inserted the following memoriam in a local paper in April 1918:

"In loving memory of my dear husband
Your last whisper I should have liked to have heard
And to breathe in your ear just one loving word
Only those who have suffered are able to tell
The pain of the heart in not saying farewell
We miss him who loved him best"

Right:
Charles George York

Far Right:
William Christopher White

Sergeant William Ernest Horton *8th Bn Somerset Light Infantry*
Service No.   26060   Age: 35
Place of Birth: Trowbridge, Wiltshire   Home Country: England
Date of Death: 18/04/1917   Cause of death: Killed in action
Memorial: Trowbridge
War cemetery: Arras Memorial
Theatre of war: France
Next of Kin: Bessie Horton (wife) - William & Elizabeth Horton (parents)
Address: 9 Tymore Terrace, Oldfield Park - 112 Mortimer Street, Trowbridge

Labourer William joined the Somerset Light Infantry. He was killed in action at Beaufort near Arras while his unit were in preparation for the Second Battle of the Scarpe on Wednesday 18 April 1917. He is remembered on the Arras Memorial and has no known grave. His brother Herbert Claude Horton was killed in June 1915.

Gunner William Christopher White *108th Siege Bty RGA*
Service No.   61562   Age: 25
Place of Birth: North Bradley, Wiltshire Home Country: England
Date of Death: 18/04/1917   Cause of death: Died of wounds
Memorial: Not known
War cemetery: Tilloy British Cemetery Tilloy Les Mofflaines
Theatre of war: France
Next of Kin: James & Eliza White
Address: Mount Pleasant, Trowbridge

William, known as Chris, was the youngest son of James and Eliza White and was employed as a grocer with Stratton, Sons and Mead of Melksham. He regularly attended the North Bradley Baptist Church and was described as having a bright and cheery nature. He joined the Royal Garrison Artillery in November 1915 and was sent to France in September 1916. He was wounded east of Arras and died as a result of these wounds on Wednesday 18 April 1917.

19 APRIL 1917 - SECOND BATTLE OF GAZA, PALESTINE

Lance Coporal Herbert Hatherall   *1/8th TF Bn Hampshire Regiment*
Service No.: 331378
Age: 20
Place of Birth: Chippenham, Wiltshire
Home Country: England
Date of Death: 19/04/1917
Cause of death: Killed in action
Memorial: Trowbridge
War cemetery: Gaza War Cemetery
Theatre of war: Egypt
Next of Kin: Alfred & Susan Hatherall
Address: 6 Shails Lane, Trowbridge

Herbert, known as Bert, originally joined the Wiltshire Regiment but was transferred to the Hampshire Regiment. He was killed in action on Thursday 19 April 1917 most likely near the position of Khashm Sihan near Gaza in Palestine when the British attacked Turkish forces.

Private Henry Turner   *7th Bn Wiltshire Regiment*
Service No.: 3/509
Age: 56
Place of Birth: Brecon, Wales
Home Country: England
Date of Death: 19/04/1917
Cause of death: Died
Memorial: Trowbridge
War cemetery: Trowbridge Cemetery
Theatre of war: Home
Next of Kin: Ellen Turner (wife)
Address: 126 Mortimer Street, Trowbridge

Henry was a railway carter employed by Norris & Son of Trowbridge. He rejoined the colours in September 1914 and saw service in France arriving in September 1915 and was then sent to Salonika. He was sent back to England being unfit for duty and treated at Manchester and Wingfield. He died at home on Thursday 19 April 1917 and is not listed on the Commonwealth War Graves Commission web site or in the soldiers died in the Great War listing.

Far left: Henry Turner

Left: Albert Victor Sartin

> *20 April 1917 - British Forces occupy Sammarah, 60 miles north of Baghdad*

Private Albert Victor Sartin	*1/8th Bn Royal Warwickshire Regt.*
Service No. 306863	Age: 19
Place of Birth: Trowbridge, Wiltshire	Home Country: England
Date of Death: 20/04/1917	Cause of death: Killed in action
Memorial: Trowbridge	
War cemetery: Thiepval Memorial	
Theatre of war: France	
Next of Kin: John & Ellen Sartin	
Address: 21 Newtown, Trowbridge	

Albert, known as Victor, was employed at Wilts United Dairies and was a keen member of the Wesley Road Sunday School. He joined the army under the Derby Scheme and enlisted on 27 March 1916 arriving in France on 25 July 1916. At the start of April 1917 he sent a letter to his parents and enclosed some snow drops and violets and said that he would send some war relics, one of which arrived the next day. It was in the shape of a French crucifix and Victor had picked it up outside a church in a recaptured French Village. On Friday 20 April 1917 Victor was fatally shot while on patrol, when his body was brought in he was found to have a booklet of the Wesley Road Sunday School 1916 anniversary hymns, which had the appearance of having much use. Lieutenant Epins wrote the following letter to John and Ellen Sartin:

"As your sons platoon commander, I have the most unpleasant duty of writing to you to inform you that he was killed in action on the morning of the 20 April. I can only say he was one of the most willing men in my platoon. He was out on patrol when the sad event happened but we managed to get him in. Will you please accept sincere sympathy of the officers, N.C.O.'s and men of B Company."

Victor was just nineteen when he met his death, he was killed near Peronne, France and the patrol he was on was probably probing the German Hindenburg defensive line. He is remembered on the Thiepval Memorial and has no known grave.

Private Hubert Greenland	*13th Bn Royal Fusiliers*
Service No. 51405	Age: 37
Place of Birth: Trowbridge, Wiltshire	Home Country: England
Date of Death: 23/04/1917	Cause of death: Killed in action
Memorial: Not known	
War cemetery: Arras Memorial	
Theatre of war: France	
Next of Kin: Minnie Greenland (wife) - Henry & Anne Greenland (parents)	
Address: 103 Rosslyn Crescent, Wealdstone - Bradford on Avon	

Hubert was the twin son of Henry and Anne Greenland, he was a plasterer prior to the war but took employment with a munitions manufacturer at the outbreak of hostilities. He was conscripted into the army in 1916 joining the Royal Fusiliers and after completing his training was sent to France. Hubert was killed in action on Monday 23 April 1917 during the Second Battle of the Scarpe near Arras. He is remembered on the Arras Memorial and left a widow and five young children.

Far Left: John Potter

Left: Frederick Blake Deverall

Private John Potter		*7th Bn Wiltshire Regiment*	
Service No.	10754	Age:	26
Place of Birth:	Edington, Wiltshire	Home Country:	England
Date of Death:	24/04/1917	Cause of death:	Killed in action
Memorial:	Trowbridge		
War cemetery:	Doiran Memorial		
Theatre of war:	Salonika		
Next of Kin:	George & Pheobe Potter		
Address:	28 Bradford Road, Trowbridge, Wiltshire		

John worked as a bottler and volunteered for service with the 7th Service Battalion Wiltshire Regiment arriving in France on 21 September 1915. In November 1915 they were sent to Salonika, Greece and he was reported missing on Tuesday 24 April 1917 during an attack south of Doiran on Bulgarian trenches. The Wiltshires were held up by the Bulgarian barbed wire and had very heavy casualties. John is remembered on the Doiran Memorial and has no known grave. His brothers Arthur and Robert were also killed on active service.

Lance Coporal Frederick Blake Deverall		*9th Bn Kings Royal Rifle Corps*	
Service No.	R/20702	Age:	29
Place of Birth:	Trowbridge, Wiltshire	Home Country:	England
Date of Death:	26/04/1917	Cause of death:	Died
Memorial:	Melksham - Trowbridge		
War cemetery:	St. Sever Cemetery Extension Rouen		
Theatre of war:	France		
Next of Kin:	Minnie Deverall (wife) - Cornelius & Louisa Deverall (parents)		
Address:	11 West Street, Trowbridge		

Frederick was well known at Holy Trinity Church and had been a leading boy chorister of the Trowbridge Company of the Church Lads Brigade. He was an excellent shot and had taken a keen interest in the Air Rifle League. He was employed in the furnishing store H. J. Knee's and was the manager at the Melksham store. At the end of the year 1913 he married Minnie

Stevens and in May 1915 he volunteered for service joining the Church Lads Battalion at Banbury. He was then transferred to the 9th Service Battalion K.R.R. after arriving in France in 1916. Frederick was wounded during the British advance on the German Hindenburg line in April 1917 and died of his wounds at No. 12 General Hospital at Rouen. In May 1918 his parents inserted the following memoriam in a local paper:

"In memory of my boy
Ye that live on mid English pastures green.
Remember us, and think what might have been".

Lance Coporal Herbert George Beaven   *15th Bn Royal Scots*
Service No.   7369   Age: 33
Place of Birth: Trowbridge, Wiltshire   Home Country: England
Date of Death: 28/04/1917   Cause of death: Killed in action
Memorial: Trowbridge
War cemetery: Arras Memorial
Theatre of war: France
Next of Kin: Agnes Annie Beaven (wife) – Thomas Beaven (parent)
Address: 44 New Road, Trowbridge, Wiltshire

Regular soldier Herbert had originally enlisted with the Wiltshire Regiment before joining the Royal Scots on 15 January 1901. He left the army in 1905 and was transferred to the reserve and married Agnes Annie Hillman at North Bradley on 2nd June 1906. Prior to the war Herbert was employed as a Postman and at the out break of hostilities he was called up and rejoined the 2nd Battalion Royal Scots. He arrived in France on 7 September 1914 and was wounded at La Bassee on 24 October 1914. After his recovery he returned to France on 6 July 1916, transferring to the 15th Royal Scots. Herbert was listed as missing in action on Saturday 28 April 1917 during fighting east of Arras as the British attacked the German positions of the Hindenburg line. He is remembered on the Arras Memorial and has no known grave. Agnes Beaven inserted the following memoriam in a local paper in April 1918:

"In loving memory of my dear husband
A loving husband good and kind
He proved to be in heart and mind
A bitter grief a shock severe
To part with him we love so dear
Our loss is great we'll not complain
But hope in heaven to meet again
Ever remembered by his wife and children"

Herbert George Beaven

Private George Cecil Slade		*2nd RM Bn RN Div RMLI*	
Service No.	PO/17928	Age:	19
Place of Birth:	East Ham, London	Home Country:	England
Date of Death:	28/04/1917	Cause of death:	Killed in action
Memorial:	Not known		
War cemetery:	Arras Memorial		
Theatre of war:	France		
Next of Kin:	Albert & Louie Slade		
Address:	14 York Buildings, Trowbridge		

Nineteen year old George was a chauffeur and the youngest son of Albert & Louie Slade; he enlisted with the marines on 30 September 1914. He was sent to the Island of Murdos, Greece in early 1916 but after becoming ill he was evacuated and returned to England. Once recovered he was sent to France. He was listed as missing in action on Saturday 28 April 1917 at Oppy Wood near Arras. Later George was assumed to have died, and he is remembered on the Arras Memorial and has no known grave. In May 1919 his parents inserted the following memoriam:

"He lays at rest in an unfamiliar land
England he went for you
O England sometimes think of him of those thousands only one
In the dawning of the new day or setting of the sun
As once he thought of you
Sadly missed and ever mourned by his Mother, Dad, Brother and Bessie"

Private George Robert Rowe		*1st RM Bn RN Div RMLI*	
Service No.	PO/16412	Age:	24
Place of Birth:	Studley, Wiltshire	Home Country:	England
Date of Death:	28/04/1917	Cause of death:	Killed in action
Memorial:	Salisbury		
War cemetery:	Arras Memorial		
Theatre of war:	France		
Next of Kin:	John & Jane Rowe		
Address:	87 Gigant Street, Salisbury		

Prior to his enlistment George worked with a blacksmith but joined the Marines on 12 August 1912. He was sent to the Greek Island of Murdos in December 1915 and he was then sent to France in May 1916. Here he was wounded with a gun shot wound to the left foot during fighting on 19 November 1916. He was listed as missing in action on Saturday 28 April 1917, most likely in the Gavrelle area and it was later assumed he had been killed on that day. He is remembered on the Arras Memorial and has no known grave.

Private Stanley George Dude Covey		*2/4th Bn Ox and Bucks Light Infantry*	
Service No.	200445	Age:	20
Place of Birth:	Trowbridge, Wiltshire	Home Country:	England
Date of Death:	28/04/1917	Cause of death:	Killed in action
Memorial:	Not known		
War cemetery:	Thiepval Memorial		
Theatre of war:	France		
Next of Kin:	George Harry & Annie Covey		
Address:	19 Barrett Street, Osney, Oxfordshire		

Stanley was the oldest son of George & Annie Covey and it is likely he was conscripted into the army. He was killed in action on Saturday 28 April 1917 when the Ox & Bucks conducted a large scale raid on German trenches at Fayet near St. Quentin, France. After the initial success and the clearing of the German Front line the Ox & Bucks encountered stiff opposition from the German Reserve Trenches and many of the British casualties occurred when the British were falling back to their own lines. One of these casualties was Stanley, he is remembered on the Thiepval Memorial and has no known grave.

Private Albert Jack Harding   *47th Bn Western Ontario Regiment*
Service No. 645381
Age: 31
Place of Birth: Trowbidge, Wiltshire
Home Country: Canada
Date of Death: 02/05/1917
Cause of death: Died of wounds
Memorial: Not Known
War cemetery: Sunderland Ryhope Road Cemetery
Theatre of war: Home
Next of Kin: Gertrude Emmeline Harding (wife) - Henry J.& Louisa Harding (parents)
Address: 1900 Broadway West, Vancouver, British Columbia

Albert was a cook and had emigrated to Canada prior to the Great War and volunteered for service with the Canadian Army on 16 January 1916. On 28 May 1916 he married Gertrude Emmeline Day at Vancouver, Canada most probably just before he sailed for Europe. He was wounded in fighting at Vimy Ridge, evacuated to England and sent to a hospital in Sunderland where he succumbed to his wounds on Wednesday 2 May 1917.

Lieutenant Henry Featherstone Clark   *11th Bn Devonshire Regiment*
Service No N/A
Age: 23
Place of Birth: Kingsclere, Hampshire
Home Country: England
Date of Death: 03/05/1917
Cause of death: Killed in action
Memorial: Not Known
War cemetery: Chapelle British Cemetery Holnon
Theatre of war: France
Next of Kin: Henry Atwood Clark & Julia Marion Clark
Address: Buckland Monachorum, Devon

Henry was the only Grandchild of Henry Clark of Trowbridge. He was educated at Christ's Hospital and was a sub editor with the Manchester Guardian when he joined the University and Public School Brigade in September 1914. He obtained a commission in the Devon Regiment in December 1914 and was attached to the 2/6th Gloucester Regiment going to the front in June 1916. He was killed in action on Thursday 5 May 1917 to the West of St. Quentin, France.

Private William Fred Culverhouse   *1/7th Bn Middlesex Regiment*
Service No. TF/202966
Age: 30
Place of Birth: North Bradley, Wiltshire
Home Country: England
Date of Death: 04/05/1917
Cause of death: Killed in action
Memorial: North Bradley
War cemetery: Arras Memorial
Theatre of war: France
Next of Kin: Frank & Ann Susanna Culverhouse
Address: Scotland, North Bradley, Wiltshire

William was a farmer and joined the army on 28 April 1916 and was sent to France in November 1916. He was killed in action east of Arras on Friday 4 May 1917. Williams' mother received the following letter from Lieutenant Frank Muxon, his company commander:

"It is a sad duty of mine to write and inform you that your son was killed in action on the 4 May 1917. It is to be of some little consolation for you to know that death was instantaneous. Your son was a good soldier and a very brave one too, and we can ill afford to lose such a man. He was quite a favourite in the company and liked by all. The burial took place the same day, a cross on which is inscribed his name and regiment being erected on his last resting place. All the officers and men send their deepest sympathy and I his company commander send my deepest sympathy."

Driver Edwin George Hillman — *281st Bde Royal Field Artillery*
Service No.   59505
Place of Birth: Trowbridge, Wiltshire
Date of Death: 07/05/1917
Memorial: Trowbridge
War cemetery: Bucquoy Road Cemetery Ficheux
Theatre of war: France
Next of Kin: Edward & Alice Hillman
Address: 24 Thomas Street, Trowbridge, Wiltshire

Age: 25
Home Country: England
Cause of death: Died of wounds

Regular soldier Edwin arrived in France on 19 August 1914. He was wounded in action during fighting near Arras, France and was taken to VII Corps Main Dressing Station at Ficheux. He died of his wounds four days before his 26th Birthday.

Private Henry Joseph Salvidge — *1/4th TF Bn Wiltshire Regiment*
Service No.   200228
Place of Birth: Chelsea, London
Date of Death: 08/05/1917
Memorial: Devizes
War cemetery: Kirkee 1914-1918 Memorial
Theatre of war: India

Age: 22
Home Country: England
Cause of death: Died

Far left: Edwin George Hillman

Left: Herbert John Hawkins

Next of Kin:	Henry Chard & Louisa Julia Salvidge
Address:	Trederwyn Bradley Rd, Trowbridge

Henry, known as Harry, had been a keen scout before joining the Wiltshire territorials. At the outbreak of war he was employed by an engine erector and as a territorial soldier was sent to serve in India. His term of service with the territorials expired in 1916 and he wrote to his mother expressing a wish to return to England and join another regiment. His mother however asked him to remain with the Wiltshires which he did. In April 1917 he was moved from Delhi to serve at Poona and wrote to his mother telling her that he was in good health. On 10 May a local vicar received a telegram from Lieutenant Redman informing him that Harry had died of diphtheria on Tuesday 8 May 1917 and asking him to break the news to Louisa Salvidge. Harry was Louisa's third and only surviving son. He is remembered on the Kirkee 1914-1918 Memorial.

Sapper Herbert John Hawkins		*505th Field Coy Royal Engineers*
Service No.	508233			Age:		33
Place of Birth:	Melksham, Wiltshire	Home Country:	England
Date of Death:	09/05/1917		Cause of death:	Died of wounds
Memorial:	Trowbridge
War cemetery:	Erquinghem Lys Churchyard Extension
Theatre of war:	France
Next of Kin:	Cecilia Sarah Hawkins (wife) – James & Louisa Hawkins (parents)
Address:	9 Thomas Street, Trowbridge - Bowerhill, Melksham

Herbert was a carter on a farm and had married Cecilia Sarah Blower in 1906. It is likely Herbert was conscripted into the army. He died of wounds on Wednesday 9 May 1915 at a field ambulance based at Erquinghem-Lys west of Armentieres, France and was buried at a churchyard of the same name. He left a widow and five young children. His brothers George and Alfred had been killed earlier in the war.

Private Bertie George Gray		*2nd Bn Wiltshire Regiment*
Service No.	21169			Age:		22
Place of Birth:	Motcombe, Dorset	Home Country:	England
Date of Death:	09/05/1917		Cause of death:	Died of wounds
Memorial:	Hilperton
War cemetery:	Mont Huon Military Cemetery Le Treport
Theatre of war:	France
Next of Kin:	George Edwin and Sarah Gray
Address:	New Cottages, Whaddon, Trowbridge

Bertie was an agricultural labourer and it is likely he was either called up under the Derby Scheme or conscripted into the army. He was wounded in action and taken to the 16th General Hospital at Le Treport, France where he died of his wounds on Wednesday 9 May 1917.

Private George William Bishop		*5th Bn Wiltshire Regiment*
Service No.	25763			Age:		30
Place of Birth:	Trowbridge, Wiltshire	Home Country:	England
Date of Death:	11/05/1917		Cause of death:	Died of wounds
Memorial:	Trowbridge
War cemetery:	Basra War Cemetery

Far left: Bertie George Gray

Left: George William Bishop

Theatre of war: Mesopotamia
Next of Kin: Mabel Eugene Bishop (wife) - Alfred Henry & Mary E Bishop (parents)
Address: 21 Seymour Road, Stapehill, Bristol

George was employed at the gas works in Trowbridge prior to the war and had married Mabel Hulbert at the start of 1914. He was a prominent member of the Salvation Army, acting as the standard bearer. He enlisted with the Wiltshires in May 1916 and was sent to Mesopotamia in November of the same year. He was wounded in action on 29 March 1917 at the Nahrwan Canal at Baghdad in modern day Iraq and conveyed to a base hospital at Basra where he died of his wounds on Friday 11 May 1917. A few hours previous to receiving official War Office notification of her husband's death, Mabel received a letter from an army chaplain stating that George was making progress.

Private Harold Francis Cosser   *1/4th TF Bn Wiltshire Regiment*
Service No.   200122   Age: 22
Place of Birth: Donhead St Mary, Wiltshire   Home Country: England

Far left: Harold Francis Cosser

Left: Tom Wheeler

Date of Death: 22/05/1917	Cause of death: Died
Memorial: Bratton	
War cemetery: Basra Memorial	
Theatre of war: Mesopotamia	
Next of Kin: George & Anna L Cosser	
Address: Edington	

Harold was the youngest son of George & Anna Cosser and had served an apprenticeship in the ironmongery department of H.J.Knee. He volunteered for service in 1914 joining the Wiltshire Territorials and was sent to India. While on service he again volunteered, this time for service in Mesopotamia arriving on 25 August 1915. He was wounded at the Battle of Cestiphon and evacuated to Kut where he was captured by Turkish forces in April 1916. He died most likely of sickness or disease on Tuesday 22 May 1917 at a hospital in Adana, Turkey and is remembered on the Basra Memorial in Modern day Iraq. In May 1918 his parents inserted the following memoriam in a local paper:

"Love cannot die; although one year
Since our great sorrow fell
Still in our hearts we mourn the loss
Of him we loved so well."

Private Tom Wheeler   *2nd Bn Wiltshire Regiment*

Service No.	32663	Age:	32
Place of Birth:	Devizes, Wiltshire	Home Country:	England
Date of Death:	03/06/1917	Cause of death:	Died of wounds
Memorial:	Trowbridge		
War cemetery:	Lijssenthoek Military Cemetery		
Theatre of war:	Belgium		
Next of Kin:	Rose Wheeler (wife) – Fanny Wheeler (parent)		
Address:	126 Mortimer Street, Trowbridge		

Tom was employed as a stoker at the Wilts United Daries and married Rose Turner in October 1916. He was called up for service early in 1917 and arrived in France during April 1917. He was wounded in action on 2 June 1917 and was taken to one of the base hospitals based at Lijssenthoek, Belgium where he died the following day. Rose Wheelers' father had died a few weeks earlier and in June 1918 she inserted the following memoriam in a local paper:

"In ever loving memory of my dear husband
Days of sadness still come o'er us
Secret tears do often flow,
Memory keeps are loved one near to us,
Though it's now one year ago.

I often think and talk of him
And think how he died;
To think I could not say goodbye
Before he closed his eyes.
Could I but kneel beside his grave,
And shed a silent tear-
But now he sleeps somewhere in France
The one I love so dear"

Private Harold Butcher   *15th Bn Royal Warwickshire Regiment*

Service No.	18595
Place of Birth:	Trowbridge, Wiltshire
Date of Death:	04/06/1917
Memorial:	Trowbridge
War cemetery:	Etaples Military Cemetery
Theatre of war:	France
Next of Kin:	Daisey A. Butcher
Address:	Nolans Cottage, Yatesbury, Wiltshire.
Age:	26
Home Country:	England
Cause of death:	Died of wounds

Harold was employed as a carriage builder by Mr W Pike in Trowbridge. In 1915 he married Daisey Cook. Having enlisted in March 1916 either under the Derby scheme or conscripted, he was posted to the 15th Service Battalion Warwickshire Regiment and sent for training on the Isle of Wight. In the autumn of 1916 he went with his Regiment to France and took part in many engagements during the winter of 1916-17. He was severely wounded by shrapnel in the head in early May 1917 and died at the General Hospital in Etaples, France.

7 JUNE 1917 - THE BATTLE OF MESSINES, BELGIUM

Private Henry Charles Champion   *6th Bn Wiltshire Regiment*

Service No.	23762
Place of Birth:	North Bradley, Wiltshire
Date of Death:	07/06/1917
Memorial:	Trowbridge
War cemetery:	Klein-Vierstraat British Cemetery
Theatre of war:	Belgium
Next of Kin:	Charles & Mary Champion
Address:	The Rank, North Bradley
Age:	17
Home Country:	England
Cause of death:	Killed in action

Seventeen year old Henry, known as Charles, was an under age soldier. Prior to the war he was employed by Salter and Co. but had been desperate to join the Navy but an affection to the throat debarred him. When the war broke out he repeatedly tried to join the army and was

Far left: Harold Butcher

Left: Henry Charles Champion

accepted on his seventh application in January 1916 and was sent to France in February 1917. He was killed in action on Thursday 7 June 1917 while serving with the 6th Battalion Wiltshire Regiment at the capture of Hollande Salient at Messines Ridge. Charles Chapman senior received the following letter from his sons' platoon commander:

"He had not been with us very long, but he was certainly one of the most promising of the younger members of the platoon. He was always smart willing and courageous and was very popular with everybody. He would have certainly been promoted had he been spared longer. I hope that it may be some consolation to you in your bereavement to reflect that he died the death of an honourable and gallant man for his King and country"

Corporal Egbert Taylor   *1st Bn Wiltshire Regiment*

Service No.	6754	Age:	31
Place of Birth:	Compton Bassett, Wiltshire	Home Country:	England
Date of Death:	07/06/1917	Cause of death:	Died of wounds
Memorial:	Trowbridge & Blacklands		
War cemetery:	Bailleul Communal Cemetery Extension Nord		
Theatre of war:	France		
Next of Kin:	Ethel F Taylor (wife) - Thomas & Emily Taylor (parents)		
Address:	Steeple Ashton, Wiltshire - Cherhill, Wiltshire.		

Egbert was employed as a farm labourer by Tom Tucker at Mill Farm, Steeple Ashton, where he took a keen intelligent interest in his work. In a ploughing competition organised by the Wiltshire Agricultural Education Committee at Keevil he won first prize and a special certificate. As a reservist, he was called to the colours on the outbreak of war and went over with the British Expeditionary Force. He was wounded in November 1915 by shrapnel in the chest and other parts of his body. He returned to France in the following June, but had only been with his regiment for a few weeks when he was again wounded and was treated at Chatham. On his recovery he was transferred to Weymouth, where after doing duty at the reinforcement camp, he again left for the fighting line in September 1916. After repeatedly refusing promotion, upon his return to France he was prevailed upon to accept the non commissioned officers stripes, and became a corporal. During the following eight months he saw much service with the Wiltshires and took part in every engagement, ultimately meeting his death on Thursday 7 June 1917, the date of his 31st birthday.

The information was conveyed in a letter from Sister McPherson, in charge of a base hospital, who writing to Ethel Taylor said;

"I am extremely grieved to tell you that your husband, Corporal Taylor, was admitted to this hospital with multiple wounds of his body and hands. He was collapsed on admission, and although everything was done for him he never recovered, but passed peacefully away at 2.30pm the same day. He did not leave any message, as he was quite unconscious."

Lieutenant Swayne, Egbert's commanding officer also wrote to Ethel expressing his regret and sympathy and said;

"Corporal Taylor was appointed brigade orderly and put there especially so as to be safer, as we realized his worth and the gallant services he had rendered, and we were hoping to get him a months leave due to him as a time-expired soldier."

It is likely that Egbert was wounded during the preparation for an attack on Messines Ridge

Left: Harry Prosser

Far left: Egbert Taylor

and evacuated to the hospital at Baileul, France. Egbert had three brothers in the army. One, who had also served in the army before the war had been captured in 1914 and was held in a German prisoner of war camp. Ethel had lost two brothers during the Great War Albert, who is remembered on Keevil war memorial and John who is remembered on Bulkington war memorial.

Sergeant Harry Prosser   *1st Bn Wiltshire Regiment*
Service No. 6972
Age: 33
Place of Birth: Westbury, Wiltshire
Home Country: England
Date of Death: 11/06/1917
Cause of death: Killed in action
Memorial: Trowbridge
War cemetery: Messines Ridge British Cemetery
Theatre of war: Belgium
Next of Kin: Mary Ann Prosser (parent)
Address: 20 Prospect Place, Trowbridge

At the outbreak of the war Harry was a bicycle tyre maker and it is likely that he was a member of the national reserve and was called up on 7 August 1914, arriving in France on 14 August 1914 where he was promoted to sergeant. He was reported missing on Messines Ridge on Monday 11 June 1917 at a position near Odious trench where the Wiltshires were subjected to German snipers, machine guns and shelling. Official news of Harry's death was received by his mother in May 1918.

Private William John Boscombe   *2nd Bn Wiltshire Regiment*
Service No. 3/9201
Age: 22
Place of Birth: Westbury, Wiltshire
Home Country: England
Date of Death: 12/06/1917
Cause of death: Died
Memorial: Trowbridge
War cemetery: Niederzwehren Cemetery
Theatre of war: Germany
Next of Kin: Frederick W & Mary Jane Boscombe
Address: Aspley House, Queenswood Road, Stockbridge, Hampshire

William John Boscombe

Twenty two year old William was a dairy man at Hobbs Bottom Farm at Atworth. He joined up at the outbreak of hostilities and arrived in France on 7 October 1914. He was captured by Germans at Beselare, Belgium on 24 October 1914 and taken to a prison camp in Hamelin, Germany. In 1916 news was received that William was in hospital but two official postcards were received later stating that his health was improving. After leaving hospital William continued to write home but in May 1916 the letters ceased. No definite information could be obtained until November 1918 when a notification of his death from illness or disease was received presuming that he had died on Tuesday 12 June 1917 at Gohlis, Germany. It is likely that his grave was relocated at the end of the war to Niederzwehren Cemetery.

Private Cecil Francis Deacon　　　　　　　　　*1st Bn North Staffordshire Regiment*
Service No.　　23307　　　　　　　　　Age:　　　　　20
Place of Birth:　Heath, Derbyshire　　　　Home Country:　England
Date of Death:　19/06/1917　　　　　　　Cause of death:　Killed in action
Memorial:　　　Not known
War cemetery:　Ypres Menin Gate
Theatre of war:　Belgium
Next of Kin:　　Frank Joseph & Elizabeth Deacon
Address:　　　10 Warner Street, Hasland Road, Chesterfield, Derbyshire

Cecil was the grandson of Joseph Deacon of Eastbourne Road, Trowbridge. He joined the army on 27 April 1916 and after training he was sent to France on 2 June 1917. At just twenty years of age Cecil was killed in action on Messines Ridge on Tuesday 19 June 1917, fifteen days after he arrived on the continent. He is remembered on the Ypres Menin Gate and has no known grave.

Sergeant John Clifford Drinkwater　　　　　　　*2nd Bn Honourable Artillery Company*
Service No.　　7701　　　　　　　　　　Age:　　　　　21
Place of Birth:　Trowbridge, Wiltshire　　　Home Country:　England
Date of Death:　28/06/1917　　　　　　　Cause of death:　Killed in action
Memorial:　　　Trowbridge
War cemetery:　Mory Abbey Military Cemetery

Theatre of war: France
Next of Kin: Edward James & Harriett Catherine Drinkwater
Address: 33 St George Terrace, Stallard Street, Trowbridge

John, known as Jack, was the second son of Edward and Harriet Drinkwater, Cloth Merchants at Fore Street, Trowbridge. He was an old High School Boy and worked with his father in the family business. In 1915 he obtained the bronze medal and in 1916 the silver medal for woollen and worsted designing and weaving, missing the presentation of the silver medal because of his military service. Jack joined the army on 22 May 1916 and after completing his training he was sent to France on 2nd October 1916. He was promoted in the field attaining the rank of sergeant in May 1917 and was recommended for the Military Medal. The first intimation of Jack's death came in the following letter on 4 July 1917 from a personal friend of his, one Private Gilbert Blanks:

"It is with the most profound grief that I inform you of the death of your son Jack. He was killed by a shell last evening, and death was instantaneous. He was a magnificent character and a splendid companion and gallant soldier. As a man and as a sergeant he was greatly beloved by all who came into contact with him and we in his platoon and in the whole of the Company, mourn his loss deeply. Personally I have lost one of my dearest chums and I cannot express in words how I feel. My pain and grief are intense."

A further letter was received from an army Chaplain explaining that Jack had been killed by a shell at Bapaume, France and the same shell had killed the platoon officer and another sergeant. He also stated that the bodies were recovered and buried well behind the lines. In October 1917 Jack's father Edward wrote to the army asking for Jack's personal property and especially his wrist watch, diary and fountain pen. Unfortunately the items were not recovered and the only items that were returned were some letters, a purse, nail clippers and some coins.

Sergeant Philip Stanleigh Belcher   *26th Field Coy Royal Engineers*
Service No.: 21026   Age: 26
Place of Birth: Trowbridge, Wiltshire   Home Country: England
Date of Death: 10/07/1917   Cause of death: Killed in action
Memorial: Trowbridge

Far left: John Clifford Drinkwater

Left: Philip Stanleigh Belcher

War cemetery: Nieuport Memorial
Theatre of war: Belgium
Next of Kin: George T & Mary A Belcher
Address: 24 Gloucester Road, Trowbridge

Regular soldier Philip was sent to the continent on 17 August 1914, he was listed as missing in action during fierce fighting at the Battle of the Dunes on the coast near Nieuport, Belgium. Philip was later assumed to have been killed on Tuesday 10 July 1917. He is remembered on the Nieuport Memorial and has no known grave.

Private Job Holloway   *1st Bn Wiltshire Regiment*
Service No.   3/561   Age: 39
Place of Birth: Southwick, Wiltshire   Home Country: England
Date of Death: 15/07/1917   Cause of death: Killed in action
Memorial: Trowbridge
War cemetery: Menin Road South Military Cemetery
Theatre of war: Belgium
Next of Kin: John & Annie Holloway
Address: 22 Timbrell Street, Trowbridge, Wiltshire

Job was the sixth son of John and Annie Holloway and joined the Army in 1898, spending 10 years in India. He received his discharge after 12 years service and at the outbreak of hostilities he rejoined the Wiltshires arriving in France on 23 October 1914. In July 1917 the Wiltshires were at Bellewarde to the east of Ypres, Belgium and while they were in the line they were subjected to considerable amount of German shell fire of both high explosives and gas. Job was one of two soldiers killed in action on Sunday 15 July 1917. In July 1918 his family inserted the following memorial in a local paper:

"No one stood beside him to bid him a last farewell
Although his grave is far away he did his duty well
He is gone but not forgotten often his name we recall
But there is nothing left to answer but his photo on the wall
Ever remembered by Father Sisters and Brothers"

Far left: Job Holloway

Left: Frank Snelgrove

Private Frank Snelgrove   *M T Wksp Army Service Corps*

Service No.	M2/201339	Age:	31
Place of Birth:	Sutton Veny, Wiltshire	Home Country:	England
Date of Death:	21/07/1917	Cause of death:	Died
Memorial:	Trowbridge & Sutton Venny		
War cemetery:	Baghdad North Gate War Cemetery		
Theatre of war:	Mesopotamia		
Next of Kin:	Florence Snelgrove (wife) - Charles & Maria Snelgrove (parents)		
Address:	12 Upper Alma Street, Trowbridge		

Frank was a delivery man for a grocery shop and married Florence Emm in 1909. He joined the Army on 7 August 1916 and after seven weeks training was sent to Mesopotamia, without being given the opportunity to say farewell to his wife and child. Florence received many letters from Frank stating he was in good health but he found the climate very hot. At the beginning of August 1917 Florence received the news of the death of her husband in hospital from heat stroke. Before Frank joined the army he taught Florence how to drive a motor vehicle and she took over Frank's job as a delivery driver.

Driver Merville Victor Knee   *South African Service Corps*

Service No.	MT-1705	Age:	25
Place of Birth:	Trowbridge, Wiltshire	Home Country:	South Africa
Date of Death:	22/07/1917	Cause of death:	Died
Memorial:	Trowbridge		
War cemetery:	Thaba Tshwane Old No 1 Military Cemetery		
Theatre of war:	Africa		
Next of Kin:	Henry J & Rosina Knee		
Address:	Rose Rank, Gloucester Road, Trowbridge		

Melville was the second son of Henry and Rosina Knee of Knee's Department Store. He was a well known all round sportsman especially playing football, cricket and lawn tennis. As a footballer with Trowbridge Town Football Club he was a popular player and could play in any position but was remembered for his role as a half back and his tricky tackling and powerful kicking. He left for South Africa soon after the outbreak of war, not knowing how the conflict would escalate. As the threat of the war grew he volunteered for service with the South African army as a motor transport driver. He saw active service in the fever ridden districts of German East Africa and was himself struck down with illness spending five months in hospital in Durban suffering from enteric fever and dysentery. After convalescence he returned to duty and in late July 1917 Melville's parents received news that he had died of pneumonia at Roberts Heights, Pretoria. Henry and Rosina Knee inserted the following memoriam in a local paper:

"Can we forget him? No, we loved him too dearly
For his memory to fade from our lives like a dream
Our lips need not speak, for our hearts mourn sincerely
For grief often dwells where it is seldom seen
God knows how much we miss him
He sees the tears we shed
But whispers: Hush! he only sleeps
For your loved one is not dead
Always remembered by his sorrowing Mother, Father, Sisters and Brother."

Private Herbert Culverhouse   *13th Bn Welsh Regiment*

Service No.	55031	Age:	32
Place of Birth:	North Bradley, Wiltshire	Home Country:	England
Date of Death:	22/07/1917	Cause of death:	Died of wounds
Memorial:	North Bradley & Southwick		
War cemetery:	Bard Cottage Cemetery		
Theatre of war:	Belgium		
Next of Kin:	Evelyn Culverhouse (wife) - Enoch & Mary Culverhouse (parents)		
Address:	2 Frome Road, Southwick		

Herbert, a bricklayer, married Evelyn Gerrish after the outbreak of war in 1914. He joined the army in 1916 initially joining the Wiltshire Regiment but was then transferred to the Welsh Regiment. He was wounded on 21 July 1917 and succumbed to his wounds on Sunday 22 July 1917 north of Ypres, Belgium, most likely when the 13th Welsh were in preparation for the Third Battle of Ypres. In July 1918 Herbert's wife Evelyn inserted the following memoriam in a local paper:

"Twelve months gone how I miss him
Some may think the wound is healed
But little do they know the sorrow
that lies within my heart concealed"

Corporal Harold Joseph Preen   *1st Bn Welsh Guards*

Service No.	1824	Age:	21
Place of Birth:	Pembroke Dock, Glamorgan	Home Country:	England
Date of Death:	23/07/1917	Cause of death:	Killed in action
Memorial:	Trowbridge		
War cemetery:	Berles New Military Cemetery		
Theatre of war:	France		
Next of Kin:	Charles & Mary Preen		
Address:	9 Clarks Place, Ashton Street, Trowbridge		

Harold, known as Joseph, was a milk seller and it is likely he joined the army during 1916. He was killed in action on Monday 23 July 1917 near Arras, France.

Far left: Merville Victor Knee

Left: Harold Joseph Preen

Corporal Albert Thomas Hamblin		*218th Siege Bty RGA*	
Service No.	87620	Age:	36
Place of Birth:	Holcombe, Somerset	Home Country:	England
Date of Death	24/07/1917	Cause of death:	Killed in action
Memorial:	Frome		
War cemetery:	Bus House Cemetery		
Theatre of war:	Belgium		
Next of Kin:	Alice Selina Hamblin (wife) - Edward J. & Louisa Eliza Hamblin (parents)		
Address	2 Bythesea Road, Trowbridge – Keyford Dairy, Frome, Somerset		

Prior to the war Albert was a malsters foreman and in the spring of 1906 he married Alice Selina Hayward at Frome in Somerset. He enlisted in the army under the Derby Scheme on 11 December 1915, was called up on 1 June 1916 and after completing his training he arrived in France on 17 January 1917. He was killed during German shelling in the early hours of the morning of Tuesday 24 July 1917 while engaged in the construction of a gun pit east of Ypres Belgium, in preparation for the Third Battle of Ypres.

Private Harry Vardy		*2/4th TF Bn Wiltshire Regiment*	
Service No.	202000	Age:	31
Place of Birth:	Yetminster, Dorset	Home Country:	England
Date of Death:	27/07/1917	Cause of death:	Died
Memorial:	Trowbridge St James Church Memorial		
War cemetery:	Basra War Cemetery		
Theatre of war:	Mesopotamia		
Next of Kin:	William George & Mildred L Vardy		
Address:	Brister End, Yetminster, Dorset		

Harry was a railway porter and a Wiltshire territorial and at the commencement of hostilities he was sent to India to replace regular British army units. While in India he volunteered for service in Mesopotamia and it is likely he arrived during 1916. He died on Friday 27 July 1917 at one of the base hospitals at Basra in modern day Iraq most likely from illness or disease.

Private William Parsons		*13th Bn Welsh Regiment*	
Service No.	55042	Age:	19
Place of Birth	Trowbridge, Wiltshire	Home Country:	England
Date of Death:	29/07/1917	Cause of death:	Killed in action
Memorial:	Trowbridge		
War cemetery:	Ypres Menin Gate		
Theatre of war:	Belgium		
Next of Kin:	Frank & Laura Parsons		
Address:	4 West Ashton Road, Trowbridge		

Nineteen year old William was employed at Yates & Company wire mattress manufacturers. He volunteered for service with the Wiltshire Regiment in February 1916 and after completing his training was sent to the continent in February 1917. He was then transferred from the Wiltshire Regiment to the 13th Battalion Welsh Regiment. William was killed in action on Sunday 29 July 1917 most likely by German shelling near Ypres, Belgium, while the 13th Welsh were preparing for the Third Battle of Ypres. Frank and Laura Parsons received the following letter from Captain Richards of the 13th Welsh:

"Your son served under me and I thought quite a lot of him. He was always so very cheerful

Far left: William Parsons

Left: Arthur Henry Carr

and will be greatly missed by all the boys in the Regiment."

In August 1918 William's parents inserted the following memoriam in a local paper:

"We were not there to see him die
The one we loved so dear
But we know he died a hero
And died without a fear
He fought for King and Country
He died a hero's death
He's now with our Heavenly Father
God Grant him peace and rest.

10
PASCHENDAELE

31 July 1917 - The Start of the Third Battle of Ypres Known as Paschendaele

Sapper Arthur Henry Carr
Service No. 183127
Place of Birth: Edington, Wiltshire
Date of Death: 31/07/1917
Memorial: Trowbridge
War cemetery: Ypres Menin Gate
Theatre of war: Belgium
Next of Kin: Emily F Carr (wife)
Address: 11 Gladstone Road, Trowbridge

422nd Field Coy Royal Engineers
Age: 40
Home Country: England
Cause of death: Killed in action

Arthur, a carpenter, had married Emily Florence Gifford in 1899 and was well known as a skilled tradesman. He worked on many local buildings including Winsley Sanatorium and County Offices in Trowbridge where he was appointed foreman in charge of the carpenters. In June 1916 he was called up but was placed on reserve and sent home. He was recalled on 26 October 1916 and sent to North Wales. In April 1917 he was sent to France and was transferred to the West Lancashire Engineers. Emily received a letter from Arthur on Tuesday 31 July 1917 stating he was going up the line for the second time after a few days rest. Unfortunately Arthur was killed in action on the same day that his wife had received the letter on the first day of the Third Battle of Ypres. He is remembered on the Ypres Menin Gate and has no known grave. He left a widow and five young children.

Private Arthur William Maill
Service No. 3/9949
Place of Birth: Clyffe Pypard, Wiltshire
Date of Death: 31/07/1917
Memorial: Trowbridge
War cemetery: Ypres Menim Gate
Theatre of war: Belgium
Next of Kin: Albert Herbert & Alice Maill
Address: 5 Kemp's Buildings, Mortimer Street, Trowbridge, Wiltshire

2nd Bn Wiltshire Regiment
Age: 26
Home Country: England
Cause of death: Killed in action

Regular soldier Arthur was the only son of Albert and Alice Maill and had worked in a foundry prior to enlisting in the Wiltshire regiment some months before the outbreak of war. He arrived in France on 23 October 1914 and saw a good deal of action. William was wounded four times and on one occasion he was so seriously injured his father journeyed to France to see him in

Right: Arthur William Maill

Far right: Eli Job Rose

hospital. He was killed in action by a shell on Tuesday 31 July 1917 during the first attacks of the Third Battle of Ypres. He is remembered on the Ypres Menin Gate and has no known grave.

2nd Lieutenant Henry Geoffrey Nelson Tarrant MC *6th Bn Royal Berkshire Regiment*
Service No.   N/A   Age: 22
Place of Birth: Bromley, Kent   Home Country: England
Date of Death: 31/07/1917   Cause of death: Killed in action
Memorial: Not known
War cemetery: Hooge Crater Cemetery
Theatre of war: Belgium
Next of Kin: Walter Tarrant
Address: 73 Croyden Road, Anerley, Kent

Henry known as Geoffrey was the grandson of Mr Hayden of Trowbridge. At the outbreak of war he volunteered for service with the Artists Rifles the 28th London Regiment and was sent to France on 27 March 1915. On 22 November 1916 he received a commission with the Royal Berkshire Regiment and while serving with them he won a Military Cross for bravery. He was killed in action on Tuesday 31 July 1917 near Zillebeke, Belgium when the Royal Berkshire attacked German positions north of the Ypres Menin Road.

Lance Corporal Reginald George Moseley   *1st Bn Wiltshire Regiment*
Service No.   18926   Age: 20
Place of Birth: Stanford Headley, Hampshire   Home Country: England
Date of Death: 01/08/1917   Cause of death: Killed in action
Memorial: West Ashton
War cemetery: Railway Dugouts Burial Ground
Theatre of war: Belgium
Next of Kin: Lewis & Jane Moseley
Address: Edgerley Cottage, Glastonbury, Somerset

Reginald was employed as a servant. He volunteered for service with the Wiltshire Regiment and arrived in France on 9 August 1915. He was one of five men killed in action on Wednesday

1 August 1917 by German shell fire near Bellewarrde Lake east of Ypres, Belgium, as the Wiltshires relieved the 1st Battalion Sherwood Foresters on the Westhoek Ridge.

Corporal Eli Job Rose   *10th Bn Royal West Surrey Regiment*

Service No.	T/23069
Place of Birth:	Trowbridge, Wiltshire
Date of Death:	04/08/1917
Memorial:	Trowbridge
War cemetery:	Ypres Menin Gate
Theatre of war:	Belgium
Next of Kin:	Minnie Adelaide Rose (wife) - William & Ellen Rose (parents)
Address:	10 Allen Road, Trowbridge
Age:	33
Home Country:	England
Cause of death:	Killed in action

Eli worked with his parents in a grocers shop in Bond Street, Trowbridge, he had married Minnie Adelaide Sumption in 1908 and was a keen member of the Upper Studley Baptist Church and Sunday School. Eli voluntarily enlisted in the Army Service Corps and after passing a trade test at Aldershot was promoted to the rank of corporal. In spring 1917 orders were received by Northern Command that all men in the Army Service Corp, irrespective of rank, who were passed fit for general service, were to be transferred to the infantry and Eli was reduced to the rank of a private soldier and sent to the training reserve. He was given leave in June 1917 and visited Trowbridge before being sent to France at the end of the same month. He was transferred to the Border Regiment and sent to the front. On reaching the front line he was again transferred, to the West Surrey Regiment, who were preparing to attack the following morning. He was killed in action during his first time under fire at Langemark, Belgium. Minnie Rose received the following letter from 2nd Lieutenant K. R. Weame of the West Surreys:

"It is with extreme sorrow that I have to inform you that your husband was killed in action whilst doing his duty on the 4th August. His death was instantaneous. Although he had not been with the company long, it was long enough to prove him a good and willing soldier, and his loss is felt by all in the company. I trust that your grief will be lighted by the knowledge of the noble manner of his death."

Eli left a widow and two children and is remembered on the Ypres Menin Gate and has no known grave.

Gunner Edward Howard Pickard MM + Bar   *4th Field Ambulance A.A.M.C.*

Service No.	10083
Place of Birth:	Southwick, Wiltshire
Date of Death:	04/08/1917
Memorial:	Not known
War cemetery:	Godewaersvelde British Cemetery
Theatre of war:	France
Next of Kin:	Thomas & Martha Pickard
Address:	Dilly Brook Farm, North Bradley
Age:	44
Home Country:	England
Cause of death:	Died of wounds

At the outbreak of the Great War Edward was a poultry farmer; he had been a seaman and settled in Australia. He enlisted with the Australian artillery on 15 September 1915 leaving Sydney on 17 December 1915. He was initially sent to Egypt and in June 1916 arrived in Marseilles, France. In December 1916 he transferred to the 4th Australian Field Ambulance and attached to duty with the 10th Australian Artillery. He was awarded the Military Medal for bravery on 20 June 1917 and later was awarded a Bar for another act of bravery. He was

Right: Edward Howard Pickard

Far right: Walter Shrapnell

wounded in action on 28 July 1917 with multiple gun shot wounds and was taken to the 4th Australian Field Ambulance. He was then transferred to No. 41 Casualty Clearing Station where he died on Saturday 4 August 1917. His personal property was returned to his next of kin consisting of letters, pipe cleaner, 2 numerals and 2 badges.

Rifleman Walter Shrapnell   *1/5th Bn London Regiment*

Service No.	315056
Place of Birth:	Trowbridge, Wiltshire
Date of Death:	06/08/1917
Memorial:	Trowbridge
War cemetery:	Ypres Menin Gate
Theatre of war:	Belgium
Next of Kin:	Mabel G M Shrapnell (wife) - Charles & Agnes Kate Shrapnell (parents)
Address:	43 Mountfield Road, Ealing, London - 6 Eastbourne Terrace, Trowbridge

Age: 32
Home Country: England
Cause of death: Killed in action

Walter, a domestic gardener, married Mabel G. M. Jones in 1912 in Kent. It is likely he joined the army in 1916, joining the London Regiment. He was killed in action on Monday 6 August 1917 north of Ypres, Belgium. He is remembered on the Ypres Menin Gate and has no known grave.

Private Charles Edward Robbins   *5th Wiltshire Regiment*

Service No.	25844
Place of Birth:	Trowbridge, Wiltshire
Date of Death:	09/08/1917
Memorial:	Trowbridge
War cemetery:	Baghdad North Gate War Cemetery
Theatre of war:	Mesopotamia
Next of Kin:	Annie L Robbins (wife) - Edward & Emily Robbins (parents)
Address:	4 Ffrwd Terrace Hirwain, Aberdare, Glamorgan - Bradford on Avon

Age: 30
Home Country: Wales
Cause of death: Died

Charles, a baker and pastry cook, had been employed by Elloways and the Cooperative Society and had married Annie L. Box in the spring of 1914. His character was described as cheery and it was difficult to be dull for long in his presence. He joined the army in May 1916 and was sent to Mesopotamia in September 1916. For several months Charles was ill and although his wife wrote every week he had only received seven letters since leaving England and parcels which had been sent on regular intervals were also not received. In mid August 1917 Annie Robbins received an official telegram informing her that Charles had died of dysentery on Thursday 9 August 1917. He left a widow and a two year old little boy.

Private John Abner Oliver   *2nd Bn Devonshire Regiment*

Service No.	26019
Place of Birth:	Newbury, Berkshire
Date of Death:	16/08/1917
Memorial:	Trowbridge
War cemetery:	Tyne Cot Memorial
Theatre of war:	Belgium
Age:	32
Home Country:	England
Cause of death:	Killed in action
Next of Kin:	Elizabeth Oliver (wife) - Frederick & Mary Oliver (parents)
Address:	3 Court Street, Trowbridge - 107 Elm Park Road, Reading, Berkshire

John was a painter in the employ of Mr W. Hussey and a prominent member of the Salvation Army which he had been associated with for 17 years and he had been a member of the Reading Corps prior to moving to Trowbridge. He was an enthusiastic musician and a band sergeant and band master of the young people's section. John married Elizabeth Gordon Mclean at Reading in the spring of 1908 and he joined the army in June 1916. After completing his training he was sent to France in July 1917. He was killed in action on Thursday 16 August 1917 as the 2nd Devons attacked German positions at the east of Ypres, Belgium near the river Habebeck. He is remembered on Tyne Cot Memorial and has no known grave.

Lance Corporal Graham Strange Whiting   *1/8th Bn Royal Warwickshire Regt*

Service No.	306642
Place of Birth:	Trowbridge, Wiltshire
Date of Death:	17/08/1917
Memorial:	Trowbridge
War cemetery:	Tyne Cot Memorial
Theatre of war:	Belgium
Age:	31
Home Country:	England
Cause of death:	Killed in action

Far left: John Abner Oliver

Left: Graham Strange Whiting

Next of Kin: Abraham & Ruth Whiting
Address: 25 Gloucester Road, Trowbridge

Graham was a livery stable coachman. It is likely he joined the army in 1916 and was sent to France in 1917. He was posted as missing in action on Friday 17 August 1917 at St. Julian, north east of Ypres, Belgium. Later it was assumed Graham had died on the same day. He is remembered on Tyne Cot Memorial and has no known grave.

Signaller Alfred James Butcher   *7th Bn British Columbia Regiment*
Service No. 790792   Age: 20
Place of Birth:, Ontario   Home Country: Canada
Date of Death: 18/08/1917   Cause of death: Died of wounds
Memorial: Not Known
War cemetery: Longuenesse St.Omer Souvenir Cemetery
Theatre of war: France
Next of Kin: Mark & Lillie Butcher
Address: 403 9th Street, New Westminster, British Columbia

Alfred, a student, was the grandson of Alfred & Elizabeth Butcher of North Bradley and enlisted with the Canadian army on 6 March 1916. He was wounded with gunshot wounds, most likely in the fighting at Vimy Ridge, Belgium and was evacuated to a hospital at St.Omer, France where he died of his wounds on Saturday 18 August 1917.

Lance Coporal William Thomas Dunlop   *1/8th Bn Royal Warwickshire Regt*
Service No. 306604   Age: 26
Place of Birth: Trowbridge, Wiltshire   Home Country: England
Date of Death: 27/08/1917   Cause of death: Killed in action
Memorial: Trowbridge
War cemetery: Poelcapelle British Cemetery
Theatre of war: Belgium
Next of Kin: Annie Dunlop (wife) - Thomas & Agnes Dunlop (parents)
Address: 18 St Margaret Street, Bradford on Avon - 87 Park Street, Trowbridge

Right: William Thomas Dunlop

Far right: Frank Reynolds

William, known as Billy, was a travelling draper and he married Annie Mason in October 1915 joining the army two months later. He was called up on 16 March 1916 and after completing his training he was sent to France on 7 September 1916. He was killed in action on Monday 27 August 1917 at St. Julian, Belgium. In August 1918 Annie Dunlop inserted the following memoriam in a local paper:

"Sleep on, dear Billy, in a far off land
In a grave we will never see
But as long as life and memory last
I will remember thee
From his wife"

Private Frank Reynolds   *1/8th Bn Royal Warwickshire Regt*
Service No.: 306687
Age: 39
Place of Birth: Trowbridge, Wiltshire
Home Country: England
Date of Death: 27/08/1917
Cause of death: Killed in action
Memorial: Trowbridge
War cemetery: Tyne Cot Memorial
Theatre of war: Belgium
Next of Kin: Eli & Hannah Reynolds
Address: 30 Bradford Road, Trowbridge

Frank was employed by Sirdar Rubber Mills in Bradford on Avon prior to the war and joined the army in March 1916. After completing his training he was sent to France in June 1916 serving with the Warwickshire Regiment. On 26 August 1917 Hannah Reynolds received a letter from Frank explaining that he expected to come home on leave very soon. Early in September Hannah received official notification from the record office in Warwick that her son had been killed in action on Monday 27 August 1917. Frank was killed at St.Juliaan, Belgium and is remembered on the Tyne Cot Memorial. He has no known grave.

Private William Henry Gay   *2nd/3rd Field Amb RAMC Corps*
Service No.: 497418
Age: 21
Place of Birth: Staverton, Wiltshire
Home Country: England
Date of Death: 29/08/1917
Cause of death: Killed in action
Memorial: Staverton & Nestle Anglo Swiss Milk Company Roll of Honour
War cemetery: Divisional Collecting Post Cemetery and Extension
Theatre of war: Belgium
Next of Kin: Hubert John & Alice Gay
Address: Factory Lodge, Staverton, Wiltshire

William was a butter maker at the Nestle Anglo Swiss Milk Company factory at Staverton. He volunteered for service with the Royal Army Medical Corps on 21 April 1915 and arrived in France on 25 January 1917. He was killed in action on Wednesday 29 August 1917. His personal possessions that were returned to his parents consisted of a 9 carat gold signet ring (bent), small silver watch (damaged) in metal case, silver cigarette case (damaged), purse – wallet one and three quarters francs – 25 centimes, photos and cards.

Driver George Alford   *2nd Field Sqdn Royal Engineers*
Service No.: 15171
Age: 31
Place of Birth: Melksham, Wiltshire
Home Country: England
Date of Death: 28/08/1917
Cause of death: Died

Right: George Alford

Far Right: Francis Henry Blower

Memorial:	Trowbridge
War cemetery:	Trowbridge Cemetery
Theatre of war:	Home
Next of Kin:	William & Hannah Alford
Address:	19 Shails Lane, Trowbridge

George originally enlisted in the army on 23 June 1906 and on his completion of his service in 1908 he was transferred to the reserve and took employment in the collieries of South Wales. At the outbreak of war he was called up and arrived in France on 17 August 1914, where he served until 17 July 1915 when he was sent back to England. He was discharged from the army on 15 June 1916 suffering from deafness which at his medical board was not attributed to military service. He died most likely of illness in August 1917 and was buried in Trowbridge Cemetery. George is not remembered by the Commonwealth War Grave Commission.

Sapper Francis Henry Blower *227th Field Coy Royal Engineers*

Service No.	19781		Age:	26
Place of Birth:	Bradford on Avon, Wiltshire		Home Country:	England
Date of Death:	20/09/1917		Cause of death:	Killed in action
Memorial:	Trowbridge			
War cemetery:	Tyne Cot Memorial			
Theatre of war:	Belgium			
Next of Kin:	Henry & Anne Blower			
Address:	2 Ansties's Court, Mortimer Street, Trowbridge			

Regular soldier Francis was the only son of Henry and Annie Blower and lived with his grandmother in Trowbridge. He had served several years in India and in January 1917 he was invalided home and spent 6 months at the depot in Chatham before being sent to France in July 1917. While on active service he sent a letter home explaining whilst at work his officer and two men were killed beside him and two others were severely wounded, but he had escaped unhurt. In early October 1917 Francis's grandmother received the following letter from Lieutenant McRae of the Royal engineers dated 24 September:

"It is with deep regret that I have to advise you that your grandson was killed in action on the

morning of the attack on the 20 September. I was his section officer, and he was one of the party to accompany me in a reconnaissance of our new front line. We were heavily shelled and took refuge in some dugouts. Shortly afterwards a shell burst in the entrance of the dug out, and he was badly wounded. We did all we could for him, but he died almost immediately. As it was impossible to do anything else we buried him on the battlefield. No words of mine can comfort you in your great sorrow, but no man can die better than to die for his country facing the foe. I only had your son a short time with me, but I invariably found him brave, cheerful and willing to do his duty whenever the call came. Please accept from myself and all the officers and men of this Company our heartfelt sympathy."*

Francis is remembered on the Tyne Cot Memorial and has no known grave.

Private William Arthur Wheeler   *13th Bn Durham Light Infantry*
Service No.: 203433
Age: 24
Place of Birth: Trowbridge, Wiltshire
Home Country: England
Date of Death: 20/09/1917
Cause of death: Killed in action
Memorial: Devizes & Potterne
War cemetery: Tyne Cot Memorial
Theatre of war: Belgium
Next of Kin: Emily E D Wheeler (wife) - Arthur J & Mary A Wheeler (parents)
Address: Glinton, The Down, Trowbridge - Longcroft Road Devizes.

William was a house painter and employed by F. Walters of New Park Street, Devizes. He married Emily E D Sheppard early in 1915 prior to joining the army and after completing his training he was sent to France in 1916. In mid October 1917 Emily Wheeler received the following letter from W.J. Acres, Williams platoon officer:

"It is with the greatest sorrow that I notify you that your husband was killed in action on 20 September 1917. As his platoon officer, I can speak of him as a most willing and cheerful soldier and he is mourned amongst his many comrades. I am very pleased to be able to inform you that he was buried and a cross erected by his comrades, which will be carefully looked after."

William was killed in action during fighting at Menin Road, near Bellewarde east of Ypres, Belgium on Thursday 20 September 1917. His grave was not looked after but lost during subsequent fighting, he is remembered on the Tyne Cot Memorial.

Corporal Albert Victor Lloyd   *124th Coy Machine Gun Corps*
Service No.: 27677
Age: 21
Place of Birth: Trowbridge, Wiltshire
Home Country: England
Date of Death: 20/09/1917
Cause of death: Killed in action
Memorial: Frome
War cemetery: Tyne Cot Memorial
Theatre of war: Belgium
Next of Kin: Henry & Mary Ann Lloyd
Address: 32 Catherine Street, Frome, Somerset

Albert, known as Bertie, was a letter press printer and originally enlisted with the Somerset Light Infantry and later transferred to the Machine Gun Corps. He was killed in action during fighting on the Menin Road near Bellewarde east of Ypres, Belgium on Thursday 20 September 1917. He is remembered on the Tyne Cot Memorial and has no known grave.

Sergeant Arthur Henry Mead MID *3rd Bn Wiltshire Regiment*
Service No.   5928   Age: 33
Place of Birth: Trowbridge, Wiltshire   Home Country: England
Date of Death: 24/09/1917   Cause of death: Accident
Memorial: Trowbridge
War cemetery: Melcombe Regis Cemetery
Theatre of war: Home
Next of Kin: Beatrice Eva Mead (wife) - George & Eliza Mead (parents)
Address: 6 Barnett's Court, Mortimer Street, Trowbridge

Arthur had originally joined the militia on 25 February 1902 and would have received regular military training. He was employed as a steam roller driver and in 1906 married Beatrice Eva Dunn. As a reservist he was called to the colours at the outbreak of the Great War arriving in France on 12 September 1914 and serving with the 1st Battalion Wiltshire Regiment. He was mentioned in Sir John French's dispatches in 1915 for his gallant and distinguished service in the field, for carrying a message to the firing line after German forces had broken through the British lines. He was wounded at Festubert, France in June 1915 and was wounded again in December 1915 at Hooge, Belgium and evacuated to England. On his recovery he was transferred to the 3rd Battalion Wiltshire Regiment at Weymouth as a First Class instructor. At 11am on Monday 24 September 1917 the Wiltshires were demonstrating a bombing (hand grenade) attack at the training camp in Weymouth to General Sclater when a bomb exploded mortally wounding Arthur. Sergeant Thomas Wildman who had also been taking part in the demonstration and was 25 to 30 yards away, disposed of his last bomb and heard Arthur calling to him. When he arrived on the scene he could see Arthur had multiple injuries including fractures to both legs. Arthur was conscious and gasped instantaneous bursts. Lieutenant Truman explained that the bombs they were using were lit with a port light which was like those used for fire works. After setting the fuse of the bomb alight the bomb was thrown, which then exploded in four and a half seconds. He doubted the cause was an instantaneous burst even though many bombs were known to have faulty fuses. Lieutenant Truman believed that the port light had dropped molten drops on to several bombs at Arthur's feet causing them to explode and his injuries were a testament to these facts. Arthur was taken to hospital where he died soon after. Arthur was buried with full military honours at Weymouth with the Wiltshires band leading the cortege. Arthur's coffin was borne on a gun carriage drawn by men of the Wiltshires and followed by nearly 200 soldiers, many of whom were carrying wreaths and crosses. Arthur left a widow and four young children.

Private Howard Stephen Rees *2nd Bn Wiltshire Regiment*
Service No.   23668   Age: 22
Place of Birth: Trowbridge, Wiltshire   Home Country: England
Date of Death: 26/09/1917   Cause of death: Died of wounds
Memorial: Trowbridge
War cemetery: Trowbridge Cemetery
Theatre of war: Home
Next of Kin: Stephen & Annie Rees
Address: 3 Nursery Villas, Bemerton, Wiltshire

Howard volunteered for service on 7 September 1914 but was discharged on 26 September being described as quite unfit for a soldier with very poor physique and a speech impediment. However he was determined to join the army and registered under the Derby Scheme and was called up in February 1916. He left England for France on 22 June 1916 and was wounded in October 1916. He then took part in engagements at Messines on 9 April 1917 and was again

Howard Stephen Rees and his grave in Trowbridge Cemetery

wounded at Arras on 23 April 1917 and evacuated to England. He succumbed to his wounds on Wednesday 26 September 1917 at Bath War Hospital.

Corporal Fred Hudd   *332nd Siege Bty RGA*
Service No.   125696
Place of Birth: Hilperton, Wiltshire
Date of Death: 28/09/1917
Memorial: St. Andrews Church & Chippenham
War cemetery: Dozinghem Military Cemetery
Theatre of war: Belgium
Next of Kin: Ada Hudd (wife) - Samuel & Emily Hudd (parents)
Address: 20 Athelstan Road, Clive Vale, Hastings – Chippenham

Age: 34
Home Country: England
Cause of death: Died of wounds

Fred, a solicitor's clerk, was the eldest son of Samuel and Emily Hudd of Foghamshire Nursery, Chippenham. In January 1896 at the opening of Chippenham Secondary School Fred was no.1 on the secondary school register and on leaving school was employed as a clerk with Wood and Audrey Solicitors and was also a teacher at the Wesleyan Sunday School in the Causeway Chippenham. In 1901 he became a clerk with Gaby Stapleton and Smith of Bexhill and in 1906 he married Ada Ward in Bromley, Kent. He was badly wounded on 14 September 1917 and succumbed to his wounds at a hospital at Dozinghem, Belgium on Friday 28 September 1917. He left a widow and two small children.

Private Albert John Lampy Batten   *1/4th TF Bn Dorsetshire Regiment*
Service No.   202935
Place of Birth: Holt, Wiltshire
Date of Death: 28/09/1917
Memorial: Holt & Trowbridge St. James Church Memorial
War cemetery: Basra Memorial
Theatre of war: Mesopotamia
Next of Kin: Edward & Emily Batten
Address: Holt, Wiltshire

Age: 28
Home Country: England
Cause of death: Killed in action

Albert was employed at the Avon Rubber works in Melksham he was a pupil of Holt

Congregational School and was a valued player of Holt Football Club. He joined the 2/4th Battalion Wiltshire Regiment in September 1914 and after completing his training was sent to India on 10 December 1914. He remained on garrison duties for nearly two yeas and in September 1916 a call was made for volunteers to serve in Mesopotamia and Albert was transferred to the 1/4th Battalion Dorset Regiment. He took part in the battles that proceeded the capture of Baghdad in conflict against Turkish Forces. He was killed in action on Friday 28 September 1917 at the fighting at Ramadi Ridge in modern day Iraq, the day before his 29th birthday. Albert is remembered on the Basra Memorial and has no known grave.

Corporal Frederick Dobson Beaven *2/6th Bn Sherwood Foresters*
Service No.: 241775
Place of Birth: Trowbridge, Wiltshire
Date of Death: 28/09/1917
Memorial: Not known
War cemetery: Tyne Cot Cemetery
Theatre of war: Belgium
Next of Kin: Frederick William & Catherine Beaven
Address: Priestcliffe, Taddington, Buxton, Derbyshire
Age: 23
Home Country: England
Cause of death: Killed in action

Frederick, known as Fred, was the eldest son of teachers Frederick and Catherine Beaven. It is likely he joined the army in 1916 and was sent to the continent in 1917. He was killed in action on Friday 28 September 1917 during a British attack on the Gravenstafel Road, near Paschendaele, Belgium.

Private Walter Stanley Jones *8th Bn Yorkshire Light Infantry*
Service No.: 37597
Place of Birth: Westbury, Wiltshire
Date of Death: 29/09/1917
Memorial: Southwick
War cemetery: Tyne Cot Memorial
Theatre of war: Belgium
Next of Kin: Frank & Jane Jones
Address: Church Street, Southwick
Age: 25
Home Country: England
Cause of death: Killed in action

Right: Albert John Lampy Batten

Far right: Walter Stanley Jones

Prior to the Great War Walter was employed in the gardens at Wingfield House. He joined the army in September 1916 and after completing his training went to France in August 1917 with the Suffolk Regiment. Shortly after his arrival he was transferred to the King's Own Yorkshire Light Infantry and was sent to Belgium. He was killed in action on Saturday 29 September 1917 in trenches near Polygon Wood, East of Ypres Belgium, during a very heavy German bombardment. Walter's platoon sergeant wrote to Frank and Jane Jones explaining that during the bombardment Walter was struck by a piece of shell just above the heart and he passed away a few minutes afterwards. He was one of six men to be killed by the same shell. The Sergeant wrote:

"I hope it will be of some comfort and help to console you to know that he was a very brave lad, and gave his life fighting for his life for the dear ones at home, never failing to do his duty, no matter how hard or great the risk always ready and willing to do his best. I cannot express my own personal loss in so brave and gallant a lad, for he was dearly loved by one and all in the platoon."

Walter's Commanding Officer also wrote the following to Frank and Jane Jones:

"It is with great sorrow to me to have to inform you of the death of Private W. S. Jones, which happened last night, caused by a shell just one hour before we were relieved from the trenches. All of us felt the loss very much, but of course it will be a greater blow to you, and I hope you may find some consolation in the fact that he fell doing his duty. Trust in the Almighty and you will find some solace to heal the wound this great loss has caused, and out of the darkness may you see some light believing that God's will be done."

Walter is remembered on the Tyne Cot Memorial and has no known grave

Private Charles Edward Marmont   *7th Bn Gloucestershire Regiment*
Service No.   23413   Age: 37
Place of Birth: Minchinhampton, Gloucestershire   Home Country: England
Date of Death: 02/10/1917   Cause of death: Killed in action
Memorial: Trowbridge
War cemetery: Basra Memorial
Theatre of war: Mesopotamia
Next of Kin: Maude Marmont (wife) - Albert J & Susanah Marmont (parents)
Address: Brinscombe, Gloucestershire - 14 Lower Alma Street, Trowbridge

Charles a cloth miller had married Maude White in 1899, he volunteered for service with the Gloucestershire Regiment and after training he was set to Gallipoli where he arrived on the 14 November 1915. He was killed in action during fighting in Mesopotamia in modern Iraq. He has no known grave and is remembered on the Basra Memorial.

Private George Henry Fry   *9th Bn Yorkshire Light Infantry*
Service No.   44026   Age: 31
Place of Birth: Broughton Gifford, Wiltshire   Home Country: England
Date of Death: 04/10/1917   Cause of death: Killed in action
Memorial: Trowbridge & Broughton Gifford
War cemetery: Hooge Crater Cemetery
Theatre of war: Belgium
Next of Kin: Ellen Louisa Fry (wife) - Francis & Mary Fry (parents)
Address: 58 Dursley Road, Trowbridge - Broughton Gifford

George was employed by the Trowbridge Cooperative Society as a van man and he married Ellen Louisa Stillman at the start of the year in 1910. At the outbreak of the Great War he joined the Royal Field Artillery but was later transferred to the King's Own Yorkshire Light Infantry. He arrived in France in December 1916 and was killed in action near Polygon Wood, Belgium on Thursday 4 October 1917. George's Commanding Officer wrote to Ellen Fry speaking in high terms of her husband's abilities as a soldier and added he was reverently buried behind the lines.

Private Henry Fergus Willis — *113th Bn Labour Corps*
Service No.   67665
Place of Birth: Trowbridge, Wiltshire
Date of Death: 04/10/1917
Memorial: Trowbridge
War cemetery: Abbeville Communal Cemetery Extension
Theatre of war: France
Next of Kin: Gideon & Mary J Willis
Address: 18 Bond Street, Trowbridge
Age: 31
Home Country: England
Cause of death: Died

Henry was the manager of a Lewis Warner Boot Shop and was the younger son of Gideon and Mary Willis. He joined the Queens Regiment in June 1916, was sent to France in February 1917 and was then transferred to the Labour Corps. He died of sickness on Thursday 4 October 1917 at the Third Australian General Hospital. Chaplain Harris wrote the following to Henry's mother:

"It is with feelings of deep sympathy that I write concerning the death of your son, which took place on the 4th of this month. When he came in he was quite conscious, but not suffering much, and although he was put on the dangerously ill list, one always has a hope of recovery. He got no better, however, and was quite resigned at the last, trusting in the loving mercy of the Almighty, and passed quietly away. He sent his fondest love to you and wished that you would not grieve over much, for he was going to the rest where we shall all go. In spite of your grief may you feel proud of having been the mother of a boy when his country called did not shirk, but answered it, even to the shedding of his life blood. He is not altogether lost, not when we believe in the Resurrection of the Life Everlasting, and we look forward to that happy time

Right: Henry Fergus Willis

Far right: Herbert Samuel Young

when we shall join our loved ones again. His body was laid to rest in the Abbeville Military Cemetery, where those of so many of his fellow soldiers lie, waiting the call of the last trumpet. That He who is the Light of the world, and who knows all our cares and sorrows, may give you strength and comfort and light in your darkness of grief, is the earnest prayer."

Private Herbert Samuel Young *1st Bn Devonshire Regiment*
Service No.   205152   Age: 33
Place of Birth: Trowbridge, Wiltshire   Home Country: England
Date of Death: 04/10/1917   Cause of death: Killed in action
Memorial: Trowbridge
War cemetery: Tyne Cot Memorial
Theatre of war: Belgium
Next of Kin: Florence Young (wife) – Samuel & Sarah Young (parents)
Address: 50 Islington, Trowbridge - 36 Islington, Trowbridge

At the start of the war Herbert had a grocers business at the Down, Trowbridge and in summer of 1915 he married Florence Bloodworth and took employment with Haden and son's. He was conscripted into the army in January 1917 and after training was sent to the continent to serve with the Devonshire Regiment. He was posted as missing on Thursday 4 October 1917 when the Devons attacked over boggy waterlogged ground near Polder Hoek Chateau east of Ypres, Belgium. Florence received the following letter from an army chaplain:

"I am afraid your husband was killed in the battle a week ago today; at least his name appears in the provisional list of casualties, although that is always liable to correction. It is more sad, as he joined us so recently. I am a Wesleyan chaplain to the brigade, and made his acquaintance at services held when we were out for a rest. I pray that God our Father may comfort you in your great trouble."

Florence Young inserted the following memoriam in a local paper:

"We did not know the pain he bore
We did not see him die
We only know he passed away
And never said goodbye
From his sorrowing wife and friends"

Herbert is remembered on the Tyne Cot Memorial and has no known grave.

Lance Corporal Joseph Robert Pearce *1/4th Bn Dorsetshire Regiment*
Service No.   202959   Age: 20
Place of Birth: Bishops Cannings, Wiltshire   Home Country: England
Date of Death: 05/10/1917   Cause of death: Died of wounds
Memorial: Bishops Cannings & Trowbridge St James Church Memorial
War cemetery: Baghdad North Gate War Cemetery
Theatre of war: Mesopotamia
Next of Kin: Henry Robert Pearce
Address: Coate, Wiltshire

Twenty year old Joseph was a farm labourer and a Wiltshire Territorial. He was sent to India at the commencement of hostilities and while there volunteered for service in Mesopotamia with the Dorset Regiment. He died of wounds at a military hospital in Baghdad on Friday 5 October 1917.

Private John Wheeler   *8th Bn Somerset Light Infantry*

Service No.	17771	Age:	19
Place of Birth:	Witham Friary, Somerset	Home Country:	England
Date of Death:	11/10/1917	Cause of death:	Died of wounds
Memorial:	Witham Friary		
War cemetery:	Outterstreene Communal Cemetery Extension Bailleul		
Theatre of war:	France		
Next of Kin:	Henry W & Annie Wheeler		
Address:	Witham Friary, Somerset		

Under age soldier John, known as Jack, was a farm labourer and lived in Trowbridge prior to joining the army. He volunteered for service at seventeen years of age with the Somerset Light Infantry and after completing his training he arrived in France on 4 October 1915. He was wounded most likely in fighting in Belgium and died of his wounds at a casualty clearing station at Outterstreene on Thursday 11 October 1917.

Bombardier Ernest Prevett Godden   *40th Bde Royal Field Artillery*

Service No.	68976	Age:	20
Place of Birth:	Trowbridge, Wiltshire	Home Country:	England
Date of Death:	12/10/1917	Cause of death:	Killed in action
Memorial:	Not known		
War cemetery:	Tyne Cot Memorial		
Theatre of war:	Belgium		
Next of Kin:	Lilian Jane Vyle		
Address:	106 Crewe Street, Derby		

Under age regular soldier Ernest arrived in France on 19 August 1914 at 17 years of age. Prior to joining the army he was a butcher's errand boy. He was killed in action during the Third Battle of Ypres, Belgium. He is remembered on the Tyne Cot Memorial and has no known grave.

Private Arthur Stanley Farr   *37th Bn Training Reserve*

Service No.	TR8/2024	Age:	18
Place of Birth:	Trowbridge, Wiltshire	Home Country:	England
Date of Death:	15/10/1917	Cause of death:	Died
Memorial:	Trowbridge		
War cemetery:	Trowbridge Cemetery		
Theatre of war:	Home		
Next of Kin:	Arthur J & Lily Farr		
Address:	6 Islington, Trowbridge		

Eighteen year old Arthur, known as Stanley, was employed at Wilts Insurance Committee's office prior to being called up in mid 1917 and was training at Sutton Veny. His father, also Arthur, had been fighting with the Wiltshires for over two years and having been granted leave was hoping he could meet his son and sent a letter enquiring if Stanley could also get leave from the army. Stanley wrote to his father explaining that he was being sent to Larkhill and that he had applied for leave and expected to come home when they had settled into his new quarters. However on the afternoon of Monday 15 October 1915 Arthur senior received a telegram stating that their son was dead. Soon after a letter arrived from Stanley which had been sent on Sunday 14 October and stated he hoped to be home the following day. Arthur left Trowbridge for Larkhill hoping a mistake had been made. He found his son had reported

Far left: Arthur Stanley Farr

Left: Thomas Percival Carpenter

sick at 9am on Monday 15 October and had been taken to hospital at 12.20pm where he died some 20 minutes later of double pneumonia. In October 1918 his parents inserted the following memoriam in a local paper:

"One year has passed since that day
When one we loved was called away
His loving ways his smiling face
No one can fill that vacant place
Sweet be your rest dear Stanley
Tis sweet to breathe your name
In life we loved you dearly
In death we do the same
Sadly missed by his sorrowing Father, Mother, Brothers and Sister"

Private Thomas Percival Carpenter		*1/4th Bn Dorsetshire Regiment*	
Service No.	202991	Age:	19
Place of Birth:	Melksham, Wiltshire	Home Country:	England
Date of Death:	21/10/1917	Cause of death:	Died of wounds
Memorial:	Trowbridge		
War cemetery:	Baghdad North Gate War Cemetery		
Theatre of war:	Mesopotamia		
Next of Kin:	Alfred & Emily Carpenter		
Address:	Trowbridge		

Under age soldier Thomas had joined the Wiltshire Territorials on 24 August 1914 and had left England for India in March 1916. He volunteered for service in Mesopotamia with the Dorsets and arrived there in October 1916. He was wounded in action on 28 September 1917 at Tel el Rayan near Baghdad in modern day Iraq and died of his wounds on Sunday 21 October 1917 at a military Hospital at Baghdad. His brother Joseph Edward Carpenter was to die in 1918.

Sapper Lewis George Elling		*21st Light Railway Op.Coy R.E.*	
Service No.	256313	Age:	28
Place of Birth:	Warminster, Wiltshire	Home Country:	England

Date of Death:	21/10/1917
Memorial:	Not known
War cemetery:	Reninghelst New Military Cemetery
Theatre of war:	Belgium
Next of Kin:	Louisa Elling (wife) - Alice Elling (parent)
Address:	20 Hilperton Road, Trowbridge - Codford St. Mary

Cause of death: Killed in action

Lewis, a carpenter and joiner, originally joined the army on 9 March 1909, leaving on 1 January 1913 and while serving in the army he married Louisa Seviour in 1911. It is likely he rejoined the army at the beginning of hostilities, and was called to the colours and sent to the continent in March 1917 with the 21st Light Railway Operating Company. He was killed in action most likely by German shell fire south west of Ypres Belgium on Sunday 21 October 1917.

Gunner Charles Edward Westall — *103rd Bde Royal Field Artillery*

Service No.	198546	Age:	31
Place of Birth:	Aldbourne, Wiltshire	Home Country:	England
Date of Death:	22/10/1917	Cause of death:	Killed in action
Memorial:	Trowbridge		
War cemetery:	La Clytte Military Cemetery		
Theatre of war:	Belgium		
Next of Kin:	Rosina Westall (wife) - Jacob & Hannah Westall (parents)		
Address:	11 York Buildings, Timbrell Street, Trowbridge - Aldbourne, Wiltshire		

Charles, a labourer, originally volunteered for service with the Wiltshire Regiment on 21 August 1914 but was discharged on 22 September 1914 being declared unfit for service. He was then conscripted into the Royal Engineers in 1916 and married Rosina Taylor in January 1917 being transferred to the Artillery before being sent to France in May 1917. In mid November 1917 Rosina received a letter from an army chaplain Rev. A.W. Chute which stated Charles had been killed in action on Monday 22 October 1917 and went on to explain:

"He was serving with the guns. The position was a dangerous spot as it was always liable to hostile shelling. On this occasion your husband was resting in a dugout with several of his companions when a shell burst on the very spot, and breaking through into the place where they were, he and three others were killed. I think it will be of some relief to know that his death was probably quite instantaneous, so that he would have been saved any suffering. I can only say how sorry I am to have to write you this sad news. Your husband had been such a short time with us and it seems hard that he should have been taken like this, but you will feel satisfaction, perhaps, in some small degree in knowing that he fell while doing his duty, and while serving the cause he knew to be right, and if it was to be, he could not have died more nobly. We held his funeral, which I conducted myself in a cemetery some seven miles behind the firing line. It is a quiet little spot and a cross will be placed to mark the grave. I think it will help you to bear this blow if you remember after all, though he is parted from you for a time he is not really dead, but has only passed on into a new and fuller life the other side of the grave."

Private Herbert John Owen — *2nd Bn Gloucestershire Regiment*

Service No.	Not known	Age:	24
Place of Birth:	Trowbridge, Wiltshire	Home Country:	Wales
Date of Death:	27/10/1917	Cause of death:	Died of wounds
Memorial:	Trowbridge		
War cemetery:	Not known		

Far left: Charles Edward Westall

Left: Harry Loxley

Theatre of war: Not Known
Next of Kin: Frank Henry & Fances A Owen
Address:, CWM, Monmonthshire

Herbert was a hewer at a colliery and he joined the forces and saw service in France and Salonika. He died on Saturday 27 October 1917 and is listed on the Trowbridge War Memorial and in the Roll of Honour. He is not remembered by the Commonwealth War grave Commission.

31 OCTOBER 1917 - BRITISH OCCUPY BEERSHEBA, MESOPOTAMIA

Private Reginald Arthur Stanley Stockting *256th Machine Gun Corps*
Service No. 113274 Age: 27
Place of Birth: Frome, Somerset Home Country: England
Date of Death: 01/11/1917 Cause of death: Died
Memorial: Hilperton Church Memorial & St. John's Church, Frome
War cemetery: Basra War Cemetery
Theatre of war: Mesopotamia
Next of Kin: Charles James & Ellen Stockting
Address: High Street, Hilperton

Reginald was a draper. He volunteered for service in 1915 with the Somerset Light Infantry and was sent to France in 1916. After three months service in Belgium he was evacuated to England with trench foot and after his recovery was sent to India. His family were informed he died of malarial fever on Thursday 1 November 1917 at Dingpore. The Commonwealth War Graves Commission states he is buried at Basra War Cemetery in modern day Iraq.

Private Harry Loxley *1/4th TF Bn Wiltshire Regiment*
Service No. 200313 Age: 33
Place of Birth: Trowbridge, Wiltshire Home Country: England

Date of Death: 02/11/1917	Cause of death: Killed in action
Memorial: Trowbridge	
War cemetery: Gaza War Cemetery	
Theatre of war: Egypt	
Next of Kin: Edith E Loxley (wife) - Louisa Marshman (parent)	
Address: 109 Newtown, Trowbridge	

Harry was employed by Herbert Harris as a plasterer and was also a Wiltshire Territorial. After the commencement of hostilities he was sent to India for garrison duties. In September 1917 the 1/4th Battalion Wiltshire Regiment were sent to Egypt and then onto to Palestine to fight the Turkish forces. Harry was killed in action by Turkish shell fire most likely as he slept on Friday 2 November 1917 in trenches at Lees Hill near Gaza.

Private Joseph Charles Pickard *1/4th TF Bn Wiltshire Regiment*

Service No.	200623	Age:	25
Place of Birth:	Trowbridge, Wiltshire	Home Country:	England
Date of Death:	02/11/1917	Cause of death:	Killed in action
Memorial:	Trowbridge		
War cemetery:	Gaza War Cemetery		
Theatre of war:	Egypt		
Next of Kin:	Job & Mary A Pickard		
Address:	Vine Cottage, Wingfield, Wiltshire		

Joseph known as Joe who was employed by Palmer and Mackay's woollen mills, had joined the Wiltshire Territorials and was at the summer camp when the war broke out. He was a keen village cricket and Football player. He was sent to India for garrison duties and in September 1917 the 1/4th Battalion Wiltshire Regiment were sent to Egypt and then onto to Palestine to fight the Turkish forces. Joe was killed in action by Turkish shell fire on Friday 2 November 1917 in trenches at Lees Hill near Gaza. Job and Mary Pickard received the following letter from Lieutenant D. Sainsbury:

"It is my very painful duty to have to write to inform you of the death of your son, on the night of November 1 – 2. He was killed by shell fire while our trenches were being heavily bombarded by the enemy, but it may be of some consolation to know that he suffered no pain as he was asleep at the time of his death and it was instantaneous. We buried him in the morning in a cemetery just in the rear of our lines. I should like to offer my most heartfelt sympathy in the sorrow which this news will cause you. As your son's platoon officer I have come into contact with him very much lately, and a more willing and reliable fellow it would be hard to find. His loss is deeply felt through the whole platoon and company and we all extend to you our sympathy in your great trouble."

Job and Mary also received a letter from Captain Pye-Smith stating:

"I had known Joe for a long time and he was always a good soldier who so far from giving any trouble, few of our fellows do that, he was most helpful on all occasions."

Joe's brother Thomas William was killed on 7 November while fighting in the same area. The brothers are buried in Gaza War Cemetery.

6 NOVEMBER 1917 - PASSENDAELE WAS CAPTURED BRINGING TO AN END THE THIRD BATTLE OF YPRES, BELGIUM

Far left: Joseph Charles Pickard

Left: John Henry Mackett

Private Charles James Cockerell   *1st Bn Duke of Cornwall's Light Inf.*
Service No. 29458
Place of Birth: Trowbridge, Wiltshire
Date of Death: 06/11/1917
Memorial: Not known
War cemetery: Tyne Cot Memorial
Theatre of war: Belgium
Next of Kin: George Charles & Sarah Ann Cockerell
Address: 7 West Quay, Bridgewater, Somerset
Age: 24
Home Country: England
Cause of death: Killed in action

Charles was a cabinet maker and a member of the 2/1st Somerset Yeomanry. He was called up and transferred to the Duke of Cornwalls Light Infantry. He was killed in action on Tuesday 6 November 1917 during an attack through the sticky Belgium mud at Polder Hoek Chateau at the Second Battle of Paschendaele. He is remembered on the Tyne Cot Memorial and has no known grave.

7 NOVEMBER 1917 - BRITISH CAPTURE GAZA, PALESTINE

Sergeant John Henry Mackett   *1/4th TF Bn Wiltshire Regiment*
Service No. 200216
Place of Birth: Alverstoke, Hampshire
Date of Death: 07/11/1917
Memorial: Trowbridge
War cemetery: Gaza War Cemetery
Theatre of war: Egypt
Next of Kin: William H & Martha Mackett
Address: Clarendon, Trowbridge
Age: 25
Home Country: England
Cause of death: Killed in action

John, known as Jack, was a clerk for the County Council Accountants department and also a Wiltshire Territorial. He was the youngest son of William and Martha Mackett, a well known footballer and cricketer and also an admirable chess player. He was sent to India for garrison duties and in September 1917 the 1/4th Battalion Wiltshire Regiment were sent to Egypt and then on to Palestine to fight the Turkish forces. Jack was one of eight men killed in action by Turkish shelling on Wednesday 7 November as the Wiltshires advanced to Fryer hill near Gaza.

Lance Corporal Thomas William Pickard   *1/4th TF Bn Wiltshire Regiment*

Service No.	200739	Age:	24
Place of Birth:	Southwick, Wiltshire	Home Country:	England
Date of Death:	07/11/1917	Cause of death:	Killed in action
Memorial:	Trowbridge		
War cemetery:	Gaza War Cemetery		
Theatre of war:	Egypt		
Next of Kin:	Job & Mary A Pickard		
Address:	Vine Cottge, Wingfield, Wiltshire		

Thomas, known as Tom, was employed by S. Collier woollen merchants at the outbreak of hostilities and volunteered for service with the Wiltshire Territorials. He was an all round sportsman playing for the village cricket and football clubs and had been called on many times to play for both Bradford on Avon clubs. He was also, for several years, a chorister at Wingfield Church. Tom was sent to India for garrison duties and in September 1917 the 1/4th Battalion Wiltshire Regiment were sent to Egypt and then on to Palestine to fight the Turkish forces. Jack was one of eight men killed in action by Turkish shelling on Wednesday 7 November as the Wiltshires advanced to Fryer Hill near Gaza. Tom's brother Joseph died on 2 November in the same area, the brother's are buried in the same cemetery just 7 graves apart.

Private Victor William Frederick Dallimore   *1/4th TF Bn Wiltshire Regiment*

Service No.	202096	Age:	28
Place of Birth:	Trowbridge, Wiltshire	Home Country:	England
Date of Death:	13/11/1917	Cause of death:	Died of wounds
Memorial:	Trowbridge		
War cemetery:	Jerusalem Memorial		
Theatre of war:	Egypt		
Next of Kin:	Agnes Dallimore (wife) -Frank & Annie Dallimore (parents)		
Address:	Church Street, Westbury - 124 Bradford Road, Trowbridge		

Victor was employed by the Trowbridge Cooperative Society at Westbury and was the eldest son of Frank and Annie Dallimore. He married Agnes E Hulbert at the end of 1913 and had been a prominent player with Trowbridge Football Club. He joined the army in April 1916 and left for India in November 1916. In September 1917 the 1/4th Battalion Wiltshire Regiment

Right: Thomas William Pickard

Far right: Victor William Frederick Dallimore

were sent to Egypt and then on to Palestine to fight the Turkish forces. He was fatally wounded in action as the Wiltshires fought up the Gaza Strip at El Mesmiyeh on Tuesday 13 November 1917. He is remembered on the Jerusalem Memorial and has no known grave. Victor left a widow and a young child.

Lance Coporal Arthur Edward Bevins　　　*1/4th TF Bn Wiltshire Regiment*
Service No.　　201107　　　　　　　　　Age:　　　　　34
Place of Birth:　Ingersby, Leicestershire　　Home Country:　England
Date of Death:　13/11/1917　　　　　　　Cause of death:　Killed in action
Memorial:　　　North Bradley
War cemetery:　Jerusalem Memorial
Theatre of war:　Egypt
Next of Kin:　　Thomas Northover & Jane Bevins
Address:　　　Broadleigh House, North Bradley

Arthur, known as Edward, was the only son of Thomas and Jane Bevins. It is likely he was a Wiltshire Territorial and was sent to India for garrison duties. In September 1917 the 1/4th Battalion Wiltshire Regiment were sent to Egypt and then on to Palestine to fight the Turkish forces. He was one of ten men killed in action on Tuesday 13 November 1917 at El Mesmiyeh, Palestine, as the Wiltshires attacked Turkish positions they were constantly shelled during the two mile advance. He is remembered on the Jerusalem memorial and has no known grave.

Corporal Ewart Frederick Parfitt　　　*1/4th TF Bn Dorsetshire Regiment*
Service No.　　202958　　　　　　　　　Age:　　　　　19
Place of Birth:　Salisbury, Wiltshire　　　Home Country:　England
Date of Death:　13/11/1917　　　　　　　Cause of death:　Died
Memorial:　　　Salisbury & Trowbridge St James Church Memorial
War cemetery:　Baghdad North Gate War Cemetery
Theatre of war:　Mesopotamia
Next of Kin:　　Frank H & Eveline A Parfitt
Address:　　　12 Albany Road, Salisbury

Nineteen year old Ewart was a Wiltshire Territorial and was sent to India on garrison duties. He volunteered for service in Mesopotamia and was transferred to the Dorset Regiment. He died on Tuesday 13 November 1917 of sickness or disease at a military hospital base in Baghdad in modern day Iraq.

A British Tank

11
CAMBRAI

On 20 November 1917 the British mounted a surprise tank attack between the River Scarpe and St. Quentin, France. This was the first time a massed tank attack had taken place and 378 machines went into action at what was to be known as the Battle of Cambrai. Initially the advance was successful but the British failed to take advantage and the Germans mounted counter attacks retaking much of the ground that had been captured.

Private Harry Percival Perryman   *6th Bn Ox & Bucks Light Infantry*
Service No.   23663
Place of Birth: Bath, Somerset
Date of Death: 20/11/1917
Memorial: Trowbridge
War cemetery: Cambrai Memorial Louverval
Theatre of war: France
Next of Kin: Katherine Perryman (wife) - Charles & Mary Perryman (parents)
Address: Banbury, Oxfordshire - Arundel, 47 Bradford Road, Trowbridge

Age: 29
Home Country: England
Cause of death: Killed in action

Harry had been an officer's steward in the Royal Navy which he left in the spring of 1914, starting a carriers business and marrying Katherine Osborne. He was the second son of Charles and Mary Perryman and enlisted in the army in June 1916. He was killed in action near the Gonnelieu Spur, La Vacquerie, France, on Tuesday 20 November 1917, the first day of the Battle of Cambrai, when the British used massed tanks for the first time. He is remembered on the Cambrai Memorial Louverval with over 7,000 men who died in the Battle of Cambrai and have no known grave. He left a widow and young daughter.

Rifleman Alfred Pocock   *12th Bn Royal Irish Rifles*
Service No.   45009
Place of Birth: Hilperton, Wiltshire
Date of Death: 20/11/1917
Memorial: Hilperton & Hilpertom Church
War cemetery: Cambrai Memorial Louverval
Theatre of war: France
Next of Kin: Mary Pocock (wife) - Henry and Sarah Pocock (parents)
Address: Horse Road, Hilperton Marsh, Hilperton

Age: 31
Home Country: England
Cause of death: Killed in action

Before the war Alfred worked in the family florist business and married Mary Austin in the spring of 1915. It is likely he was conscripted into the army in 1916 joining the Rifle Brigade and was then transferred to the Royal Irish Rifles. He was killed in action near Havrincourt, France, on Tuesday 20 November 1917, and is remembered on the Cambrai Memorial Louverval.

Far left: Harry Percival Perryman

Left: Alfred Pocock

Private Hugh Henry Tozer   *2/6th TF Bn Devonshire Regiment*
Service No. 65046   Age: 20
Place of Birth: Boscombe, Hampshire   Home Country: England
Date of Death: 22/11/1917   Cause of death: Accident
Memorial: Trowbridge St James Church Memorial
War cemetery: Amara War Cemetery
Theatre of war: Mesopotamia
Next of Kin: Thomas William & Annie Meaby Tozer
Address: Whaddon Farm, Alderbury, Wiltshire

Hugh was the eldest son of William and Annie Tozer and a Wiltshire Territorial. He was sent to India for garrison duties and later volunteered for service in Mesopotamia and transferred to the Devonshire Regiment. He was killed by an accident on Thursday 22 November 1917 at Shiekh Saad in modern day Iraq and buried at Y Cemetery at the same place. His remains were later moved to Amara War Cemetery.

Driver Albert Henry Hodge   *56th Bde Royal Field Artillery*
Service No. 97010   Age: 22
Place of Birth: Devizes, Wiltshire   Home Country: England
Date of Death: 23/11/1917   Cause of death: Died of wounds
Memorial: Trowbridge
War cemetery: Baghdad North Gate War Cemetery
Theatre of war: Mesopotamia
Next of Kin: Edwin & Elizabeth Hodge
Address: 26 Newtown, Trowbridge

Prior to the war Albert was employed as a collier hewer at Penygraig, South Wales and volunteered for service in 1914. After training at Kildare and Basingstoke he was sent to Gallipoli arriving on 21 July 1915 and after the evacuation of the peninsular was sent to Egypt, then Mesopotamia. Edwin and Elizabeth Hodge received the news on 29 November 1917 that their son had died of wounds in action on 23 November 1917. His family inserted the following memoriam in a local paper:

*"Fondly we loved him; he is dear to us still.
But in grief we must bend to God's Holy Will.
Our Sorrow is Great, and our loss is hard to bear;
But angels will guard our dear loved one with care.
Ever remembered by his sorrowing Dad, Brother and Sister"*

Lance Coporal George Jesse Dorey Hunt   *1/4th TF Bn Wiltshire Regiment*

Service No.	201217	Age:	31
Place of Birth:	Trowbridge, Wiltshire	Home Country:	England
Date of Death:	23/11/1917	Cause of death:	Died of wounds
Memorial:	Trowbridge		
War cemetery:	Jerusalem War Cemetery		
Theatre of war:	Egypt		
Next of Kin:	Glibert Edwards & Eliza Hunt		
Address:	Heath Bank, Newtown, Trowbridge		

George was employed by the Bristol Drapery Company in Silver Street, Trowbridge and was the only surviving son of Gilbert & Eliza Hunt. He volunteered for service at the start of the war joining the Wiltshire Territorials and was sent to India for garrison duties. In September 1915 he was invalided home but after a short furlough he rejoined the home service battalion. After being declared fit for foreign service he was returned to India in March 1916 and in September 1917 the 1/4th Battalion Wiltshire Regiment were sent to Egypt and then onto to Palestine to fight the Turkish forces. He was wounded in action most likely during fighting at Bi'r 'Umrān, near Jerusalem, and died of his wounds on Friday 23 November 1917.

Private George Job Dunn Martin   *1/4th TF Wiltshire Regiment*

Service No.	201701	Age:	28
Place of Birth:	Netherbury, Dorset	Home Country:	England
Date of Death:	23/11/1917	Cause of death:	Killed in action
Memorial:	Trowbridge		
War cemetery:	Jerusalem War Cemetery		
Theatre of war:	Egypt		
Next of Kin:	Arthur & Tabitha Martin		

Right Albert Henry Hodge

Far right: George Jesse Dorey Hunt

Left: Far left: John Thomas Smith

Far left: George Job Dunn Martin

Address: Faverlands Farm, Salwayash, Dorset

Ironmonger George was a Wiltshire Territorial and was sent to India for garrison duties at the start of the war. In September 1917 the 1/4th Battalion Wiltshire Regiment were sent to Egypt and then on to Palestine to fight the Turkish forces. He was one of three men killed in action on Friday 23 November 1917 during fighting at Bi'r 'Umrān, near Jerusalem. The Wiltshires also had 3 men missing two of which were stretcher bearers who had volunteered to go and look for wounded of the Somerset Light Infantry.

Private Samuel Charles Pollard *12th Bn South Wales Borderers*
Service No.:   30452
Place of Birth: Trowbridge, Wiltshire
Date of Death: 25/11/1917
Memorial: Not known
War cemetery: Cambrai Memorial Louverval
Theatre of war: France
Next of Kin: May Pollard (wife) - Samuel & Sarah Pollard (parents)
Address: 1 Turner Road, Cardiff, Glamorganshire – Trowbridge

Age: 38
Home Country: Wales
Cause of death: Killed in action

Samuel, known as Charles, was a barman and had married Mary Jane Sloper in South Wales in 1907. It is likely he was conscripted into the army joining the South Wales Borderes. He was killed in action at Bourlon Wood, France, during the Battle of Cambrai. He is remembered on the Cambrai Memorial Louverval and has no known grave.

Sapper Edward Charles Watts *24th Div Signals Royal Engineers*
Service No.:   90829
Place of Birth: Semington, Wiltshire
Date of Death: 29/11/1917
Memorial: Not Known
War cemetery: St Pierre Cemetery Amiens
Theatre of war: France
Next of Kin: Charles & Agnes Watts

Age: 24
Home Country: England
Cause of death: Died

Address: 13 High Street, Semington

Edward known as Teddy, a farm labourer, volunteered for service soon after the commencement of hostilities and after completing his training was sent to France on 30 August 1915. He was given home leave during 1917 and on his return to France he was taken ill and sent to a base hospital near Amiens, France, where he died on Thursday 29 November 1917.

Corporal John Thomas Smith   *L Bty Royal Horse Artillery*

Service No.	65303	Age:	25
Place of Birth:	Christchurch, Sussex	Home Country:	England
Date of Death:	30/11/1917	Cause of death:	Died of wounds
Memorial:	Trowbridge		
War cemetery:	Cambrai Memorial Louverval		
Theatre of war:	France		
Next of Kin:	Edith Reynolds (sweetheart) - James R & Jane Anne Smith (parents)		
Address:	37 Waterworks Road, Trowbridge – Bexhill, Sussex		

John, known as Jack, was a baker's delivery man and enlisted with the artillery on 25 April 1911 at Eastbourne and was later posted to H Battery in Trowbridge, where he met Edith Reynolds. At the outbreak of hostilities Jack and L Battery was sent to France on 15 August 1914, taking part in the action at Nery, France involing Lionel Hastings where a number of Victoria Crosses were won. After serving in France Jack was sent to Gallipoli arriving in October 1915 and leaving for Egypt in November 1915. After serving in Egypt he returned to England for home leave and was then sent back to France. He was reported wounded and missing on Friday 30 November 1915 during the German Counter attack at the Battle of Cambrai. On 16 October 1918 Jack was presumed to have died on or since the date he was declared missing. In November 1918 Edith inserted the following memoriam in a local paper:

"Peacefull be thy rest, dear Jack,
it is sweet to breathe thy name;
In life I loved you dearly,
In death I'll do the same.
No one knows the silent heartache,
Only those can tell
Who have lost their best and dearest,
Without saying farewell.
From his devoted Sweetheart, Edith"

Sergeant Reginald Tom Moore   *91st Bde Royal Field Artillery*

Service No.	16237	Age:	24
Place of Birth:	Westwood, Wiltshire	Home Country:	England
Date of Death:	01/12/1917	Cause of death:	Killed in action
Memorial:	Not known		
War cemetery:	Cambrai Memorial Louverval		
Theatre of war:	France		
Next of Kin:	Mabel N. Moore (wife) - Albert & Annie Moore (parents)		
Address:	Broad Street, Trowbridge - Upper Westwood		

Reginald, a farm labourer, volunteered for service with the Royal Artillery and after completing his training was sent to France on 24 July 1915. While home on leave he married Mabel N. Pinchin in the spring of 1917. He was killed in action on Saturday 1st December 1917 during

Above: An abandoned British tank

Left: Reginald Thomas Moore

the German counter attack at the Battle of Cambrai. He is remembered on the Cambrai Memorial Louverval and has no known grave. In December 1918 his family inserted the following memoriam in a local paper:

"We shall never forget his loving face
as he bid us his last goodbye;
and left his home forever,
On the battle field to die,
But the hardest part has yet to come
When the hero's all reach home,
We shall miss amongst those cheering lads
The face of our own loved one
But some day in a better land
We shall meet again and understand.
From his ever loving father, mother, sisters and brothers.

Private Stephen Smith *1st Bn Wiltshire Regiment*
Service No. 3/8072 Age: 27
Place of Birth: Hilperton, Wiltshire Home Country: England
Date of Death: 01/12/1917 Cause of death: Died
Memorial: Not known
War cemetery: Trowbridge Cemetery
Theatre of war: Home
Next of Kin: Beatrice Smith (wife) - Thomas & Sarah Smith (parents)
Address: 14 Lower Broad Street, Trowbridge

Stephen enlisted with the Wiltshire Militia on 16 December 1904 and re-enlisted with the 3rd Battalion Wiltshire Regiment on the 14 June 1908. He married Beatrice Harding on 30 August 1908 at the Baptist Church in Trowbridge. At the outbreak of hostilities he was called to the colours and was sent to France on 12 September 1914 with the 1st Battalion Wiltshire Regiment. He was wounded with a gun shot wound to the right foot at Richbourg, France on 19 October and evacuated to England being sent to Manchester War Hospital. He was discharged from the Army on 15 April 1916 being medically unfit and on 4 July 1917 he attended a medical board

Right:
Stephen Smith

Far right:
Herbert Abrams

having developed tuberculosis which had been aggravated by his military service. He died from the disease on Saturday 1 December 1917 and was buried in Trowbridge Cemetery later in December 1917. Stephen is not remembered by the Commonwealth War Graves Commission.

Sergeant Herbert Abrams		*2nd Bn Wiltshire Regiment*	
Service No.	19041	Age:	19
Place of Birth:	Trowbridge, Wiltshire	Home Country:	England
Date of Death:	03/12/1917	Cause of death:	Killed in Action
Memorial:	Trowbridge		
War cemetery:	Hooge Crater Cemetery		
Theatre of war:	Belgium		
Next of Kin:	Joseph & Lavinia Abrams		
Address:	10 St. Thomas Passage, Trowbridge		

Under age soldier Herbert, known as Bert, had voluntarily enlisted in 1915 at sixteen years of age. He had joined the Trowbridge Church Lads Brigade in 1910 and was an apprentice of the Cooperative Society at the Mortimer Street Branch. He was also an active member of St. Thomas' Church Sunday School. He was sent to France in 1916 and was twice wounded being sent home to recover. At the age of nineteen he had attained the rank of sergeant. Bert was killed in action on Monday 3 December 1917 while the Wiltshires were in trenches near Polderhoek Chateau. New Zealand Infantry attacked the Chateau and the Germans retaliated by shelling the Wiltshire's support line trenches and back area causing seven casualties. Joseph & Lavinia Abrams received letters from Captain A.J. Smart and 2nd Lieutenant F. J. E. Spencer extracts from which are below:

"He was a splendid example of a man and you have every reason to be proud of him. He was hit by a piece of shell and killed instantaneously."

"I cannot praise him too highly for his work in the platoon of which I am in command. His name, I can assure you will not be forgotten by his comrades and myself. He was a very keen sportsman and helped me many times to organise games, and concerts and sports, for the welfare of the platoon."

Private Albert Wareham   *2nd Bn Wiltshire Regiment*

Service No.	10958	Age:	31
Place of Birth:	Hinton, Wiltshire	Home Country:	England
Date of Death:	03/12/1917	Cause of death:	Killed in action
Memorial:	Bulkington & Keevil		
War cemetery:	Hooge Crater Cemetery		
Theatre of war:	Belgium		
Next of Kin:	James & Elizabeth Wareham		
Address:	Oxenleaze Farm, Keevil, Wiltshire		

Farm labourer Albert volunteered for service with the 2nd Battalion Wiltshire Regiment and arrived in France on 26 January 1916. He was killed in action on Monday 3 December 1917 while the Wiltshires were in trenches near Polderhoek Chateau. New Zealand Infantry attacked the Chateau and the Germans retaliated by shelling the Wiltshire's support line trenches and back area causing seven casualties.

2nd Lieutenant George Victor Blake   *1st Bn Shropshire Light Infantry*

Service No.	N/A	Age:	30
Place of Birth:	Trowbridge, Wiltshire	Home Country:	England
Date of Death:	03/12/1917	Cause of death:	Killed in action
Memorial:	Trowbridge		
War cemetery:	Marcoing British Cemetery		
Theatre of war:	France		
Next of Kin:	Nancy Eva Blake (wife) - Henry Blake JP & Catherine Blake(parents)		
Address:	Fairhavens, Oswestry, Shropshire – Elmhurst, Trowbridge		

George was a solicitor and the fourth son of Henry & Catherine Blake he married Nancy Eva Sheather in Oswestry in 1913. At the outbreak of hostilities he joined the Shropshire Royal Engineers Officer Training Corps and received a commission. He Joined the Shropshires in February 1917 and was sent to the 6th Divisional Training Company, returning to his regiment on 26 March 1917. He was killed in action on Monday 3 December 1917, the day after his birthday, during the German counter attack while in trenches on the east side of the St. Quentin Canal, east of Marcoing Station at the Battle of Cambrai. The Shropshires withstood the first attack but during the second the Germans broke through the British lines and fierce hand to hand fighting ensued forcing the Shropshires to withdraw. He left a widow and small child.

Private Wilfred Frederick Stanley Groves   *2nd Bn Wiltshire Regiment*

Service No.	24213	Age:	19
Place of Birth:	Trowbridge, Wiltshire	Home Country:	England
Date of Death:	04/12/1917	Cause of death:	Killed in action
Memorial:	Trowbridge & Trowbridge United Free Church		
War cemetery:	Tyne Cot Memorial		
Theatre of war:	Belgium		
Next of Kin:	Emma Groves (grandmother)		
Address:	6 Newtown, Trowbridge		

Nineteen year old Wilfred volunteered for service on 10 May 1915 and was wounded at Messines in 1917. He was killed in action on Tuesday 4 December 1917 while in trenches near the Polderhoek Chateau, Belgium. His Grandmother received the following letter from 2nd Lieutenant Gerald M. Jeans:

Right: George Victor Blake

Far right: Wilfred Frederick Stanley Groves

"It is with the greatest sorrow that I write to inform you that your grandson was killed at 10am on the 4 December by a bursting shell in the front line. It may be some little consolation and comfort to know that he died a painless death. He was under my command and I found him to be a splendid fellow and absolutely trustworthy and always willing to undertake any work, both dangerous and otherwise. Three night's before his death I was sent out on patrol for a certain purpose. I took my servant with me and asked for one volunteer from my platoon to accompany me. Your grandson immediately stepped forward and volunteered to go with me. I was more than grateful. With his assistance we accomplished the work we had to in 'No Man's Land' within an hour, and then returned to our lines. He made the greatest sacrifice of all. You may rest assured he has done his duty most nobly and fearlessly for his country and battalion, and it grieves me to lose him from my platoon. He was not alone when the great call came, and another splendid fellow was killed, while others were wounded by the same shell. May I again offer my deepest sympathy in your loss."

Wilfred is remembered on the Tyne Cot Memorial and has no known grave. His grandmother inserted the following memoriam in December 1918:

"One year has passed since that day,
When one we loved was called away.
His loving ways and smiling face;
No one can fill his vacant place.
Sweet be your dreams dear Wilfred;
'Tis sweet to breathe your name.
In life we loved you dearly,
In death we do the same.
Sadly missed by his sorrowing grandmother, uncle and aunt, Will and Ada"

Gunner Arthur Francis Griffin   *248th Siege Bty RGA*

Service No.	110612	Age:	20
Place of Birth:	Hilperton, Wiltshire	Home Country:	England
Date of Death:	06/12/1917	Cause of death:	Died of wounds
Memorial:	Hilperton – Hilperton Church & Methodist Church Memorial		
War cemetery:	St Sever Cemetery Extension Rouen		

Theatre of war: France
Next of Kin: Henry & Sarah Griffin
Address: Horse Road, Hilperton

Twenty year old Arthur was the youngest son of Henry & Sarah Griffin, it is likely Arthur was conscripted into the army and arrived in France on 16 February 1917. He was wounded in action on 26 October 1917 and evacuated to No. 9 General Hospital, Rouen where he succumbed to his wounds on Thursday 6 December 1917.

9 DECEMBER 1917 - JERUSALEM SURRENDERS TO BRITISH FORCES

Private Norman William Harding — *Dorset Yeomanry*
Service No. 230901
Place of Birth: Frome, Somerset
Date of Death: 12/12/1917
Memorial: Mere
War cemetery: Alexandria Hadra War Memorial Cemetery
Theatre of war: Egypt
Next of Kin: Harry Thomas & Emma Eliza Harding
Address: North Bradley, Wiltshire
Age: 22
Home Country: England
Cause of death: Died of wounds

Norman's father had been the master of Mere workhouse and Norman served as his clerk. He died of wounds received in fighting in Palestine, at a military hospital in Alexandria, Egypt, on Wednesday 12 December 1917.

Captain Christopher Ken Merewether — *1/4th TF Bn Wiltshire Regiment*
Service No N/A
Place of Birth: North Bradley, Wiltshire
Date of Death: 19/12/1917
Memorial: Salisbury & North Bradley
War cemetery: Port Said War Memorial Cemetery
Age: 27
Home Country: England
Cause of death: Died of wounds

Right: Arthur Francis Griffin

Far right: Christopher Ken Merewether

Theatre of war: Egypt
Next of Kin: Rev. Wyndham Arthur Seinde & Harriot Edith Merewether
Address: Langton House, Salisbury

Christopher was the only child of the Rev. W A S Merewether, Vicar of St. Thomas of Canterbury, Salisbury, and grandson of the late Henry Alworth Merewether, Q.C., of Bowden Hill, Chippenham, formerly chairman of the Wiltshire Quarter Sessions and Recorder of Devizes. He was educated at St Aubyn's, Rottingdean and Winchester College, where he was in the senior Division Sixth Book and head of his house. Matriculating at Oriel College, Oxford, he took honours in modern history, and when leaving the university was selected by the directors of the White Star Line of Liverpool for training as an assistant manager. Having passed through the Officers Training Corps at Winchester, he was appointed to the command of the Bradford-on-Avon half company of the Wilts Territorials, and on the outbreak of war he left his appointment with the White Star Company and joined the Wilts Regiment, with which he served continuously from August, 1914. Christopher took a prominent place in all school games, played for his college XI, was a member of the Vincent's and Authentic's Cricket Club, and at hockey represented Oxford University against Cambridge. He was an original member of the Cavendish Club, London.

He was wounded in the fighting about Katrah and Mughar on November 13, and was subsequently admitted to Kantara Hospital, from which he was transferred to the 31st General Hospital at Port Said. He was reported dangerously wounded in the right shoulder and spine, and on Monday 26 November 1917, news was received stating that his condition was grave, but that he was cheerful and had practically no pain. Christopher died on Wednesday 19 December 1917 of wounds received in action.

Private Frederick John Overton *8th Bn East Yorkshire Regiment*
Service No.: 28889
Age: 27
Place of Birth: Semington, Wiltshire
Home Country: England
Date of Death: 26/12/1917
Cause of death: Killed in action
Memorial: Trowbridge
War cemetery: Mory Abbey Military Cemetery Mory
Theatre of war: France
Next of Kin: Richard & Bessie Overton

Frederick John Overton

Address: 48 Bradford Road, Trowbridge

It is likely Fred, a farm labourer, was conscripted into the army originally joining the Artillery and was then transferred to the 8th Battalion East Yorkshire Regiment. He was Killed in action on Boxing Day 1917 as the Germans pushed the British back from the gains they had made during the Battle of Cambrai. In December 1918 his parents inserted the following memoriam in a local paper:

" Sleep on dear Fred in a far off land
In a grave we shall never see
As long as life and memory last
We will remember thee
From Mother Brothers and Sister"

Gunner Reginald Charles Rogers — *93rd Bde Royal Field Artillery*
Service No.	176310	Age:	27
Place of Birth:	West Ashton, Wiltshire	Home Country:	England
Date of Death:	28/12/1917	Cause of death:	Killed in action
Memorial:	Edington		
War cemetery:	Hermines Hill British Cemetery		
Theatre of war:	France		
Next of Kin:	Frank & Clara Helen Rogers		
Address:	Priory Farm, Edington		

Reginald worked on his parents farm and was the second son of Frank & Clara Rogers. He joined the Wiltshire Yeomanry on 7 March 1910 and served with them until 6 March 1916 when he was transferred to the Royal Artillery. He was killed in action on Friday 28 December 1917 during fighting after the German counter attack following the Battle of Cambrai.

12
1918

Private Stanley Oliver Gomm — *1st Bn Essex Regiment*
Service No.   39516
Age: 19
Place of Birth: High Wycombe, Bucks
Home Country: England
Date of Death: 01/01/1918
Cause of death: Died of wounds
Memorial: Trowbridge
War cemetery: Bois Guillaume Communal Cemetery Extension
Theatre of war: France
Next of Kin: William Free & Sarah Ann Gomm
Address: 28 Gloucester Road, Trowbridge, Wiltshire

Nineteen year old Stanley originally joined the Army service corps but it is likely he was transferred to the Essex Regiment when there was a need for more infantry men. He was probably wounded during fighting at the Battle of Cambrai and died of his wounds on New Years day 1918 at No.8 General Hospital at Bois-Guillaume, near Rouen, France. His brother Ernest Arthur Gomm had died of wounds on 2 January 1916.

Chaplain 4th Class Cyril Narramore Were — *Royal Army Chaplains Department*
Service No.   N/A
Age: 36
Place of Birth: North Bradley, Wiltshire
Home Country: England
Date of Death: 09/01/1918
Cause of death: Died
Memorial: Not Known
War cemetery: Outterstreene Communal Cemetery Extention Bailleul

Right: Stanley Oliver Gomm

Far right: Sidney Herbert Griffin

Theatre of war: France
Next of Kin: Mildred Gladys Were (wife) - Edward Ash & Julia Leite Were (parents)
Address: 14 Christchurch Road, Reading, Berkshire.

Cyril was the second son of Edward Ash and Julia Leite Were and was born in North Bradley when his father was the Vicar of North Bradley. In 1907 he married Mildred Gladys Trip at Derby and he arrived in France on 4 December 1912. Official records indicate he died suddenly on Wednesday 9 January 1918 and it is interesting to note the dates in the following account the Rev. F.R.Barry D.S.O. wrote to Cyril's wife:

"He went up with his battalion into supports on the night of 6-7 January 1918, the first night he had been up in the line, and appeared to be perfectly well. When his servant went to his dugout on the morning of the 8 January he found him lying dead on his bed, apparently through heart failure. It was only just a month since he succeeded the Rev. O.A. Holden (who was killed in action on 1 December 1917), and he had already made a great impression and won the affection of both the officers and men amongst whom he worked."

The Bishop of Southwark to whom Cyril was a domestic chaplain, wrote:

"He was like a son to me, and only those who knew him most intimately could understand how truly he was one of God's saints. I never knew a man more entirely pure of heart and meek in spirit, more utterly unselfish and filled with the love of fellow men. I can never forget all he has been to me and done for me. I am most thankful the officers and men so soon came to appreciate him."

Cyril is buried in Outterstreene Communal Cemetery Extension, he left a widow and son.

Able Seaman Sidney Herbert Griffin   *HM Tug Mercantile Marine Res.*
Service No. 890568
Place of Birth: Trowbridge, Wiltshire
Date of Death: 20/01/1918
Memorial: Trowbridge
War cemetery: Plymouth Naval Memorial
Theatre of war: At Sea
Next of Kin Albert & Eliza Griffin
Address: 8 Allen Road, Trowbridge

Age: 19
Home Country: England
Cause of death: Killed in action

Sidney was the youngest son of Albert and Eliza Griffin and had attended the National Nautical School to train to be a seaman. In January 1918 he was serving on HMS Louvain which had started life as the Harwich Ferry which had previously been SS Dresden. She was converted to an armed boarding steamer and was sunk on Sunday 20 January 1918 while sailing in the Aegean Sea by the German submarine UC22. The Louvain sank with the loss of 224 lives and 1950 bags of mail and parcel post. Sidney is remembered on the Plymouth Naval Memorial. In January 1919 his brothers and sisters inserted the following memoriam in a local paper:

"We mourn for you dear brother
But not with outward show
For the heart that mourns sincerely
Mourn silently and low
Ever remembered by his loving sisters and brothers"

Sapper Harry Meaden   *Inland Water Transport R.E.*

Service No.	WR/504215
Place of Birth:	Tilshead, Wiltshire
Date of Death:	27/01/1918
Memorial:	Trowbridge
War cemetery:	Dunkirk Town Cemetery
Theatre of war:	France
Next of Kin:	Joseph Meaden (grandfather)
Address:	Tilshead, Wiltshire

Age:	25
Home Country:	England
Cause of death:	Accident

Prior to the outbreak of hostilities Harry was a carter on a farm and resided at 42 Newtown, Trowbridge. He was accidentally drowned at Dunkirk on Sunday 27 January 1918.

Private Andrew Boa   *226th Coy Machine Gun Corps*

Service No.	122723
Place of Birth:	Thurlow, Suffolk
Date of Death:	01/02/1918
Memorial:	Trowbridge
War cemetery:	Lijssenthoek Military Cemetery
Theatre of war:	Belgium
Next of Kin:	Lilian Boa (wife) – Andrew & Margaret Boa (parents)
Address:	4 Tewkesbury Terrace, London - 52 Avenue Road, Trowbridge

Age:	32
Home Country:	England
Cause of death:	Died of wounds

Andrew was a bank clerk and had studied at Albert Memorial College Framlingham, St Michael and Saxted in Suffolk. He married Lilian A S Stangroom in 1910 at Great Yarmouth, Norfolk. It is likely he was conscripted into the army initially serving with the Royal Fusiliers and then transferring to the Machine Gun Corps. He was wounded at Passchendaele on 5 January 1918 and succumbed to his wounds at a Military hospital at Lijssenthoek east of Ypres, Belgium on Friday 1 February 1918.

Captain Harold Conquest Clar kMC   *2nd Bn Wiltshire Regiment*

Service No	N/A.
Place of Birth:	Trowbridge, Wiltshire
Date of Death:	07/02/1918
Memorial:	Trowbridge - Staverton & Hilperton Church Memorial
War cemetery:	Noyon New British Cemetery
Theatre of war:	France
Next of Kin:	Dorothy Violet Clark (wife) – William Perkins & Alice Clark
Address:	Wyke House, Hilperton Marsh, Trowbridge

Age:	36
Home Country:	England
Cause of death:	Died of wounds

Harold was the eldest son of William and Alice Clark and had arrived in France in January 1915. He was wounded in 1916 when a mine exploded, burying him, and it took men five hours to free him. He was evacuated to England covered in bruises and suffering from shell shock. In February 1917 he was posted to the 2nd Battalion Wiltshire Regiment and in September 1917 he was awarded the Military Cross from the King. He received the decoration for leading a patrol to the German lines on Wednesday 27 June 1917 in Belgium. The Wiltshires War diary for this day explains the circumstances:

"2/Lieuts WG FIELD and HC CLARK and 32 other ranks had a successful patrol, and obtained identification of the Battalion opposite our trenches. No prisoners were taken as the enemy proved recalcitrant. 3 were bayoneted (killed) and the remainder wounded. A shoulder title and cap were, however secured, and a safe withdrawal effected, although hotly pressed from

Far left: Andrew Boa

Left: Harold Conquest Clark

the rear by strong enemy reinforcements with rifle fire and bombs."

In late November 1917 while on leave Harold married Dorothy Violet Foley at Christchurch Paighton and after a short honeymoon at Ivybridge he returned to the front. Harold was wounded in the thigh and leg by German shell fire on 5 February 1918 while serving in the trenches in France on what was described by the War Diary as a 'quiet day'. He was evacuated to a military hospital at Noyon, France, where it was found he had partially severed arteries in his leg. The surgeon did everything possible for him but Harold's leg had to be amputated. During the next 48 hours he rapidly grew weaker and succumbed to his wounds on Thursday 2 February 1918 Colonel Martin of the Wiltshire's wrote the following:

"All the regiment will mourn his loss. He was a most popular officer and regarded with affection by all his brother officers. He was buried in the little cemetery joining the hospital where he died, and a little cross will be erected over his grave to mark the spot where he lies."

Driver Sidney Reeves		*K Bty13th Res Bde. RHA*	
Service No.	38980	Age:	30
Place of Birth:	Penton, Hampshire	Home Country:	England
Date of Death:	08/03/1918	Cause of death:	Died of wounds
Memorial:	Trowbridge		
War cemetery:	Trowbridge Cemetery		
Theatre of war:	Home		
Next of Kin:	Mabel Reeves (wife) - Richard & Emma Reeves (parents)		
Address:	20 British Row, Trowbridge		

Sidney had been stationed at Trowbrigde with the Royal Horse artillery and had left the army and married Mable Jenkins in 1908. At the outbreak of hostilities Sidney was a member of the reserves and was called back to the colours arriving in France on 15 August 1914. After two years and six months service in France Sidney was sent home on account of illness and spent he next ten months under hospital treatment. He was waiting discharge from the army at barracks in London, when a starlight aeroplane raid took place. Shortly after midnight Sidney was struck by a splinter from an aerial bomb. The missile struck him in the back and legs and he was heard to cry out "Oh my poor legs." He was wounded so seriously that the London police made a telephonic communication to Trowbridge police who then notified Mabel Reeves. On being told the information Mabel went to London by the first train only to find that Sidney had died at 4am on Friday 8 March 1918. Sidney left a widow and three children.

Private William George Jones   *10th Bn Royal Fusilers*
Service No. 36387
Place of Birth: Potterne, Wiltshire
Date of Death: 09/03/1918
Memorial: Trowbridge
War cemetery: Tyne Cot Memorial
Theatre of war: Belgium
Next of Kin: Florence Gertrude K Jones (wife) – Ernest and Elizabeth Jones (parents)
Address: 3 Council House, Great Cheverell – Trowbridge

Age: 31
Home Country: England
Cause of death: Killed in action

William was one of the composing staff at the Wiltshire Times before the war and in 1910 he had married Florence G K Heath. It is likely he was conscripted into the army joining the 10 Battalion Royal Fusilers known as the Stockbrokers because they had originally been made up of business men from the City of London. William was killed in action in the early hours of the morning of Saturday 9 March 1918 when the Fusiliers repelled a German attack at Polderhoek Chateau, Belgium. He is remembered on the Tyne Cot Memorial and has no known grave. His brother Laurence Herbert was killed in 1915.

Lieutenant Leonard Vincent Southwell   *Royal Flying Corps*
Service No. N/A
Place of Birth: Bath, Somerset
Date of Death: 14/03/1918
Memorial: Trowbridge & Bath
War cemetery: Longuenesse St.Omer Souvenir Cemetery
Theatre of war: France
Next of Kin: Edward Smith & Edith Mary Southwell
Address: Pembroke House, 13 Norfolk Buildings, Bath

Age: 28
Home Country: England
Cause of death: Died of wounds

Right Sidney Reeves

Far right: William George Jones

Leonard, a clerk, had been a member of the Royal Navy and left England for Canada arriving on 11 September 1912. Soon after his arrival he joined the militia, then volunteered for oversea's service on 17 April 1916 and was discharged from the Canadian army on 15 May 1916, transferring to the Royal Flying Corps. He died of wounds on Thursday 14 March 1918 at a military hospital at St.Omer. In March 1915 one of Leonard's comrades inserted the following memoriam in a local paper:

"A very Gallant gentleman"

Gunner William Trower Chivers		*166th Siege Bty RGA*	
Service No.	66174	Age:	21
Place of Birth:	Trowbridge, Wiltshire	Home Country:	England
Date of Death:	17/03/1918	Cause of death:	Killed in action
Memorial:	Trowbridge		
War cemetery:	Vielle-Chappelle New Military Cemetery Lacouture		
Theatre of war:	France		
Next of Kin:	Blanche Chivers		
Address:	19 Westbourne Road, Trowbridge		

William, a clerk, enlisted with the Royal Garrison Artillery on 15 December 1915 and after completing his training was sent to France on 12 September 1916. He was appointed battery signaller and injured his back in an accident on 7 October 1918. After a short time in hospital he returned to his unit. He was granted home leave in December 1917 most likely returning to Trowbridge. William was killed in action on Sunday 17 March 1918 near Vielle Chappelle, the bombardment was the prelude to the German attack on 23 March 1918. In March 1919 his mother inserted the following memoriam in a local paper:

"What's brave what's Noble he did it
And made death proud to take him
A soul so fiery sweet can never die
But lives and loves and works through all eternity
Ubique quo fas et gloria docunt"

Driver William Walter John Davis		*119th Brigade Royal Field Artillery*	
Service No.	W/4380	Age:	21
Place of Birth:	Standerwick, Somerset	Home Country:	England
Date of Death:	19/03/1918	Cause of death:	Died of wounds
Memorial:	Trowbridge		
War cemetery:	Mendinghem Military Cemetery		
Theatre of war:	Belgium		
Next of Kin:	Walter & Ada A Matilda Davis		
Address:	4 Allen Road, Trowbridge		

Twenty one year old William was the eldest son of Walter and Ada Davis and it is likely he was conscripted into the army joining the Royal field Artillery. He died of wounds on Tuesday 19 March 1918, at a Military Hospital at Mendinghem, Belgium.

Private Arthur Frederick Fluke		*133rd United States Army*	
Service No.	Not known	Age:	28
Place of Birth:	Trowbridge, Wiltshire	Home Country:	USA

Arthur Frederick Fluke

Date of Death: 19/03/1918
Memorial: Trowbridge
War cemetery: Rosehill Cemetery (Chicago)
Theatre of war: America
Next of Kin: Frank & Mary Fluke
Address: 48 Drynham Road, Trowbridge

Cause of death: Died

Arthur arrived in the United States on 22 August 1907. He joined the U.S. army and in 1918 he was with 133rd Field Hospital, 100th Sanitary Train, Camp Cody, Denning, New Mexico. He was taken sick while on a hike in the Ozark Mountains and died of pneumonia on Tuesday 19 March 1918. His remains were shipped to Chicago in the charge of sergeant Titus which was a distance of over 1,000 miles. He was buried in Rosehill Cemetery with full military honours. The coffin was covered with the Stars and Stripes and six men from the 333rd Machine Gun Company, to which his brother Walter belonged, acted as pall bearers.

Private William Thomas Stanley Maple *2/6th TF Bn Devonshire Regiment*

Service No.: 268438
Place of Birth: Devizes, Wiltshire
Date of Death: 19/03/1918
Memorial: Devizes & Trowbridge St James Church Memorial
War cemetery: Kut War Cemetery
Theatre of war: Mesopotamia
Next of Kin: William & Mary Maple
Address: 1 Farleigh Place, Devizes

Age: 19
Home Country: England
Cause of death: Accident

William was the youngest son of William & Mary Maple and originally joined the 2/4th Battalion Wiltshire Regiment and it is likely he was sent to India on garrison duties. At some time after this he was transferred to the 2/6th Battalion Devonshire Regiment arriving in Mesopotamia in September 1917. He was accidentally killed in a bomb (hand grenade) explosion on Tuesday 19 March 1918.

13
KAISERSCHLACT

21 MARCH 1918 - THE GERMANS LAUNCH THEIR SPRING OFFENSIVE

Sapper Howard William Davis — *400th Field Coy Royal Engineers*
Service No.   213621
Place of Birth: Trowbridge, Wiltshire
Date of Death   21/03/1918
Memorial: Trowbridge
War cemetery: Arras Memorial
Theatre of war: France
Next of Kin: Samuel & Anne Davis
Address: 51 Timbrell Street, Trowbridge

Age: 37
Home Country: England
Cause of death: Killed in action

Howard was a master builder and it is likely he was conscripted into the army to serve with the North Staffordshire Regiment and when it was realized he had building skills he was transferred to the Royal Engineers. He was killed in action on Thursday 21 March 1918 in the Cambrai area when the Germans mounted an overwhelming attack. He is remembered on the Arras Memorial and has no known grave.

Gunner Herbert Ernest Hutton — *76th Siege Bty RGA*
Service No.   165980
Place of Birth: Cricklade, Wiltshire
Date of Death: 21/03/1918
Memorial: Trowbridge
War cemetery: Arras Memorial
Theatre of war: France
Next of Kin: Ernest & Mary Hutton
Address: 51 Crocker Street, Newport, Hampshire

Age: 24
Home Country: England
Cause of death: Killed in action

Herbert, known as Bert, was the eldest son on Ernest and Mary Hutton and came from a military family; his father had served with the Cameronian Scottish Rifles and Bert himself had served as a signal boy with the Royal Navy on the H.M.S. Africa. It is likely he arrived in France on 31 March 1916 and was killed in action on Thursday 21 March 1918 near St. Quentin, France, when the Germans mounted an overwhelming attack. He is remembered on the Arras Memorial and has no known grave. Bert's family inserted the following memoriam in a local paper:

"One year has passed since that sad day
When one we loved fell in the fray
His loving voice his smiling face
No one can fill my dear one's place

Right: Herbert Ernest Hutton

Far right: Albert Bray

Sleep on dear Bert in an unknown grave
Your life for your country you nobly gave
Only those who have suffered are able to tell
The pain in the heart at not saying farewell
From his sorrowing mother, sisters, brother, uncle and aunt"

Private Albert Bray   *2nd Bn Royal Inniskilling Fusiliers*
Service No.   41599   Age: 30
Place of Birth: Trowbridge, Wiltshire   Home Country: England
Date of Death: 21/03/1918   Cause of death: Died of wounds
Memorial: Not known
War cemetery: Pozieres Memorial
Theatre of war: France
Next of Kin: Annie Bray (wife) – James & Emily Bray (parents)
Address: 15 Phillip Street, Mountain Ash, Glamorganshire – Trowbridge

Albert had originally joined the Army Service Corps and it is likely he was transferred to The Royal Inniskilling Fusiliers because of a lack of Infantrymen. He was wounded and taken prisoner during the Germans attack near St. Quentin on Thursday 21 March 1918. He died the same day as a prisoner of war. He is remembered on the Pozieres Memorial, with over 14,000 men killed between March and April 1918 and has no known grave.

Private Amor Geoffrey Pike   *2nd Bde Tank Corps*
Service No.   92755   Age: 22
Place of Birth: Hilperton, Wiltshire   Home Country: England
Date of Death: 22/03/1918   Cause of death: Killed in action
Memorial: Hilperton & Hilperton Church Memorial
War cemetery: Pozieres Memorial
Theatre of war: France
Next of Kin: Amor Mullins & Constance Pike
Address: Church Farm, Hilperton

Amor was the eldest son of Amor & Constance Pike and initially joined the Royal Wiltshire

Yeomanry before transferring to the Tank Corps. He was killed in action near St. Quentin on Friday 22 March 1918 during the overwhelming German attack. He is remembered on the Pozieres Memorial and has no known grave.

Private William John Holloway   *1st Bn Wiltshire Regiment*
Service No.   21283   Age: 19
Place of Birth: Trowbridge, Wiltshire Home Country: England
Date of Death: 23/03/1918   Cause of death: Killed in action
Memorial: Trowbridge
War cemetery: Arras Memorial
Theatre of war: France
Next of Kin: John & Eliza Jane Holloway
Address: 1 Burbridges Yard, Upper Broad Street, Trowbridge

Prior to the commencement of hostilities William was employed at Trowbridge sawmill, he was the elder son of John and Eliza Holloway. He enlisted in July 1915 at sixteen years of age and arrived in France on 9 December 1915. Being under age he was sent home in January 1916 but was sent back to France in November 1916. He was wounded during the battle of Messines on 5 June 1917 and came home on sick leave, returning to the front on his recovery. On Saturday 23 March 1918 the Wiltshires were in trenches east of Fremicourt near Bapaume, France. During the morning they were subjected to a 3 hour bombardment followed by two attacks by German infantry both of which were repulsed and during the afternoon they were again subjected to heavy shell fire causing many casualties. It is likely William was killed by German shell fire. he is remembered on the Pozieres Memorial and has no known grave.

Lance Coporal Frank Arthur Sherwood   *6th Bn Wiltshire Regiment*
Service No.   22958   Age: 26
Place of Birth: Trowbridge, Wiltshire Home Country: Wales
Date of Death: 23/03/1918   Cause of death: Killed in action
Memorial: Trowbridge
War cemetery: Arras Memorial
Theatre of war: France
Next of Kin: Emma Elizabeth Sherwood
Address: 41 Copplestone Street, Mountain Ash, Glamorganshire

Far Left: William John Holloway

Left: Frank Arthur Sherwood

Frank, a factory worker, had married Emma Gregory at the start of 1918 in South Wales. It is likely he joined the Wiltshires and arrived in France in 1916-17. He was posted as wounded and missing on Saturday 23 March 1918 when the 6th Battalion Wiltshire made a stand against the German attack at Morchies, East of Bapaume. He is remembered on the Arras Memorial and has no known grave.

Lance Coporal Frederick Alfred Clift   *1st Bn Wiltshire Regiment*

Service No.	19084	Age:	18
Place of Birth:	Windsor, Berkshire	Home Country:	England
Date of Death:	24/03/1918	Cause of death:	Killed in action
Memorial:	Trowbridge		
War cemetery:	Arras Memorial		
Theatre of war:	France		
Next of Kin:	Frederick & Annie Clift		
Address:	Hilperton Marsh, Trowbridge		

Under age soldier Frederick was employed by Frederick Rose a confectioner who himself was to die from wounds as a prisoner in April 1918. He was the fourth son of Mr and Mrs Clift and was a member of the Loyal Mount Ararat Juvenile Lodge of Odd fellows. He joined the army at the age of fifteen and a half years in March 1915 and arrived on the Gallipoli Peninsular on 4th December 1915. He was invalided home with dysentery and after his recovery was sent back to France where he was attached to the Lewis Gun section and promoted to Lance Corporal. On Sunday 24 March 1918 the Wiltshires were east of Fremicourt near Bapaume, France, where they had been shelled during the day. At 4pm the Germans attacked and were repulsed on the immediate front and the Wiltshires were ordered to retire; but at the same time the British Troops on the left of the Wiltshires were pushed back leaving the Wiltshire's flank exposed. The Wiltshires front line companies then attempted to retire but were practically exterminated by German machine gun fire. Frederick was posted as missing and in December 1918 his parents were informed that he had been killed in action on the day he was reported missing. He is remembered on the Arras Memorial and has no known grave.

Private Bernard Newman Cottle   *1st Bn Wiltshire Regiment*

Service No.	18149	Age:	19
Place of Birth:	Melksham, Wiltshire	Home Country:	England
Date of Death:	24/03/1918	Cause of death:	Killed in action

Right: Frederick Alfred Clift

Far right: Bernard Newman Cottle

Memorial:	Trowbridge
War cemetery:	Arras Memorial
Theatre of war:	France
Next of Kin:	William N & Kate M Cottle
Address:	121 Mortimer Street, Trowbridge

Under age soldier Bernard attended Trowbridge boys high School and after completing his education went to learn farming with Mr Guley. He volunteered for service in 1914 at 16 years of age and arrived in France on 27 April 1915. He was killed in action on Sunday 24 March 1918 when the Wiltshires were east of Fremicourt near Bapaume, France in the same action as Fredrick Clift. He is remembered on the Arras Memorial and has no known grave.

Private Charles Frederick Mooney — *2nd Bn Ox & Bucks Light Infantry*

Service No.	25450	Age:	28
Place of Birth:	Trowbridge, Wiltshire	Home Country:	England
Date of Death:	24/03/1918	Cause of death:	Died of wounds
Memorial:	Trowbridge		
War cemetery:	Arras Memorial		
Theatre of war:	France		
Next of Kin:	Eliza Mooney		
Address:	St.Thomas's Passage, Trowbridge		

Charles, known as Charlie, worked in a butchers shop and it is likely he was conscripted into the army joining the Worcestor Regiment then being transferred to the 2nd Battalion Oxfordshire and Buckinghamshire Light Infantry. He was reported wounded and missing in France on Sunday 24 March 1918 and was last seen walking towards Bapaume, France, one hour before the town was captured by German forces. In February 1919, Eliza Mooney inserted an advert in a local paper asking for information concerning her son. It was assumed later that Charlie had died of wounds on the day he was reported missing. He is remembered on the Arras Memorial and has no known grave.

Private Charles Henry Field — *2nd Bn Devonshire Regiment*

Service No.	30938	Age:	19
Place of Birth:	Coleford, Somerset	Home Country:	England
Date of Death:	25/03/1918	Cause of death:	Killed in action
Memorial:	Trowbridge		
War cemetery:	Roye New British Cemetery		
Theatre of war:	France		
Next of Kin:	Charles & Mary Field		
Address:	129 Rock Road, Trowbridge		

Nineteen year old Charles was a farm labourer and it is likely he was conscripted into the army joining 2nd Battalion Devonshire Regiment. He was killed in action on Monday 25 March 1918 most likely as the Devons withdrew eastwards between Misery and Villers Cabonnel south of Peronne, France.

Private Hubert Harold Chappell — *2nd RM Bn RN Div R.M.L.I.*

Service No.	PLY/13088	Age:	33
Place of Birth:	Wells, Somerset	Home Country:	England
Date of Death:	27/03/1918	Cause of death:	Killed in action
Memorial:	Trowbridge		

Right: Charles Henry Field

Far right: Hubert Harold Chappell

War cemetery: Hedauville Communal Cemetery Extension
Theatre of war: France
Next of Kin: William & Annie Chappell
Address: 5 Bond Street, Trowbridge

Hubert, known as Bert, joined the Royal Marine Light Infantry on 17 October 1904 and when on leave he played football for Trowbridge Town. He saw service in many parts of the world and at the commencement of hostilities he was serving on the Light Cruiser H.M.S. Dartmouth which saw action in the Indian Ocean and at the Dardenelles. Bert then volunteered for land service and was sent to Greece and then on to France. He was wounded at Martinsart, east of Thiepval, France on Wednesday 27 March 1918 and taken to one of the field ambulances based at Hedauville, where he succumbed to his wounds. In March 1919 his family inserted the following memoriam in a local paper:

"Only a year has passed since that sad day
When one we loved fell in the fray
His loving voice his smiling face
No one can fill our dear son's place
Sleep on dear Bert in a far off grave
Only those who have suffered are able to tell
The pain in the heart in not saying farewell"

Rifleman Leonard Samuel Young   *2nd Bn New Zealand Rifle Brigade*
Service No. 42858   Age: 24
Place of Birth: Petone, New Zealand   Home Country: New Zealand
Date of Death: 31/03/1918   Cause of death: Died of wounds
Memorial: Not known
War cemetery: Engelbelmer Communal Cemetery Extension
Theatre of war: France
Next of Kin: Mr. E. Young & Alice Young
Address: 59 Victoria Street, Petone, Wellington, New Zealand

Leonard was the grandson of James & Sarah Prince of Bond Street, Trowbridge, and had left New Zealand on 2 April 1917. He died of wounds on Sunday 31 March 1918 at the field ambulance station at Englebelmer, France.

Private Frederick Job Rose   *2/6th Bn South Staffordshire Regt*

Service No.	46542	Age:	35
Place of Birth:	Trowbridge, Wiltshire	Home Country:	England
Date of Death:	03/04/1918	Cause of death:	Died of wounds
Memorial:	Trowbridge		
War cemetery:	Liege Robermont Cemetery		
Theatre of war:	Belgium		
Next of Kin:	Florence E Rose (wife) - Job & Emily Rose (parents)		
Address:	16 Duke Street, Trowbridge		

Frederick owned a wholesale confectionary business and was a member of Emanuel Church where he was missionary secretary in the Sunday school and treasurer of the Brotherhood. He married Florence Ellen Barnes in 1905 and was a member of the local volunteers. Frederick was conscripted into the Army Service Corps in March 1917 and was first sent to serve in Ireland and he was transferred to the Infantry in August 1917. He was then sent to France in December 1917 joining the South Staffordshires and the last news received from him was a field card on 20 March 1918, two days before the German advance. Some weeks later he was officially posted as missing since 21 March. Frederick was wounded and captured during the German advance. He was taken to the Reserve Hospital at Liege, Belgium, where he succumbed to his wounds on Wednesday 4 April 1918.

Private Charles Henry Robert Damon   *11th Bn Royal Sussex Regiment*

Service No.	G/17076	Age:	19
Place of Birth:	Trowbridge, Wiltshire	Home Country:	England
Date of Death:	03/04/1918	Cause of death:	Killed in action
Memorial:	Not Known		
War cemetery:	Pozieres Memorial		
Theatre of war:	France		
Next of Kin:	Henry & Jane Damon		
Address:	Farleigh Hungerford, Somerset		

Ninteen year old Charles was the eldest son of Henry and Jane Damon. He was reported missing between 21 and 30 March 1918 following the Battle of Bapaume, France, during the German offensive. Some time after 1921 he was officially posted as killed in action on Wednesday 3 April 1918 and is remembered on the Pozieres Memorial and has no known grave.

Frederick Job Rose

9 APRIL 1918 - 'GEORGETTE' THE SECOND GERMAN SPRING OFFENSIVE IS LAUNCHED

Lance Coporal Albert Edward Ash *6th Bn Wiltshire Regiment*
Service No.   204229
Place of Birth: Holt, Wiltshire
Date of Death: 10/04/1918
Memorial: Trowbridge – Holt – Hilperton -Staverton
War cemetery: Tyne Cot Memorial
Theatre of war: Belgium
Next of Kin: Maggie I. Ash (wife) - Edwin J & Polly Ash (parents)
Address: 12 Hilperton Marsh, Trowbridge - The Midlands, Holt

Age: 25
Home Country: England
Cause of death: Killed in action

Albert was a leather dresser and he married Maggie I Gerrish in 1911. He was a member of Wiltshire Yeomary and in September 1917 the Yeomanry were amalgamated with the 6th Battalion Wiltshire Regiment. On Wednesday 10 April 1918, the Wiltshires were in trenches east of Messines on Wytshaete Ridge where they were subjected to an intense bombardment by the Germans consisting of high explosives and gas shells. The British line to the right of the Wiltshires was subjected to a German attack under cover of mist. This attack eventually forced the Wiltshires to retreat. Albert was killed during this attack on Messines. He is remembered on the Tyne Cot Memorial and has no known grave. In April 1919 Maggie Ash inserted the following memoriam in a local paper:

"Sleep on dear one in an unknown grave
Your life dear one you nobly gave
No loved ones were with you to say goodbye
But safe in God's keeping now you lie
From his loving wife and children"

Private Robert Henry Shimmon   *1/4th TF Bn Wiltshire Regiment*
Service No.   201922   Age: 33
Place of Birth: Holloway, London   Home Country: England

Right: Albert Edward Ash

Far Right: Robert Henry Shimmon

Date of Death: 10/04/1918 Cause of death: Killed in action
Memorial: Trowbridge
War cemetery: Ramleh War Cemetery
Theatre of war: Egypt
Next of Kin: Mabel Shimmon (wife) - Robert Henry & Sophia Shimmon (parents)
Address: 25 Bradley Road, Trowbridge

Robert, a warehouseman, had originally joined the Territorials on 9 July 1906 enlisting in the Royal artillery. At the end of the year in 1915 he married Mabel Hunt and afterwards joined the Wiltshire Territorials. He was sent to India for garrison duties and in September 1917 the 1/4th Wiltshires were sent to Egypt and then on to Palestine. On Wednesday 10 April 1918 the Wiltshires attacked the Sheikh Subih ridge near Jaffa in modern day Israel and were shelled heavily by Turkish forces as they advanced. It is likely Robert was killed during this attack.

Private Arthur Ernest Davis *6th Bn Wiltshire Regiment*
Service No. 36095 Age: 18
Place of Birth: Trowbridge, Wiltshire Home Country: England
Date of Death: 11/04/1918 Cause of death: Killed in action
Memorial: Salisbury - Salisbury St Pauls Church Memorial – Dews Methodist Mem.
War cemetery: Tyne Cot Cemetery
Theatre of war: Belgium
Next of Kin: Hedley Herbert & Lucy Miles Davis
Address: 53 St Pauls Road, Salisbury

Arthur was a member of the Trowbridge Boy's Brigade Bugle Band and he was an under age soldier joining the Wiltshires in 1916 at 16 years of age but after a few months service he was sent home until he reached the age of 18 years. He was returned to France in April 1918 and within a week was reported missing on Thursday 11 April 1918. Arthur's parents were informed officially in September 1918 that he was missing and later in August 1919 it was assumed he had died. He was killed during fighting when the Wiltshires were in trenches east of Messines on Wytshaete Ridge where they were subjected to an intense bombardment by the Germans consisting of high explosives and gas shells. The British line to the right of the Wiltshires was subjected to a German attack under cover of mist. This attack eventually forced the Wiltshires to retreat.

Private Wilfred James Frederick Griffin *25th Coy Machine Gun Corps*
Service No 23062 Age: 20
Place of Birth: Chippenham, Wiltshire Home Country: England
Date of Death: 11/04/1918 Cause of death: Killed in action
Memorial: Trowbridge
War cemetery: Ploegsteert Memorial
Theatre of war: Belgium
Next of Kin: Frederick & Clara J. Griffin
Address: 39 Wyke Road, Trowbridge

At the outbreak of hostilities Wilfred was employed at the Trowbridge Club and being a member of the special reserve was called up. He arrived in France with the Wiltshire Regiment on 6 July 1915 at 17 years of age and served nearly three years in France. He was transferred to the Machine Gun Corps and was killed in action, being shot through the neck during heavy fighting in Belgium on Thursday 11 April 1918. He is remembered on the Ploegsteert Memorial and has no known grave. His brother Gilbert William Frank Griffin wasto be killed on 21 May 1918.

Far right: Wilfred James Frederick Griffin

Right: Frederick Herbert Curtis

Private Frederick Herbert Curtis		*9th Bn Yorkshire Light Infantry*	
Service No.	36593	Age:	22
Place of Birth:	Battersea, London	Home Country:	England
Date of Death:	12/04/1918	Cause of death:	Died of wounds
Memorial:	Trowbridge		
War cemetery:	Villers-Faucon Communal Cemetery Extension		
Theatre of war:	France		
Next of Kin:	Alfred & Alice Curtis		
Address:	Drynam Villa, 53 Dynnham Road, Trowbridge		

Frederick, known as Fred, was an office clerk and the eldest son of Alfred and Alice Curtis. He originally joined the Wiltshire Regiment; was transferred to the Royal Berkshire Regiment and then to the Yorkshire Light Infantry. He was wounded and captured during the German offensive in March 1918 and succumbed to his wounds at a German temporary hospital near Peronne, France on Friday 12 April 1918. In April 1919 his parents inserted the following memoriam in a local paper:

"Not now but in the coming years
It may be in a better land
We'll read the meaning of our dears
We'll meet again and understand
From his sorrowing father, mother and brothers"

Private Albert William Bainton		*1st Bn Wiltshire Regiment*	
Service No.	18031	Age:	38
Place of Birth:	Wingfield, Wiltshire	Home Country:	Wales
Date of Death:	12/04/1918	Cause of death:	Died of wounds
Memorial:	Not known		
War cemetery:	Ploegsteert Memorial		
Theatre of war:	Belgium		
Next of Kin:	Harriet Malinda Bainton (wife) - William and Jane Bainton (parents)		
Address:	Woodfield Terrace, Penrhiwceiber, Glamorganshire – Trowbridge		

Albert was a coal miner in South Wales and in 1900 married Harriet Malinda Beecham. At the outbreak of war he volunteered for service with the 5th Battalion Wiltshire Regiment and arrived at Gallipoli on 15 July 1915. He was wounded in September 1915 and was evacuated to England and after his recovery he was sent to the 1st Battalion Wiltshire Regiment. He was wounded most likely by German shelling on Friday 12 April 1918 at Neuve Eglise, Belgium, he died soon after. He is remembered on the Ploegsteert Memorial and has no known grave. He left a wife and three children.

Private Percy Reginald Randall   *10th Bn Worcestershire Regiment*
Service No. 51303
Age: 18
Place of Birth: Trowbridge, Wiltshire
Home Country: England
Date of Death: 14/04/1918
Cause of death: Died of wounds
Memorial: Trowbridge
War cemetery: La Clytte Military Cemetery
Theatre of war: Belgium
Next of Kin: William & Fanny Randall
Address: 25 New Road, Mortimer Street, Trowbridge

It is likely eighteen year old Percy, the youngest son of William and Fanny Randall, was conscripted into the army joining the Worcester Regiment. He was wounded in fighting in Belgium and died of those wounds on Sunday 14 April 1918.

Private Charles Richard Winter   *6th Bn Wiltshire Regiment*
Service No. 35066
Age: 18
Place of Birth: Bermondsey, London
Home Country: England
Date of Death: 15/04/1918
Cause of death: Killed in action
Memorial: Trowbridge
War cemetery: Tyne Cot Memorial
Theatre of war: Belgium
Next of Kin: Charles & Eliza Ann Winter
Address: 19 Polebarn Road, Trowbridge

Eighteen year old Charles was the eldest son of Charles senior and Eliza Winter. He attended Trowbridge Boy's High School and on leaving was employed in the office of A.H. and S. Bird Coal Merchants. He joined the army on 1 November 1917 soon after attaining military age and was sent to France in the first week of April 1918. He was killed in action on Monday 15 April 1918 near the Kemml-Wytschaete road, Belgium, most likely by German shelling. He is remembered on the Tyne Cot Memorial and has no known grave.

Gunner Henry William Bull   *12th Siege Bty RGA*
Service No. 110760
Age: 34
Place of Birth: Yatton Keynell, Wiltshire
Home Country: England
Date of Death: 17/04/1918
Cause of death: Died of wounds
Memorial: Trowbridge & Corsham
War cemetery: Etaples Military Cemetery
Theatre of war: France
Next of Kin: Annie Bull (wife) - John & Isabella Bull (parents)
Address: 60 Mortimer Street, Trowbridge - Broadstone Corsham

Henry was a bricklayer and a popular sportsman. He was the captain of Corsham Football Club for three years and he led the team to three victories in the League Cup. He was also well known for his bowling skills for Corsham Cricket Club. He attested under the Derby Scheme on 12

Right: Charles Richard Winter

Far right: Henry William Bull

February 1916 and married Mary Ann Brewer at St. Thomas' Church Trowbridge on t 5 June 1916. He was called up in August 1916 and after training he was sent on a signals course. He arrived in France in May 1917 and was wounded in the abdomen on 9 April 1918 while going to the aid of a wounded comrade. He succumbed to his wounds on Wednesday 17 April 1918 at the Canadian Hospital Etaples, France. Henry's parents received the following letter from Lieutenant A. C. Hampson:

"Probably by this time you will have received news of your son. I feel it is useless for one to say what our feelings are when compared with what yours must be, but I must say that he was a man beloved, and better still, respected by all of us. It may come as some consolation to you to know that you have every reason to be proud of him. He received his wound when carrying in a wounded comrade under observation and fire of the enemy. Such acts have a far more reaching effect than the actual saving of life which he undoubtedly effected. These are the sacrifices which build up the moral of our Army. No one of whatever constitution, can fail to live up to such an example.
May I, on behalf of his officers and comrades offer you our sincere sympathy. I know how empty words are. I wish I could force into them some of our feelings of "one who has also known adversity," and may we in the light of these glorious achievements of our friends play the game as they have played it for the honour of our country and our Battery."

Private Thomas White   *52nd Bn Australian Infantry AIF*
Service No. 2005A   Age: 29
Place of Birth: Mackay, Queensland   Home Country: Australia
Date of Death: 17/04/1918   Cause of death: Killed in action
Memorial: Mackay, Queensland
War cemetery: Villers Bretonneux Military Cemetery
Theatre of war: France
Next of Kin: Violet Mary White (wife) – William & Charlotte White (parents)
Address: 9 Havelock Street, Trowbridge – Australia

Thomas, a labourer, enlisted with the Australian army on 11 January 1916 and after completing his training travelled to England via Egypt arriving on 16 August 1916. He was sent to France in November 1916 and evacuated to England shortly thereafter. On 26 September 1917 he

Far left: Thomas White

Left: William George Wickham

married Violet Mary Holloway at Holy Trinity Church, Trowbridge returning to France in November 1917. On 5 April 1918, the 52nd Battalion at Dernancourt assisted in the repulse of the largest German attack mounted against Australian troops during the war. He was killed in action on Wednesday 17 April 1917 in fighting near Villers Bretonneux, France.

Corporal William George Wickham   *1st Bn Worcestershire Regiment*
Service No.   55272   Age: 29
Place of Birth: Trowbridge, Wiltshire   Home Country: England
Date of Death: 25/04/1918   Cause of death: Died of wounds
Memorial: Trowbridge
War cemetery: Crouy British Cemetery Crouy Sur Somme
Theatre of war: France
Next of Kin: George & Anna Maria Wickham
Address: 86 Dursley Road, Trowbridge

William was the eldest son of George and Anna Wickham, he was employed by Bowyer, Philpott and Payne as a butcher. He was an active member Wesley Road Wesleyan Church and Sunday school and was a keen football and cricket player. He enlisted with his brother in the Gloucester Regiment and for over two years he was the acting seargeant instructor in physical training. In 1918 he was transferred to the Worcestershire Regiment and was given the rank of Corporal, he arrived in France at Easter 1918. He died of wounds inflicted by German shell fire at 47th casualty clearing station based at Crouy, France on Thursday 25 April 1918. In April 1919 William's family inserted the following memoriam in a local paper:

"No day light dawns no night begins
But what we think of you
A son so loving a brother so kind
A beautiful memory left behind
Never forgotten by his loving father, mother, brothers and sisters"

Private Arthur Tom Carrier   *820th Coy Army Service Corps*
Service No.   M2/183564   Age: 37
Place of Birth: Bradford on Avon, Wiltshire   Home Country: England

Date of Death:	25/04/1918	Cause of death:	Died
Memorial:	Corsham		
War cemetery:	Mikra British Cemetery		
Theatre of war:	Balkans		
Next of Kin:	Jessie Harriett Carrier (wife) - Tom & Martha Carrier (parents)		
Address:	5 Thomas Street, Walcot, Somerset – Sladesbrook, Bradford on Avon		

Prior to the war Arthur was a chauffeur to the Rev. J Penrose the Vicar of West Ashton and married Jessie Harriett Macey in 1909. He joined the army on 2 June 1916 and was sent to Salonika, Greece, on 21 May 1917. He died on Thursday 25 April 1918 of jaundice malaria at a military hospital at Salonika. In 1919 his family inserted the following memoriam in a local paper:

"The midnight stars are shining
Upon his lonely grave
The one we love is sleeping
The one we could not save
May the heavenly winds blow softly
O'er that sweet and hallowed spot
Though the sea divides his grave from us
He will never be forgot RIP"

Private Arthur Lewis Davis　　　　　　　　　*6th Bn Wiltshire Regiment*

Service No.	24139	Age:	25
Place of Birth:	Trowbridge, Wiltshire	Home Country:	England
Date of Death:	28/04/1918	Cause of death:	Killed in action
Memorial:	Trowbridge		
War cemetery:	HAC Cemetery Ecoust-st Mein		
Theatre of war:	France		
Next of Kin:	Rose Davis (wife) - Hiram & Fanny Davis (parents)		
Address:	9 Prospect Place, Trowbridge - 28 Thomas Street, Trowbridge		

Arthur was an engine cleaner and married Rose Lucas in the spring of 1915. It is likely he was conscripted into the army joining the 6th Battalion Wiltshire Regiment. He was posted as missing on 23 March 1918 during the German attack at Baupaume. In February 1919 Rose Davis inserted an advert in a local paper asking for information about her missing husband. Official information was received that Arthur had been killed in action on Sunday 28 April 1918, it is likely during the confusion of the German offensive Arthur became detached from the Wiltshire's and died fighting with another unit.

Private Arthur Bull　　　　　　　　　*1/4th TF Bn Wiltshire Regiment*

Service No.	200626	Age:	29
Place of Birth:	Trowbridge, Wiltshire	Home Country:	England
Date of Death:	10/05/1918	Cause of death:	Killed in action
Memorial:	Trowbridge		
War cemetery:	Ramleh War Cemetery		
Theatre of war:	Egypt		
Next of Kin:	Annie Maria Bull (wife) – James & Sarah Bull (parents)		
Address:	23 St.Thomas Road, Trowbridge		

Arthur was a plasterer and tiler and married Annie Maria Beaverstock in 1907, he was also a

Far left: Arthur Tom Carrier

Left: Arthur Bull

Wiltshire Territorial. In October 1914 he was sent to India for garrison duties and in September 1917 the 1/4th Wiltshires were sent to Egypt and on to Palestine. Arthur was employed as a cook while with the Wiltshires and was killed by a shell during a Turkish barrage on Friday 10 May 1918 near Rafat and was originally buried at Ballut. Arthur left a widow and two young children. He was killed by the same shell burst that killed William Edwards.

Private William George Edwards   *1/4th TF Bn Wiltshire Regiment*

Service No.	200665	Age:	35
Place of Birth:	Melksham, Wiltshire	Home Country:	England
Date of Death:	10/05/1918	Cause of death:	Killed in action
Memorial:	Holt – Hilperton & Hilperton Church Memorial		
War cemetery:	Ramleh War Cemetery		
Theatre of war:	Egypt		
Next of Kin:	Emma Louisa Edwards (wife) - Herbert and Eliza Edwards (parents)		
Address:	Horse Road, Hilperton – Trowbridge		

Prior to the Great War William was employed building the milk factory at Staverton and had married Emma Reynolds at Robourne, near Malmesbury at the end of the year in 1908. He was also a Wiltshire Territorrial and in October 1914 he was sent to India for garrison duties and in September 1917 the 1/4th Wiltshires were sent to Egypt and on to Palestine. While with the Wiltshires he was employed as a cook, was wounded in November 1917 and returned to his regiment in March 1918. He was killed by a shell during a Turkish barrage on Friday 10 May 1918 near Rafat and was originally buried at Ballutt. William was killed in the same burst that killed Arthur Bull. Emma Edwards received the following letter from Lieutenant Colonel Armstrong:

"He gave his life for others, and could not have died a nobler death. I do hope that it may be of some little comfort to you to know how deeply we all sympathise with you."

In May 1919 Emma Edwards inserted the following memoriam in a local paper:

"I cannot think you dead it must only be
That you have travelled far
And while I find my path on earth more lonely

My sky has gained a star
A star whose place in heaven I see more plainly
Because with me, tis night
Yet through my tears I sometimes seek vainly
And cannot find its light
Ever remembered by his sorrowing wife"

Private Charles James Norris   *34th Bn Royal Fusiliers*
Service No.   31411   Age: 37
Place of Birth: Trowbridge, Wiltshire   Home Country: England
Date of Death: 13/05/1918   Cause of death: Died of wounds
Memorial: Trowbridge – Hilperton & Hilperton Church Memorial
War cemetery: St Sever Cemetery Rouen
Theatre of war: France
Next of Kin: Lisetta Broughton Norris (wife) - James and Emily Norris (parents)
Address: 64 Ashton Street, Trowbridge

Charles, known as James, was employed by Beaven's tanyard at Holt and had married Lisetta Cantello at the end of 1915. He enlisted in March 1916 with the Devon Regiment and was transferred to the 101st Labour Battalion, Royal Fusiliers. He died of gas poisoning on Monday 13 May 1918 at No. 10 General Hospital. Chaplain Agnew wrote the following letter to Lisetta Norris:

"I have very sad and painful news to break to you. Your husband came into this hospital so badly gassed with mustard gas shells that he died shortly afterwards yesterday. The loss of your husband must be a very grievous one for you to bear, but I know you will always be proud of him in that he surrendered his life on the altar of duty for his King and country. But your great consolation must be that which the Christian religion affords that those who believe in Christ shall never really die, but enjoy the life everlasting. We believe, too, that even on earth there is communion with those who have crossed the Veil. May God be with you in this your deep affliction, and may the sunshine of His love appear to you even in the darkness of your sorrow."

Corporal Alec James Hudd   *4th Sqdn Royal Air Force*
Service No.   320229   Age: 25
Place of Birth: Trowbridge, Wiltshire   Home Country: England

Right: William George Edwards

Far right: Alec James Hudd

Date of Death:	14/05/1918	Cause of death:	Died
Memorial:	Trowbridge - Hilperton Church & Methodist Church - Staverton		
War cemetery:	Longuenesse St.Omer Souvenir Cemetery		
Theatre of war:	France		
Next of Kin:	Marguerite Hudd (wife) - James & Elizabeth Hudd (parents)		
Address:	Streatham Common London - The Nurseries Hilperton Marsh		

Alec was the youngest son of James and Elizabeth Hudd and worked with his father at Hilperton Nurseries. In 1915 he married Marguerite Hudd in London and he was a member of the Wiltshire Yeomanry. He transferred to the Royal Flying Corps, which on 1 April 1918 became the Royal Air Force. He died of lobar pneumonia on Tuesday 14 May 1918 at No .9 Casualty Clearing Station at St.Omer, France.

Private Charles George White *1st R.M. Bn. R.N. Div RMLI*

Service No.	CH/2201(S)	Age:	19
Place of Birth:	Hilperton, Wiltshire	Home Country:	England
Date of Death:	19/05/1918	Cause of death:	Killed in action
Memorial:	Hilperton		
War cemetery:	Hamel Military Cemetery Beaumont Hamel		
Theatre of war:	France		
Next of Kin:	Samuel & Florence White		
Address:	Dymont Square, Hilperton		

Charles was a labourer and enlisted with the Marines on 23 March 1917 at 18 years of age arriving in France in June 1917. He received a gunshot wound to the head on 7 April 1918 while serving at Englebelmer, south west of Beaumont Hamel, France and after his recovery he rejoined his unit on 22 April 1918. During the early hours of Sunday 19 May 1918 the Marines took part in a raid proceeded by a short bombardment on German lines aiming to capture prisoners or identify the units opposing them at Hamel sector. Charles was posted as missing in action assumed dead and later officially reported to have been killed in the raid. The Marines war diary gives an account of the state of the German positions:

"When however the objective was reached it was found to have been absolutely evacuated by the enemy, & unfortunately we were unable to obtain identification of any kind. Dugouts & shelters were effectively bombed & fired after being searched & much damage was done. Our casualties were remarkably small".

Private Peter Gane *2/4th TF Bn Wiltshire Regiment*

Service No.	202538	Age:	34
Place of Birth:	Newton, Wiltshire	Home Country:	England
Date of Death:	19/05/1918	Cause of death:	Died
Memorial:	Tisbury & Trowbridge St James Church Memorial		
War cemetery:	Madras 1914 1918 War Memorial Chennai		
Theatre of war:	India		
Next of Kin	Emily Gane (parent)		
Address:	Newtown, Tisbury, Wiltshire		

Peter a Wiltshire Territorial, was sent to India for garrison duties and died of illness or disease at Allahabad, India and was buried in Allahabad New Cantonment Cemetery. The Commonwealth War Graves Commision do not tend the graves of British soldiers in many cemeteries in India and Peter is remembered on the Madras 1914-1918 War Memorial Chennai.

Signaler Gilbert William Frank Griffin   1/5th Bn South Lancashire Regt

Service No.	4066	Age:	19
Place of Birth:	Hilperton, Wiltshire	Home Country:	England
Date of Death:	21/05/1918	Cause of death:	Died of wounds
Memorial:	Trowbridge		
War cemetery:	Pernes British Cemetery		
Theatre of war:	France		
Next of Kin:	Frederick and Clara J. Griffin		
Address:	39 Wyke Road, Trowbridge		

Prior to the Great War Gilbert was employed by the Anglo Swiss milk factory at Staverton. He originally volunteered for service with the 2/3rd Home Counties Field Ambulance of the Royal Army Medical Corps on 15 April 1915 and was discharged on 24 September 1915, presumably because he was not suitable for military service. He attested for military service under the Derby Scheme, joining the Royal Wiltshire Yeomanry on 10 March 1917 and was sent to France arriving on 15 April 1918. He was then transferred to the South Lancashires on 17 April 1918 serving as a signaler. Gilbert was wounded by a shell burst on Monday 20 May 1918 and succumbed to his wounds the following day. Clara Griffin received the following letter from Lieutenant Harold Davis:

"I should like to express to you on behalf of his comrades and his officers the deep sympathy which we all feel for you in the loss of your son. I am taking this first opportunity, after coming out of the line, to let you know what few particulars I have been able to obtain about the sad occurrence. It was on his last tour in the line, when just leaving rest billets to proceed into the trenches on the evening of the 19 May, that a shell burst in the midst of the company to which your son was attached, killing one man and wounding several more. Your son was severely wounded and removed to hospital straight away, where everything possible was done to ease his last hours. He died the following day in hospital at Pernes where he is buried. In the short time that he had been with the signal section your son had already done valuable work. He was an excellent signaler and a fine soldier, cool, brave and confident, and he had rapidly endeared himself to his comrades by his unfailing cheerfulness and good humour in the hardships and difficulties of life in the field."

Gilbert's brother Wilfred had been killed in action in April 1915.

Right: Gilbert William Frank Griffin

Far right William George Thomas Loveday

Private Henry Ernest Shipway   *6th Bn Shropshire Light Infantry*
Service No.   14779   Age: 39
Place of Birth: Trowbridge, Wiltshire   Home Country: England
Date of Death: 21/05/1918   Cause of death: Died
Memorial: Not known
War cemetery: Chauny Communal Cemetery British Cemetery Extension
Theatre of war: France
Next of Kin: Eliza Shipway (parent)
Address: Trowbridge

Ernest was employed as a coal miner in South Wales. He volunteered for service and arrived in France on 28 September 1915. He died most likely due to illness or disease on Tuesday 21 May 1918.

27 May 1918 - 'Blucher' the Third German Spring Offensive

Private William George Thomas Loveday   *4th Bn South Staffordshire Regt*
Service No.   43589   Age: 19
Place of Birth: Swindon, Wiltshire   Home Country: England
Date of Death: 27/05/1918   Cause of death: Killed in action
Memorial: Trowbridge
War cemetery: Soissons Memorial
Theatre of war: France
Next of Kin: Thomas G & Laura Loveday
Address: 6 Stanmore Street, Swindon

Nineteen year old William was the eldest son of Thomas & Laua Loveday and was employed by Mr Darling of Fore Street, Trowbridge delivering parcel's for Sutton and Co. He enlisted in May 1917 and was trained at Sandhill Camp, Felixstowe. He was sent to France on 31 March 1918 and was killed in action at the Battle of the Aisne on 27 May 1918. He is remembered on the Soissons Memorial and has no known grave. In May 1919 his family inserted the following memoriam in a local paper:

"Farewell dear one to all our hearts so dear
Oft do we breathe your memory with a tear
Short was thy life but long thy rest
God called thee soon because he thought it best
From his loving Grandmother, Brother and Sister"

Lance Coporal Frederick Walter Bartholomew   *106th Field Coy Royal Engineers*
Service No.   186305   Age: 21
Place of Birth: Dorchester, Dorset   Home Country: England
Date of Death: 28/05/1918   Cause of death: Killed in action
Memorial: Trowbridge
War cemetery: Soissons Memorial
Theatre of war: France
Next of Kin: Edith Emma Drewett (parent)
Address: 3 Brickley Lane, Devizes

It is likely Frederick, known as Fred, was conscripted into the army joining the Royal Engineers

Right: Frederick Walter Bartholomew

Far right: Frank Holton

and was killed in action during the Battle of the Aisne at Jonchery sur Vesle between Soissons and Rheims, France. He is remembered on the Soissons Memorial and has no known grave.

Sapper Frank Holton		*105th Field Coy Royal Engineers*	
Service No.	153874	Age:	36
Place of Birth:	Trowbridge, Wiltshire	Home Country:	England
Date of Death:	30/05/1918	Cause of death:	Died of wounds
Memorial:	Trowbridge - No 15 Shop Memorial Swindon Railway Museum		
War cemetery:	City of Paris Cemetery Pantin		
War cemetery:	City of Paris Cemetery Pantin		
Theatre of war:	France		
Next of Kin:	Edward & Sarah Holton		
Address:	3 Martins Buildings, The Halve, Trowbridge		

Frank was the youngest son of Edward and Sarah Holton and was an employee of the Great Western Railway Works in Swindon, where he worked as a plumber in No 15 Shop in the carriage department. He joined the Army enlisting with the Royal Engineers and was wounded during fighting at the Battle of the Aisne on 27 May 1918. He succumbed to his wounds on Thursday 30 May 1918 at a French hospital in Paris.

Lance Corporal Charles Wyndham Barnes		*2nd Bn Wiltshire Regiment*	
Service No.	11257	Age:	33
Place of Birth:	Westbury, Wiltshire	Home Country:	England
Date of Death:	01/06/1918	Cause of death:	Killed in action
Memorial:	Heywood		
War cemetery:	Soissons Memorial		
Theatre of war:	France		
Next of Kin:	Violet Blanche Barnes (wife) - Frank W. & Helena Barnes (parents)		
Address:	The Beeches, Yarnbrook - Hill Nest, Heywood		

Charles was a law clerk and the eldest son of Frank Wyndham and Helena Barnes and married Violet Eyers at the end of 1914. He volunteered for service with the Wiltshire Regiment and arrived in France on 19 July 1915. On Saturday 1 June 1918 the Wiltshires were at Chambrecy, France and were expecting an attack. To their left was a French regiment and the Wiltshires had agreed with them to inform each other if they were going to retreat. The Germans heavily attacked the French during the morning and at 2pm the French informed the Wiltshires they were about to retire, the Wiltshires received no orders and stayed in position. At 4.30pm German machine gunners crept up on the left of the Wiltshires and opened fire but the Wiltshire had to wait until 7.30pm until the order came to withdraw. It is likely that Charles was killed in action at this time. He is remembered on the Soissons memorial and has no known grave.

Private Harry Jefferies — 6th Bn Wiltshire Regiment
Service No.: 204200
Age: 31
Place of Birth: Trowbridge, Wiltshire
Home Country: England
Date of Death: 03/06/1918
Cause of death: Died
Memorial: Trowbridge
War cemetery: Birmingham Lodge Hill Cemetery
Theatre of war: Home
Next of Kin: Henry Jefferies
Address: 12 Yerbury Street, Trowbridge

Harry had originally joined the Wiltshire Yeomanry and in September 1917 they were merged with the 6th Battalion Wiltshire Regiment. He died of illness or disease on Monday 3 June 1918 at a hospital in Birmingham.

Private Walter George Parsons — 2/4th TF Bn Wiltshire Regiment
Service No.: 202576
Age: 39
Place of Birth: Chippenham, Wiltshire
Home Country: England
Date of Death: 05/06/1918
Cause of death: Died
Memorial: Chippenham & Trowbridge St James Church Memorial
War cemetery: Madras 1914 1918 War Memorial Chennai
Theatre of war: India
Next of Kin: Thomas & Elizabeth Parsons
Address: 51 Lowden, Chippenham

Walter was a Wiltshire Territorial was sent to India for garrison duties. He died of illness or disease at Allahabad, India and was buried in Allahabad New Cantonment Cemetery. The Commonwealth War Graves Commission do not tend the graves of British soldiers in many cemeteries in India and he is remembered on the Madras 1914-1918 War Memorial Chennai.

Private Edward Charles Hoddinott — 2/4th TF Bn Wiltshire Regiment
Service No.: 202431
Age: 31
Place of Birth: Warminster, Wiltshire
Home Country: England
Date of Death: 07/06/1918
Cause of death: Died
Memorial: Trowbridge St James Church Memorial - Warminster
War cemetery: Madras 1914-1918 War Memorial Chennai
Theatre of war: India
Next of Kin: Charles & Maud Mary Hoddinott
Address: Church Road, Silton, Zeals, Wiltshire

Edward, a Wiltshire Territorial, was sent to India for Garrison duties and died of illness or disease at Lebong, India. He was buried in Lebong New Cantonment Cemetery. The Commonwealth War Graves Commission do not tend the graves of British soldiers in many cemeteries in India and he is remembered on the Madras 1914-1918 War Memorial Chennai.

Right: Harry Jefferies

Far right: Robert Stanley Potter

Private Robert Stanley Potter	*1st Bn Hampshire Regiment*
Service No. 45840	Age: 19
Place of Birth: Poonamalee, India	Home Country: England
Date of Death: 08/06/1918	Cause of death: Died of wounds
Memorial: Trowbridge	
War cemetery: Pernes British Cemetery	
Theatre of war: France	
Next of Kin: William Henry & Lydia Annie Potter	
Address: 40 Frome Road, Trowbridge	

Robert was employed by Sainsbury & Co. as a lorry driver and on reaching 18 years of age he joined the Hampshire Regiment in May 1917 and was sent to France at Easter of the same year. He was severely wounded in the chest on Saturday 8 June 1918 and succumbed to his wounds the same day at No. 6 Casualty Clearing Station at Pernes en Artois, France. His brother Charles William Potter had been killed in January 1916.

Sapper Herbert Cecil Charles Knowler	*Base Depot Royal Engineers*
Service No. 346907	Age: 24
Place of Birth: Trowbridge, Wiltshire	Home Country: England
Date of Death: 13/06/1918	Cause of death: Suicide
Memorial: Trowbridge	
War cemetery: Baghdad North Gate War Cemetery	
Theatre of war: Mesopotamia	
Next of Kin: Sarah Williams (mother)	
Address: 16 Upper Broad Street, Trowbridge	

Herbert a blacksmith attested under the Derby Scheme on 10 December 1915 and was called up on 18 April 1916 joining the Somerset Light Infantry. He was then transferred to the Royal Artillery and was sent to Mesopotamia arriving in Basra on 21 September 1917. In May 1918 Herbert was compulsorily transferred to the Royal Engineers. In July 1918 Herbert's mother Sarah, received official news that her son had died of wounds at the British General Hospital in Baghdad. She then wrote to the records office asking for information about his death and if it had been accidental. In December 1918 Sarah received the following reply from the Royal

Far left: Herbert Cecil Charles Knowler

Left: Ernest James Garfield Belbin

Engineers records office:

"Madam, your letter to the O.C. British General Hospital, Baghdad, has been passed to this office for reply as your late son 346907 Sapper H.C. Knowler, R.E., did not die in that hospital. I regret to have to inform you the Injury from which he died (Gun Shot wound Face and Head) were self inflicted. A Court of Enquiry was held, but there was no evidence to prove why he did it. It took place during the night in his sleeping tent."

Private Percy Shrapnell		*1/7th Royal Warwickshire Regiment*	
Service No.	306640	Age:	25
Place of Birth:	Bath, Somerset	Home Country:	England
Date of Death:	15/06/1918	Cause of death:	Killed in action
Memorial:	North Bradley		
War cemetery:	Magnaboschi British Cemetery		
Theatre of war:	Italy		
Next of Kin:	Joseph & Ellen Shrapnell		
Address:	Yarnbrook, Wiltshire		

Percy was a brick layers labourer and it is likely he joined the army during 1917. He was sent to Italy with the 1/7th Warwickshire Regiment and was killed in action on Saturday 15 June 1918, when the Austrians heavily shelled the British trenches at Magnaboschi with both high explosive and gas shells.

Lance Corporal Ernest James Garfield Belbin		*503rd Field Coy Royal Engineers*	
Service No.	504536	Age:	22
Place of Birth:	Swindon, Wiltshire	Home Country:	England
Date of Death:	27/06/1918	Cause of death:	Died of wounds
Memorial:	Trowbridge		
War cemetery:	Pernois British Cemetery		
Theatre of war:	France		
Next of Kin:	Ernest & Martha Belbin		
Address:	25 Innox Road, Trowbridge		

Ernest a labourer enlisted with the Royal Engineers on 7 October 1915 and after completing his training he was sent to France. On 8 March 1918 he was granted 14 days leave to go to England and returned to France just before the German Offensive. He was wounded with bomb wounds to the head and back on Wednesday 26 June 1918 and succumbed to his wounds the following day at the 41 Casualty Clearing Station. His personal possessions were returned to his parents consisting of disc, letters, photos, letter case, silver watch and strap, knife and cards.

Private William Henry Haines   *4th Bn Wiltshire Regiment*
Service No. 201551
Age: 20
Place of Birth: Trowbridge, Wiltshire
Home Country: England
Date of Death: 03/07/1918
Cause of death: Died
Memorial: Melksham
War cemetery: Melksham Church Cemetery
Theatre of war: Home
Next of Kin: Harry & Mary Jane Haines
Address: 40 Forest Road, Melksham

William was the eldest son of Harry and Mary Jane Haines and died of illness or disease at a London hospital on Wednesday 3 July 1918. He was buried in Melksham Cemetery with full military honours organised by Melksham Volunteer Corp and a wounded soldier played the last post.

Corporal John Howard Cherry   *59th Bn Australian Infantry AIF*
Service No. 2144
Age: 22
Place of Birth: Camberwell, Victoria
Home Country: Australia
Date of Death: 04/07/1918
Cause of death: Killed in action
Memorial: Not Known
War cemetery: Mericourt Labbee Communal Cemetery Extension
Theatre of war: France
Next of Kin: Gladys Cherry (wife) – Major Thomas Cherry (parent)
Address: 2 Lower Alms Street, Trowbridge

John, a student, enlisted with the Australian army on 15 April 1916. After completing his training he left Melbourne in August 1916 and arrived in England in 6 December 1916 being sent to France the following day. He was sent to Codford, England in November 1917 and on 12 January 1918 he married Gladys Greenland at Codford St Mary. John returned to France in April 1918 and was killed in action near Mericourt, France on Thursday 4 July 1918. Gladys Cherry inserted the following memoriam in a local paper in July 1919:

"Into the fields of battle he bravely took his place
And fought and died for England the honour of his race
He lies not in his native land but under a foreign sky
Far from friends who loved him but in a hero's grave he lies"

Sapper Frederick Guy Norris   *18th Div. Signal Coy. Royal Engineers*
Service No. 267994
Age: 34
Place of Birth: Trowbridge, Wiltshire
Home Country: England
Date of Death: 06/07/1918
Cause of death: Died
Memorial: Corsham
War cemetery: Terlincthun British Cemetery Wimille
Theatre of war: France

Next of Kin: Frederick & Emma Norris
Address:, Trowbridge

Frederick was a post office clerk and widely known in the the Melksham area as a piccolo player. He joined the Royal Engineers in 1915 and after completing his training was sent to France. He died of pneumonia on Saturday 6 July 1918 at No. 54 Field Hospital at Boulogne. The Commonwealth War Grave Commission list the date of Frederick's death as 6 July 1919.

Captain William Charles Strong   *2/4th TF Bn Wiltshire Regiment*
Service No.: N/A
Age: 47
Place of Birth: Warminster, Wiltshire
Home Country: England
Date of Death: 26/07/1918
Cause of death: Died
Memorial: Trowbridge St James Church Memorial - Warminster
War cemetery: Madras 1914 - 1918 War Memorial Chennai
Theatre of war: India
Next of Kin: Marion Strong (wife) - Robert & Louisa Strong (parents)
Address: 30 Boreham Road, Warminster

Prior to the war William was a clerk at Longleat estate office. He married Marion Chinn in 1904 and had been Quarter Master Sergeant in the Volunteer Corps. He was sent to India soon after the outbreak of war and died of illness or disease at Allahabad, India and was buried in Allahabad New Cantonment Cemetery. He is remembered on the Madras 1914-1918 War Memorial Chennai. He left a widow and six children.

Sergeant Allen Naylor Waterhouse   *16th Balloon Coy Royal Air Force*
Service No.: 2440
Age: 33
Place of Birth: Bradford, Yorkshire
Home Country: England
Date of Death: 27/07/1918
Cause of death: Killed in action
Memorial: Not known
War cemetery: St Pierre Cemetery Amiens
Theatre of war: France
Next of Kin: Ella G Waterhouse (wife) - John & Grace E Waterhouse (parents)
Address: 21 Wylie Rd, Trowbridge

Allen, a chauffeur, married Ella Jumbo in the spring of 1912. He volunteered for service with the Royal Flying Corps and arrived in France on 10 October 1915. He was a member of 16 Balloon Company with the balloons being used for artillery observation. He was killed in action on Sunday 27 July 1918 near Amiens, France

Private William Charles Burnell   *1st Garrison South Staffordshire Regt*
Service No: 204709
Age: Not Known
Place of Birth:, Not known
Home Country: England
Date of Death: 31/07/1918
Cause of death: Died
Memorial: Trowbridge St James Church
War cemetery: Kirkee 1914-1918 Memorial
Theatre of war: India
Next of Kin: Not Known
Address: Not Known

William, a Wiltshire Territorial, was sent to India for garrison duties and was transferred to the South Staffordshire Regiment. He died of illness or disease on Wednesday 31 July 1917.

The Commonwealth War Graves Commission do not tend the graves of British soldiers in many cemeteries in India and he is remembered on the Madras 1914-1918 War Memorial Chennai.

Allen Naylor Waterhouse

14
A BLACK DAY FOR THE GERMAN ARMY

8 AUGUST 1918 - THE SECOND BATTLE OF AMIENS

Private John Perkins (Cutmore)   *19th Central Ontario Regiment*
Service No.   800030   Age: 22
Place of Birth: Trowbridge, Wiltshire   Home Country: England
Date of Death: 08/08/1918   Cause of death: Killed in action
Memorial: Trowbridge
War cemetery: Crucifix Corner Cemetery Villiers Bretonneux
Theatre of war: France
Next of Kin: Ethel Helen Perkins
Address: 23 Union Street, Trowbridge, Wiltshire

John, a labourer, had emigrated to Canada prior to the commencement of hostilities and joined the Canadian army on 5 February 1916. He was killed in action on Thursday 8 August 1918 near Villiers Bretonneux, France during the Second Battle of Amiens. His name is given as Cutmore on the Trowbridge war memorial but he served under the name of Perkins.

Rifleman Precival George Warr   *9th Bn London Regiment*
Service No.   391399   Age: 28
Place of Birth: Dulwich, London   Home Country: England

Right: John Perkins (Cutmore) - Below: German prisoners

Date of Death: 10/08/1918   Cause of death: Died of wounds
Memorial: Not known
War cemetery: Beacon Cemetery Sailly Laurette
Theatre of war: France
Next of Kin: Mabel Warr (wife) - Henry George & Harriet Warr (parents)
Address: 9 New Road Court, Trowbridge – London

Percy was a clerk to a master printer. He married Mabel E Cartwright in the spring of 1915 and joined the 9 London Regiment known as Queen Victoria's rifles. He died of wounds on Saturday 10 August 1918 near Sailly-Laurette, France during the second battle of Amiens.

21 AUGUST 1918 - THE SECOND BATTLE OF ALBERT

Private Henry Charles Smith   *47th Coy Machine Gun Corps*
Service No.   53732   Age: 21
Place of Birth: Melksham, Wiltshire   Home Country: England
Date of Death: 23/08/1918   Cause of death: Killed in action
Memorial: Trowbridge
War cemetery: Dernancourt Communal Cemetery Extension
Theatre of war: France
Next of Kin: Charles & Mary A. Smith
Address: 37 The Furlong, Trowbridge

Henry, known as Harry, was employed by J. & T. Clark of Trowbridge and joined the Wiltshire Regiment in July 1915. He was sent to France in 1916 and transferred to the Machine Gun Corps. He was killed in action on Friday 23 August 1918 near Derncourt, France during the recapture of Albert.

Private Frederick Arthur Johnston Nelson   *28th Artists Rifles London Regiment*
Service No.   766816   Age: 19
Place of Birth: Rathfriland, County Down Home Country: England
Date of Death: 22/08/1918   Cause of death: Died of wounds

Right: Herny Charles Smith

Far right: Frederick Arthur Johnston Nelson

Memorial:	Trowbridge
War cemetery:	Bagneux British Cemetery Gezaincout
Theatre of war:	France
Next of Kin:	William & Rachel Nelson
Address:	New Sarum 54 Bradley Road, Trowbridge, Wiltshire

Frederick was the only son of William and Rachel Nelson. He was a keen musician and an accomplished player of the piano having also been the organist at the Emanuel Baptist Church. He enlisted in August 1917 soon after his eighteenth birthday and had been recommended for a commission. He was waiting for orders to come through when news of the German advance was received in March 1918. Frederick volunteered to go to France even though he was only eighteen. In May 1918 one of Frederick's comrades, Charles Mott, died of wounds and Frederick had written letters home of how at a concert in a village café, Charles sang favourite songs and Frederick accompanied him on the piano. Another letter Frederick wrote explained his feelings about fighting for his country, he wrote:

"I am most uncomfortable in front line trenches, in a state of filth, not having washed or shaved for eight days, but I am merry and bright under the camouflage. A man will have a bad time out here if he is inclined to be pessimistic. I am sure you have wondered if my keenness has suffered since I have been out here, where the work is terribly hard and dispiriting. I can honestly say that I still posses the spirit of keenness - patriotism, call it what you will, with which I joined the army. Though my whole body aches with hard work, though my head and eyes be heavy through lack of sleep, I am happy, for I believe it is for England. I am prepared to die out here and think it an honour, I would not be without that feeling for anything; it is worth more than another man's strength to me."

Frederick died of gunshot wounds to the chest at a casualty clearing station based at Gezaincout, France on Thursday 22 August 1918.

Private Cecil Dean Early   *24th Bn Royal Fusilers*

Service No.	STK/2027	Age:	28
Place of Birth:	Southampton, Hampshire	Home Country:	England
Date of Death:	23/08/1918	Cause of death:	Killed in action
Memorial:	Southampton		
War cemetery:	Railway Cutting Cemetery Courcelles Le Comte		
Theatre of war:	France		
Next of Kin:	Egbert R. & Ellen E. Early		
Address:	Shirley, Southampton, Hampshire		

Cecil was a bank clerk at Capital and Counties Bank, Fore Street, Trowbridge. He joined the 24 Battalion Royal Fusiliers known as the Sportsman's Battalion. He was killed in action near Courcelles-le-Comte, north west of Bapaume, France on Friday 23 August 1918.

Bombardier William Alec Ransom   *F Bty 14th Bde Royal Horse Artillery*

Service No.	67947	Age:	24
Place of Birth:	Hastings, Sussex	Home Country:	England
Date of Death:	24/08/1918	Cause of death:	Killed in action
Memorial:	Trowbridge		
War cemetery:	St. Amand British Cemetery		
Theatre of war:	France		
Next of Kin:	Florence Emily Ransom (wife) - William & Margret Ransom (parents)		

Address: 26 Lower Studley, Trowbridge – Crowborough, Sussex

Regular soldier William had been based in Trowbridge prior to the war and before the conflict commenced he was sent to India. He was then sent on to France in September 1914 and remained on active service until he was evacuated to England with a poisoned foot early in 1917. While in England he married Florence Hopkins of Lower Studley and after his recovery in 1917 he returned to France. He was then sent to Italy and then back to France again and was expected home on leave when the news arrived of his death. William was killed in action on Saturday 24 August 1918 with 4 comrades while carrying a badly wounded sergeant who had lost an arm and a leg to a dressing station. A shell fell amongst the group killing the whole party instantly. William and his comrades are buried in the same cemetery. His brother Arthur had been killed in August 1916.

Private Charles Styles   *5th Bn Wiltshire Regiment*
Service No.   25810   Age: 28
Place of Birth: Farringdon, Berkshire   Home Country: England
Date of Death: 24/08/1918   Cause of death: Accident
Memorial: Trowbridge
War cemetery: Basra Memorial
Theatre of war: Mesopotamia
Next of Kin: Florence Mabel Styles (wife) - Richard & Annie Styles (parents)
Address: 1 Hardings Yard, Newtown, Trowbridge - Highworth

Charles married Florence M Edmonds in the summer of 1915 and it is likely he joined the army soon after being sent to Mesopotamia to serve with the 5 Battalion Wiltshire Regiment. He drowned accidentally on Saturday 24 August 1915. He is remembered on the Basra Memorial and has no known grave.

Private Herbert Greenhill   *Princess Patricia's Canadian L.I.*
Service No.   2260915   Age: 29
Place of Birth: Farleigh Hungerford, Wiltshire   Home Country: Canada
Date of Death: 26/08/1918   Cause of death: Killed in action
Memorial: Trowbridge

Right: William Alec Ransom

Far Right: Charles Styles

War cemetery: Vis En Artois British Cemetery Haucourt
Theatre of war: France
Next of Kin: Arthur & Elizabeth Ann Greenhill
Address: 119 Newtown, Trowbridge

Herbert, a steward, was the third son of Arthur & Elizabeth Greenhill and had emigrated to Canada prior to the Great War. He joined the Canadian army on 29 June 1917 at Toronto, Canada. He was killed in action on Monday 26 August 1918 during the Scarpe Offensive east of Monchy le Preux, France, a German strong point, while taking part in a bombing attack.

2nd Lieutenant Bruce James Sloper MC *3rd Machine Gun Corps*
Service No.: N/A   Age: 26
Place of Birth: Devizes, Wiltshire   Home Country: England
Date of Death: 31/08/1918   Cause of death: Killed in action
Memorial: Devizes & Trowbridge St. James Church Memorial
War cemetery: Mory Abbey Military Cenetery Mory
Theatre of war: France
Next of Kin: Marler Kell & Mary Maud Sloper
Address: Delldene, Devizes

Bruce was the third son of Marler and Mary Sloper and worked for his father in a tailors and drapers shop in Trowbridge, he was also a Wiltshire Territorial. It is likely he was sent to India at the outbreak of war. He transferred to the Machine Gun Corps and returned to England where he received a Commission on 25 August 1917 and was sent on to France on 28 September 1917. During the German advance in 1918 he received the Military Cross, and the following citation appeared in the London Gazette:

"For conspicuous gallantry and devotion to duty. With two guns on the right of an infantry brigade inflicted severe losses on the enemy, who made several determined attacks. When the forward defences were penetrated - and he was practically surrounded he successfully withdrew his men and guns to a fresh position, holding up and eventually repulsing the attack."

Bruce was killed in action near Mory a village between Arras and Bapaume, France, on Saturday 31 August 1918. His brother Reginald Sloper, a cadet with the Flying Corps, had died in January 1918.

Far left: Herbert Greenhill

Left: Hugh Deane Smith

Private Hugh Deane Smith   *6th Bn Dorsetshire Regiment*

Service No.	30769	Age:	20
Place of Birth:	Bristol, Gloucestershire	Home Country:	England
Date of Death:	01/09/1918	Cause of death:	Killed in action
Memorial:	Trowbridge		
War cemetery:	Vis En Artois Memorial		
Theatre of war:	France		
Next of Kin:	Frederick & Mary E. Smith		
Address:	32 Roundstone Street, Trowbridge		

Hugh was the only son of Frederick & Mary Smith. He attempted to join the army several times and was rejected until in May 1917 his attempt was successful. During his training he was promoted to the rank of corporal and was offered a role in England as a Lewis gun instructor but he chose to go to France snd was transferred as a private to the Dorset Regiment. On Sunday 1 September 1918 the Dorsets were north of Lesbouefs, France which was a neat area where the Dorsets had served during the winter of 1916 - 1917. Hugh and some other men of the Dorsets were in a trench when a German shell dropped amongst them, killing five and wounding four others. One of Hugh's comrades wrote the following to Frederick & Mary Smith:

"We have been over the top about five times during the last fortnight, and we have had a very trying time in the big advance, but I never heard Hugh have a wrong word with anyone, and I am only voicing the opinions of all our platoon when I say we have lost one of the quietest lads in the company. He was the best lad bar none, in the battalion."

Hugh was killed a within a few days of his 21st birthday and is remembered on the Vis En Artois Memorial and has no known grave.

Able Seaman William George Marshman   *Hawke Bn RN Division RNR*

Service No.	R/1561	Age:	21
Place of Birth:	Trowbridge, Wiltshire	Home Country:	England
Date of Death:	03/09/1918	Cause of death:	Killed in action
Memorial:	Trowbridge		
War cemetery:	Vis En Artois British Cemetery Haucourt		
Theatre of war:	France		
Next of Kin:	Florence A Marshman (wife) - William. G & Rose Marshman (parents)		
Address:	19 Timbrell Street, Trowbridge - 114, Lower Studley, Trowbridge		

William was the eldest son of William sr. and Rose Marshman and before the Great War he was a goods checker on the Trowbridge and Frome railway. He attested under the Derby Scheme and was placed on the army reserve in January 1916 being called up on 8 June 1917. He was sent to France on 20 August 1917 and at Christmas 1917 he was invalided home to England with trench foot. In the spring of 1918 William married Florence A Edwards and returned to France on 6 August 1918. He joined Hawke Battallion on 28 August 1918 and was killed in action on Tuesday 3 September 1918, east of Haucourt, France on the day the Battle of the Scarpe ended and the Germans retreated to the Hindenburg line. William left a widow and a young daughter.

Private William Charles Hector Bennett   *15th Bn Hampshire Regiment*

Service No.	28909	Age:	18
Place of Birth:	Trowbridge, Wiltshire	Home Country:	England
Date of Death:	04/09/1918	Cause of death:	Killed in action

Far left: William George Marshman

Left: William Charles Hector Bennett

Memorial:	Hilperton & Hilperton Church
War cemetery:	Voormezeele Enclosure No 3
Theatre of war:	Belgium
Next of Kin:	Joseph James and Ethel Bennett
Address:	Horse Road, Hilperton

William was employed at the Staverton Milk Factory. He originally joined the Wiltshire Regiment but in mid August was sent to France and transferred to the Hampshire Regiment. William was shot through the head and killed instantly during an attack east of Vierstraat on Wednesday 4 September 1918.

Driver William Beaverstock   *29th Reserve Park ASC*

Service No.	T/212685	Age:	32
Place of Birth:	Trowbridge, Wiltshire	Home Country:	England
Date of Death:	04/09/1918	Cause of death:	Died

William Beaverstock

Memorial:	Trowbridge
War cemetery:	Salonika Lembet Road Military Cemetery
Theatre of war:	Salonika
Next of Kin:	Mary Beaverstock
Address:	10 Edinburgh Buildings, The Halve, Trowbridge

Wiliiam was a coal carter and volunteered for service on 7 September 1914 serving two years in England before being sent to Salonika in August 1916. He died of an intra cranial haemorrhage at a base hospital on Wednesday 4 September 1918. His mother Mary on application for a pension for her son received 4 shillings. Williams' name appears as Baverstock on the Trowbridge War Memorial.

Bombardier Edward William Rogers   *316th Siege Bty RGA*

Service No.	85343	Age:	34
Place of Birth:	Bermondsey, Surrey	Home Country:	England
Date of Death:	06/09/1918	Cause of death:	Killed in action
Memorial:	Steeple Ashton		
War cemetery:	Magnaboschi British Cemetery		
Theatre of war:	Italy		
Next of Kin:	Mrs E Rogers (wife) - Edward & Hester Rogers (parents)		
Address:	The Common, Steeple Ashton		

Edward known as Eddie, was employed by Massey & Co. as a carpenter and painter. He was well known in Torwbridge and had been a recognised player with the football team and was described as generous and unselfish. He was also a bell ringer in Steeple Ashton and well respected in the village. Eddie had arrived in Italy early in 1917 and was hoping to come home on leave. He was killed instantaneously by a shell on Friday 6 September 1918 and was buried with full military honours at the English Cemetery among the Italian mountains.

Ordinary Seaman Stanley William Gardener   *H.M.S.Victory Royal Navy*

Service No.	SS/9218	Age:	18
Place of Birth:	Congresbury, Somerset	Home Country:	England
Date of Death:	06/09/1918	Cause of death:	Died
Memorial:	Staverton		
War cemetery:	Haslar Royal Naval Cemetery		
Theatre of war:	Home		
Next of Kin:	William Albert & Florence Beatrice Gardener		
Address:	Staverton		

Stanley was the second son of William and Florence Gardener. He died on Friday 6 September 1918 of illness or disease at the Haslar Military Hospital, Portsmouth.

2nd Lieutenant Percy William Bowles MC MM   *C Battery 219th Bde RFA*

Service No.	N/A	Age:	25
Place of Birth:	Great Yarmouth, Norfolk	Home Country:	England
Date of Death:	10/09/1918	Cause of death:	Killed in action
Memorial:	Bradford on Avon		
War cemetery:	Manchester Cemetery Riencourt Les Bapaume		
Theatre of war:	France		
Next of Kin:	Dorothy E Bowles (wife) - William & Hannah Bowles (parents)		
Address:	21 Frome Road, Trowbridge, Wiltshire		

Percy was the son of William & Hannah Bowles, boat owners of Yarmouth, Norfolk. Before the war he was a sergeant serving with the Royal Horse Artillery at Trowbridge Barracks. From the outbreak of war he served continuously in Belgium, France and Gallipoli, including Mons. He received the Military Medal as a sergeant and soon after was promoted to 2nd Lieutenant and later awarded the Military Cross. In 1915 he married Dorothy Hibberd at Bradford on Avon. He was killed by a German while sleeping after an arduous nights work on Tuesday 10 September 1918. Dorothy Bowles received the following letter from Brigadier General Walshe:

"Your husband had not been with us long when his turn came to join those honoured ones who have given their lives for their country. Short though the time was, we had all learnt to esteem and respect him as a good officer and a jolly good fellow. He was always cheery and willing and most able as a commander and good at his work. His Colonel told me he was equally good with the horses and the guns and that is not common nowadays. As an old Horse Artilleryman I had a special bond of sympathy with your husband, I shall be so pleased if you can write to me and let me know if there is anything I can do to help you in any way. With the greatest sympathy to you and your family in the great loss you have suffered."

Private Arthur Flower   *152nd Coy Labour Corps*

Service No.	90773		Age:	39
Place of Birth:	Trowbridge, Wiltshire		Home Country:	England
Date of Death:	13/09/1918		Cause of death:	Accident
Memorial:	Not known			
War cemetery:	Ecoust St Mein British Cemetery			
Theatre of war:	France			
Next of Kin:	Henry & Emma Flower			
Address:	6 Shails Lane, Trowbridge			

Arthur was a haulier and had been conscripted into the army on 9 May 1916 originally joining the Royal Berkshire Regiment and then transferred to the Devon Regiment on 9 June 1916. He arrived in France on 14 June 1916 and in May 1917 was transferred to the Labour Corps. He died of injuries to the thighs, buttock, back and left arm, after an accident with a bomb (hand grenade) on Friday 13 September 1918.

Far left: Reginald Arthur Evans

Left: Reginald Colin Rose

Private Reginald Arthur Evans   *1/5th South Lancashire Regiment*

Service No.	54065	Age:	19
Place of Birth:	Trowbridge, Wiltshire	Home Country:	England
Date of Death:	17/09/1918	Cause of death:	Killed in action
Memorial:	Trowbridge		
War cemetery:	Guards Cemetery Windy Corner Cuinchy		
Theatre of war:	France		
Next of Kin:	Jack & Alice Evans		
Address:	2 Thomas Street, Trowbridge		

Reginald, known as Reg, was employed by H.J.Knees Ltd. and on reaching the age of eighteen joined the army on 5 March 1917 enlisting with the Royal Wiltshire Yeomanry. On 11 April 1918 he was sent to France and transferred to the South Lancashire Regiment. He was killed in action on Tuesday 17 September 1917 near Cuichy when a German mine exploded under the shelter where he was taking refuge.

Private Reginald Colin Rose   *2nd Bn Wiltshire Regiment*

Service No.	36320	Age:	19
Place of Birth:	Trowbridge, Wiltshire	Home Country:	England
Date of Death:	17/09/1918	Cause of death:	Died of wounds
Memorial:	Trowbridge		
War cemetery:	Lapugnoy Military Cemetery		
Theatre of war:	France		
Next of Kin:	Albert & Rhoda Rose		
Address:	8 Havelock Street, Trowbridge		

It is likely Reginald joined the Wiltshire Regiment in 1917 and was sent to France in 1918. He died of wounds on Tuesday 17 September 1917 at No. 32 Casualty Clearing Station at Lapugnoy, west of Bethune, France.

Private Walter George Portingale   *1/4th TF Bn Wiltshire Regiment*

Service No.	200495	Age:	33
Place of Birth:	Monkton Deverill, Wiltshire	Home Country:	England
Date of Death:	19/09/1918	Cause of death:	Killed in action
Memorial:	Not known		
War cemetery:	Ramleh War Cemetery		
Theatre of war:	Egypt		
Next of Kin:	Ada Portingale		
Address:	4 Carpenters Alms Yard, Roundstone Street, Trowbridge		

Walter, known as George, was a carter on a farm and a Wiltshire Territorial. He married Ada Hulbert at the start of 1915 most likely leaving for India soon after. In September 1917 the 1/4th Wiltshires were sent to Egypt and then on to Palestine. George was killed in action on Thursday 19 September 1918 as the Wiltshires fought their way through modern day Israel. His brother Archie Portingale had been killed in August 1917.

2nd Lieutenant Harry Colston Collings   *284th Siege Bty RGA*

Service No.	N/A	Age:	32
Place of Birth:	Bristol, Gloucestershire	Home Country:	England
Date of Death:	19/09/1918	Cause of death:	Killed in action

Above: Hooge Village, Belgium in 1918 - Right: Harry Colston

War cemetery: Marteville Communal Cemetery Attilly
Theatre of war: France
Next of Kin: Thomas Henry & Annie Collings
Address: 1 The Avenue, St. George, Bristol

As a boy Harry was at St. Barnabas School, Bristol and having won a scholarship he went on to Merchant Venturers College. On completing his education in Bristol he went to Carmarthen College where he was a keen cricket and football player and he remained here until 1907. He then became an assistant master at Holy Trinity School, Trowbridge. He was well known in the town for being a fast bowler and also played for Trowbridge football club. He married Clara F. Jones in the summer of 1914, but she sadly died in 1917. Harry had joined the artillery in May 1916 and qualified as a signaler being sent to France on 8 February 1917. He returned to England and passed through the Trowbridge cadet school obtaining a commission in December 1917, returning to France in March 1918. He was killed in action on Thursday 19 September 1918 near St. Quentin, France.

Private Albert Samuel White   *2nd Bn Leinster Regiment*
Service No. 1317
Age: 33
Place of Birth: Trowbridge, Wiltshire
Home Country: Wales
Date of Death: 28/09/1918
Cause of death: Killed in action
Memorial: Not known
War cemetery: Hooge Crater Cemetery
Theatre of war: Belgium
Next of Kin: Frederick & Sarah Jane White
Address: 27 Lady Tyler Terrace, Rhymney, Monmouthshire

Albert was a haulier and married Elizabeth Stevens in South Wales in 1907, he volunteered for service with the Wiltshire Regiment but at the time the Wiltshires had too many recruits while the Irish Regiment were in need of recruits and he was transferred to the Leinster Regiment. He served in Gallipoli arriving on 9 July 1915 and shortly after returning to Europe he was posted as wounded and missing on Saturday 28 September 1918 and at some point later his remains were located and he was officially listed as killed in action.

Sergeant Henry Snook MSM   *Royal Canadian Regiment*
Service No.: 477867
Place of Birth: Hilperton, Wiltshire
Date of Death: 29/09/1918
Memorial: Not known
War cemetery: Quarry Wood Cemetery Sains Les Marquion
Theatre of war: France
Next of Kin: Jonah & Pheobe Snook
Address: Woodside, West Ashton, Wiltshire
Age: 45
Home Country: Canada
Cause of death: Killed in Action

Henry a master tailor was the only son of Jonah and Pheobe Snook and had emigrated to Canada prior to the Great War. He volunteered for service on 23 August 1915. He then returned to Europe while serving with the Royal Canadians, was promoted to sergeant and won the Meritous Service Medal. Henry was killed in action near Cambrai on Sunday 29 September 1918.

Sergeant Harry Webb   *2nd Bn Hampshire Regiment*
Service No.: 28050
Place of Birth: Corsham, Wiltshire
Date of Death: 30/09/1918
Memorial: Trowbridge & Broughton Gifford
War cemetery: Hooge Crater Cemetery
Theatre of war: Belgium
Next of Kin: Lilian Nellie Webb (wife) - Frederick & Mary Webb (parents)
Address: Ashton Street, Trowbridge - Broughton Gifford
Age: 23
Home Country: England
Cause of death: Killed in action

Harry was a gardener. It is likely he was conscripted into the army joining the Wiltshire Regiment, was transferred to the Duke of Cornwalls Light Infantry and then to the Hampshire Regiment. In the summer of 1918 Harry married Lilian Nellie Pike at Baradford on Avon. He was killed in action on Monday 30 September 1918 at Gheluvelt during the British advance through Belgium.

Private Albert Charles Perrett   *32nd Coy Machine Gun Corps*
Service No.: 133781
Place of Birth: Bulkington, Wiltshire
Date of Death: 02/10/1918
Memorial: Not known
War cemetery: Vis En Artois British Cemetery Haucourt
Theatre of war: France
Next of Kin: Charles & Fanny Perrett
Address: Littlemarsh, Semington
Age: 19
Home Country: England
Cause of death: Killed in action

Nineteen year old Albert was the second son of Charles and Fanny Perrett and it is likely he joined the Army on his eighteenth birthday. He was killed in action at the Battle of St. Quentin Canal on Wednesday 2 October 1918.

Private William James Hawkins   *19th Bn Australian Infantry A I F*
Service No.: 6570
Place of Birth: Trowbridge, Wiltshire
Date of Death: 03/10/1918
Memorial: Trowbridge
War cemetery: Estrees Communal Cemetery
Age: 26
Home Country: Australia
Cause of death: Killed in action

Theatre of war: France
Next of Kin: Thomas & Eliza Jame Hawkins
Address: 23 Innox Terrace, Bradford Road, Trowbridge

As a boy William had been a member of the Manvers Street Wesleyan Sunday School and Church and went to school in Newtown. He served an apprentiship as a French Polisher with H.J. Knee Ltd. and in 1913 he emigrated to Australia. He joined the Australian army on 20 November 1916 and arrived in England in April 1917. He injured his foot in January 1918 and was evacuted to England, he returned to his unit and the front in April 1918. William was killed in action near Estrees, France, on Thursday 3 October 1918. In January 1919 Thomas and Eliza Hawkins received the following letter from Captain W. J. Tenerry:

"He was killed during an attack at Estrees, by an enemy machine gun. Later his body was recovered and buried at the cemetery in Estrees by his comrades. Your boy was my batman for a few months and I thought a great deal of him, as he had the qualities of a good man. I understand the company commander, who was acting for me had written to you. As we have been broken up and transferred to other companies and units, everyone has been out of touch with things. My sympathy to you in your sorrow, for tis even harder to bear on the eve of victory."

William's family inserted the following memoriam in a local paper in 1919:

"Somewhere in France our loved one is sleeping ,
While angels bright are watching near,
Still at home are hearts are aching,
For we have lost a son most dear.
All his suffering now ended,
His wounded body is at rest,
His soul, from every ill defended,
Reposes on his Saviours breast.
Ever remembered by his father, mother, sisters and brother"

Sergeant Reginald Stanley Fulford   *104th Coy Machine Gun Corps*
Service No.   151388   Age: 26
Place of Birth: Longbridge Deverill, Wiltshire   Home Country: England
Date of Death: 05/10/1918   Cause of death: Died
Memorial: Trowbridge
War cemetery: Haringhe (Bandaghem) Military Cemetery
Theatre of war: Belgium
Next of Kin: William L & Ellen Fulford
Address: Shortwood, 49 Bradley Road, Trowbridge

Reginald, known as Reg, was employed in a drapers shop in Oxford Street, London and was the youngest son of William and Ellen Fulford. He was a keen sportsman with interest in boating, tennis and was a good shot. He was a member of the City of London Yeomanry, the Rough Riders and volunteered for overseas service at the outbreak of hostilities. He was sent to Egypt and Palestine and was at the Battle for Jerusalem transferring to the Machine Gun Corps. After four years on overseas service he returned to England in August 1918 and visited Trowbridge. He was drafted to France and was wounded while defending a cross roads with a machine gun. He was taken to the military hospital at Bandaghem, Belgium, but was too ill to leave a message. He succumbed to his wounds on the same day, Saturday 5 October 1918.

Right: William James Hawkins

Far right: Reginald Stanley Fulford

2nd Lieutenant Edward Frank Ponting   *21st Bn Manchester Regiment*
Service No.: N/A
Place of Birth: Trowbridge, Wiltshire
Date of Death: 05/10/1918
Memorial: Not known
War cemetery: Prospect Hill Cemetery Gouy
Theatre of war: France
Next of Kin: Eva Frances Talmage Ponting (wife) - Edward & Ellen Ponting (parents)
Address: Box - 3 Downhayes Road, Trowbridge

Age: 30
Home Country: England
Cause of death: Killed in action

Edward was employed by the Cooperative Wholesale Society in their Woolens Department and was the second son of Edward and Ellen Ponting. In 1913 he married Eva F T Street at Box and volunteered for service with the Royal Garrison Artillery in May 1915. He was commissioned with the Manchester Regiment in August 1917 and was sent to France in October 1917. He was then sent to Italy and was granted home leave in summer 1918 and visited his parents in Trowbridge. He returned to Italy and on 17 September 1918 he was transferred back to France. Edward was killed in action south of Gouy, France on Saturday 5 October 1918. He left a widow and young child.

Right: Edward Frank Ponting

Far right: John Herbert Graham

Pioneer John Herbert Graham   *A Sig.Depot (Bedford) R.E.*

Service No.	255049
Place of Birth:	Trowbridge, Wiltshire
Date of Death:	06/10/1918
Memorial:	Not known
War cemetery:	Stretford Cemetery
Theatre of war:	Home
Next of Kin:	Amy Beatrice Graham (wife) - John Long & Elizabeth Graham (parents)
Address:	Rushmoor Lane, Bristol - Hilperton Road, Trowbridge
Age:	42
Home Country:	England
Cause of death:	Died

John was a clerk and the eldest son of John and Elizabeth Graham and married Amy Beatrice Snailum in 1904. He joined the army under the Derby Scheme on 29 November 1915 and was called up on 16 June 1916. After completing his training as a signaler he was sent to France and arrived on 27 November 1916. He was gassed in April 1918 during the German advance and was evacuated to England on 24 April 1918. On 21 September 1918 John was admitted to the 1st Eastern General Hospital at Cambridge with what was described as tonsillitis. He died of septicaemia following an operation on Sunday 6 October 1918. He left a widow and three children.

Able Seaman Charles Llewellyn Down   *Hood Bn Royal Naval Division R.N.V.R.*

Service No.	R/6721
Place of Birth:	Trowbridge, Wiltshire
Date of Death:	08/10/1918
Memorial:	Trowbridge
War cemetery:	Flesquieres Hill British Cemetery
Theatre of war:	France
Next of Kin:	Annie E.Down (wife) - James & Mary Down (parents)
Address:	1 Whitehorse Cottages, Bratton - 7 Union Square, Trowbridge
Age:	30
Home Country:	England
Cause of death:	Killed in action

Charles married Annie E Carr in 1911 and joined the army under the Derby Scheme on 15 November 1915, being called up on 24 April 1918. After completing his training he was sent to France arriving on 3 September 1918. He was killed in action at Cambrai, France on Tuesday 8 October 1918. He left a widow and young son, and in November 1918 his wife inserted the following memoriam in a local paper:

"The only comfort that I have is we shall meet again,
His smiling face will greet me when the gate I enter in.
I prayed that god would keep a watch and shield him in the fray,
But, alas, my hopes were blighted when the sad news came that day.
He died for me
Sadly missed by his wife and little son"

Private Reginald Henry Lucas   *15th Bn Cheshire Regiment*

Service No.	67408
Place of Birth:	Trowbridge, Wiltshire
Date of Death:	09/10/1918
Memorial:	Not Known
War cemetery:	Terlincthun British Cemetery Wimille
Theatre of war:	France
Next of Kin:	Henry James & Edith Lucas
Address:	40 Hanover, Stalybridge, Cheshire
Age:	19
Home Country:	England
Cause of death:	Died of wounds

Reginald was a joiner and was conscripted into the army being called up on 24 August 1917 and sent to the training reserve. He was transferred to the Cheshire Regiment and sent to France at the start of April 1918. He was wounded with a gun shot wound to the head received during fighting on 6 October 1918 and was evacuated to the Canadian General Hospital at Boulogne. His parents were sent a telegram informing them that Reginald was dangerously ill but they were refused permission to visit him. Soon after Henry and Edith Lucas received another telegram informing them their son had succumbed to his wounds on Wednesday 9 October 1918.

Private Charles George Perryman *1st Garrison Worcestershire Regiment*
Service No.   26652   Age: 28
Place of Birth: Bath, Somerset   Home Country: England
Date of Death: 10/10/1918 Cause of death: Died
Memorial: Trowbridge
War cemetery: Not known
Theatre of war: Home
Next of Kin: Charles & Mary Perryman
Address: Arundel, 47 Bradford Road, Trowbridge

Charles, known as George, was a butler and the third son of Charles & Mary Perryman. He joined the army on 21 February 1916 but on 27 July 1916 he was discharged from the army with the comment:

"Flat feet, and poor physique, impossible to walk any distances with a pack on his back, and not likely to improve with training. Recommended for discharge by travelling Medical Board as not likely to become an efficient soldier"

Charles died from tuberculosis of the lungs on Thursday 10 October 1918, his brother Harry Percival Perryman was killed in November 1917. Charles is not remembered by the Common Wealth War Graves Commission.

Lance Coporal Frederick Mathew Purnell   *1/8th Bn TF Royal Warwickshire Regt*
Service No.   306709   Age: 27
Place of Birth: Trowbridge, Wiltshire   Home Country: England

Right: Charles George Perryman

Far right: Frederick Mathew Purnell

Date of Death:	10/10/1918	Cause of death:	Killed in action
Memorial:	Trowbridge		
War cemetery:	Maurois Communal Cemetery		
Theatre of war:	France		
Next of Kin:	George & Mary Purnell		
Address:	87 Lower Studley, Trowbridge		

Frederick was a van man with the Trowbridge Cooperative Society and had joined the army in July 1916 after the death of his brother, George Henry Purnell, while serving with the Welsh Regiment. He was sent to Italy in November 1917 and returned to France in September 1918. His parents received the following letter from Frederick's commanding officer:

"Lance Corporal Purnell was struck on the head by a piece of shrapnel and killed instantly while advancing on the German position. He was buried in the division cemetery and a cross has been erected bearing his rank and name. Corporal Purnell was always a good soldier and was liked and highly respected by all. As an N.C.O. he did some valuable work."

Frederick was killed in action on Thursday 10 November 1918 between Honnechy and St Benin, South of Le Cateau, France.

Private William Alfred Mattock   *9th Bn Royal Irish Fusiliers*

Service No.	42194	Age:	34
Place of Birth:	Seend, Wiltshire	Home Country:	England
Date of Death:	11/10/1918	Cause of death:	Killed in action
Memorial:	Seend		
War cemetery:	Tyne Cot Memorial		
Theatre of war:	Belgium		
Next of Kin:	Nellie Mattock (wife) - Alfred & Emmeline Mattock (parents)		
Address:	Seend View, Seend - 6 Innox Road, Trowbridge		

William was a groom and he married Nellie Kate Froude on 25 March 1913 at Wantage in Berkshire. He attested under the Derby Scheme on 10 December 1915 and was called up on 31 May 1916 being sent to the 3rd Wiltshire Battalion at Weymouth. Because of his experience with horses he was transferred to the army Service Corps in 1917 and was sent to France in April 1918. Due to a shortage of infantry men he was compulsorily transferred to the Royal Irish Fusiliers and was twice wounded in September 1918, the second time by barbed wire. He was killed in action during fighting near Ypres on Friday 11 October 1918 and is remembered on the Tyne Cot memorial. He has no known grave and left a widow and young son.

Bandsman Herbert Scrine   *2nd Bn Wiltshire Regiment*

Service No.	7681	Age:	29
Place of Birth:	Holt, Wiltshire	Home Country:	England
Date of Death:	12/10/1918	Cause of death:	Died
Memorial:	Trowbridge & Holt		
War cemetery:	Niederzwehren Cemetery		
Theatre of war:	Germany		
Next of Kin:	Francis & Jane Scrine		
Address:	33 Mount Pleasant Corifree, Trowbridge		

Old soldier Herbert joined the Wiltshires in 1906 at the age of seventeen years and ten months. At the outbreak of war he was serving with the Wiltshires in Gibraltar and after returning to

England he and the Wiltshires landed at Zeebrugge on 7 October 1914. Herbert was captured by the Germans during the British retreat and spent the next four years in captivity as a prisoner of war and was forced to work in salt mines. He died most likely from malnutrition and bad treatment in Germany on Saturday 12 October 1918.

Private William Walter Neat *1st Garr. Bn South Staffordshire Regt*
Service No.   204600
Place of Birth: Westbury, Wiltshire
Date of Death: 12/10/1918
Memorial: Trowbridge St James Church Memorial
War cemetery: Kirkee 1914-1918 Memorial
Theatre of war: India
Next of Kin: Henry George & Clara Neat
Address: Westbury Leigh, Westbury

Age: 21
Home Country: England
Cause of death: Died

Walter was the oldest son of Henry & Clara Neat, he volunteered for service with the 2/4th Battalion Wiltshire Regiment and was sent to India to serve on garrison duties. While serving he was transferred to the South Staffordshire Regiment and in 1918 he became ill. He died of bronchial pneumonia at Deolai Hospital on Saturday 12 October 1918. The Commonwealth War Grave Commission do not tend many of the graves in India and Bernard is remembered on the Kirkee 1914-1918 Memorial. His name on the St. James Memorial is spelt Neate.

Private Victor Baker *7th Bn Wiltshire Regiment*
Service No.   18771
Place of Birth: Melksham, Wiltshire
Date of Death: 16/10/1918
Memorial: Trowbridge
War cemetery: Pommereuil British Cemetery
Theatre of war: France
Next of Kin: James & Ellen L Baker
Address: Semington Lane, Melksham

Age: 20
Home Country: England
Cause of death: Killed in action

Right: William Walter Neat

Far right: Victor Baker

Victor joined the 7th Battalion Wiltshire Regiment and was initially sent to Salonika in Greece and then returned to France in July 1918. He was killed in action on Wednesday 16 October 1918 between St.Souplet and St. Bennin south of Le Cateau. France.

Sapper Frederick Stephen D. Land　　　　　　*250th Tunneling Company R.E.*
Service No.　　　139208　　　　　　　　Age:　　　　　　32
Place of Birth:　　Trowbridge, Wiltshire　　　Home Country:　England
Date of Death:　　17/10/1918　　　　　　　Cause of death:　Killed in action
Memorial:　　　　Trowbridge
War cemetery:　　La Gorgue Communal Cemetery
Theatre of war:　　France
Next of Kin:　　　Elthel Land (wife) - Mary Land (parent)
Address:　　　　 29 Shails Lane, Trowbridge

Frederick, known as Fred, was a hawker and the only son of Mary Land. He married Ethel Louisa Perrott in 1905. He volunteered for service with the Wiltshire Regiment in January 1915 and was sent to France on 23 June 1915. He transferred to the 250th Tunnelling Company Royal Engineers in October 1915, and was killed while removing a German mine on Thursday 17 October 1918.

Private Percy Tavener　　　　　　　　　*2/6th TF Bn Devonshire Regiment*
Service No.　　　268430　　　　　　　　Age:　　　　　　24
Place of Birth:　　Bristol　　　　　　　　　Home Country:　England
Date of Death:　　20/10/1918　　　　　　　Cause of death:　Died
Memorial:　　　　Trowbridge St James Church Memorial
War cemetery:　　Kirkee 1914-1918 Memorial
Theatre of war:　　India
Next of Kin:　　　Arthur & Sarah Tavener
Address:　　　　 45 Gooch Street, Swindon

Percy was a machine man at the Loco and Carriage department of the Great Western Railway Works in Swindon. He originally joined the 2/4th Wiltshire regiment and was sent for garrison duties in India, and was later transferred to the Devonshire Regiment. He died of illness or disease on Sunday 22 October 1918 and is buried in a Cemetery in India. The Commonwealth War Grave Commission do not tend the graves of many soldiers who died in India and Percy is remembered on the Kirkee 1914-1918 Memorial.

Private Joseph Edward Carpenter　　　　　*1st Bn Somerset Light Infantry*
Service No.　　　50407　　　　　　　　　Age:　　　　　　37
Place of Birth:　　Trowbridge, Wiltshire　　　Home Country:　England
Date of Death:　　24/10/1918　　　　　　　Cause of death:　Killed in action
Memorial:　　　　Trowbridge
War cemetery:　　Verchain British Cemetery
Theatre of war:　　France
Next of Kin:　　　Alfred & Emily Carpenter
Address:　　　　 17 Newtown, Trowbridge

Joseph was a finisher in a cloth mill, he married Elizabeth Ada Gillard in Bristol in 1903 and it is likely that he was conscripted into the army, joining the Somerset Light Infantry. He was drowned in the Ecaillon River, France, when the Somerset attacked the Ferm de Bonveneule

Right: Frederick Stephen D. Land

Far right: Joseph Edward Carpenter

south east of Monchaux, France, on Thursday 24 October 1918. Small bridges were supposed to have been put in place across the river to aid the Somersets attack, however there were difficulties getting the bridges in place and the Somersets were caught in a German bombardment. Some of the Somersets chose to swim the river and it is likely Joseph was drowned at this time. His brother Thomas Carpenter had died in Mesopotamia in October 1917.

Trooper Curtis Henry Neave	*104th Coy Machine Gun Corps*
Service No. 151583	Age: 31
Place of Birth: Great Yarmouth, Norfolk	Home Country: England
Date of Death: 24/10/1918	Cause of death: Killed in action
Memorial: Trowbridge	
War cemetery: Ingoyghem Military Cemetery	
Theatre of war: Belgium	
Next of Kin: Daisey Nora Neave (wife)	
Address: The Halve, Trowbridge	

Old soldier Curtis had arrived in France with the British Expeditionary Force with the 2nd

Right: Curtis Henry Neave

Far right: Gideon James Slade (Hancock)

Dragoons on 15 August 1914 and was wounded at Mons and evacuated to England. He married Daisey Nora Pepler in 1916 and on his recovery was drafted to Egypt and Palestine transferring to the Machine Gun Corps and taking part in the fighting when Jerusalem was captured. In 1918 he was granted home leave and following this was sent to France. He was killed in action on Thursday 24 October 1918 during fighting at Oteghem, Belgium. His wife received the following letter from 2nd Lieutenant W. Edwards:

"I have much regret that it is my painful duty to inform you of the death in action of your husband in the early morning of October 24. Fortunately death was instantaneous, and he could not have possibly suffered pain. He was buried in pleasant surroundings and a small cross marks his grave. He was a splendid fellow, always cheerful under the most trying circumstances, and a valuable asset to my section. His loss has been greatly felt by us all, and I have been asked to convey to you the deepest sympathy of all his friends. Please accept my heartfelt sympathy in you bereavement."

Sergeant Harold James Merritt   *8th Bn East Surrey Regiment*
Service No.: 14995
Place of Birth: Cold Walham, Sussex
Date of Death: 24/10/1918
Memorial: Southwick
War cemetery: Honnechy British Cemetery
Theatre of war: France
Next of Kin: James & Eliza Merritt
Address: Frome Road, Southwick
Age: 28
Home Country: England
Cause of death: Killed in action

Harold was a factory hand was the third son of James and Eliza Merritt. It is likely he was conscripted into the army joining the East Surrey Rgiment. He was killed in action on Thursday 24 October 1918 during the Battle of the Selle, south of Cateau, France.

Private Gideon James Slade (Hancock)   *Canadian Army Medical Corps*
Service No.: 3206982
Place of Birth: Trowbridge, Wiltshire
Date of Death: 29/10/1918
Memorial: Not known
War cemetery: Edmonton Mount Pleasant Cemetery
Theatre of war: Canada
Next of Kin: Jessie Slade (wife) - James & Mary Hancock
Address: Buena Park, California - 19 Hilperton Road, Trowbridge
Age: 34
Home Country: Canada
Cause of death: Died

Gideon used his mothers' maiden name of Slade and was a graduate nurse, before emigrating first to Australia and then on to the United States of America in 1906. He had served in the Royal Navy. While in America he married his wife and on 16 February 1918 he enlisted with the Canadian army. He died of illness or disease in a hospital in Canada.

Signaler Alfred John Earl   *1st Bn Gloucestershire Regiment*
Service No.: 27178
Place of Birth: Trowbridge, Wiltshire
Date of Death: 01/11/1918
Memorial: Trowbridge
War cemetery: Mont Huon Military Cemetery Le Treport
Theatre of war: France
Age: 29
Home Country: England
Cause of death: Died of wounds

Next of Kin: Edith Earl (wife) – Alfred John & Kate Laura Earl (parents)
Address: 30 Colston Road, Bristol - 14 Gladstone Road, Trowbridge

Alfred, a clerk, was the eldest son of Alfred senior and Kate Earl. He had married Edith Gregory in Bristol in 1911 and lived with his wife and young daughter at Lower Easton in Bristol. It is likely he was conscripted into the army joining the Gloucester Regiment. He was seriously wounded at the end of October 1918 while attached to the Royal Engineers 1st Engineering Company. News was received by his family on Thursday 24 October 1918 and Alfred's wife and father went to the military hospital at Le Treport, France to be with him. However Alfred did not regain consciousness and died on the evening of Friday 1 November 1915.

Private James Andrews	*1/4th TF Wiltshire Regiment*
Service No. 1327	Age: 24
Place of Birth: Trowbidge, Wiltshire	Home Country: England
Date of Death: 01/11/1918 *(approximate date)*	Cause of death: Died
Memorial: Trowbridge	
War cemetery: Trowbridge Cemetery	
Theatre of war Home	
Next of Kin: William & Elizabeth Andrews	
Address: 29 Islington, Trowbidge, Wiltshire	

James was an engine fireman employed by the Great Western Railway and joined the Wiltshire Territorials in August 1910 at the age of 17 years and four months. At the outbreak of hostilities he volunteered for overseas service and arrived in India on 9 October 1914. While serving in India he developed malaria and was sent home in October 1915 and the following month was discharged from the army. He died at home in November 1918 from the effects of malarial fever contacted on service. He was buried in Trowbridge cemetery on 6 November 1918. James is not remembered by the Commonwealth War Graves Commission.

Driver Albert Edward Gibbs	*5th Bde Royal Horse Artillery*
Service No. 51861	Age: Not Known
Place of Birth: Bristol, Glocestershire	Home Country: England
Date of Death: 02/11/1918	Cause of death: Died

Right: James Andrews

Far right: Albert Edward Gibbs

Memorial:	Trowbridge
War cemetery:	St Sever Cemetery Extension Rouen
Theatre of war:	France
Next of Kin:	Not known
Address:	2 North View Cottage Mortimer Street, Trowbridge

Albert, known as Edward, was an old soldier and had been stationed at Trowbridge prior to the commencement of hostilities. He arrived in France on 15 August 1918 and was a member of the L Battery that took part in the action at Nery, France. He died of illness or disease on Saturday 2 November 1918 at a Military hospital at Rouen France.

Private John Loxley   *929th Area Emp.Coy. Labour Corps*

Service No.	107037	Age:	30
Place of Birth:	Trowbridge, Wiltshire	Home Country:	England
Date of Death:	02/11/1918	Cause of death:	Died
Memorial:	Trowbridge		
War cemetery:	Etaples Military Cemetery		
Theatre of war:	France		
Next of Kin:	Margaret F Loxley (wife) - Frank & Elizabeth Loxley (parents)		
Address:	14 Wentworth Road, Harborne, Birmingham - Trowbridge		

John was the only son of Frank and Elizabeth Loxley and a brush maker. He had learned his trade from Mr Newth of Trowbridge and before the war took a position in Birmingham instructing blind people. At the start of 1917 John married Margaret F. Priday and soon after was conscripted into the army joining the Hampshire Regiment. He was later transferred to the Labour Corps and in October 1918 John was diagnosed with a cerebral haemorrhage. He died on Saturday 2 November 1918 at No. 26 General Hospital, Etaples, France.

Lieutenant Robert John Matthews   *4th Bn Norfolk Regiment*

Service No.	N/A	Age:	21
Place of Birth:	Trowbridge, Wiltshire	Home Country:	England
Date of Death:	02/11/1918	Cause of death:	Died
Memorial:	Trowbridge & Hilperton		
War cemetery:	Grantham Cemetery		
Theatre of war:	Home		
Next of Kin:	Henry & Rose Matthews		
Address:	The Cottage, Hilperton Road, Trowbridge		

Robert was the youngest son of Henry & Rose Matthews and attended Trowbridge High School. Soon after his seventeenth birthday he joined the army and obtained a commission with the Norfolk Regiment and was attached to the Machine Gun Corps arriving in France on 12 July 1917. He was wounded at Merville, France in March 1918 and was evacuated to England. He had almost recovered from his wounds when he contracted influenza and returned to hospital. He died of pneumonia on Saturday 2 November 1918, within a day of his 21st birthday. He was buried at Grantham with full military honours.

Corporal Kirwin Barnes Sweetland   *1st Bn Somerset Light Infantry*

Service No.	11987	Age:	22
Place of Birth:	Trowbridge, Wiltshire	Home Country:	England
Date of Death:	02/11/1918	Cause of death:	Killed in action

A BLACK DAY FOR THE GERMAN ARMY

Right: Kirwin Barnes Sweetland

Far right: Montague W Colcomb

Memorial: Box
War cemetery: Preseau Communal Cemetery Extension
Theatre of war: France
Next of Kin: Samuel Morgan & Laura Mary Sweetland
Address: Box, Wiltshire

Kirwin was a clerk working for the railway and volunteered for service on 4 September 1914, being sent to France on 21 May 1915. He was wounded near Ypres in September 1915 and after recovering in hospital he returned to the front. He was killed in action on Saturday 2 November 1918 near Preseau, France, during the Battle of Valenciennes.

Lance Coporal Montague W Colcomb   *Inland Water Transport R.E.*
Service No. WR/553571   Age: 24
Place of Birth: Bristol   Home Country: England
Date of Death: 04/11/1918   Cause of death: Died
Memorial: Trowbridge
War cemetery: Basra War Cemetery
Theatre of war: Mesopotamia
Next of Kin: Wesley & Margaret Colcomb
Address: 33 Innox Road, Trowbridge

Montague was a fitter with Great Western Railway and had joined Royal Artillery Territorials in January 1912 and at the commencement of hostilities was sent to India for garrison duties. On 1 January 1917 he was transferred to the regular army and in the same year he was again transferred to the Royal Engineers. He was sent to Basra Mesopotamia, in modern day Iraq, to work in the dockyard. On 3 November 1918 he was taken to hospital suffering from malaria where he died at 9.30pm the following day. His personal effects were returned to his parents consisting of 2 discs, wallet, photos, belt and letters.

Staff Sergeant Albert Edward Dowding MSM MID   *Army Service Corps*
Service No .S/20969   Age: 31
Place of Birth: Peshawar, India   Home Country: England
Date of Death: 04/11/1918   Cause of death: Died
Memorial: Trowbridge

War cemetery: Ste. Marie Cemetery Le Harvre
Theatre of war: France
Next of Kin: Frederick Matthias & Mary Agnes Dowding
Address: Templemore 64 Newtown, Trowbridge

Regular soldier Albert had enlisted in the Army Service Corps in 1903 and was sent to France on 8 August 1914. He was mentioned in Sir Douglas Haig's dispatches in 1917 and in August 1918 he was awarded the Meritous Service Medal and had been given home leave in October 1918. He was admitted to the Palais Regales 2nd General Hospital, Le Harve on 24 October 1918 after contracting influenza and died of broncho-pneumonia on Monday 4 November 1918. His parents inserted the following memoriam in a local paper:

"We loved him, oh, no tongue can tell
How much we loved him and how well
God loved him too, and thought it best
To take him home with Him to rest"

Lance Coporal Edward Joseph Hollis   *Military Foot Police RMP*
Service No.: P/8999
Age: 42
Place of Birth: Witney, Berkshire
Home Country: England
Date of Death: 06/11/1918
Cause of death: Died
Memorial: Trowbridge
War cemetery: Trowbridge Cemetery
Theatre of war: Home
Next of Kin: Rose Annie Hollis (wife) - Edward Joseph Hollis (parent)
Address: Watercress House, Farleigh Hungerford

Edward was an excavator and married Rose Annie Banks on 20 January 1907 at Trowbridge. It is likely he was conscripted into the army joining the Devonshire Regiment and transferring to the Military Police where he served on home duties. He died of illness or disease at Chiseldon Military Hospital on Wednesday 6 November 1918.

Private Albert James Davis   *1st Bn Devonshire Regiment*
Service No.: 72266
Age: 37
Place of Birth: Pangbourne, Berkshire
Home Country: England
Date of Death: 07/11/1918
Cause of death: Killed in action

Far left: Albert Edward Dowding

Left: Edward Joseph Hollis

Memorial: Not known
War cemetery: St Sever Cemetery Extension Rouen
Theatre of war: France
Next of Kin: Maud Eliza Davis (wife) - Walter Thomas & Elizabeth Davis (parents)
Address: 57 Park Street, Trowbridge

Albert was a clerk working for a leather manufacturer. It is likely he was conscripted into the army joining the Lincolnshire Regiment then transferring to the Devonshire Regiment and then to 116th Company Chinese Labour Corps, where he was given the rank of sergeant. He was killed in action on Thursday 7 November 1917.

Private Thomas Henry Pepler   *Royal Army Medical Corps*
Service No.   497486   Age: 33
Place of Birth: Trowbridge, Wiltshire   Home Country: England
Date of Death: 08/11/1918   Cause of death: Died
Memorial: Trowbridge
War cemetery: Trowbridge Cemetery
Theatre of war: Home
Next of Kin: Emily Pepler (wife) - Henry & Rose Pepler (parents)
Address: 29 Adcroft Street, Trowbridge

Prior to the Great War Thomas was a rubber worker in Bradford on Avon and was the eldest son of Henry & Rose Pepler. He married Emily Draper in South Wales in 1906 and they had four children. He volunteered for service with the medical corps on 6 May 1915 and was sent to France on 25 January 1917. He was invalided home in January 1918 and after his recovery was sent to work at the 4th Northern General Hospital at Lincoln where he contacted influenza and died of bronchitis on Friday 8 November 1918. He was buried with full military honours at Trowbridge Cemetery.

Private Albert Victor Rodgers   *Base Depot Wiltshire Regiment*
Service No.q   20729   Age: 21
Place of Birth: Westwood, Wiltshire   Home Country: England
Date of Death: 08/11/1918   Cause of death: Died
Memorial: Trowbridge

Right: Thomas Henry Pepler

Far right: Albert Victor Rodgers

War cemetery: Trowbridge Cemetery
Theatre of war: Home
Next of Kin: Edward & Elizabeth Rodgers
Address: 85 Mortimer Street, Trowbridge

Albert volunteered for service in May 1915 and after completing his training was sent to Mesopotamia with the Wiltshire Regiment. In October 1917 he was sent home suffering from dysentery and was sent to various hospitals, seven months being spent at Trowbridge Red Cross Hospital. In the spring of 1918 he was transferred to the Bristol and Almondsbury Hospital where he died on Friday 8 November 1918. His sister Amy died on the same day and brother and sister were buried in the same grave in Trowbridge Cemetery. Their father Edward Patrick Rodgers had died in January 1916. On the Trowbridge War Memorial his name is spelt *Rogers*.

Private Donald Robert Keates		*MT Army Service Corps*	
Service No.	M2/200812	Age:	26
Place of Birth:	Yarnbrook, Wiltshire	Home Country:	England
Date of Death:	10/11/1918	Cause of death:	Died
Memorial:	Bradford on Avon & North Bradley		
War cemetery:	Terlincthun British Cemetery Wimille		
Theatre of war:	France		
Next of Kin:	Ebenezer & Rosina Keates		
Address:	Yarnbrook		

Donald was a motor mechanic and the sixth son of Ebenezer and Rosina Keates and was well known in the area. Prior to being conscripted into the army he had gone to many tribunals stating his skill was essential to the local community and he had shown petitions signed by nearly all the motor vehicle owners in Bradford on Avon. However, he was eventually called up in July 1916 joining the Army Service Corps. Donald contracted influenza and was admitted to No. 83 General Hospital where he died of pneumonia on Sunday 10 November 1918. His brother Roland had died in 1915.

Donald Robert Keates

15
ARMISTICE DAY - MONDAY 11 NOVEMBER 1918

The War is Over but the Deaths Continue:

Private John Howard Barnes		*Royal West Surrey Regiment*	
Service No.	35238	Age:	29
Place of Birth:	Trowbridge, Wiltshire	Home Country:	England
Date of Death:	11/11/1918	Cause of death:	Died
Memorial:	Not Known		
War cemetery:	Trowbridge Cemetery		
Theatre of war:	Home		
Next of Kin:	Ethel Winifred Barnes (wife) - George & Eliza Barnes (parents)		
Address:	21 Richmond Terrace Clifton, Bristol - 16 Duke Street Trowbridge		

John, known as Howard, was a grocers' assistant and married Ethel Winifred Slade on 12 May 1915 at the Tabernacle, Trowbridge. He joined the army under the Derby Scheme attesting on 10 December 1915 and was called up on 30 May 1916 joining the Royal West Surrey Regiment. While in training he was found to have a heart weakness which was aggravated by the physical exercise. He was discharged from the army on 23 October 1917 and declared unfit for military service. He was awarded a pension but died on Monday 11 November 1918 from the strain that had been placed on his heart.

Acting Bombardier William Stanley U Bush		*87th Bde Royal Field Artillery*	
Service No.	8475	Age:	24
Place of Birth:	Bradford on Avon, Wiltshire	Home Country:	England
Date of Death:	21/11/1918	Cause of death:	Died of wounds
Memorial:	Trowbridge		
War cemetery:	Sollesmes British Cemetery		
Theatre of war:	France		
Next of Kin:	Henry George & Agnes Annie Bush		
Address:	The Kings Arms Inn, Castle Street, Trowbridge		

Before the start of the war William was a fireman with the Great Western Railway and was the the eldest son of Henry and Agnes Bush. He enlisted in 1914 and was sent to France on 17 July 1917. William had served through most of the Great War and was expected to return home shortly after the armistice. Unfortunately he contracted influenza and was admitted to 42nd Casualty Clearing Station where he died of pneumonia on Thursday 21 November 1918.

Far Left: William Stanley U Bush

Left: William Bailey

Corporal William Bailey   *90th Sqdn Royal Air Force*
Service No. 79047   Age: 40
Place of Birth: Trowbridge, Wiltshire   Home Country: England
Date of Death: 22/11/1918   Cause of death: Died
Memorial: Trowbridge
War cemetery: Trowbridge Cemetery
Theatre of war: Home
Next of Kin: Rose Bailey (wife) – Robert & Matilda Bailey (parents)
Address: 15 Wingfield Road, Trowbridge

William was a carpenter and married Rose Hayward at the beginning of 1915. He joined the Royal Air Force on home service and died of pneumonia at the 4th Northern General Hospital Lincoln on Friday 22 November 1918.

Boy 2nd Class William Clement Bray   *HMS Powerful Royal Navy*
Service No. J/87718   Age: 18
Place of Birth: Trowbridge, Wiltshire   Home Country: England
Date of Death: 25/11/1918   Cause of death: Died
Memorial: Trowbridge
War cemetery: Trowbridge Cemetery
Theatre of war: Home
Next of Kin: Frederick & Annie Elizabeth Bray
Address: 3 George Street, Trowbridge

Seventeen year old William joined the Royal Navy in April 1918. He was the second son of Frederick and Annie Bray. After just 20 days service on H.M.S. Powerful he was taken ill with pneumonia and emphysema and admitted to hospital. He died after a long and painful illness on Monday 25 November 1918 at the Royal Naval Hospital Plymouth. Annie Bray had already lost a brother and two nephews in the war.

Private Harry Martin   *2/4th TF Bn Wiltshire Regiment*
Service No. 35244   Age: 33
Place of Birth: Bishopsteignton, Devon   Home Country: England

Right: William Clement Bray

Far Right: Jesse Herbert Lester

Date of Death: 25/11/1918 Cause of death: Died
Memorial: Trowbridge St James Church memorial
War cemetery: Madras 1914-1918 War Memorial Chennai
Theatre of war: India
Next of Kin: Frances Martin (mother)
Address: The Triangle, Bishopsteignton, Devon

Harry was a domestic gardener and a Wiltshire Territorial. He served on garrison duties in India and died of illness or disease on Monday 25 November 1918 and was buried in Benares Cantonment Cemetery. The Commonwealth War Graves Commission do not tend many of the graves in India and Harry is remembered on the Madras 1914-1918 War Memorial Chennai.

Driver Jesse Herbert Lester *2nd Bde Royal Field Artillery*
Service No. 1461 Age: 45
Place of Birth: Trowbridge, Wiltshire Home Country: England
Date of Death: 28/11/1918 Cause of death: Died
Memorial: Trowbridge
War cemetery: Trowbridge Cemetery
Theatre of war: Home
Next of Kin: Eliza Lester (wife) - John & Annie Lester (parents)
Address: 2 Havelock Street, Trowbridge

Old soldier Jesse had joined the artillery on 27 May 1892. He married Eliza Clark at the start of 1903 and left the service in 1904. In civilian life he worked as a mine hewer and volunteered for service on 1 October 1914 and was promoted to acting bombardier. He was sent to France on 20 November 1915, on Christmas Day 1915 Jesse was reduced to the rank of driver for drunkenness and neglect of duty. He was then sent to Egypt and arrived in February 1916. In October 1916 he was admitted to hospital with valvular disease of the heart and shortly after evacuated to England. He was discharged from the army on 22 December 1916, declared unfit for service and given a pension. Jesse died on Thursday 28 November 1918.

Private John Albert Gulliver *3rd Bn Hampshire Regiment*
Service No. 27810 Age: 40
Place of Birth: Steeple Ashton, Wiltshire Home Country: England

Far left: John Albert Gulliver

Left: Percy Herbert C. Baber

Date of Death: 30/11/1918 Cause of death: Died
Memorial: Hilperton
War cemetery: Hilperton Cemetery
Theatre of war: Home
Next of Kin: John & Ruth Gulliver
Address: Horse Road Hilperton Marsh, Hilperton

John was a builders' labourer and the eldest son of John and Ruth Gulliver. It is likely he was conscripted into the army joining the Duke of Cornwall's Light Infantry, before transferring to the Hampshire Regiment then the 442nd Agricultural Coy of the Labour Corps. He died on Sunday 30 November 1918 from disease contracted on service in France.

Lance Coporal Percy Herbert C. Baber *22nd Bn Rifle Brigade*
Service No. 204543 Age: 42
Place of Birth: Trowbridge, Wiltshire Home Country: England
Date of Death: 05/12/1918 Cause of death: Died
Memorial: Trowbridge & Trowbridge United Free Church
War cemetery: Mikra British Cemetery
Theatre of war: Salonika
Next of Kin: Lily Baber (wife) - James & Martha Baber (parents)
Address: 30 New Road Mortimer Street, Trowbridge

Percy was a brush maker and married Lily Chamberlain on the 1 August 1914. It is likely he was conscripted into the army and sent to Salonika. He died at No.50 General Hospital Salonika of illness and disease on Thursday 5 December 1918. His medals were never claimed and were sent for disposal.

Able Seaman Arthur Frederick Shrapnell *H.M.S.Cassandra Royal Navy*
Service No. J26736 Age: 22
Place of Birth: Trowbridge, Wiltshire Home Country: England
Date of Death: 05/12/1918 Cause of death: Died
Memorial: Trowbridge
War cemetery: Plymouth Naval Memorial

Theatre of war: At sea
Next of Kin: Alice Shrapnell
Address: 5 Apple Gates Yard, Court Street, Trowbridge

Arthur was the only son of Alice Shrapnell and on Thursday 5 December 1918 he was serving on the Light Cruiser H.M.S. Cassandra in the Baltic Sea travelling between the Baltic capitals. The Cassandra hit a mine which had been laid during the war and sank. Arthur is remembered on the Plymouth Naval Memorial.

Sergeant Wilfred Jeffery Baker   *1st Bn Wiltshire Regiment*
Service No. 10432
Place of Birth: Trowbridge, Wiltshire
Date of Death: 07/12/1918
Memorial: Trowbridge
War cemetery: Trowbridge Cemetery
Theatre of war: Home
Next of Kin: William J & Annie S Baker
Address: 15 Avenue Road, Trowbridge
Age: 24
Home Country: England
Cause of death: Died

Wilfred was the second son of William and Annie Baker. He was a pupil of Newtown School and won a county scholarship, continuing his education at the Secondary School. On leaving he was employed by Mr W. N. Ledbury before working for the County Council Land Agent. Wilfred volunteered for service on 1 September 1914 and was sent to France on 26 January 1916. He was wounded being shot in the arm on August Bank Holiday 1915 near Dickebusche, Belgium and was evacuated to England being sent to Brighton Hospital and then to Wingfield House Red Cross Hospital. After being in service for 4 years Wilfred was struck down with influenza which developed into Pneumonia and his death on Saturday 7 December 1918 at a Military hospital at Aylesford, Kent. His body was brought home to Trowbridge where he was buried with full military honours.

Private Stephen Walter Dyer   *2/4th TF Bn Wiltshire Regiment*
Service No. 202075
Place of Birth: Salisbury, Wiltshire
Age: 21
Home Country: England

Wilfred Jeffery Baker and his grave in Trowbridge Cemetery

Date of Death:	09/12/1918	Cause of death:	Died

Memorial: Salisbury - St Pauls, Salisbury - Trowbridge St James Church
War cemetery: Madras 1914 -1918 War Memorial Chennai
Theatre of war: India
Next of Kin: James & Emily Dyer
Address: Salisbury, Wiltshire

Stephen was a Wiltshire Territorial and was sent to India for garrison duties. He died most likely due to illness or disease and was buried in Allahabad New Cantonment Cemetery. The Commonwealth War Grave Commission do not tend many of the graves in India and Stephen is remembered on the Madras 1914-1918 War Memorial Chennai.

Corporal Frank William Cox *10th Bn Hampshire Regiment*
Service No.: 43818
Age: 27
Place of Birth: Melksham, Wiltshire
Home Country: Egypt
Date of Death: 16/12/1918
Cause of death: Died
Memorial: Trowbridge
War cemetery: Mikra British Cemetery
Theatre of war: Salonika
Next of Kin: Frank William Cox
Address: 11 Innox Road, Trowbridge

Frank originally joined the 7th Battalion Wiltshire Regiment and was sent to France arriving on 21 September 1915. He was then sent to Salonika where he was transferred to the Hampshire Regiment. He died of illness or disease on Monday 16 December 1918.

Private Frederick William Noble Pocock *2/4th TF Bn Wiltshire Regiment*
Service No.: 202477
Age: 43
Place of Birth: Bradfield, Berkshire
Home Country: England
Date of Death: 22/12/1918
Cause of death: Died
Memorial: Trowbridge St James Church Memorial
War cemetery: Madras 1914-1918 War Memorial Chennai
Theatre of war: India
Next of Kin: Clara Marian Pocock (wife) - Frederick and Harriet Pocock (parents)
Address: 14 Council Houses, Ludgershall

Frederick was a shop assistant in an ironmongers and also a Wiltshire Territorial, he married Clara Marian Meddows in Warwick in 1903. Frederick was sent to India for garrison duties and died of illness or disease on Sunday 22 December 1918 being buried at Benares Cantonment Cemetery. The Commonwealth War Grave Commission do not tend many of the graves in India and Frederick is remembered on the Madras 1914-1918 War Memorial Chennai.

Private John Poynter P Say *2/4th TF Bn Wiltshire Regiment*
Service No.: 202557
Age: 29
Place of Birth: Trowbridge, Wiltshire
Home Country: England
Date of Death: 26/12/1918
Cause of death: Died
Memorial: Trowbridge
War cemetery: Madras 1914-1918 War Memorial Chennai
Theatre of war: India
Next of Kin: Asaph & Fanny Say

ARMISTICE DAY - MONDAY 11 NOVEMBER 1918

Right: John Poynter P. Say

Far right: James Rees Cole

Address: 8 Park Street, Trowbridge

John was a foundry clerk, a Wiltshire Territorial and the only son of Asaph and Fanny Say. He was sent to India for garrison duties and died from enteric fever on Boxing Day 1918 at the Stationary Hospital Allahabad, India. He was buried in Allahabad New Cantonment Cemetery. The Commonwealth War Grave Commission do not tend many of the graves in India and John is remembered on the Madras 1914-1918 War Memorial Chennai.

1919

Gunner James Rees Cole   *2nd Siege Res Bde. (Catterick) R.G.A.*

Service No.	163614	Age:	37
Place of Birth:	Chanery, Cardiganshire	Home Country:	England
Date of Death:	01/01/1919	Cause of death:	Died

Memorial: Bradford on Avon -Bradfrod on Avon Christchurch - Trowbridge
War cemetery: Bradfrod on Avon Christchurch Churchyard
Theatre of war: Home
Next of Kin: Bessie Susan Cole (wife) – Thomas & Jane Cole (parents)
Address: 164 Oxford Road, Reading - 40 Bradley Road Trowbridge

James was an ironmonger and married Bessie Susan Livings on 26 November 1911 at Christ Church, Bradford on Avon where he had been a member of the choir for 17 years. He enlisted under the Derby Scheme on 11 December 1915 and was called up on 25 June 1917. In August 1918 he injured his foot and after treatment in France he was evacuated to England and hospital in Reading and then on to Catterick. While at Catterick he developed influenza and was thought to be making a good recovery when he had a relapse. He died on New Years Day 1919. A post mortem discovered that James had pleurisy and death was due to an embolism of the brain. His body was brought to Bradford on Avon and buried with full military honours at Christ Church Bradford on Avon. He left a widow and two children.

Private Ralph Richard Bray   *1/4th TF Bn Wiltshire Regiment*
Service No.   201356   Age: 23
Place of Birth: Trowbridge, Wiltshire   Home Country: Egypt

Date of Death: | 04/01/1919 | Cause of death: | Died
Memorial: | Trowbridge
War cemetery: | Kantara War Memorial Cemetery
Theatre of war: | Egypt
Next of Kin: | Daisey Mead (fiancee) - Benjamin & Charlotte Bray (parents)
Address: | Bradford Road, Trowbridge - 19 Mortimer Street, Trowbridge

Ralph was employed by W.R.Stephens in Castle Street, Trowbridge, as a coach painter and was the youngest son of Benjamin and Charlotte Bray. He joined the 1/4th Wiltshires on 5 November 1914 and was sent to India for garrison duties spending some time at Delhi. In September 1917 he was sent to Egypt and then served during the campaign in Palestine without injury. In November 1918 he was treated in hospital for malaria. He returned to his unit and was recovering when he was taken ill again. He died from broncho – pneumonia on Saturday 4 January 1919 at No.44 Stationary Hospital, Kantara, Egypt.

Private John Albert Sartin   *7th Duke of Cornwalls Light Infantry*

Service No. | 38846 | Age: | 19
Place of Birth: | Trowbridge, Wiltshire | Home Country: | England
Date of Death | 07/01/1919 | Cause of death: | Died
Memorial: | Trowbridge
War cemetery: | Doullens Communal Cemetery Extension No.1
Theatre of war: | France
Next of Kin: | John A & Ellen A Sartin
Address: | 21 Newtown, Trowbridge

John, known as Jack, was a shoe maker and the youngest son of John and Ellen Sartin. He enlisted with the Warwickshire Regiment in June 1917 and was later transferred to the Duke of Cornwall's light Infantry. He died of pneumonia on Tuesday 7 January 1919 at No.18 Casualty Clearing Station. Jack was nineteen years of age and his brother, Albert Victor, was killed in April 1917 while serving with the Warwickshire Regiment.

Private Thomas Morris   *1st Bn Wiltshire Regiment*

Service No. | 26301 | Age: | 38
Place of Birth: | Bradford on Avon, Wiltshire | Home Country: | England

Far left Richard Bray

Left:John Albert Sartin

ARMISTICE DAY - MONDAY 11 NOVEMBER 1918

Date of Death: 11/01/1919   Cause of death: Died
Memorial: Trowbridge
War cemetery: Bradford on Avon Cemetery
Theatre of war: Home
Next of Kin: Annie Morris (wife) - Henry & Eliza Morris (parents)
Address: 17 Shails Lane, Trowbridge – Bradford on Avon

Thomas was a maltster's labourer and he married Annie Britten at the beginning of 1903. He joined the Wiltshires after the beginning of the war and had seen active service in France. He was at home on a short leave when he fell ill with influenza and was taken to Sutton Veny Military Hospital where he developed pneumonia and died on Saturday 11 February 1919. His body was brought to Bradford on Avon and he was buried with a full military funeral. He left a widow and seven children.

Lance Corporal Clifford Frank Wheeler   *16th Bn Kings Royal Rifle Corps*
Service No.: C/1639
Place of Birth: Trowbridge, Wiltshire
Date of Death: 19/01/1919
Memorial: Trowbridge
War cemetery: Trowbridge Cemetery
Theatre of war: Home
Next of Kin: John Potter & Elizabeth Wheeler
Address: 69 Park Street, Trowbridge
Age: 22
Home Country: England
Cause of death: Died of wounds

Clifford was an under gardener at Highfield and joined the Rifle Corps toward the end of 1915. He served for two and a half years in France and was wounded three times. The first time was in the leg and the second when fortunately the bullet struck his ammunition pouch first. The third in October 1918 was more serious when he lost his leg after being hit with what was thought to be an explosive bullet. He was evacuated to England and was taken to Bristol then on to the Red Cross Hospital in Trowbridge. It was found it was necessary for Clifford to undergo a further operation to remove protruding bones. The operation was thought to be successful however Clifford did not recover and died the following day on Sunday 19 January 1919 from heart failure. Clifford was the first patient to die at Trowbridge Red Cross Hospital and was buried in Trowbridge Cemetery with full military honours.

Right: Clifford Frank Wheeler

Far right: William George Brittain

Sapper William George Brittain   *Tyne Electrical Engineers R.E.*
Service No.   327816   Age: 36
Place of Birth: Strood, Kent   Home Country: England
Date of Death: 28/01/1919   Cause of death: Died
Memorial: Trowbridge
War cemetery: Trowbridge Cemetery
Theatre of war: Home
Next of Kin: Rose A. Brittain (wife) - Frederick & Ellen Brittain (parents)
Address: 1 Cox's Yard, Castle Street, Trowbridge

William had served at home with the Royal Engineers during the Great War and died on Tuesday 28 January 1919 at Sutton Veny Hospital. His body was returned to Trowbridge and he was buried in Trowbridge Cemetery.

Corporal Ernest Ritchens   *160th Coy Labour Corps*
Service No.   107742   Age: 46
Place of Birth: Semington, Wiltshire   Home Country: England
Date of Death: 01/02/1919   Cause of death: Died
Memorial: Hilperton & Hilperton Church
War cemetery: Hilperton Cemetery
Theatre of war: Home
Next of Kin: Sarah Louisa Richens (wife) - Isaac & Sarah Ritchens (parents)
Address: The Rank, Hilperton - Little Marsh, Semington

Ernest was an old soldier having served in the South African campaign at the turn of the century. On leaving the army he was employed as a farm labourer and in the summer of 1907 he married Sarah Louisa York. His services were again called on in the Great War and he initially joined the Wiltshire Regiment and was then transferred to the Hampshire Regiment and finally to the Labour Corps. He died at No.1 Australian Hospital, Sutton Veny. His body was returned to his home and he was buried in Hilperton Cemetery.

Chief Motor Mechanic Howard John King   *HMS Fresh Hope R.N.V.R.*
Service No.   MB/3058   Age: 37
Place of Birth: Trowbridge, Wiltshire   Home Country: England

Far left: the grave of Ernest Ritchens in Hilperton Cemetery

Left: Harold John King

ARMISTICE DAY - MONDAY 11 NOVEMBER 1918

Date of Death: 05/02/1919   Cause of death: Died
Memorial: Trowbridge
War cemetery: Kingston Upon Thames Cemetery
Theatre of war: Home
Next of Kin: Lily Rose King (wife) - Edgar & Emily King (parents)
Address: 65 Acacia Grove, New Malden, Surrey – Trowbridge

Howard was a fitter for Oil and Gas Engines and a member of the Royal Naval Volunteer Reserve. He had married Lily Rose Davidge in Kingston upon Thames in 1906. He died of pneumonia on Wednesday 5 February 1919 at the Naval Hospital Larbert, Scotland.

Private Arthur Park MM   *2nd Bn Wiltshire Regiment*
Service No. 8084   Age: 28
Place of Birth: Devizes, Wiltshire   Home Country: England
Date of Death: 09/02/1919   Cause of death: Died
Memorial: Trowbridge
War cemetery: Trowbridge Cemetery
Theatre of war: Home
Next of Kin: Arthur & Bridget Park
Address: 83 Dursley Road, Trowbridge

Regular soldier Arthur arrived in France with the Wiltshire on 7 October 1914. He was wounded on three occasions while on active service and was awarded the Military Medal. On the day his name appeared on the list for his award he was captured by the Germans. He was repatriated in January 1919 and was taken sick while at home. He was removed to the Red Cross Hospital in Trowbridge for treatment but died of pneumonia on Sunday 9 February 1919. He was buried in Trowbridge Cemetery with full military honours

Captain John Randall   *Royal Garrison Artillery*
Service No. N/A   Age: 33
Place of Birth: Trowbridge, Wiltshire   Home Country: England
Date of Death: 17/02/1919   Cause of death: Died
Memorial: Trowbridge

Right: Arthur Park

Far right: John Randall

War cemetery: Trowbridge Cemetery
Theatre of war: Home
Next of Kin: E.M.Randall (wife) - William & Eliza Randall (parents)
Address: Homefield Cottage, Polebarn Road, Trowbridge

John, known as Jack, joined the artillery at Plymouth in 1904 and served until 1912 in India, Aden, Burma amongst other stations and returned to England as a sergeant. He went to France with one of the first siege batteries in September 1914. In August 1915 he was granted a commission and in November 1916 he was severely wounded and sent to an Officers Convalescent Home in the Isle of Wight. Jack was unfit for frontline service and was placed in charge of a reserve Brigade at Prees Heath, Shropshire and was promoted to full Lieutenant in June 1917 and Captain in November 1918. On 14 February 1919 he was taken sick with influenza and admitted to the military hospital at Prees Heath. He died of pneumonia on Monday 17 February 1919. His body was returned home and he was buried with full military honours. He left a widow and two young children, Major Begbie wrote the following letter to Mrs Randall:

"During the last year your husband has acted throughout as my second in command, and his services have been invaluable. No trouble has been too much for him, and anything he had to do he did with all his might. The great personal interest he took in them endeared him to all the men of the battery. It is a great grief you have to bear but it must be great comfort to you that you can look back with pride on the splendid example your husband set us all while he lived, though gone he will never be forgotten by us"

Private Victor Harold C Mundy　　　　　　　　　*2/4th Bn TF Wiltshire Regiment*
Service No.: 201803　　　　　　　　Age: 22
Place of Birth: Trowbridge, Wiltshire　　　Home Country: England
Date of Death: 20/02/1919　　　　　Cause of death: Died
Memorial: Trowbridge – Trowbridge UFC & Trowbridge St James Memorial
War cemetery: Kirkee 1914-1918 Memorial
Theatre of war: India
Next of Kin: Thomas Oliver & Amelia Rhoda Mundy
Address: 1 West Street, Trowbridge

Victor joined the army in 1915 and was sent to India for garrison duties. Thomas & Amelia Mundy received a letter from Victor dated 3 February 1919 stating that he was looking forward to coming home, on the same day they received the War Department notification of Victor's death. He died on Thursday 20 February 1919 of pneumonia at King George War Hospital, Poona and he was buried near Poona, India, The Commonwealth War Grave Commission do not tend many of the graves in India and Victor is remembered on the Kirkee 1914-1918 Memorial.

Sapper Cornelius Pearce　　　　　　　　　*Royal Engineers*
Service No.: 224164　　　　　　　　Age: 34
Place of Birth: Trowbridge, Wiltshire　　　Home Country: England
Date of Death: 21/02/1919　　　　　Cause of death: Died
Memorial: Trowbridge
War cemetery: Not known
Theatre of war: Home
Next of Kin: Nellie Lavinia Pearce (wife) - Cornelius & Martha Pearce (parents)
Address: 52 Ringwood Road, South Twerton - 3 Bond Street, Trowbridge

ARMISTICE DAY - MONDAY 11 NOVEMBER 1918

Right: Victor Harold C. Mundy

Far right: Cornelius Pearce

Cornelius was a carpenter and joiner and married Nellie Lavinia Weaver at the end of 1909 in Bristol. He was conscripted into the army on 22 November 1916 joining the Devon Regiment and was then transferred to the East Yorks Regiment and then to the Royal Engineers. He was sent to France where he served from 9 September 1917. In Easter 1918 while working 10 miles from Cambrai he was taken ill. He reported sick and was sent to 10th General Hospital at Rouen and from there was sent home on 1 November 1918. He was discharged from service on 17 December 1918 with valvular disease of the heart. He died of the same disease on Friday 21 February 1919. Cornelius is not remembered by the Commonwealth War Graves Commission.

Private Frederick Ernest Bertie Randall   *13th Bn Somerset Light Infantry*

Service No.	54396
Place of Birth:	Trowbridge, Wiltshire
Date of Death:	28/03/1919
Memorial:	Trowbridge
War cemetery:	Trowbridge Cemetery
Theatre of war:	Home
Next of Kin:	Levi & Emily
Address:	11 Wingfield Road, Trowbridge

Age: 48
Home Country: England
Cause of death: Died

Frederick, known as Bert, joined the army and was employed on home service with the Labour Corps. He died of illness or disease at Norwich military hospital on Friday 23 March 1919.

Driver Samuel John Culverhouse   *7th Mech. Trans. Coy. A.S.C.*

Service No.	M/201580
Place of Birth:	Trowbridge, Wiltshire
Date of Death:	30/03/1919
Memorial:	Trowbridge
War cemetery:	Abbeville Communal Cemetery Extension
Theatre of war:	France
Next of Kin:	Elizabeth Culverhouse (wife) - George & Eliza Culverhouse (parents)
Address:	48 Bond Street, Trowbridge

Age: 38
Home Country: England
Cause of death: Died

Far left: Frederick Ernest Bertie Randall

Left: Samuel John Culverhouse

Samuel was a vanman and motor driver employed by Watson and Gowen of Gloucester Road, Trowbridge and married Elizabeth Pearce in spring 1907. He was called up in 1916 and sent to Grove Park where he qualified as a first class driver and was sent to France in 1917 where he served until the armistice when he was given home leave. He returned to France to wait for demobilization. While waiting at the coast he developed a bad cold which further developed to erysipelas and he was admitted to the 3rd Australian General Hospital at Abbeville, France. He died on Sunday 30 March 1919 and left a widow and young son. In April 1919 his wife inserted the following memoriam in a local paper:

"We pictured him safe returning
We longed to grasp his hand
But god has postponed our meeting
It will be in a better land
If we could have raised his dying head
And heard his last farewell
The grief would not have been so hard
For those who loved him well
From his sorrowing wife and son"

Corporal William John Cockerton   *2/4th TF Bn Wiltshire Regiment*
Service No.   200476   Age: 22
Place of Birth: Holloway, London   Home Country: England
Date of Death: 20/04/1919   Cause of death: Died
Memorial: Trowbridge – Trowbridge St. James Church Memorial
War cemetery: Trowbridge Cemetery
Theatre of war: Home
Next of Kin: John & Elizabeth Cockerton
Address: Ivanhoe Trawle, Cockhill, Trowbridge

William was serving an apprentiship with his uncle as an ironmonger and was also a Wiltshire Territorial being called up and sent to India with the 2/th Battalion Wiltshire Regiment on 12 December 1914. While on garrison duties in India he volunteered for service in Mesopotamia. William was reported missing in February 1917 and later his family were informed that William had been severely wounded in the chest on 2 February 1917 and had died of his wounds half an hour later. His family was grief stricken and his name was placed on the Roll of Honour at Trowbridge Town Hall. Six months later in July 1917 William's parents received a card from Turkey in their son's handwriting informing them that he was a prisoner in the hands of the Turks. William returned home in January 1919 after four years and two months absence abroad, two of which as a prisoner of war. William told the story of how he became a prisoner:

"In August 1916 I was transferred to the Royal Engineers Signal Company attached to the 37th Indian Brigade. On February the 1st, 1917, I went into action with the 45th Sikhs, and after covering the trenches I was told to open up communications with the reserve regiment, the telephone lines were continually being broken, and the regiment was becoming hard pressed on the left, efforts were made to get a message through. I left the trenches in an endeavour to connect up the broken wire, but was driven back by machine gun fire, and when I returned to the trench I found that the Sikhs had retired to the left and had been captured, only dead bodies remaining. I ran to the communication trench but was hit in the shoulder, surrounded and captured. I was taken to the Turkish head quarters and my wound was dressed and I remained there for four days. Three British prisoners were brought in and about 200 Sikhs, the remnant of the regiment, all the white officers having been killed. We were marched the whole of the day until Baghdad was reached and here we were joined by about 20 of the Kut captives who had been left behind. We spent some time here and we were housed in huts by the river. We were transferred from one guard to another each of which would take possession of an article of clothing, until we were left with only trousers and shirts, not even a piece of string or braces. The arrival of a Turkish officer gave the opportunity of complaint and our boots were returned. We had high hopes of rescue, news filtered through that the British cavalry were advancing, and the Germans who were there in large numbers, began to clear out. Early on March 1st, we were paraded and marched off in the direction of Mosul. We were each given a pound of dark bread and a handful of dates, it was four days later before any other food was obtained when we were given a flat cake of bread about half a pound in weight. No water was carried and the only way of procuring a drink was by scooping water from pools we found occasionally in the sand. This march continued for 31 days across the dessert, lasting from sunrise to sunset, and only stopping twice for two days, owing to the extreme exhaustion of the men, who were mostly Sikhs. In this manner nearly 500 miles were travelled, the guards were riding on horseback and prodded with rifles any man who fell by the way.
On April 1st we reached Derhezie and were put to work on the Baghdad railway under German

William John Cockerton and his grave at Trowbridge Cemetery

engineers. The daily rations consisted of half a pound of lentils or wheat and dark coarse bread, the only liquid being dirty water from the river. As every village above turned its refuse and sewage into the stream, the water was absolutely putrid and dysentery and malarial fever were rife, many deaths occurring, especially affecting the Sikhs.

We lived in Arab tents and the daily routine went on for nearly two years, during which time I received three parcels from the Wilts Prisoners of War Fund, and they had been in transit for over twelve months. Eventually the glad tidings of the surrender were received, and on November 16 1918 a British officer arrived, and we were taken to Aleppo and we were cleaned, disinfected and refitted and then we were brought by easy stages overland to Italy and France and arrived in England on January 10 a journey of two months."

On arriving home William had the unique experience of reading his own obituary. Early in March 1919 he went to Harrow on the Hill for a holiday with his uncle. He was taken ill with malarial fever which developed into pneumonia and William died on Sunday 20 April 1919. His body was brought to Trowbridge by rail and he was buried in Trowbridge Cemetery.

Private Bernard Hibberd   *2/4th TF Bn Wiltshire Regiment*
Service No.: 201778
Age: 30
Place of Birth: Wardour, Wiltshire
Home Country: England
Date of Death: 03/06/1919
Cause of death: Died
Memorial: Tisbury – Trowbridge St. James Church Memorial
War cemetery: Madras 1914-1918 War Memorial Chennai
Theatre of war: India
Next of Kin: Samuel & Lucy Hibberd
Address:, Tisbury, Wiltshire

Bernard was a groom and a Wiltshire Territorial. He was sent to India for garrison duties and died of illness or disease at Allahabad, India and is buried at Allahabad New Cantonment Cemetery. The Commonwealth War Grave Commission do not tend many of the graves in India and Bernard is remembered on the Kirkee 1914-1918 Memorial.

Sergeant John Stephen Carter   *Indian Ordnance Department*
Service No.: 202590
Age: 27
Place of Birth: Battersea, London
Home Country: England
Date of Death: 10/08/1919
Cause of death: Died
Memorial: Trowbridge St James Church Memorial
War cemetery: Delhi Memorial India Gate
Theatre of war: India
Next of Kin: Ada R Carter (wife) - Stephen and Martha Eliza Carter (parents)
Address: 2 Belle Vue Terrace, Station Road, Westbury, Wiltshire

John was a clerk and married Ada R Player in Westbury at the beginning of 1916. He was sent to India to serve with the 2/4th Battalion Wiltshire Regiment on garrison duties and while there was transferred to the Indian Army serving with the Indian Ordnance Department. He died most likely of illness or disease on Sunday 10 August 1919. It is likey he is buried in India, and John is remembered on the Delhi Memorial India Gate.

Private Walter John Cooper   *9th P.O.W. Coy Labour Corps*
Service No.: 90178
Age: 27
Place of Birth: Trowbridge, Wiltshire
Home Country: England
Date of Death: 18/08/1919
Cause of death: Accident

Memorial:	Trowbridge
War cemetery:	Houchin British Cemetery
Theatre of war:	France
Next of Kin:	Fred & Elizabeth Cooper
Address:	32 Newtown, Trowbridge

Walter was a labourer at Chapman and Company Bedding Works and a regular member of the Wesley Road Wesleyan Bible Class. He joined the army under the Derby Scheme on 11 December 1915 and was called up on 24 March 1916 initially joining the Devonshire Regiment and then transferred to the Labour Corps. He was sent to France in June 1916 and was employed on salvage duties. Walter was killed in an accident on Monday 18 August 1919 and a court of enquiry was held, Lieutenant Harper gave the following statement:

"On the afternoon of August 18 1919, I was in charge of a working party at the Chicory Factory near Bethune. The party was engaged in cleaning the ground recently occupied by a horse transport company and also picking up any scrap iron and wire lying about. About 14.40 hrs. I saw a party off loading a hand cart near the broad gauge railway and carrying the material to the dump situated on the other side of the railway. I walked over to the dump and while my back was turned heard an explosion. I instantly turned round and saw a cloud of smoke. I ran to the spot and found both, No.10299 Pte. Carr C. and No.90178 Cooper W.J. had been injured. I summoned aid with every possible speed, and the orderly was sent for a doctor and an ambulance. Their wounds were dressed by the company medical orderly and the men were removed to No. 15 Casualty Clearing Station with every possible speed."

Private Reader witnessed the following:

"I saw Pte. Cooper pick up a piece of shell from the ground. I heard a report (explosion) and something struck me on the leg. I looked round and saw Ptes. Cooper and Carr lying on the ground. "

In his statement Lance Corporal Miller the Medical orderly explained what he found when he arrived on the scene:

"I found Pte. Cooper in a very grave condition, his eyes were gone, his nose blown off and his face was very badly smashed in, his right leg was also badly fractured."

Below: Scrap metal German steel helmets - Right: Walter John Cooper

Engine Room Art Herbert James Warburton *H.M.S.Canarvon Royal Navy*
Service No.   M/13378
Place of Birth: Trowbridge, Wiltshire
Date of Death: 17/10/1919
Memorial: Not Known
War cemetery: Gibraltar North Front Cemetery
Theatre of war: Gibraltar
Next of Kin: Florence M. Warburton (wife) - Manoah & Marion Warburton (parents)
Address: 61 Morris Street, Swindon

Age: 30
Home Country: England
Cause of death: Died

Herbert was an Engineer's Metal Turner and married Florence Hayes at the end of 1911 in Swindon. It is likely he died of illness or disease while serving on the Cadet training ship H.M.S. Carnarvon.

Private Frederick Francis *5th Wiltshire Regiment*
Service No.   23855
Place of Birth: Barford St Martin, Wiltshire
Date of Death: 23/12/1919
Memorial: Trowbridge
War cemetery: Brookwood Military Cemetery
Theatre of war: Home
Next of Kin: Lot & Sarah Martin
Address: South Street, Barford St Martin, Wiltshire

Age: 35
Home Country: England
Cause of death: Died

Frederick a maltster lodged in Trowbridge at 11 Yerbury Street and was a well known bell ringer. He joined the army and was sent to Mesopotamia. He died from pneumonia on his way home from the Middle East and his body was brought back to England and buried in Brookwood Military Cemetery.

Lance Corporal Solomon J Fry *MT Army Service Corps*
Service No.   M2/182314
Place of Birth: Foxham, Wiltshire
Date of Death: 06/01/1920
Memorial: Not Known
War cemetery: Trowbridge Cemetery
Theatre of war: Home
Next of Kin: Alice Fry (wife) – Jacob & Anne Fry (parents)
Address: 2 Court Street, Trowbridge

Age: 37
Home Country: England
Cause of death: Accident

Solomon married Alice Biggs in the summer of 1909 and was killed in a motor accident in Devizes after his discharge from the army.

Private Stafford Herbert Sidnell *Canadian Engineers*
Service No.   405593
Place of Birth: Trowbidge, Wiltshire
Date of Death: 31/01/1920
Memorial: Not known
War cemetery: Trowbridge Cemetery
Theatre of war: Home
Next of Kin: Frederick & Annie Sidnell
Address: 48 Park Street, Trowbridge, Wiltshire

Age: 31
Home Country: England
Cause of death: Died

Far left: The grave of Solomon J Fry in Trowbridge Cemetery

Left: Stafford Herbert Sidnell

Stafford was a Glass polisher had left England for Canada in 1910 and volunteered for service with the 35th Battalion Canadian Army on 5 April 1915. He returned to England with them and was stationed at Folkestone for some time after which he was sent to France taking part in operations at Arras. He was transferred to the Canadian Engineers with who he remained to the end of the war when he returned to Toronto Canada. He decided to leave Canada and arrived in England on 21 January 1920 and was reunited with his parents. A few days later he visited his sister in Bristol and whilst there he fell ill and was taken to Bath Royal United Hospital where he died a few hours later. He was buried in Trowbridge Cemetery; Stafford is not remembered by the Commonwealth War Grave Commission. Frederick and Annie Sidnell were to lose all four of their sons, Walter was killed during fighting in 1914, William died of wounds in 1916, Arthur who had been a branch manager at the Cooperative Society in Trowbridge, succumbed to pneumonia in 1918.

Gunner William George Parsons   *Royal Field Artillery*
Service No.   216076
Place of Birth: Wilton, Wiltshire
Date of Death: 22/02/1920
Memorial: Not Known
War cemetery: Trowbridge Cemetery
Theatre of war: Home
Next of Kin: Anne E Parsons (wife) - Emanuel Edward & Harriet Parsons (parents)
Address: 1 Homefield Cottages, Polebarn Road, Trowbidge – Wilton
Age: 28
Home Country: England
Cause of death: Died

William was employed by Spencer Moulton & Co. and was a talented footballer and played for Salisbury City and Bradford on Avon in 1913 where he moved to in the same year. In January 1917 he was called up joining the Royal Field Artillery and during the spring of 1917 he married Annie E McGrath. He was badly gassed near Ypres in April 1918 and after a long spell in hospital, where he never fully recovered from his injury he was demobilised in October 1918. He returned to his civilian work and took up his place as centre forward of Bradford on Avon Football Club. In 1919 he had to undergo a severe operation at Bristol which was not successful and after a painful illness he passed away on Sunday 22 February 1920. William left a widow and young daughter; he is not remembered by the Commonwealth War Graves Commission.

William George Parsons

Sergeant William James Nelson Loder   *4th Bn Wiltshire Regiment*
Service No.   200087   Age: 26
Place of Birth: Trowbridge, Wiltshire   Home Country: England
Date of Death: 24/04/1920   Cause of death: Died
Memorial: Not known
War cemetery: Holt Old Cemetery
Theatre of war: Home
Next of Kin: Angeline Annie Loder (wife) - Harry & Rosiana Loder (parents)
Address: Manor Cottage, Holt

James was a general Engineer and a Wiltshire Territorial and had married Angeline Annie Gliddon in Holt in 1917. He died most likely of disease on Saturday 24 April 1920.

Private Jesse Albert Knowles   *Yorkshire Light Infantry*
Service No.   204508   Age: 34
Place of Birth: Trowbidge, Wiltshire   Home Country: England
Date of Death: 01/07/1920   Cause of death: Died
Memorial: Trowbridge
War cemetery: Not known
Theatre of war: Not known
Next of Kin: Lucy Knowles (parent)
Address: Mortimer Street, Trowbridge, Wiltshire

Jessie a compositor joined the Yorkshire Light Infantry and served with them in France. He returned after the war and died most likely of illness or disease in the summer of 1920 at Ashford, Kent.

16
REMEMBRANCE

Left: Trowbridge War Memorial today and below the public unveiling in August 1921. Rev. Harry Sanders had first called a meeting to plan a memorial in April 1919. A poll had been taken and other memorial ideas which had been considered were public baths, a free library, or an extension of the cottage hospital (most of the poll voted for public baths.) The memorial was designed by W.H. Stanley a local architect . The bronze figure was by P.G. Bentham and was cast in bronze at Singers Ltd of Frome and the cost of the project was £1500 . The memorial was placed on the site where a n old leaning walnut tree had been a landmark for generations. A Great War Tank which had been presented to the town was moved to another site in the park.

Above left the Trowbridge Role of Honour 1500 copies were printed, the book was financed from the proceeds of a special Fete held in 1920 and by the Rev. Harry Sanders who compiled the book. He was throughout the period of the War Chairman of the Trowbridge Urban Council. - Above right The memorial in Holy Trinity Churchyard, Trowbridge, unveiled and dedicated on Sunday 3 April 1921. - Below left the memorial to the men of the 2/4th Territorial Battalion Wiltshire Regiment who fell in The Great War at St. James Church, Trowbridge. Originally it had gold lettering which over the years has been rubbed away. It was unveiled and dedicated on Sunday 2 February 1920. - Below right The memorial originally erected in the front porch of the Tabernacle Congregational Church in memory of the men who were connected with the church and Sunday School, now in the United Free Church. It was unveiled by Fred Earney on Armistice Sunday 1921, his brother William appears on the memorial.

REMEMBRANCE

The Trowbridge Tank was presented by the National War Saving Committee in December 1919 in recognition of the town's achievements for raising funds for the war. It was placed on a concrete plinth near where the war memorial stands today facing the main entrance of the park. The tank demolished part of the wall as it was driven into the park.

Above left & right: Dinners were arranged for returning service men.

Right: Hilperton War Memorial unveiled and dedicated on Saturday 30 May 1920.

Far right: Hilperton Church War Memorial unveiled and dedicated on Sunday 1 February 1920

 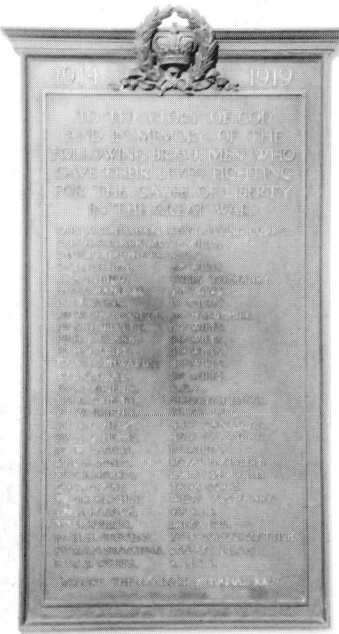

Hilperton Methodist Church Memorial now in St.Mary's Church Hilperton.

Left & above: Staverton War Memorial Lectern was unveiled and dedicated on the evening of Tuesday 18 May 1920.

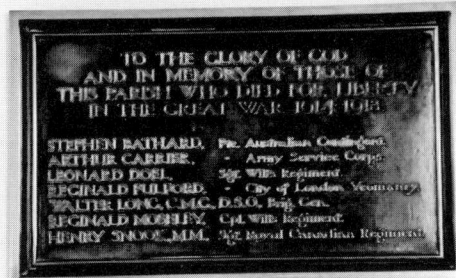

Top left: Southwick War Memorial

Top right North Bradley War Memorial unveiled and dedicated on Sunday 2 February 1920

Above: West Ashton War Memorial

Right: Heywood & Hawkridge Memorial unveiled and dedicated on the evening of Sunday 14 March 1920. It is now in North Bradley Church.

On Sunday 30 November 1919, Field Marshal Viscount French who had commanded the British Expedition Force at the start of the Great War unveiled a Memorial tablet in memory of the fallen of West Ashton as well as Tablet and Window in Memory of Walter Long.

Above Walter Long's memorial tablet

Left: Part of the memorial window

Below: Field Marshal Viscount French arriving at West Ashton.

TROWBRIDGE MEN NOT REMEMBERED BY THE COMMONWEALTH WAR GRAVES COMMISSION

When this book was printed in June 2010 the following men were not remembered by the CWGC. I have collated each mans documents and prepared files which have been sent to the CWGC and it is hoped that they will one day be recognised by their country and given the recognition they deserve.

George Alford	**Herbert John Owen**
James Andrews	**William George Parsons**
John Howard Barnes	**Cornelius Pearce**
Ernest Bennett	**Charles George Perryman**
William Burge	**Stafford Herbert Sidnell**
William Arthur Cox	**Stephen Smith**
Roland Keates	**Henry Turner**

The grave of Stephen Smith in Trowbridge Cemetery. He died of T.B. aggravated by military service.

Maps

The Western Front

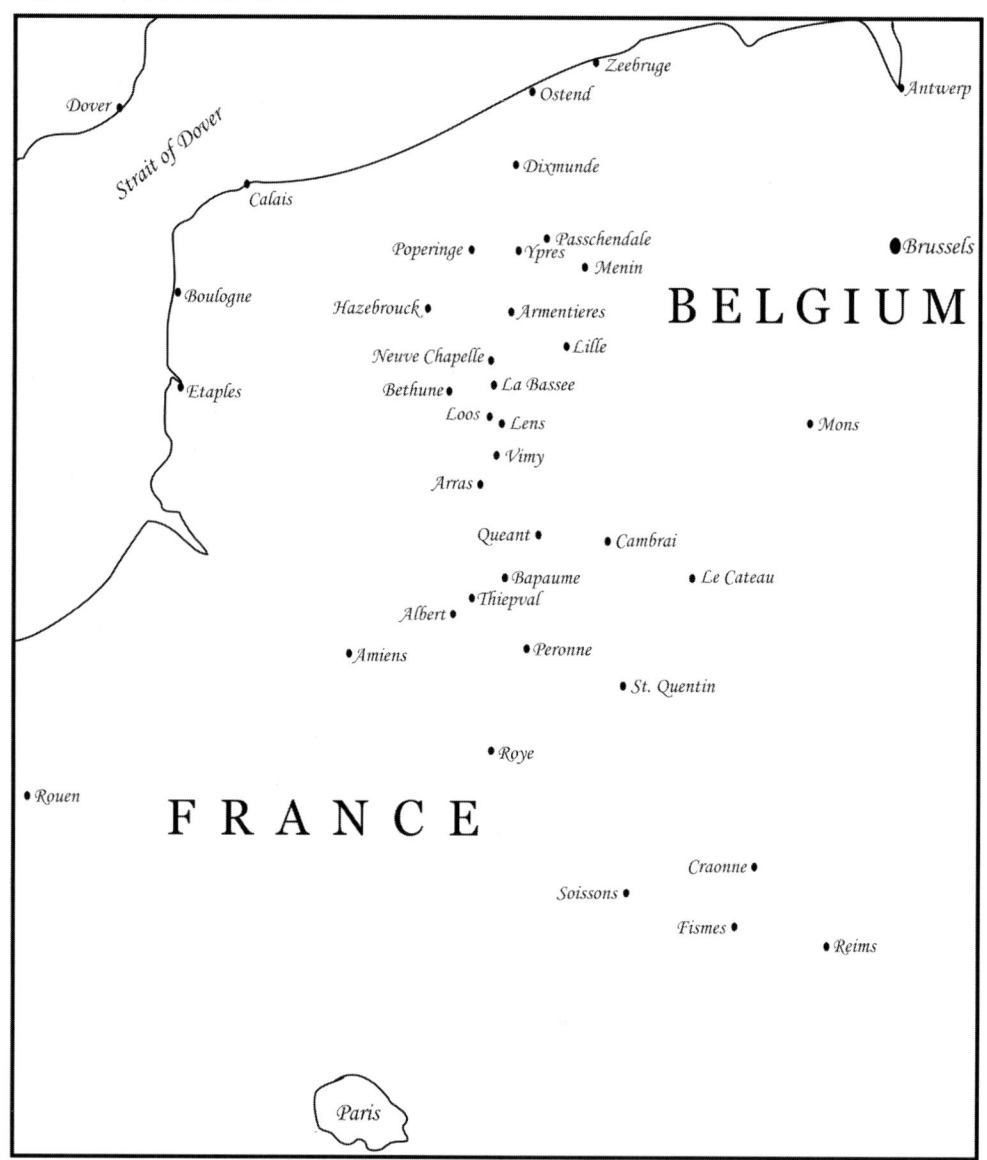

Gallipoli 1915 to 1916

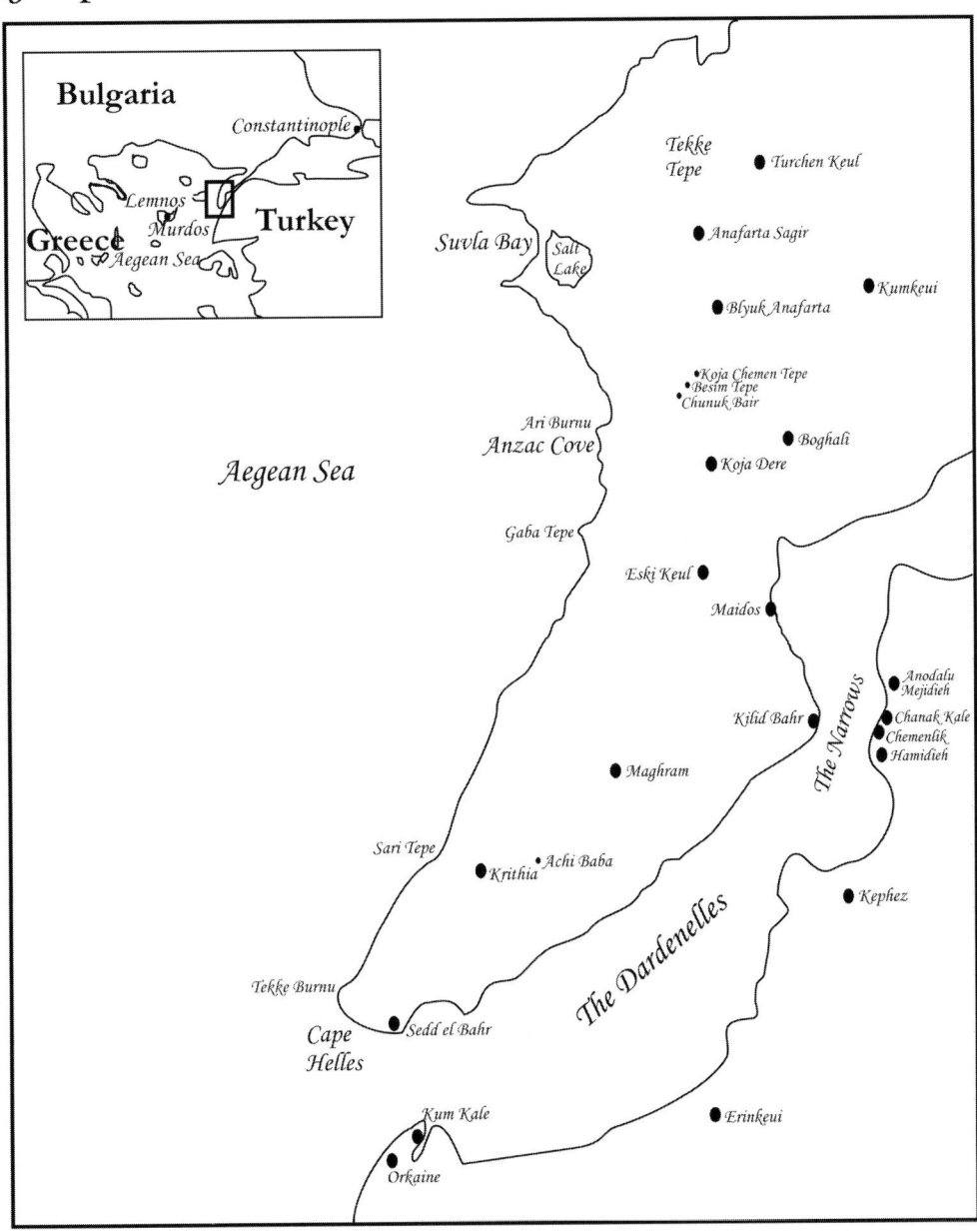

Mesopotamia 1914 to 1918

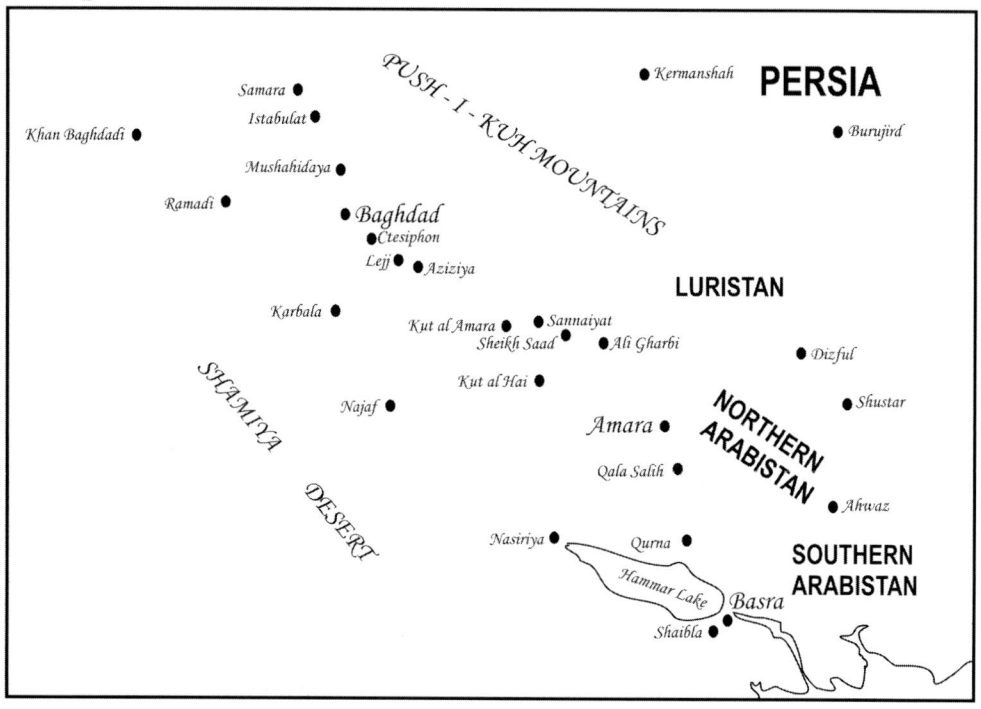

Balkans 1914 to 1918

Palestine 1914 to 1918

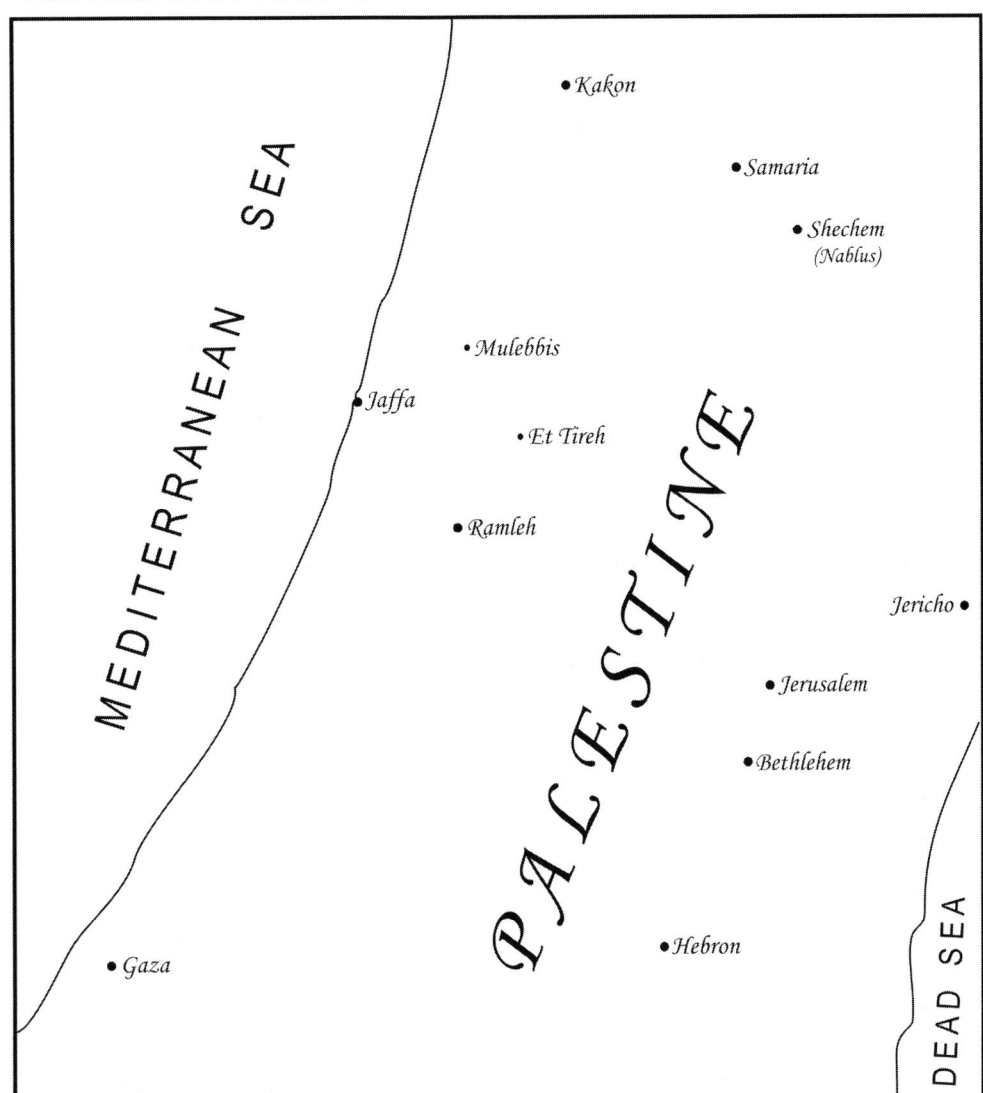

A-Z OF MEMORIALS

Abbeville Communal Cemetery Extension
Samuel John Culverhouse
Henry Fergus Willis
Leonard Doel
Aeroplane Cemetery
Charles Edward Bailey
Agny Military Cemetery
George Herbert Harman
Alexandria Chatby Cemetery
Stephen Bathard
AAlexandria Hadra War Memorial Cemetery
Norman William Harding
Amara War Cemetery
James Andrews
James Elms
William Arthur Ruddle
Rupert Charles Rowe
Howard Stanley Hillman
Andrew Lochhead
Hugh Henry Tozer
William Henry Burden
Arras Memorial
Herbert George Beaven
Frederick Alfred Clift
Bernard Newman Cottle
Howard William Davis
William John Holloway
William Ernest Horton
Herbert Ernest Hutton
Charles Frederick Mooney
Frank Arthur Sherwood
William Charles Wood
William Fred Culverhouse
George Cecil Slade
Arthur Howard Lane
William Bray
George Robert Rowe
Walter Robert Adams
Hubert Greenland
Baghdad North Gate War Cemetery
Thomas Percival Carpenter
Albert Henry Hodge
Herbert Cecil C. Knowler
Edward Ernest Preen
Charles Edward Robins
Frank Snelgrove

Baghdad North Gate War Cemetery
William Albert Baker
William Harry G. Andrews
Edward Ewart Parfitt
Joseph Robert Pearce
Percy William J Brown
Albert Ash
Joseph Harry Barnes
Bagneux British Cemetery Gezaincout
Frederick Arthur J. Nelson
Bailleul Communal Cemetery Extension Nord
Egbert Taylor
Arthur Henry Waterhouse
Arthur William Webb
Bard Cottage Cemetery
Herbert Culverhouse
Barlin Communal Cemetery
Raymond George Vincent
Baron Commuanl Cemetery
Lionel Francis H. Mundy
Basra Memorial
Alfred Charles Bishop
Herbert Reginald Clift
Leslie Gayton
Thomas Huan A. Hurley
Charles Edward Marmont
Horace William Sherman
George Nelson Smith
Charles Styles
Albert Edward Willis
Arthur George Hiscox
Willie Froom
Edgar Jesse Gregory
Robert Berrett
Harold Francis Cosser
Frederick John Sawyer
Alfred Edward V. Beck
John Hopgood
Albert John L. Batten
William Edward Archer
Henry Hutchins
Arthur Tanner
Geoffrey Hayward Manning
Levi Erasmus Garrett
George Henry Swaine

Basra War Cemetery
George William Bishop
Montague W Colcomb
Reginald Arthur S. Stockting
Harry Vardy
Beacon Cemetery Sailly Laurette
Percival George Warr
Bedford House Cemetery
George Henry Shrapnell
Berks Cemetery Extension
Walter H. Pinchin
Berles New Military Cemetery
Harold Joseph Preen
Bernfray Wood British Cemetery Montauban
John Francis Keevil
Bethune Town Cemetery
Walter Moore
William Sidnell
Samuel Starr
Birmingham Lodge Hill Cemetery
Harry Jefferies
Bois Guillaume Communal Cemetery Extension
Stanley Oliver Gomm
Boulogne Eastern Cemetery
Frederick William Hooper
Bradford on Avon Cemetery
Thomas Morris
Baradford on Avon Christchurch Churchyard
James Rees Cole
Brandhoek New Military Cemetery
William George Sainsbury
Bristol Arnos Vale Cemetery
Joseph Samuel Fincher
Bronfray Farm Military Cemetery Bray Sur Somme
Walter Slade
Brookwood Military Cemetery
Richard Carey Parsons
Frederick Francis
Browns Road Military Cemetery
George Hooper

Bucquoy Road Cemetery Ficheux
Edwin George Hillman
Douglas Robert Pinchin
Bully-Grenay Communal Cemetery French Extension
Thomas Victor Cross
Bus House Cemetery
Albert Thomas Hamblin
Cambrai Memorial Louverval
Harry Percival Perryman
John Thomas Smith
Samuel Charles Pollard
Reginald Tom Moore
Alfred Pocock
Carnoy Military Cemetery
Arthur William Firman
Chapelle British Cemetery Holnon
Henry Featherstone Clark
Chauny Communal Cemetery British Cemetery Extension
Henry Ernest Shipway
City of Paris Cemetery
Robert Henry Blake
City of Paris Cemetery Pantin
Frank Holton
Cologne Southern Cemetery
George B Banks
Couin British Cemetery Cemetery
Arthur Frederick Nicholls
Couin New British Cemetery
Walter Long
Crouy British Cemetery Crouy Sur Somme
William George Wickham
Crucifix Corner Cemetery Villiers Bretonneux
John Perkins
Delhi Memorial India Gate
John Stephen Carter
Delhi War Cemetery
Frederick John Perrett
Dernancourt Communal Cemetery Extension
Henry Charles Smith
Dickebusch New Military Cemetery
Henry Alfred George Fryer
Divisional Collecting Post Cemetery and Extension
William Henry Gay

Divisonal Cemetery
Roland John Burton
Doiran Memorial
John Potter
George Hamilton C. Jackman
Doullens Communal Cemetery Extension No 1
John Albert Sartin
Dozinghem Military Cemetery
Fred Hudd
Dunkirk Town Cemetery
Harry Meaden
East Murdos Military Cemetery
Herbert Reynolds
Ecoust St Mein British Cemetery
Arthur Flower
Edmonton Mount Pleasant Cemetery
Gideon James Slade
Elzenwalle Brasserie Cemetery
William Purnell
Embarkation Pier Cemetery
William Job White
Englebelmer Communal Cemetery Extension
Leonard Samuel Young
Erquinghem Lys Churchyard Extention
Herbert John Hawkins
Essex Farm Cemetery
Arthur Henry Hulbert
Estrees Communal Cemetery
William James Hawkins
Etaples Military Cemetery
Harold Butcher
Henry William Bull
Herbert Charles Collins
John Loxley
Leonard Percy Watson
Reginald John Yerbury
Flesquieres Hill British Cemetery
Charles Llewellyn Down
Gaza War Cemetery
Herbert Hatherall
Harry Loxley
John Henry Mackett
Thomas William Pickard
Joseph Charles Pickard

Gezaincourt Communal Cemetery Extension
George Guy Hermon Hodge
Gibraltar North Front Cemetery
Herbert James Warburton
Godewaersvelde British Cemetery
Edward Howard Pickard
Grandcourt Road Cemetery Grandcourt
Frank Oliver Stokes
Grantham Cemetery
Robert John Matthews
Great Yarmouth Gorleston Cemetery
Robert Pennington Williams
Green Hill Cemetery
William Percy Alfred Young
Guards Cemetery Windy Corner Cuinchy
Charles Gordon Bond
Reginald Arthur Evans
HAC Cemetery Ecoust-st Mein
Arthur Lewis Davis
Hamel Military Cemetery Beaumont Hamel
Charles George White
Harelbeke New British Cemetery
William Campbell Adamson
Haringhe (Bandaghem) Military Cemetery
Reginald Stanley Fulford
Haslar Royal Navel Cemetery
Stanley William Gardener
Hedauville Communal Cemetery Extension
Hubert Harold Chappell
Heilly Station Cemetery Mericourt LAbbe
Sidney Herbert Reynolds
Francis Mortimer Propert
Helles Memorial
Leonard Arthur Cox
Joseph Earle
Herbert Marshman
Arthur Charles Potter
Albert George Ricketts
William J. De Vere Scott

Helles Memorial
Charles Leonard Smart
Hubert John Clark
George Randall
George Percy Coward
William Charles Elkins
James Henry Hillman
Sydney John Chandler
Robert Michael Moffatt
Hermines Hill British Cemetery
Reginald Charles Rogers
Hilperton Cemetery
John Albert Gulliver
Ernest Ritchens
Holt Old Cemetery
William James Nelson Loder
Honnechy British Cemetery
Harold James Merritt
Hooge Crater Cemetery
Herbert Abrams
George Henry Fry
Harry Webb
Henry Geoffrey Nelson Tarrant
Albert Wareham
Albert Samuel White
Houchin British Cemetery
Walter John Cooper
Ingoyghem Military Cemetery
Curtis Henry Neave
Jerusalem Memorial
Victor William F. Dallimore
Arthur Edward Bevins
Jerusalem War Cemetery
George Jesse Dorey Hunt
George Job Dunn Martin
Kantara War Memorial Cemetery
Ralph Richard Bray
Karasouli Military Cemetery
Alfred Smith
Kemmel Chateau Military Cemetery
Samuel Henry Billett
Kingston Upon Thames Cemetery
Howard John King
Kirkee 1914-1918 Memorial
Victor Harold C Mundy
Henry Joseph Salvidge
William Harold Singer
Stanley John Swayne
William George L. Marshman

Kirkee 1914-1918 Memorial
Frank Woodward
Percy Tavener
George Hillier
Frederick Henry Sparey
William Walter Neat
Edward Leonard Sutton
William Charles Burnell
Klein-Vierstraat British Cemetery
Henry Charles Champion
Kut War Cemetery
William Thomas S. Maple
Albert Walter Cullimore
La Brique Military Cemetery No2
Walter Foyle
La Clytte Military Cemetery Pennyco
Percy Reginald Randall
Charles Edward Westall
La Ferte Sous Jouarre Memorial
Walter Herbert Noyes
La Gorgue Communal Cemetery
Frederick Stephen D. Land
Lala Baba Cemetery
Paul Aloysius Kenna
Lapugnoy Military Cemetery
Reginald Colin Rose
William Edward Hodges
Le Touquet Paris Plage Communal Cemetery
Sidney Edwards
Le Touret Memorial
Thomas Pritchard Adlam
William Ewart Earney
Edwin Stephen Ford
William Albert Hurn
Albert Ernest Little
Walter Sidnell
William Avons
William Lewington
Ernest Meaden
George Blackman
William Henry Forsyth
Stanley Alfred Elkins
Liege Robermont Cemetery
Frederick Job Rose

Lijssenthoek Military Cemetery
Andrew Boa
Tom Wheeler
Liverpool Anfield Cemetery
Sydney Ernest J Green
Longuenesse St.Omer Souvenir Cemetery
Alec James Hudd
Leonard Vincent Southwell
Alfred James Butcher
Loos Memorial
William Edwin Jenkins
William Tom Jefferies
Frank Thompson
Madras 1914 1918 War Memorial Chennai
John Poynter P. Say
Walter George Parsons
Stephen Walter Dyer
Edward Charles Hoddinott
Peter Gane
Frederick William N.Pocock
Bernard Hibberd
William Charles Strong
Harry Martin
Magnaboschi British Cemetery
Percy Shrapnell
Edward William Rogers
Manchester Cemetery Riencourt Les Bapaume
Percy William Bowles
Marcoing British Cemetery
George Victor Blake
Maroc British Cemetery
Arthur Henry Bailey
Henry Arthur White
Marteville Communal Cemetery Attilly
Harry Colston Collings
Maurois Communal Cemetery
Frederick Mathew Purnell
Melcombe Regis Cemetery
Arthur Henry Mead
Melksham Church Cemetery
William Henry Haines
Mendinghem Military Cemetery
William Walter John Davis

Menim Road South Military Cemetery
Job Holloway
Mericourt Labbee Communal Cemetery Extension
John Howard Cherry
Merville Communal Cemetery
Ernest Arthur Gomm
Richard Thomas Knight
Mesnil Ridge Cemetery Mesnil-Martinsart
Charles Elms
Messines Ridge British Cemetery
Harry Prosser
Mikra British Cemetery
Percy Herbert C Baber
Frank William Cox
Arthur Tom Carrier
Mont Huon Military Cemetery Le Treport
Alfred John Earl
Bertie George Gray
Mory Abbey Military Cenetery
John Clifford Drinkwater
Frederick John Overton
Bruce James Sloper
Mountain Ash Maesyrarian Cemetery
George Henry Shrapnell
Nesle Communal Cemetery
Charles George York
Netley Military Cemetery
Sidney Percy Hartley
Neuville-Vitasse Road Cemetery
Arthur John Ayres
John Elms
Niederzwehren Cemetery
William John Boscombe
Herbert Scrine
Nieuport Memorial
Albert Higgs Vinson
Philip Stanleigh Belcher
Nouex Les Mines Communal Cemetery
Benjamin Daly
Noyon New British Cemetery
Harold Conquest Clark
Osmondwall Cemetery
Harry J Burbidge

Outterstreene Communal Cemetery Extention Bailleul
John Wheeler
Cyril Narramore Were
Pernes British Cemetery
Gilbert William Frank Griffin
Robert Stanley Potter
Pernois British Cemetery
Ernest James Garfield Belbin
Perth Cemetery China Wall
William Joseph Bennett
Pieta Military Cemetery
Charles Brinkworth
Ploegsteert Memorial
Wilfred James F. Griffin
Felix C. H. Hanbury-Tracy
Albert William Bainton
Plymouth Navel Memorial
Sidney Herbert Griffin
Robert Potter
Arthur John Richards
Arthur Frederick Shrapnell
Poelcapelle British Cemetery
William Thomas Dunlop
Pommereuil British Cemetery
Victor Baker
Pont Du Hem Military Cemetery La Gorgue
Frederick Dike
Port Said War Memorial Cemetery
Christopher Ken Merewether
Portianos Military Cemetery
William James Pepler
Portsmouth Naval Memorial
Rowland Herbert Stafford
John James Foreman
Edward Clifford Jones
William Alfred Wheeler
Frederick Butcher
Esley John Rawlings
Herbert Howard Rogers
Frank Tadd
Henry Woodman
Potijze Chateau Grounds Cemetery
Laurence Hubert Jones
Pozieres Memorial
Amor Geoffrey Pike
Albert Bray
Charles Henry Robert Damon

Preseau Communal Cemetery Extension
Kirwin Barnes Sweetland
Prospect Hill Cemetery Gouy
Edward Frank Ponting
Puchevillers British Cemetery
Reginald Etwell
Quarry Wood Cemetery Sains Les Marquion
Henry Snook
Railway Cutting Cemetery Courcelles Le Comte
Cecil Dean Early
Railway Dugouts Burial Ground
Reginald George Moseley
Ramleh War Cemetery
Arthur Bull
Robert Henry Shimmon
William George Edwards
Walter George Portingale
Reninghelst New Military Cemetery
Lewis George Elling
Rosehill Cemetery (Chicago)
Arthur Frederick Fluke
Roye New British Cemetery
Charles Henry Field
Salonika Lembet Road Military Cemetery
Wiliiam Beaverstock
Frederic Merritt
Sarigol Military Cemetery Kriston
Walter Frank Webb
Serre Road Cemetery No 1
Bryan Wilfred F. Maguire
Soissons Memorial
Frederick W. Bartholomew
William George T. Loveday
Charles Wyndham Barnes
Sollesmes British Cemetery
William Stanley U Bush
St. Amand British Cemetery
William Alec Ransom
St. Pierre Cemetery Amiens
Allen Llewellyn Palmer
Edward Charles Watts
Allen Naylor Waterhouse

St Sever Cemetery Extension Rouen
Albert Edward Gibbs
Frederick Blake Deverall
Arthur Francis Griffin
Charles Alfred Grant
Albert James Davis
St Sever Cemetery Rouen
Albert Ford
Charles James Norris
Staverton St.Paul Churchyard
Frank Roland Holloway
Ste. Marie Cemetery Le Harvre
Albert Edward Dowding
Stretford Cemetery
John Herbert Graham
Talana Farm Cemetery
Edward Charles Thornton
Terlincthun British Cemetery Wimille
Frederick Guy Norris
Donald Robert Keates
Reginald Henry Lucas
Thaba Tshwane Old No 1 Military Cemetery
Merville Victor Knee
Thiepval Memorial
Frank Henry Angell
Albert Edward Baker
Reginald George Box
Albert Brunker
Jack Oswald Couldridge
James Dicks
Frank Edward Elliott
Frederick Gore
William Harris
Albert Victor Lane
Walter George Lester
Edward Victor Mattock
Geoffery Raymond Palmer
George Henry Purnell
Arthur Jesse Rawlings
Walter Trollope
William Alfred G Wilkins
Albert Victor Sartin
Frederick Sidney Elliott
George Cornish
William Arthur Reynolds
Stanley George Dude Covey
Charles Edward Griffiths
George Knight
Alfred William F. Shuttleworth

Tilloy British Cemetery Tilloy Les Mofflaines
William Christopher White
Trowbridge Cemetery
Wilfred Jeffery Baker
William Clemment Bray
William George Brittain
William John Cockerton
Arthur Stanley Farr
Edward Joseph Hollis
William Jacobs
Jesse Albert Knoles
Jesse Herbert Lester
Arthur Park
Thomas Henry Pepler
John Randall
Frederick Ernest B. Randall
Sidney Reeves
Albert Victor Rodgers
Edward Patrick Rodgers
Clifford Frank Wheeler
George Victor Jim Elmes
Ernest Bennett
William Bailey
Howard Stephen Rees
Thomas Rogers
Henry James Bethell
Henry Turner
Solomon J Fry
Stephen Smith
William George Parsons
George Alford
John Howard Barnes
Stafford Herbert Sidnell
Tyne Cot Memorial
Albert Edward Ash
Francis Henry Blower
Wilfred Frederick S.Groves
Walter Stanley Jones
John Abner Oliver
Frank Reynolds
Graham Strange Whiting
Charles Richard Winter
Herbert Samuel Young
William Arthur Wheeler
William Alfred Mattock
Charles James Cockerell
Ernest Prevett Godden
Albert Victor Lloyd
William George Jones
Arthur Minchin

Tyne Cot Cemetery
Herbert James Hurn
Arthur Ernest Davis
Frederick Dobson Beaven
Verchain British Cemetery
Joseph Edward Carpenter
Vermelles British Cemetery
Charles William Potter
Vielle-Chappelle New Military Cemetery Lacouture
William Trower Chivers
Villers Bretonneux Memorial
Samuel Marshman
Villers Bretonneux Military Cemetery
Thomas White
Villers Station Cemetery Viller Au Bois Cemetery
Hubert George Helps
Villers-Faucon Communal Cemetery Extension
Frederick Herbert Curtis
Vimy Memorial
Fred Gardiner
Henry Arthur Walton
David George Parfitt
Vis En Artois British Cemetery Haucourt
William George Marshman
Herbert Greenhill
Albert Charles Perrett
Vis En Artois Memorial
Hugh Deane Smith
Voormezeele Enclosure No1 and No2
John Crabbe
Voormezeele Enclosure No 3
William Charles H. Bennett
William James Matthews
Wancourt British Cemetery
Charles Edward Miller
Warlencourt British Cemetery
Charles William Baden
William George Bendall
Herbert Nelson Reynolds
Henry Howard Purnell
Warlincourt Halte British Cemetery Saulty
Alfred Hawkins

West Ashton Church
Roland Cook Keates
Woburn Abbey Cemetery Cuinchy
Alexander James Hayter
Wulvergem Churchyard
Herbert Pictor
Ypres Menim Gate
Arthur Henry Carr
Arthur Edward Frame
Frederick Francis Frame
William Hall
Albert Harrison

Ypres Menim Gate
Herbert Claude Horton
Arthur William Maill
William Parsons
Eli Job Rose
Walter Shrapnell
Herbert Harold H. L. Stillman
Harry Turner
William James Underwood
Ebeneezer Walter T Mattock
Henry Howard Stevens
Cecil Francis Deacon
Frederick Philip Cole

Ypres Menim Gate
Ernest Pullen
Charles Bray
William Dallimore
Walter Leo Letora
John Thomas Long
Walter Powell
Wilfred Ernest Treasure
Robert Henry White
George Hawkins
George Barber
Ypres Town Cemetery Extension
Clifford Nelson Bailey

The Missing

Men remembered on local memorials who I have yet to find military details.

Name	**Memorial**
John Abbott	North Bradley
John J Allen	North Bradley
Edward Ford	North Bradley
H G Hobbs	Hilperton
Henry Maslen	2/4th Bn Wilts Memorial, Trowbridge St. James Church.
James Philips	North Bradley
John Roberts	North Bradley
C Smith	Trowbridge

A Postcard depicting the 3rd battalion Wiltshire Regiment were based at Weymouth during the Great War where many new recruits were sent for training.